*Collected
Plays and
Poems
1958–1988*

Collected Plays and Poems, *1958–1988*

J. P. Clark-Bekederemo

With an Introduction
by Abiola Irele

Howard University Press

Washington, D.C.

1991

Howard University Press, Washington, D.C. 20008

Three Plays, Ozidi: A Play, and *The Bikoroa Plays* were originally published by Oxford University Press, London, United Kingdom. *A Decade of Tongues: Selected Poems, 1958–1968, State of the Union,* and *Mandela and other poems* were originally published by Longman, Essex, United Kingdom.

Manufactured in the United States of America

This book is printed on acid-free paper.

10 9 8 7 6 5 4 3 2 1

Library of Congress Cataloging-in-Publication Data

Clark, John Pepper. 1935–
    [Selections. 1991]
    Collected plays and poems, 1958–1988 / J. P. Clark-Bekederemo;
with an introduction by Abiola Irele.
        p.   cm.
    ISBN 0-88258-128-7 (cloth) : $34.95
    1. Nigeria—Literary collections.   I. Title
    PR9387.9.C55A6   1991
    828—dc20   91-14580
                                                                              CIP

082499

CONTENTS

State of the Union

Mandela and other poems

INTRODUCTION
Abiola Irele

THIS PUBLICATION of John Pepper Clark-Bekederemo's collected works must be greeted as cause for great satisfaction. It comes at an appropriate point in a career that has been one of the most remarkable in the development of African literature. For readers who are already acquainted with Clark-Bekederemo's poetry and plays as they have appeared in various volumes over the last thirty years or so, this collection brings his imaginative work into a single focus, affording an opportunity to see it as a whole and in the full span of its development. For other readers who are coming to this work for the first time, the collection offers in convenient form an introduction to the expression of one of the most creative and forceful imaginative minds at work on the African continent at the present time.

In considering the work itself, it is perhaps best to start with a general observation, namely, that there are two distinct but related impulses behind Clark-Bekederemo's expression. The first is the necessity he felt to convey the uniqueness of his experience of place and time. This means that it was not enough for him to write in an undifferentiated and falsely "universal" way; it was imperative rather to situate his expression so precisely, in terms of subject matter and specific references, as to impress upon it the mark of an individual consciousness in immediate and active relationship to its shaping environment. From this fundamental preoccupation derives the second impulse: to find the most adequate terms in which to capture the distinctive quality of his experience and thus to establish in his work both an individual vision and a personal tone of address. These impulses, as well as the particular circumstances in which Clark-Bekederemo's work has evolved, have imposed upon him the demands of a constant experimentation with language and form, so that the continuous adjustment of his expressive means to an unfolding pattern of experience has come to represent an essential part of his creative project.

The problem of securing an original point of entry into literary expression raised by this preliminary observation is of course one that any individual contemplating a career of creative writing has to ponder, and it is even more pressing in its implications for the would-be poet, who has to reckon with the peculiar demands of the genre in the necessary effort to make new meaning, not only through the medium of a language he or she shares with the community but within a literary tradition that designates a background of significance and valuations with which every new work has, as it were, to contend, in order to establish its own area of expressive being. In the case of the modern African writer, this problem becomes especially acute, complicated as it is by the language question. The creative process in this case has to proceed from an area of tension between the structures of expression of the two languages to which the writer is related: on one hand, that of the writer's native environment, including the complex of symbols with which that language is pervaded and, on the other, the imported language, with the literary conventions that it sustains and that the African writer has been conditioned by Western education and all the other factors of the colonial experience to assimilate and to some extent internalize.

The evolution of modern Nigerian literature in English, of which Clark-Bekederemo's work represents both a major source of development and a significant instance, provides a specific illustration of the working out of this problem, of the challenge it has posed to our writers and the way in which this challenge has been met. Clark Bekederemo's work derives its interest in part from this situation, and in order fully to grasp the nature of his achievement, it is useful to examine some of the factors that constitute the ground from which his work has issued.

We must start specifically with the problem of language—from what seems at first sight the anomaly of an African writer using a European language, in this case English, for a creative purpose. This is of course a situation that has been the subject of a longstanding debate in discussions of modern African literature. The range of linguistic, ideological, and critical issues involved in this debate need not detain us here, except to emphasize the point that English occupies a position that can hardly be considered peripheral to the social and cultural interests that constitute potent forces within the process of national integration in a country like Nigeria, engaged, like all new states, in an active quest for a comprehensive mode of national identity.

The fact is that, for better or for worse, the English language has been bequeathed as a common legacy to Nigeria by history. The random pattern of colonization that brought diverse ethnic and linguistic groups together within the confines of a single political entity, combined with the imposition of English as the reference language during the colonial period, accounts for the privileged position that the language still occupies today in the national life of the country. The extreme nature of the linguistic diversity of the country has worked largely to reinforce this position, to such an extent that English serves not only as the language of government, commerce, and education but also, and as a necessary extension of its function in these spheres, as the common medium of national discourse and, more important still, of cultural expression at anything beyond the restricted level of ethnic manifestations. There is thus a real sense in which English has effectively worked its way into the fabric of the national consciousness as this began to take shape during the latter part of the colonial period and is still being constituted at the present time.

The internal role of English within Nigeria is complemented by the undoubted international scope of the language, for it must also be borne in mind that English, with its many variants, is not only a common language within Nigeria but is also a language that has become, in George Steiner's term, *extra-territorial,* and this in more than its purely utilitarian function. The significance of this fact for the African writer has often been stressed in terms of the widening of the potential audience for the African work that this situation promises. But it is by no means certain that this extrinsic factor is an important, or even a relevant, consideration in the use of English—as indeed of French and Portuguese—by African writers: the fact is that for practically all of them, they have had no choice in the matter. What is more, the emphasis on the question of audience obscures the really decisive factor in the process of literary creation with which the language question is of necessity bound up, the intrinsic one of form and modality of expression. The implications of this factor for the African writer have to do with the problematic relation that obtains between an African work in a European language and the established conventions of Western literature, and how this relation determines the modes of engagement of the writer with the African background in the effort to formulate through appropriate metaphors an experience that is authentically grounded.

The gravity of the problem is highlighted in English-speaking Africa by the fact that education in English and the familiar acquaintance with the language that such education enables places the potential writer in direct touch with what has been codified as one of the most powerful traditions in world literature, a tradition that embraces the so-called Authorized Version of the Bible, and includes the works of writers such as Chaucer, Shakespeare, Milton, Bunyan, Wordsworth, Jane Austen, George Eliot, and Charles Dickens (among many others) as its principal points of reference. It has to be borne in mind that the process of linguistic acculturation within the colonial educational system functioned in great measure through a managed encounter with the works either acknowledged or certified as classics within this literary tradition. The result was that the experience of literature itself was fostered in the educated segment of the population by an almost exclusive reference to the literary tradition of English as it had come to be represented by colonial education.

To recall these factors is to draw attention to the cultural repercussions of the colonial experience, its peculiar manifestations in the area of literary values and awareness. It also sets the background for the varying forms of approach to the use and domestication of the European languages, and in particular English, for literary purposes in the African context, especially for poetic expression. Thus, when Africans began to write poetry in the English language, they had before them as models the hymnal verses of Christian worship, with their traditional sentiments, standard rhymes, and regular ryhthms, as well as the poetry of English Romanticism. The determining impact of a conditioning to this kind of literary fare is well illustrated by the productions of the first generation of English-speaking West African poets in the years before the Second World War and of its immediate aftermath: in the poems of writers such as Ralph Armattoe, Gladys Caseley-Hayford, and Michael Dei-Anang in Ghana, Abioseh Nicol in Sierra Leone, and Denis Osadebay and Mabel Imoukhuede in Nigeria. These writers, incidentally, are well represented in the historic anthology, *West African Verse*, compiled by Olumbe Bassir and published by Ibadan University Press in the mid-fifties.

The term *pioneer* has come to be attached to this early phase in the development of West African poetry in English. It is a term that need not carry the somewhat patronizing connotation it now seems to have acquired, for although it cannot be said that these early poets were truly accomplished or produced distinguished work, a good part of this early production offered what on any fair terms must be considered interesting material. If the language of Wordsworth, Keats, Shelley and especially Tennyson provided these poets with norms of expression, it did not by any means determine a facile imitation but served rather as the touchstone of a poetics that came readily to hand for the expression of preoccupations that were fundamental to the self-awareness of the poets. These preoccupations were articulated mainly through the themes of cultural discomfort, leading to self-discovery, on which much of this early poetry turned. Above all, the pioneer poets demonstrated that English could serve—indeed, *had* to serve— as a serviceable medium for the imaginative exploration of their lived situation.

It is now possible in retrospect to see how limiting in its possibilities was the idiom that was available to these early poets. It is not so much that this idiom had become outdated even as these poets were deploying its resources to address issues arising from their situation; the problem was that it could not sustain their expression beyond a certain range of perceptions and responses. It is this limitation that accounts for the impression of rhetorical flatness this poetry evinces for us today, a limitation that the succeeding generation of poets knew it had to overcome if it was to produce work of more enduring value. This is the generation that arose in the late fifties, and having become conversant with more recent developments in the metropolitan literature, adopted in a deliberate way the new procedures these developments offered for their expression in the African situation. In so doing, they were able to expand the scope of African poetry in English and thus to impart to it a wholly new temper.

Clark-Bekederemo's work stands out in this respect. What is more, it can be said to have assumed a specific historic significance in the evolution of Nigerian, and indeed, African poetry in English, for it is indisputable that his early efforts were central to both the thematic re-orientation and profound transformation of idiom that led to the decisive advance that the new poetry came to represent. The context of development of Clark-Bekederemo's work in this new direction, which also accounts for the genesis of Nigerian literature in English, extends in its ramifications, as I hope to show, well beyond questions of literature. But it is with specific reference to his education in English literature at the University College of Ibadan, where he was a student in the late fifties, as well as the singular nature of the cultural and social ambience of his experience there, that this development must first be viewed, in order to understand the role he has played in the shaping of a poetic expression in English that rendered the language properly responsive to the promptings of his particular environment.

Like similar institutions in British colonies in other parts of the world, University College, Ibadan, as it was formally known in its early years, was founded in 1948 with the aim of preparing colonial students for degrees from the University of London in a limited range of disciplines. It was perhaps to be expected that, in the circumstances of its founding, the institution should have been conceived essentially as an academic and intellectual outpost of the British Empire, so that the curriculum was modeled closely, and in certain cases, directly, on what obtained at the sponsoring university for the various disciplines offered at Ibadan. It is therefore fortunate that in matters of literary study, London as an institution was relatively forward-looking, for the English syllabus devised for Ibadan, based on successive periods of English literary history beginning with the Renaissance, covered a range of authors and works that extended to the writers of the thirties and even beyond. The syllabus also took account of the critical reval-uations that had occurred in English literary scholarship, so that it gave due prominence to the "strong" line of English poetry that runs from Shakespeare and the metaphysicals through Robert Browning and Gerald Manley Hopkins into the moderns—Wilfrid Owen, W. B. Yeats, T. S. Eliot, Ezra Pound—and right up to the work of a later generation represented by such poets as Dylan Thomas, W. H. Auden, and Stephen Spender. The tag "Spenser to Spender" invented by the students to describe the syllabus thus provides a fair idea of its fairly comprehensive scope.

In making a large place for modern poetry, the English syllabus at Ibadan offered in particular an extensive introduction to what, in his book of that title, C. K. Stead has described as "the new poetic." This new poetic reflected a profound change in sensibility that was also manifested in other genres as a pervasive tone of vision and expression that defines the general character of modernism as a distinctive move-ment in twentieth century English literature. The novels of Joseph Conrad, D. H. Lawrence, Virginia Woolf, and James Joyce, which form a significant part of this movement, therefore also received con-siderable attention in the courses in English offered at Ibadan during this period. No less important than the primary literature was the criticism that developed alongside this movement, represented in par-ticular by the theoretical work of I. A. Richards, the essays of T. S. Eliot himself, and the criticism of F. R. Leavis. English studies at

Ibadan thus reflected the results in the postwar period of the movement toward a reorganization of the discipline as an area of serious academic endeavor.

It needs to be pointed out that the course also provided a perspective that went beyond the British literary scene. It afforded the possibility of an encounter with American literature, especially the drama of Eugene O'Neill, Tennessee Williams, and Arthur Miller, as well as with aspects of continental European literature. Apart from the corpus of classical Greek drama, which was read in translation, one could also make acquaintance in more than a random way with important texts of contemporary Western literature—the novels, say, of Albert Camus or the plays of Ibsen. The drama of Brecht in particular was a singular revelation that has left a permanent impact on the Nigerian dramatic scene.

These references have an immediate relevance for a consideration of Clark-Bekederemo's development, for they indicate the immediate influences that shaped the tenor and determined the direction of his work. For there is no question that, but for his encounter as an undergraduate with European modernism in its dynamic relation to the tradition of Western literature and in its specific extensions as evoked above, his horizons would have been confined within the narrow limits prescribed by the conventional expression in English to which he had been conditioned by his previous education. The moderns, on the other hand, introduced him to a new and distinctive experience of literature. Their poetry in particular opened up perspectives of expression that offered new possibilities in the language. It is well to consider in this respect the way in which the dimension of form, thrown into sharp relief in the more subtle exploration of the resources of imagery and the greater reliance on strategies of paradox and irony, on suggestive allusiveness, even at the risk of obscurity, came into new prominence in modernism, making for a complexity of statement that produced a more demanding kind of poetry, one that sought to formulate in language an expanded response to life, in order to achieve the wholeness of experience envisaged in the fairly prescriptive terms of Yeats's definition of creative endeavor in language: "Blood, imagination and intellect running together." And one way in which the conjunction of these elements could be assured was through a recourse to myth, which came to be viewed as the deep foundation of the imaginative consciousness itself.

The impact of the new literature on Clark-Bekederemo's work can be measured as much by its conscious assimilation of the idiom of modernism, which can be felt in the very movement of his work, especially in the early poems, as by the specific echoes which can be picked out from individual passages. The presence of such echoes further reflects a method that he took over from the moderns, Pound and Eliot in particular, and consists in the deliberate deployment of literary references in one's own work as a way of enforcing one's own meaning—a constructive use of what has come to be known as "intertextuality." Behind this method lay a conception of poetic practice that he had also come to embrace and that implied an acute consciousness of craft. The encounter with modern poetry thus entailed for him a serious apprenticeship of poetic technique, a heightened awareness of the very process involved in fashioning words into an organic unity of form in order to reflect the full press and to convey the original tonality of the poetic experience.

Perhaps more than anything, Clark-Bekederemo's initiation into the new poetic also led him to the recognition that, in the African context, the question that confronts the writer with a serious creative purpose in English becomes more than the adaptation of the imported language to the realities of the new environment, that it involves rather a total appropriation that would bring African expression into a living relation with the tradition of literature in English over its entire range of development, a gesture moreover centered especially upon the sharpest manifestations of this tradition. We might note in this respect that his attitude to the use of English goes further in its implications than that of Chinua Achebe, who speaks of making the imposed language "carry the burden" of his African experience. Clark-Bekederemo on the other hand stakes out a more extensive claim to the resources offered by the English language and its literary tradition, as is made clear by his leading essay in the collection entitled *The Example of Shakespeare*. And it is in the endeavor to make good this claim, the compulsion he felt to assume for his individual expression a linguistic and literary legacy that had become available to him, however indirectly, that Clark helped to inaugurate a new kind of Nigerian poetry in English.

The personal effort itself must, however, be related to the wider context of Clark-Bekederemo's development for an appreciation of its wider social and historical significance—to the cultural and intellectual climate that defined the collective ethos at Ibadan during his student days and from which his early work emerged. The word *renaissance* is perhaps too elevated to describe this context, but my personal recollection of the prevailing atmosphere at the university at that time is dominated by the tremendous sense of excitement with which, as students, we lived our experience of university life. That we were a tiny handful meant that we not only formed a closely knit community, we were inevitably affected by the distinct character of privilege that access to higher education took on for us in our particular circumstances and that every aspect of life at the university was designed to emphasize.

If the excitement we felt had an essentially social basis, much of it also had for some of us an intellectual source, arising from our introduction to the Humanities in their Western formulation, which we approached with an ideological innocence that was nearly complete. This attitude may appear in retrospect surprisingly naive and even inexplicable; the truth, however, is that many of us were struck with a genuine astonishment at discovering structures of knowledge and of ideas to which we came with practically no previous background or preparation, and whose impact on our minds was for that reason all the more forceful. Moreover, the very remoteness of the intellectual culture to which we were being diligently assimilated by our largely British mentors to the actualities of our environment and the conditions of our existence endowed that culture with nothing less than the appeal of an attractive ideal.

This state of mind induced by our experience at the university came, as it were, to be embodied and to assume a peculiar character in the English Department. Although there was no organized movement with a well-defined program, there existed among students of English at Ibadan a self-consciousness that came to be crystallized around *The Horn,* the student poetry magazine Clark-Bekederemo edited in its first year of publication, from 1957 to 1958. When his poems began to appear in the pages of this modest cyclostyled production, they made a strong impression in student circles, and the long poem "Ivbie," to which an entire number of the magazine was devoted, even provoked a storm due to the uncompromising boldness of its imagery. What was in evidence in these poems was their originality, deriving from their confident integration of the modern idiom. Their radical departure in relation to previous efforts at producing African poetry in English with which we were acquainted was immediately apparent to all. Moreover, the self-assurance that went with the manifested quality of his talent gave these poems first published in *The Horn* a distinctive accent among the cluster of voices that found their first expression in the magazine.

The Horn eventually developed into something more than an outlet for new poetic talent; it came as well to function as a medium of intellectual reflection and in particular as a forum among the students for debate about the place of culture in the new Nigerian society that we felt, as if on our very pulses, was coming into existence. The underlying issue in this debate was the idea of culture as the condition for the refinement of the individual spirit and even for a conception of a decent way of life, the influence of Matthew Arnold's *Culture and Anarchy* being decisive here. Though focused primarily on literature, our preoccupations concerned the place and transformative potential of the arts in our society.

The atmosphere at Ibadan in the late 1950s and early 1960s encouraged the cultural preoccupations and aesthetic inclinations the magazine highlighted. The university had become a focal point of cultural activity, oriented exclusively toward Western forms; indeed, by the late fifties, it was in effect a veritable island of Western culture amid a vibrant sea of native life. *The Horn* devoted a considerable part of its content to reviews of university productions of plays, concerts, and operas and thus reflected in its pages the intense character of this activity and its foreign orientation. In this way, and combined with its devotion to poetry, the magazine not only fostered a cult of literature but also promoted an aestheticism that came in the circumstances to be associated with the discipline of English.

Although the cultural orientation at Ibadan during this period can be said to have had its beneficial aspect, insofar as it favored the cultivation of a cosmopolitan awareness, it carried in the immediate context of its publication the grave implication of an exclusiveness whose social consequences amounted to a narrow elitism. Moreover, the heady character of the atmosphere in which we moved tended to obscure for us the moral and spiritual risk involved in the process in which we were so clearly caught up, that of the active formation of an elite taking its intellectual and cultural bearings from the West and becoming disengaged as a result from its own cultural and human milieu.

It may seem therefore paradoxical to state that *The Horn* also provided a way out of this incipient drama of alienation. For while it reflected cultural and artistic preoccupations that were oriented by Western references, it also functioned as the vehicle of a cultural nationalism that implicitly challenged the primacy of Western expressions in the modes of apprehension to which we were being conditioned by our education. Two factors seem to me to have been responsible for this possibility of its playing apparently contradictory roles. In the first place, the engagement with foreign culture, for all the genuine enthusiasm we brought to it and the unabashed satisfactions it procured for us, left us ultimately with the profound sentiment of being unhoused in the realm of culture. If therefore we were to achieve any degree of balance in our imaginative experience and in our intellectual and emotional life—in other words, any form of true integration—we had to create forms of expression that conformed as closely as possible to the genuine conditions of life within our society. These forms had furthermore to embody an originality of expression distinctive enough to exert a countervailing force to the inclination toward a simple mimetism to which we were subject.

The second factor provides an ironic reflection upon the literary culture to the promotion of which the English Department at Ibadan was committed. As a concession presumably to the African milieu in which they operated, our British teachers introduced into the syllabus some literary works written by European writers employing either wholly or in part an African setting, notably Conrad's *Heart of Darkness*, Graham Greene's *The Heart of the Matter,* and Joyce Cary's "African" novels, *Aissa Saved* and *Mister Johnson.* Our reaction against these works was predictable, and was as much a function of the largely negative image of Africa we encountered in them as of the obvious inadequacies we could immediately identify as regards their depiction of human situations in the African context, the limited and even unfeeling grasp these works displayed of the true texture of life in the African environment they sought to represent. It is instructive to recall in this connection Chinua Achebe's testimony to the effect that his motivation for writing *Things Fall Apart* was the need he felt to contradict the image of Africa and of Africans in the novels of Joyce Cary. Although Achebe had left the university well before Clark-Bekederemo entered Ibadan, his classic novel grew in part from the same reaction to the European literary discourse on Africa to which *The Horn* provided an avenue of expression.

For it is no exaggeration to affirm that the poems we published in *The Horn* represented in their own way a contestation of the literary deformation of Africa involved in European literature devoted to the continent. They were the signs of a movement toward a more authentic expression of the African milieu in literature than was afforded by these European works. There was an evident purposiveness to the efforts of the contributors to the magazine: to develop a literature in English that was a truer reflection of the context of life within which they were located.

Because, for imaginative expression, the format of the magazine could only accommodate poetry, it was in this genre that the creative elements among us responded to a need that made itself imperative. It is easy to understand the way in which the new poetic of modernism was suited to the project implicit in our endeavours, for it facilitated a reworking of the language in order to make it conform to the requirements of an expression centered upon our milieu and experience. There remained then, beyond the exhilaration of our discovery of modern literature, the challenge of applying its procedures to the expression of our particular situation, the challenge precisely that lies behind the impulse to innovation that inspired the poets of *The Horn*, and none more so than Clark-Bekederemo.

No less important in the cluster of effects that helped to foster this new literary awareness was the appearance at this time of the early numbers of the review *Black Orpheus,* edited by Ulli Beier and published by the recently established Ministry of Education of the Western Region of Nigeria at Ibadan. Through this review, located at our doorstep, as it were, we made the acquaintance of black literature in the diaspora and of the negritude movement. The review brought to us in an admittedly thin but nonetheless impressive stream excerpts in English, translations of representative samples in other languages, and critical essays devoted to the major writers. The publication of James Kirkup's sensitive English translation of Camara Laye's *The African Child* came at this time as further revelation of the possibility of an authentic literature of African inspiration. And although these writers could not feature in our academic program, we read their works as they came to us with a ready passion, so that Langston Hughes, Countee Cullen, Nicolas Guillén, Aimé Césaire, Léon Damas and Léopold Sédar Senghor soon became more than names to us; they opened up for us new horizons of thought and awareness of immediate import to our status and existence as colonial subjects. Their example promised nothing less than a form of initiation, in the truest sense of the word, into a universe of the imagination that we could enter with a wholeness of response. For we felt through their works a sense of connection to a wider community of sentiment, to an affirmative impulse in which we not only had a feeling of being participants, but also of having the seal of validity placed upon our own humble efforts.

When, therefore, in 1958, a double bill consisting of Wole Soyinka's plays, *The Lion and the Jewel* and *The Swamp Dwellers* was produced by the student Dramatic Society at the University Arts Theatre, it came as a welcome justification of our expectations. The plays went to the heart of our enthusiasms, so that we experienced the production as something of a landmark event in our cultural experience. It was about this time also that Chinua Achebe's *Things Fall Apart* appeared, confirming most impressively the point of our reaction against European fictions of Africa, and our intimations of a gathering movement toward the creation of a national literature. It must be remembered that Amos Tutuola's *The Palmwine Drinkard* had been published a few years earlier, and contrary to the impression that has been given of its having received a hostile reception in Nigeria, the work was in fact regarded with genuine admiration by the discerning part of the reading public in Nigeria, which was certainly appreciable. At all events, the appearance of these works indicated, albeit in a rather scattered fashion, the constitution of a new literary expression among us. This was a development that seemed to us at the time highly propitious, for it was closely linked in our minds with our political hopes: the genesis we were witnessing of a national heritage of literary expression original to us, we felt, could only herald the advent of the national community of our vision.

Soyinka himself, who had earlier been a student for two preliminary years at Ibadan before proceeding to Leeds for his degree, returned from England the year after the Ibadan production of his two plays to take up a position as research fellow in the English Department at Ibadan. The detail is important, for there is considerable interest in relating the fact that it was in the student room made available to him on the campus of University College, Ibadan, and against the background of the charged atmosphere of expectation in the months immediately preceding Nigerian independence, that Soyinka wrote *A Dance of the Forests,* the play with which he sought to mark, in his own individual way, the historic import of the impending occasion.

The formal end of Nigeria's colonial status to which we all looked forward duly took place on the first of October 1960. In the ten years or so before that event, Nigeria went through a process of transformation of such magnitude that the period can be considered a truly momentous one— possibly, from the social point of view, the most significant—in the country's history. Constitutional changes leading to internal self-government provided the political setting for a determined modernizing effort marked by extensive economic initiatives, an effort that was epitomized by the tremendous expansion of education in the Western Region, an example that was quickly taken up by that of the Eastern Region. The period thus witnessed a social revolution that has had far-reaching effects. But the most distinctive feature of the period was psychological in its nature and effect, marked as it was by a powerful release of energies that contributed to the euphoria of the times, a distinct collective feeling that swept the country. For we were keenly conscious of being engaged in a historic process, that of recovering the existential initiative that colonial rule had denied us.

It was inevitable that the larger political and social background of life beyond the university indicated by these factors should have had a direct impact on the outlook and thinking of students at Ibadan. The confident progress the country was making toward independence tended to have a muting effect on anticolonialist feelings in student circles, but as the ideological stance of Clark-Bekederemo's long poem "Ivbie" indicates, these feelings were not altogether absent; indeed, they might be said to have formed an undercurrent to the dominant mood of optimism that prevailed among the students. And although the privileged status conferred by our education induced in us a feeling of self-importance, this feeling went undeniably with a strong sense of responsibility for our own society, for we were also ardent nationalists, passionately committed to a vision of our country's future. It is true that the signs of ethnic tensions presaging difficulties in the process of nation building had begun even at this time to be visible, and that there was reason for a certain foreboding concerning the future. This did not, however, make any appreciable impression on our minds as we looked forward with enthusiasm to independence and to a new future for our country.

The fervid atmosphere I have evoked here was reflected in the pages of *The Horn*. It is not too much to claim, in relation to its immediate function as a channel of literary expression, that this modest student magazine had a part that was far from negligible in the education of sensibility that prepared the ground for the development and reception of a national literature in Nigeria. It is therefore not without significance to observe that the early work of Clark-Bekederemo, which was for some three years the major animating force of *The Horn*, went on to exert in this development a powerful and enduring influence. But beyond this limited perspective of the magazine's role, the cultural assertion that took place under its auspices can now be seen, despite its limited scope, as the manifestation of a profound reconversion of consciousness among the new elite of Nigeria as it was being formed at the country's foremost intellectual center.

Thus the literature that began to be produced in this period by this elite grew out of the various pressures that converged on the minds of its most articulate members, and reflected the factors at work in their objective social and cultural situation. This initial immersion of Nigerian literature in the realities of the national experience has remained a prominent feature of its subsequent development, manifested by its steady reflection of the vicissitudes that have marked the course of Nigerian history in the postcolonial era. This fact places Clark-Bekederemo's work in a particular perspective, for his work exemplifies in a remarkable way the interaction of literature with the determining factors of the Nigerian experience, their coming together to form an instructive narrative of African destiny in modern times. His work needs therefore to be viewed against the political, social and intellectual background I have sketched here for an understanding not only of its beginnings but also of its evolution in terms both of theme and form. It is to a necessarily rapid and therefore limited survey of the development of Clark-Bekederemo's work in poetry and drama that the rest of this introduction will be devoted.

Clark-Bekederemo has invoked, as the justifying principle of his creative work, an Ijaw saying that applies to his own immediate situation in the Nigerian context: "Two hands a man has." The invocation has a primary significance deriving from the intimate linguistic and cultural connections he enjoys to two of the most prominent ethnic groups in the Niger Delta, the Ijaw and the Urhobo. The fact that he has devoted his energies to a scholarly presentation of the impressive tradition of oral poetry and performing arts of these two groups attests already to the way in which this double legacy of his indigenous background has been brought into fruitful connection with the other large frame of reference established for his experience by his Western education.

The principle of complementarity suggested by the Ijaw saying also governs his creative work in English. This can be seen in the way this work conciliates the two planes of awareness and of realization—of theme and of expression—brought together in his work, enabling a mutual reinforcement of their respective modes of significance. The fact that much of his work, in particular the plays, revolves around aspects of the life and lore of the Niger Delta suggests that this area of the country, with its distinctive landscape and the symbolic associations it generates, functions not merely as a setting for his work but as its informing spirit, opening out for his imagination a singular perspective on the world.

The issue that seems to have confronted Clark-Bekederemo at the outset of his writing career was how to localize his expression by making the English language inhabit, as it were, the spirit of the Niger Delta as it communicated itself to his imagination. A clear progression can be discerned in his approach to this issue throughout the evolution of his work, a process that begins to come into view in his early poems. These poems are mostly set pieces, explorations of landscape and situation in an imaginative effort to establish a sense of place. They provide an insight into this initial direction of Clark-Bekederemo's inspiration, the way in which he begins to work his way toward an active redeployment of the English language to serve expressive ends removed from its "natural" setting, and thus to invest the adopted language with a new significance.

It is of particular interest in this respect to observe the way in which, in the poem "Night rain," we are led by the evocation and the imagery from one level of meaning to another, a transition by which its theme is dramatically amplified and its structure of imagery given an extension of reference. At an obvious level, it presents a vivid rendering of a concrete scene: that of a tropical storm and its effects on a humble household. The image of the mother filled with solicitude for her children intervenes at the central point in the movement of the poem to give focus to the descriptive details by which the poem's setting is elaborated: "roof thatch," "wooden bowls and earthenware," "roomlet and floor," "loosening mat," all suggest an appropriate background to the enactment of specific life in the poem. The conventional metaphor in which the rain drops are first perceived as beads on a rosary gives way to another that registers a more sharply perceived detail of indigenous life:

> She moves her bins, bags and vats
> Out of the run of water
> That like ants filing out of the wood
> Will scatter and gain possession
> Of the floor.

The second level of meaning in the poem emerges from this background of acute apprehensions. The transition from concrete evocation in the first part of the poem to the symbolic import of the second part is marked in the transfer from the limited sense which the word *drumming* is given in the early part of the poem to the more comprehensive meaning it acquires, denoted by "over all the land" in the latter part; the word in effect receives a new value that reflects the change in perspective that takes place within the poem. The transition it signals turns in the most natural way on the image of the mother, an image that becomes magnified in its implied association with the landscape, itself powerfully invoked at the end of the poem as its ultimate reference. The setting thus assumes a primal quality that in turn lends due force to the telluric terms of the confident affirmation of the poet's sense of being in the closing lines.

When this structure of transitions in the imagery and references of the poem is properly considered, it is not difficult to read the entire poem as a reliving of the movement of consciousness from which the whole meaning of the poem proceeds, as a statement therefore of the poet's ambivalent cultural situation and as the working out of an imaginative mode for its resolution. In this reading, the progression from the confused awareness of the opening lines ("doped out of the deep") to the exultant accents of the poem's final statement can be seen to recount an adventure with a supremely personal significance.

What emerges at once in "Night rain" is Clark-Bekederemo's assured handling of setting, a quality that is displayed even more clearly in such poems as "Fulani cattle" and "Girl bathing." In "Fulani cattle," the evocation of the long march of the cattle as they are driven on the hoof from the North to the South across the vast expanses of the Nigerian countryside affords an occasion for a graphic presentation of contemporary life in the country over a wide range of social and economic manifestations, an evocation that is then given an arrestingly contemplative turn at the end of the poem. With "Girl bathing," the pictorial associations of the title alerts us to the temptation to facile exoticism presented by the subject, a temptation deliberately con-fronted and averted in this poem, which builds on a cardboard image of Africa in order precisely to complicate and give it a fuller and richer dimension. The tone of sensousness in this poem, channelled through the play of imagery as well as through the effects of ryhme and verse design, is felt to attach as much to the bathing girl who is the imme-diate subject of the poem, as to the visual frame of her presentation. Thus, although "Girl bathing" makes no overt ideological point, the theme of renewal, which the poem intimates, can be said to involve the poet himself, so that the imagery and the meaning it sustains become expressive of his project of intense valorization on a broader front of references and allusions. The fact indeed that the poem brings to mind David Diop's "Rama Khan" and Léopold Sédar Senghor's "Femme noire" is not without significance for this reading.

The aesthetic foundation of Clark-Bekederemo's project is thrown into sharp relief by the impressionistic style of "Ibadan dawn," in which the atmospheric quality of the evocation becomes the very condition for its realized sense of ceremonial, its urging of a vital relation be-tween the communal consciousness and the immediate framework of life. We might note in passing that the notations in this poem provide the background for the compacted imagism of the justly famous shorter poem, "Ibadan." And the vitalism that is suggested in "Ibadan dawn" is elaborated into a pansexualism in "The year's first rain," a poem remarkable for its density of statement and the scope of the energies it celebrates.

It becomes obvious as we consider the pattern of imagery in these and other early poems that these are more than nature poems in the usual sense of the term; they articulate rather an active engagement of the imagination with the poet's environment. And their essential burden is their intuition of a process of coming to birth, an element of the poet's expression that is directly evocative of his own developing awareness.

It is the self-recognition implied by this element of the poems that is dramatized in "Agbor dancer." Here, the theme turns on an explicit statement of the relation between the poet's two orders of reference: the self-description "early sequestered from my tribe" stands in an inverse relation to the notation "ancestral core" associated with the female dancer, both serving as opposed terms in a dialectic of identities that unfolds in the poet's mind. Thus, the poem presents us with self-reflection in a manner approaching that of the French-speaking negritude poets. The querulous and agonized note that pervades their expression is, however, absent here; the interrogation of the final stanza does not dramatize a sense of conflict but underscores rather the affirmative insistence, emphasized by the Yeatsian ending—the comparison with the final lines of "Among Schoolchildren" is inescapable—upon the significance of the dance itself, its projection of the dynamic interaction of body and mind with the world of nature.

This observation suggests a "neo-Africanism" that is inherent in these poems—inherent rather than advertised, an underlying ground of ideas, perceptions and responses from which the thought, the themes, and the imagery proceed. We might say that an essential African sentiment animates these poems, manifested in a traditionalism that is counterpoised against a threatening estrangement of the poet's consciousness. This element of the poetry is however not worried into significance, but impresses itself on us forcefully both as the tacit recognition of an assumed background and as the effect of experience. In other words, it is not pursued as in Okigbo's *Heavensgate* into a ritual of personal initiation, developed into a drama of cultural self-retrieval, nor as in Soyinka's *Idanre*, elaborated into a comprehensive mythology proposed as a reference of a collective spirituality.

Clark-Bekederemo's "neo-Africanism" functions rather as an all-in-clusive framework of immediate perception, one that serves first and foremost to *place* his expression and thus to establish its natural context of vision, an original perspective for a reappraisal of his universe.

This unforced way of relating to the traditional background makes for the poignant interest of the poem "Abiku." There is no attempt within the poem to explicate the concept on which its theme of deprivation and weary resignation is based, to elaborate upon its meaning or to connect it with the system of belief of which it forms a part. The comparison here with Soyinka's poem of the same title becomes inevitable in this regard. That *abiku* is a Yoruba word meaning literally "born to die" and that, in the context of a high rate of infant mortality, of successive pregnancies and deliveries, it came to furnish the concept for what is believed to be the repeated reincarnations of the same child in the same woman, is for Soyinka the starting point for the weaving of an elaborate conceit around the emblems with which the capricious child is associated. With Clark-Bekedermo's poem, the meaning issues directly out of the enacted moments of the evocation. Thus, the "abiku" concept does not feature as an object of poetic or speculative interest in itself; it is endowed rather with a deep relevance to the human situation that is the subject of the poem, made to carry the burden of personal emotion. It thus appears less as an accessory than as the very foundation for the poet's meditation upon a singular form of tragic predicament.

The point here is that in none of these poems does Africa feature in a direct or self-conscious way as the subject of Clark-Bekederemo's expression. There is no deliberate approach to origins in the grand rhetorical manner of Senghor, the hieratic mode of Okigbo, or the mystical mode of Soyinka. Africa assumes a presence in these poems not as an abstraction, but within particulars that make up a texture of life, as a natural environment peopled with a human existence that the poet endeavors to bring to imaginative life.

The long poem "Ivbie," with its explicit polemical intent offers the one notable exception to this observation. "Ivbie" is a poem that deserves extended treatment for a proper clarification of its complex network of allusions and an appreciation of its deep impulses. But even a cursory reading cannot fail to point up its problematic nature. It is what we might call a protest poem, for its theme connects directly to the historical context of black literature, as this bitter allusion to the devastation of slavery and colonial exploitation make clear:

> Those unguent gums and oils
> Drawn in barrels off to foreign mills
> The soil quarried out of recognition
> As never would erosion another millennium
> The blood crying for blood spilt free
> From keels away on frothing sea
> The dark flesh rudely torn . . .

"Ivbie" lacks however the true vehemence of other works of black protest literature that come to mind. Two reasons can be advanced for what appears to be the relative detachment of tone that we observe in the poem. The first seems to me to be a function of Clark-Bekederemo's adoption of Eliot's style for much of his expression here, a move that betrays him into the occasional solemn abstraction that is at odds with the emotional requirements of his theme, as in these lines with which the second movement opens:

> In the irresolution
> Of one unguarded moment
> Thereby hangs a tale
> A tale so tall with implications
> Universal void cannot contain
> The terrible immensity
> Nor its permanence dissolve
> In the flux wash of eternity:

It is not apparent that there is a vital progression from these lines to the poet's denunciation of colonial violations quoted earlier, yet it is to this denunciation that it is meant to serve as introduction. There appears to be therefore a discrepancy between the dry manner of Eliot's style, which is here co-opted for Clark-Bekederemo's expression, and the inspirational ground of his poem. This discrepancy between matter and manner produces throughout the poem an impression of contrivance that seems to me to detract from its overall impact. The introduction of the Ijaw deity Oyin, who recalls the blind seer Tiresias in Eliot's *The Waste Land,* is a case in point: there is an arbitrariness to the device which is clearly more distracting in its effect than contributory to a proper organization of the poem's system of references and its general emotional tone.

The second reason is related to this last observation and has to do with the way the urgency of the theme of protest is diminished by the context in which we encounter the poem. The focused evocations of

Clark-Bekederemo's early poems generate such a field of collected force that the song of lament that "Ivbie" aspires to be is undermined in its significance by the spontaneous vigor which these poems communicate. We come to feel that the overwhelming sense of personal presence in the other poems has become in the long poem little more than a gesture of self-dramatization. The nature of the cultural malaise "Ivbie" gives voice to appears in this light to be somewhat factitious, too rhetorically presented (as in the echo of Shakespeare's *Macbeth*: "Sleep no more!") to come across with the proper force of conviction.

The reservations expressed here concern what appears to be the deliberate intellectualism of the poem, which results in an obvious derivativeness of its formulations. It remains true, however, that the poem's ambitious intentions are not only fully declared but are intensely realized at crucial moments in its development, as in this passage from the third movement:

> Now, where are the lightning-spokes
> That quivering should dance
> Ten thousand leagues into the limbs of things?
> Where are the broadways
> Of oriflamme that opening wide should lance
> Into the heart of darkness,
> As when trembling like a fresh
> Maid before her man,
> Moonlight distils flourescent submarine seas?

The sustaining tension of the poem becomes manifest in this passage in which the charged irony of the allusions to Ariel's song in Shakespeare's *The Tempest* and to Conrad's well-known fiction of Africa is played against the poet's deep awareness of his own primary truths, and developed into an expansive vision of their ultimate elemental significance. The double awareness that runs through "Agbor dancer" is here fully dramatized, at the level of explicit thought as well as that of expressive means. "Ivbie" can be said therefore to articulate explicitly the theme of rediscovery that informs the other poems and is made palpable in their imagery. It charts the movement of the poet's mind towards a full response to the solicitations of the local environment, the "market murmur of assembled waves," which that envrironment suggests to his imagination and which so powerfully resonates in his own expression in these early poems.

What is remarkable about these early poems is the intelligent effort of re-organization of the adopted language to the poet's situation and circumstance. It is instructive to compare this effort to that of the white South African poets who were the first to envisage the possibility of a poetry that took Africa as its subject, and whose preconceptions, tied as much to the European conditioning of their sensibilities as to their prejudicial view of Africa, proved ultimately disabling in their attempt to give credible expression to their encounter with and relation to a new landscape of human and natural life. It may be thought that, as one writing from the inside, Clark-Bekederemo enjoyed an indisputable advantage over these poets. Yet it is obvious from an examination of his versification that that these early poems involved a strenuous testing out of his medium, a conscious process of naturalization, at the level of form and composition, by which he sought to bring his language into a state of expressive equivalence with his experience.

The results of the experimentation with language he was engaged upon in these early poems are, of course, variable. Sometimes a straining after effect can readily be discerned in some of these poems, as seems to me to be the case with "The imprisonment of Obatala." At other times, the sense of ryhthm is not always consistent with the tone and general movement of the poem as required by the theme, although it should be borne in mind here that the interference from the indigenous background of voice may well constitute a value in itself for African poetry in English. As already noted, "Ivbie" suffers a softening of its tone from a self-consciousness that creates a dissonance between inspiration and formal realization. This is the kind of uneven quality that one can expect in a young poet making his way through a field of antecedent voices in quest of his own. Yet it has sometimes been used to discount the triumphs that Clark-Bekederemo is entitled to claim at this early period of his career. The rhyme scheme in "Easter" for instance is so carefully woven across the broken rhythm of the verse as to participate in the progression of the poem's thought toward its ironic conclusion. And we can feel, in poem after poem, how verbal and formal effects collaborate to render an overwhelming sense of felt life.

We might observe that the wrestling with form and language in these early poems reflects the poet's determination to invest his evocations with such vivid energy as to get them well beyond the compass of a mere exercise in "local color." In this respect, Clark-Bekederemo's debt to Hopkins has proved largely beneficial, even if some of its effects on his poetry are sometimes as disconcerting as in the original source. The alliterative pattern initiated with "doped out of the deep" in "Night rain," the precision of the imagery and of the visual notations and the whole press of language in this and other poems make this debt evident, even without its open acknowledgment in the subtitle of "Ibadan dawn." The athletic quality of Hopkin's idiom, of his vocabulary, verse rhythms, and verbal sonorities, are so appropriate to the vibrant quality of these poems that the occasional jarring note seems of little moment, judged against their overall impact. And it is not only Hopkins, but also Wilfrid Owen and W. B. Yeats whose influence can be felt as positive in giving direction to Clark-Bekederemo's exploration of poetic language. "Fulani cattle" for instance offers such a subtle variation on "Anthem for Doomed Youth" that Owen's poem can be considered to serve as its "intertext," as much in its theme as in its form, for the resourceful use of near rhymes and other features of Owen's idiom and technique contribute to the experience of Clark-Bekederemo's poem. As for Yeats, his influence is so pervasive that it can be said to have been wholly absorbed into the texture of Clark-Bekederemo's personal idiom.

It is worth insisting that Clark-Bekederemo's appropriation of these models in his early poems often vindicates a method that may have proved damaging to his individual genius. The really important point is that, far from taking his situation for granted, Clark-Bekederemo took it seriously enough to ponder the lessons that the masters of the language he was obliged to use had to offer. His effort was bent toward refining his craft sufficiently to encompass an unprecedented creative purpose. That purpose was to reconstitute in language a specific field of experience pervaded by a developed sense of his location in the world, and to endow that location with true poetic significance. It is this intention that lends to Clark-Bekederemo's early poetry its firm sense of conviction, its vitality of expression.

The achieved sense of place that *Poems* mobilizes affords the perspective from which to view *A Reed in the Tide*, the volume that follows. Poems such as "Flight across Africa," "Times Square," and "Cave call" are impressions of travel, entries in a mental diary, records of isolated moments in a widening experience of the world. They project the multiple perspectives that proceed naturally from a self-assured consciousness. A number of these poems relate to his experience during the year he spent as a visiting scholar in the United States, an acerbic account of which he has provided in his book, *America, Their America*. The poet's attitude to the materialism and consumerism associated with America, as it comes through in "Service," may seem conventional. However, when the sardonic tone of the poem is linked with the hedonistic connotation of "service" in the popular, urban culture of Nigeria, the connection with his sense of home and the meaning become clear as a willed distancing of the self. The poem is a repudiation of "the siren streets and afternoon" of a civilization with which he is unable to strike a spiritually satisfying relation, and whose spread over the globe he therefore deplores. The context of these poems does not however fully account for their general atmosphere, for although they display a variation of tone and mood, they have in common an almost whimsical restlessness, which suggests that our poet is almost by temperament unsuited for the role of "the fortunate traveller," which the Caribbean poet Derek Walcott assumes in one of his best-known collections.

The juxtaposition in *A Reed in the Tide* of poems related to external experience with other poems dealing with the internal social and political situation of the post-independence era that Nigeria had just entered at the time of their composition sets up a thematic counterpoint between the private realm of the poet's inspiration and the "public sphere" of an emerging concern with public events. The critical turn that the Nigerian situation began to take at this time imposes upon the poet's attention the claims of the social universe of his existence, which now begins to feature as a primary focus of his preoccupations.

The use of an organic image to depict the corruption in public life in "Emergency commission" establishes the moral perspective of the poet's concern and illuminates the import of the two poems that focus directly on political figures who played prominent roles in the unfolding drama of the Nigerian crisis. In "The leader" and "His Excellency the masquerader," the allusions to aspects of the traditional background bring home, so to speak, the human and social implications of the poet's preoccupations. Where in the former the agony of politics is expressed in the allegorical idiom of the folktale tradition—an idiom that the poet is to employ with great effect in the succeeding volume— in the latter, an ironic reversal of the normal healthy associations of traditional ceremonies provides the basis for a bitter satire of political behavior. These political poems more than foreshadow in theme and language and in their general atmosphere the poems of *Casualties*, his next collection, devoted entirely to the convulsions occasioned by the Nigerian Civil War of 1967–70.

The continuity of the poet's inspiration from one volume to the other is underscored in the dirge-like "Song" with which *Casualties* opens, in its recall of an earlier age of youthful idealism contrasted to a present desolation, an age

When but to think of an ill, made
By God or man, was to find
The cure prophet and physician
Did not have.

The sentiment of a shattered ideal mourned in this opening poem provides the emotional setting for the poet's stance toward the tragic course of events of which *Casualties* constitutes a searing record. The gloom that pervades the panoramic view of civil turmoil that he offers in "A photograph in *The Observer*," suggests more than a generalized feeling of emotional distress; the final refrain "night falls over us" indicates a more comprehensive grasp of the essential pathos of history as exemplified by the unfolding drama of national events. The apocalyptic terms that characterize the plangent horror of the Nigerian Civil War in "The beast" and the harrowing realism with which it is detailed in such pieces as "Season of omens" and "July wake" tend toward a confirmation of the extensive emotional range of the poems in *Casualties*.

Because several of the poems weave a tale around specific individuals, they require for their understanding some familiarity with the details of the Nigerian crisis. The effectiveness of the imagery in "The cockerel in the tale" depends for example on identifying the specific allusions in the poem to the role of Major Nzeogwu, one of the leaders of the January 1966 military coup, which unleashed the chain of events that was to culminate in the Civil War. Similarly, "The reign of the crocodile" has to be read as the poet's personal commentary on the personality and style of government of General Ironsi, whose inadequacies proved a major factor in the subsequent slide toward the Civil War that broke out in July 1967. The poem appears in this light as an expression of the poet's personal indignation at the failure of leadership during a critical period in Nigerian history.

But *Casualties* is not primarily concerned with the abstract issues of the politics that came to a head with the Nigerian Civil War. It ranges much further, into the ambiguous moral terrain where public events exert contradictory pressures on individual choices. The volume speaks directly to the personal dilemma this situation presents to the poet himself, and is remarkable for the honesty with which he confronts this dilemma in the various poems as they weave their emotional and moral thread through the volume. Nowhere is this more evident than in the sequence of three poems devoted to his relations with Emmanuel Ifeajuna, another principal actor in the events of the Nigerian Civil War who was also a personal friend. The composite portrait of Ifeajuna that emerges from "Leader of the hunt," "Conversations at Accra," and "Return home" is marked by a profound ambivalence that attests to the poet's conflict of loyalties. The three poems do more than dramatize the confusions of two troubled minds, that of the poet and the subject of his poem; they are intended to discount the abstract heroics of the public square in a severe probing of private motives, as the poet gropes toward the duty of human understanding, which the moment and the demands of a personal bond require.

Where the Ifeajuna sequence involves some elaboration, "Death of a weaverbird," an elegy to Christopher Okigbo, a fellow poet and another close friend, who was killed on the Biafran side of the Civil War, is keyed to understatement. Its refusal to dwell on the man, but rather to invoke the claims of a common pursuit, betokens a refusal to surrender to emotion, an appeal to the controlling power of art. The poem thus takes on its poignancy less from the text than from its context, its departure from the conventions of the elegiac genre serving to enforce the statement it makes of a grief larger than words.

It is thus a willingness to go behind the headlines and the rhetoric of public stances to the conflicts generated within individuals that distinguishes this volume. Against this background, the rhetorical flourish of "We are all casualties" in the title poem dedicated to Chinua Achebe understates somewhat the emotional reach of these poems, the intimate thrust of the experience of the Civil War for the poet himself and for many individuals, and which he endeavors to engage with in such poems as "Dirge" and "Night song."

The obvious public reference of the poems of *Casualties* may seem to imply that the volume is confined to the circumstances of Nigeria and thus suggest a limitation to their significance. But they do not only compose a narrative of the Nigerian Civil War, they organize themselves into a meditation upon the event. It is this aspect of the volume that accounts for its most striking formal feature, the predominance in it of animal imagery, developed throughout into a scheme of primal metaphors. The poet's construction of this scheme points to the suggestion it carries of Nigeria, the reference of the poems, as a kind of jungle, and of the civil war of which it is the theater as a drama of elementary and destructive passions. They derive in this sense a didactic function from the allegorical mode in which they are cast; this mode becomes in turn a means of displacing the public aspect of the theme in order to reinforce the introspective character of the poems.

The fact that the volume's scheme of metaphors is derived from the oral tradition becomes of the utmost importance from this point of view. It makes clear the poet's concern to address an immediate audience in terms with which it is familiar, which relate directly to its established structure of sensibility and response. Thus, while *Casualties* often documents the events and presents the characters involved in the Nigerian Civil War in factual terms, it also transposes these elements of its narrative into an imaginative register with a highly ethical resonance. In other words, these elements assume their value within the framework of a comprehensive parable that determines the didactic function of the volume, pointing to the necessity of moral values as a foundation for political and social life. The oral tradition thus serves as the formal and moral perspective for the poet's consistent angle of vision on the characters and situations that enter his meditation.

It seems fair to affirm that *Casualties* represents Clark-Bekederemo's finest accomplishment in the area of poetry. The stress of the historical moment that occasioned the composition of these poems called forth from him a "terrible beauty" of expression. It obliged him to a creative endeavor in the quest for a mode of address appropriate to the occasion, to the experience centered upon it, and to the audience it affected. It served both to sharpen the sense of responsibility inherent all along in his earlier work, as well as to inspire a new experience of poetic form that enabled him to find an original voice. The paring of his idiom for the tale of desolation he had to tell brought a firmer temper to his poetry, gave it a new dimension in which language, emotion, and imagery became finely fused within a firmly grounded and coherent aesthetic framework. *Casualties* is indeed nothing less than the triumphant demonstration of the expressive potential of the African imagination.

It is perhaps no surprise that this achievement could not be fully matched in the sequel to the volume represented by *State of the Union*, which is devoted to the social and political malaise of Nigeria in the aftermath of the Civil War. The dominant key here is related not so much to a mood of disillusionment as to a disengagement of the poet's feeling from his subject. The poems seem to develop on an even plateau of uncomplicated emotion, so that the language of the poems seems to shun the forthright rhetoric of a persuasive discourse for the indirections of a weary irony. This character of the volume makes for a subdued tone through most of the poems.

It is possible to argue that in *State of the Union*, Clark-Bekederemo has carried the stripping of his poetic language that he began in *Casualties* to its limits. Already in the "Epilogue" to this latter volume, we begin to feel that the spare, taut diction he cultivated for his narration of the Nigerian Civil War has become too plain to move us with the telling power of genuine poetry. It may be reasoned that the need he felt to testify to the ills of society justifies the unadorned garb he has chosen to give to his expression in *State of the Union*, that his objective was to communicate in the most direct way possible with his audience, which called for a language immediately accessible to them. It may also be that the nature of the subject he takes on, the failure of will in the national community, has resulted in a depressed imagination reflected directly in his language.

State of the Union is not, for all that, devoid of interest. The note of disillusionment we have remarked upon modulates into a more markedly personal mood of rueful dejection in some of the poems in the latter section of the volume, providing an insight into not only the imbrication of the public with the personal in Clark-Bekederemo's poetry but also into a certain logic of development in all his work, a point to which we shall return presently. For now, it useful to remark upon the way poems such as "Autumn in Connecticut" and "Birthday at Wesleyan, Middletown" begin to dwell upon the theme of passing time and decay, a theme whose implications provide the key to the poet's reflections upon his individual condition in "The Coming of Age." The elegiac note that predominates in this section of the volume is struck with a simple but resolute clarity in the lines that conclude the poem:

> All under spell of day
> Moves on into night.

The brooding note of the poems in the latter section of *State of the Union* runs easily into that of *Mandela and other poems*, his latest volume. The neat division into three clearly marked sections is of particular interest for a consideration of this slim but highly distinctive volume. The political subject in the first section, with its pan-Africanist vision, recovers for us some of the motivating force of his early work, emerging in a mode of exasperation in "A Letter to Oliver Tambo." The two sections that make up the rest of the volume place this political background in something of a recessive light. The second section, composed of a series of elegies, is set off against the background of hope and continued aspiration mapped out by the opening section; the poems in this section compose a somber quartet in which the enacted ritual of mortality sets the atmosphere for the extended contemplation represented by the poems in the last section of the volume. This connection makes the volume assume a retrospective significance: they are in the nature of a preliminary summing up of life and experience as the poet moves into the uncertain climate of middle age.

The volume thus traces for us the transition from the exuberance of Clark-Bekederemo's early poems to a somberness that has been lurking in his previous expression (as in "Tide-wash") and now comes fully to the fore. The poet insists upon the elegiac note in this last volume to the point where it takes him over the edge of a morbid perception in some of the poems. However, if the starkness of "Death of a Lady" and "A Passing at the New Year" seems so obviously opposite to a romantic imagination, the poems are not as far removed from the questing spirit of romanticism as they appear at first sight. For all their bleakness, they represent less a gesture of despair than a reasoned activity of the poetic mind engaged in sustained interrogation of accumulated experience, a seeking for the essential meaning of an individual life in relation to that of others.

Mandela and other poems throws a sharp light from this point of view on the personal voyage traced by the progression of Clark-Bekederemo's themes, which takes us from the delight in the world and sensuous excitement of his early poems to the pensive and measured gravity of his latest work. At one level, that of public reference, this progression runs parallel to his country's history and registers the descent toward a mood of social despair. But at a more profound level of consciousness, it involves the sober recognition of the inevitable scourge of time, the inexorable process of decay in the world of nature that is at the same time the condition for its renewal.

It is no accident that the dominant image in his poetry relates to the tides of the Niger Delta, the manifestation in a familiar landscape of the idea of changeability, the experience of transition, of the natural phases that govern the movement of life. Nature in its closest guise to the poet offers here a dramatic illustration of all existence as a continuous flux, within which humanity itself appears as indeed "a reed in the tide." The conclusion to "Streamside exchange" is especially suggestive of this entrenched position in his imaginative thought. What seems like an awkward rhyme in the final lines of the poem acquires a singular force here: it works perfectly to give a matter of fact tone to the Bird's response and thus to underscore the grim finality of the apprehension it registers:

> You cannot know
> And should not bother;
> Tide and market come and go
> And so has your mother.

We become aware then, as we consider the development of his poetry, that a tragic vision is integral to Clark-Bekederemo's aesthetic consciousness. We might explain the thematic progression of his poetry by observing that this vein of his imagination is at first obscured by the enthusiasms of his beginnings, but that once he came into full possession of his language, it only needed the confirming effect of events and of personal experience to uncover and bring this vein into stark prominence. And whatever our attitude to the view of life Clark-Bekederemo proposes to us in his poetry, we can have no doubt that it provides the theme that accounts for the direct power of his expression.

Clark-Bekederemo's plays provide an expanded framework for the expression of the tragic vision that runs through his poetry. There is a clear affective and aesthetic solidarity between the two aspects of his work, which is emphasized by the fact that the Niger Delta is the setting for all the plays. This fact prompts a preliminary observation that places the plays themselves in a general perspective. The natural environment of his native region assumes significance here as the theater in which the drama of the human condition is acted out. For while each play is self-contained, they tend to be structurally linked. This appears to be the playwright's way of insisting upon the essential unity of their inspiration. They represent in this light individual instances of a comprehensive structure of tragic apprehension.

Clark-Bekederemo's reputation as a playwright rests largely on the success of his first play, *Song of a Goat*. The play had an immediate impact when first produced, because its theme of domestic tragedy, centered upon questions having to do with fertility and procreation, had appeal for a Nigerian audience, for whom such questions have a primordial importance. The ploy, which consists in the ritual slaying of a goat as part of the dramatic action, was calculated to impress, even if its motivation was not a crude sensationalism, but to awaken in the audience the sense of drama as communal rite. Besides its theme, the appeal of this play derives essentially from the playwright's robust vitality of language with its remarkable consistency of tone, his impressive handling of atmosphere, and the successful realization of the play's moral focus. The compactness of the play, with its swift movement of its action toward a tragic climax, contributes to an overwhelming tightly wrought tension.

Although the action of the play is not overtly concerned with the issue of culture conflict that dominated African writing for a time, the two levels at which it develops, that of the psychological and the social, suggest an interpretation that places it squarely within the context of a breakdown of the rules of custom. The heart of the problem the play deals with is quite simply the variable hold of social constraint on the individual. The Masseur speaks for the needs of society with his constant reminder of a convention that stresses the survival of the clan, appealing through this reminder to Zifa's sense of community against his sense of personal identity. His words, "The soil is sacred, and no one man may dispose of it," express an all-encompassing ethos by which the clan has given coherence to its collective existence. Zifa's reluctance to accept the dictates of this ethos, despite his disability, amounts to an insistence on the claims of the individual against those of society, an attitude that threatens the very conception his society continues to entertain of its organic life.

Ebiere's distraught condition is, in this view of the play, much less a function of her sexuality than of her husband's intransigence, which denies her the possibility of reconciling her personal physical and emotional needs with her instinctive adherence to the conventions of her own society. Her sense of wrong on these two counts comes through in a speech whose formulation derives its meaning from its context. When she refers to herself in these words:

> I who have suffered neglect and
> Gathered mold like a thing of sacrifice
> Left out in sun and rain at the crossroads.

the imagery brings out a sentiment of frustration that operates at more than a purely personal level. The life-enhancing properties of the sun and rain are in fact invoked as part of a religious consciousness that links the ritual of sacrifice with the solidarity of the clan and the communal well-being. Her grievance comes down to the acute sense of marginality she is made to feel by being thwarted in her creative function and thus being denied a role she has wholeheartedly identified with in maintaining the continued life of the community.

The fact that the character of Tonye is merely sketched in within the drama has been seen as a failure of craft on the part of the playwright. This view cannot, however, be sustained, for the portraiture of Tonye conforms entirely with the formal scheme of the play. Tonye's role emphasizes the imponderable nature of the drama in which all the characters are caught up: he is merely the accessory of its tragic unfolding, the hapless victim of what is manifestly a dilemma of transition. The point is that the conflict enacted in this play transcends the two main characters: it revolves essentially around the norms by which their society will live in the new dispensation, hinted at if not fully established in the play.

Song of a Goat has been compared with Eugene O'Neill's *Desire under the Elms*, but as noted already, the theme of sexuality is not as central in Clark-Bekederemo's play as it is in Eugene O'Neill's. A more appropriate parallel is that between the theme of Clark-Bekederemo's play and Garcia Lorca's two plays, *Yerma* and *Blood Wedding*. Clark-Bekederemo himself has given assurance that he had not read Lorca when he wrote his own play, and we can give full credence to this assurance and accept that the observed parallel between his work and that of Lorca is purely fortuitous. A valid comparison between the Nigerian playwright's work and that of the Spaniard can easily be sustained without assuming an influence from one writer to the other, however. For both were writing about a community in which the harshness of the environment conditioned an ideological emphasis on communal survival and consequently determined a preoccupation, often anguished and certainly pregnant with tragic possibilities, with the fundamentals of life.

It is a preoccupation of this order that receives prominence in *Song of a Goat*, whose text is one long figuration on the idea of growth and vitality; that a sense of the reciprocities between blood and soil becomes, as it were, a natural extension of this presiding idea emerges from the theme and action of the play. The close parallel between the imagery of "The year's first rain" and *Song of a Goat*'s first act alerts us to the interaction between the poet's habit of sensibility and his projections in the play as these are embodied in his characters. It is essential in this respect to attend closely to the formal design of the play as a verse drama, a feature that connects it directly to Clark-Bekederemo's early poems, whose reference it expands within the scheme of a developed dramatic action.

This formal connection between Clark-Bekederemo's poetry and his dramatic work is perhaps most evident in *The Masquerade*. The lyricism of the courting scene in the first act effectively transforms this scene into one long poem, a paean to youth and to the land, an affirmation of life in the exultant spirit of "Girl bathing." The evocations in this scene take their place in the dramatic context of the play as the poetic background for the tragedy of star-crossed lovers presented by the play. And as in this kind of play, it is the opposition between the welcoming attitude to life natural to youth in its first flush of bloom and the hideboundedness of the older people, the loss of the capacity for response to life's promptings, that produces a tragic outcome.

From the point of view of structure and dramatic action, *The Raft* is certainly the most compact of Clark-Bekederemo's plays. There is a continuous flow of the action that contributes to the impression of concision already determined by the reduced world of the raft, which serves as its scenic framework, and the unified temporal scheme—twenty-four hours from one sunset to another—within which the whole action of the play is enclosed. At the same time, the tight construction of the play is able to accommodate a full account both of the life of its characters, down to the technical details of their profession on which the play depends for its action and its symbolism, and of aspects of contemporary experience that place the action in a wider perspective of reference.

The Raft has been interpreted as a parable of Nigeria, its four characters representing the four regions of the Federation in the pre-Civil War era. In this interpretation, the play is seen to contain a clear message to a country adrift in a political storm and heading toward disaster. The allusions to the prevailing social and political circumstances in Nigeria at the time the play was written are many and specific enough to justify the view that the playwright's concerns as a citizen find a large measure of expression in this play, as indeed they do in his poetry, as we have seen. Thus, a reading of the work as direct commentary on Nigeria is indeed plausible, but it is one with which we cannot rest content. For one thing, the correspondence between the action of the play and the social and political situation it addresses is far from being as simple as this reading would allow. The expressionist cast of the play is enough to preclude a hasty analogy of the play with any kind of univocal political or social statement. Moreover, the wider ramifications of the play are expressly indicated in the headings the playwright has appended to the text in each of its four tableaux. These headings suggest a more elevated scope to the playwright's intention than is allowed by a narrow political interpretation of his play.

We come to an idea of this intention once again by way of the poetry. The far from idyllic tone of the poem "Return of the fishermen" anticipates in its evocation much of the human and natural atmosphere of the play. The use of dramatic irony in the first tableau is central to the drama: the enveloping fog that is given a simple mention in an early scene of the play deepens in meaning later in Kengide's cry: "The fog is everywhere," and prolonged in its anguish by the words "has shut up the world/Like a bat its wings." The ominous import of this cry is at once made explicit in the words "All is blindness and scales!" The scene in which this utterance takes place forms part of a consistent pattern in the play's dramatic movement, in which a good deal of comic business seems to go on, only to be punctuated at intervals by a sudden awareness by the four characters of their enormous plight. The parallel of this pattern to those moments of lucid insight that sometimes assail us within the random, uncharted flow of human experience hardly needs dwelling upon.

This parallel places Clark-Bekederemo's play in a perspective in the light of which it becomes possible to grasp its proper dimension. *The Raft* strikes us as nothing less than a meditation on the precariousness of the human condition. There is nothing portentous about the way the play goes about what we may take to be its demonstration: indeed, the very setting is appropriate to such a demonstration, founded upon a conception of the Niger Delta as a properly elemental environment, one that lends itself readily to a drama of extreme situations apt to test men's mettle and thus to wring from them a recognition of their true place in the universe. The straightforward symbolism of the whirlpool both features the actual menacing quality of the environment and figures the cosmic terror it induces. The play rings a series of variations on the expression of this terror. Kengide's cry quoted above is earlier voiced more trenchantly by Ibobo's morose reflection on his own existential situation:

> I try to shut my eyes, gateways to my head
> Which is one great cage where misfortune,
> Like an alligator trussed within, batters
> At my temples, forehead and back.

When later in the play, Kengide alludes to the bitterness of the kolanut as a metaphor of life, it is to generalize from the particular experience of the characters to that of mankind at large, whose agony is presented in the play as being a dramatic representation.

The play's pessimistic vision affords no place for a comforting view of life. The heading "Iron and Fire" for the third tableau establishes a grim equivalence between the malevolence of man and the destructive potential of machine that the action plays out. The deliberate ambiguity of the heading "Call of Land" for the final tableau alludes at once to the fugitive hope of the characters and the inescapable fact of human mortality, providing a highly ironic comment on the vanity of worldly agitations. A desperate recognition of the absurdity of human existence thus runs through the play, summed up in these lines:

> No, each day some poor fellow is either
> Going out with a hiss or making his brief
> Entrance with a howl, and the women wail
> Going to bed and wake up wailing, for their seeds
> Are eaten up by the black beetle.

It is not clear to what extent, in the writing of this play, Clark-Bekederemo can be considered to have been indebted to a certain tradition of modern European theater. What seems at one level of its development to be its loose structure—the seemingly rambling dialogue and unfocused action of the play—conforms to this tradition insofar as it affords a formal pointer to the conventions of what Martin Esslin has called "Theater of the Absurd." But these elements are in fact highly organized towards a statement that is in immediate relation to the playwright's experience of background and handling of setting. For if *The Raft* is so profoundly concerned with the existential predicament of humankind, it is as a function of a deep reflection prompted not in the least by a disenchantment with modern civilization, less still by a nihilist vision, but by a disciplined insight, the fruit of the playwright's contemplation of the immense vistas offered to his vision by the living framework of sea and sky, land and water in which human existence has its immediate location in the Niger Delta. The play is thus essentially an expression of a grounded awe of the obscure forces of the universe. In this sense, *The Raft* gives an original dimension, of a properly metaphysical nature, to the modern preoccupation with the absurd: it is by taking a measure of humanity, against the scale of the natural world, which forms the background of his own experience, that the playwright proffers his dread understanding of the human condition.

The total integration of setting into the dramatic movement of *The Raft* for a philosophical reflection points to its foundation in a coherent view of the world, in a cosmology that serves as the constant reference for the complex interaction of the lives that Clark-Bekederemo evokes in his plays with the environment. It was inevitable that he should have been led to draw directly upon the dramatic resources offered by myth and legend among his own people for his next play, *Ozidi,* based on the Ijaw epic he recorded, transcribed, and edited. Part of the interest of this play derives from its relation to its source in the Ijaw oral tradition, a fact that prompts a comparison between the play and the original epic. It needs to be stressed however that the play is not a mere adaptation of the epic for the modern stage, but in fact a transposition of the traditional material, which makes the play an autonomous dramatic work. It needs therefore to be viewed as a restatement by the playwright, in personal terms, of the significance he attaches to the traditional epic.

Ozidi is without question Clark-Bekederemo's most fully realized play; it is at the same time the work in which he seems to have attained full mastery of his idiom. It is obvious that the conception of the play came to him fully formed from his living so long with the material in its original version. The full coincidence of Clark-Bekederemo's genius with his subject becomes evident in the way the clear linearity of the action is orchestrated in a complex elaboration of the material he took over from the traditional background.

As is so well demonstrated in the Elizabethan drama with which Clark-Bekederemo was familiar from his English studies, the revenge theme in itself offers excellent prospects for effective theater. The heroic dimension that the theme receives in the national epic of his own people gave a pronounced lift to the playwright's imagination, which becomes fully attuned to the spirit of the Ijaw story, to the tremendous energy of its original manifestation in the traditional epic. It is this quality that Clark-Bekederemo has endeavored to capture, as much in language as in the total design and movement of the play. The location of the action partly in the world of myth, similar in some respects to that which we encounter in Tutuola's novels, gives the play a large dimension that comes through in the following passage in which the Story-Teller reports the collaboration of the elements at the birth of Ozidi junior:

> In the seventh month of Orea seeing
> Her belly, she bore the dead Ozidi
> A son safe away in her mother's town
> Ododama. That day it rained barrels
> Of water through a sieve of sunshine. You
> Could say of the storm that a giant wind
> Had taken the sea as an orange by the mouth
> And sucking it, had spat in face of the sun
> Who winced lightning, and then hurled it all back
> At earth as rain and bolts of thunder.

Despite this mythic background, the play bears most directly on the moral dilemmas of our human universe. An important factor that appears to be operative in the writing of the play is the profound fascination that the personality of the national hero of the Ijaw people and that of his grandmother, Oreame, exercised upon the playwright's imagination. The appeal of these two characters served to stimulate what amounts to a personal re-assessment on his part of their linked moral adventure. For *Ozidi* can be considered a modern morality play, concerned most essentially with the place of hubris in human affairs.

The play's focus on Oreame's formidable resolution serves as the playwright's mode of exploration of this problem. It is important to bear in mind in this respect that in most African languages, the connotation of the word translated as *witch* has a more positive ring than is suggested by its English equivalent. It designates quite simply one who happens to be endowed with extraordinary powers, which can be applied for good or ill. Oreame herself is in fact presented at one moment in the play in her normal role as healer, so that what we witness is an inversion of the humane function she fulfils in her community. It is not without interest in our consideration of this point to note the way in which her male counterpart and collaborator, the Old Man Wizard, is thoroughly humanized in the play:

> I am, oh,
> I am by the look of the setting sun.
> My brain has frozen within the skull; it now
> Knocks like a dry nut in its shell.

Ozidi presents us with a character study of the utmost psychological and moral interest. Oreame's inflexible will makes her the embodiment of the driving principle of Ozidi's passion and, at the same time, the externalized figure of his lack of growth in moral awareness. Despite his role as the ostensible hero of the play, Ozidi's immaturity is sufficiently dwelt upon to instruct us about the true character of his hubris: the awful contrast between his unusual physical attributes and his undeveloped consciousness makes the point that the play is concerned with the destructive course of an impersonal force to the point where, like a storm in nature, it has to play itself out for a restoration of order in the world. The public disavowal of Ozidi's frenzy occurs appropriately at the moment when it reaches its highest moment, in the duel between him and Ofe, when he stands all alone with his grandmother in their victory. This scene, taken with the subsequent ones that illustrate the progressive corruption of the moral purpose of Oreame and her grandson, highlights the ambiguous relation between the claims of justice they represent at the outset and the habit of violence they have adopted as their unfailing response to situations. And it is only when Ozidi is divested of his passion that he can be welcomed back into the company of men.

As in the epic from which it is derived, the formal organization of Clark-Bekederemo's play serves to point up the human significance of the Ozidi story. The elaborate pageantry through which the plot moves in the epic is reproduced in the play in the context of a lively interaction between the text and the extra- and para-textual effects that both lend dramatic support to the action and contribute to its affective quality.

All the indications are that, in his conception of the play, Clark-Bekederemo had firmly before him the operative principle of African art as a mode of total performance, and that he sought to actualize this principle in his play within the framework of modern dramatic practice.

This observation raises the question of the technical demands of the play. It has often been objected that these demands cannot reasonably be met in the modern theater. But as anyone who has seen the film of the original epic made by Frank Speed soon comes to realize, there is nothing in the play as conceived and written by Clark-Bekederemo that is beyond the resources of a reasonably equipped theater company. For all its limitations, the film clarifies many of the technical issues raised by the play. Apart from the fact that the context is often presented directly in the dialogue, which takes on much of the burden of scene-painting, it soon becomes apparent that the conventions of realistic drama are out of place in a work that relies primarily on the device of stylization for its most important effects.

The examples abound of the way in which, through its formal organization, the play aspires to the condition of total drama. The assignation to the drums of the "cauldron music" of Ozidi's bowels as they rumble in anger is only one instance of the various devices which tend to this end. We might mention in particular the great scene of self-recognition by the young Ozidi, which depends for its dramatic impact less on dialogue than on the stage business from which it is worked out. Other scenes require particular effects and specific skills from the actors. The scene in act two in which Oreame takes Ozidi to the forest grove to be fortified by Old Man Wizard calls for choreographic skills that the playwright was well aware were well developed among the traditional artists of his own people and those of other ethnic groups in Nigeria, as for instance the famous acrobatic dancers of the Ishan people in Midwestern Nigeria. He could have no hesitation therefore in writing this scene as he did. For the rest, the use of mime and costumed masque is expressly indicated for many other episodes. All that is necessary therefore to bring the play alive is proper acquaintance with the principles and conventions of African artistic expression and some imagination on the part of the producer.

These technical considerations are essential for an appreciation of the playwright's deepest intention, for the purpose of any production of the play must be to restore to full view of the audience Clark-Bekederemo's conception of his work as a form of communal celebration. *Ozidi* seems designed to provide something of a complement to

The Raft in its immediate political significance as well as in its further metaphysical resonances: the bleak landscape of the earlier play becomes in the later one the cosmic backdrop for a drama of immense proportions. The outcome of this drama, in which the character of Ozidi attains an ironic but true form of transcendence, that implied by his reduction to the level of ordinary mortal, gives the transformation an affirmative purpose, the character of a celebration of the common humanity he shares with his people.

Clark-Bekederemo's *Ozidi* might be said to work ultimately toward a projection of the emblematic significance of the Ijaw epic onto the contemporary national scene, as a means of engendering the sentiment of a common bond in time and space. There is a real sense in which the play has meaning as the effort to convert a tribal into a national consciousness. If the Ijaw saga enacts for its original audience a ritual of collective consecration through the celebration of a legendary figure and the invocation of the mythic imagination, the modern play seeks to enforce, in secular form, a collective consciousness in the new context of an urgent project of national integration.

This purposive direction of the play's symbolism becomes explicit in the final scene that seeks to involve the national psyche in its meaning. The final procession of actors and audience takes on a wider significance from this point of view and must be interpreted both as the joyous acceptance of a restoration of harmony in the imaginative world of the play itself and as its symbolic anticipation in the real world of national coexistence inhabited by its contemporary audience. It is, moreover, a scene that underscores the playwright's sense of his artistic mission, the emphasis he places upon the function of drama as the means of a collective therapeutic.

There is a noticeable drop in dramatic pace and intensity as we move from this first group of plays to the three plays that constitute the Bikoroa trilogy. The return to the theme of domestic tragedy already treated in *Song of a Goat* gives the trilogy a simplicity of outline that makes for a certain concentration of effect. These plays seem to me ideally suited for performance over a three-day period, so that the pathos that runs through the trilogy can be more keenly felt to flow as a continuous stream from one play to the next. Besides, their triadic scheme virtually makes them into a single play in three extended movements, not only linked thematically by the working out through their development of an inexorable destiny in the fortunes of a single family but also unified by a reflective point of view. The fifty-year temporal span of the plays is projected, as it were, across the rootedness of the community the play deals with, stressing the permanence of the human impulses operating within it, against the background of developments in the wider world.

The real point of concentration in the trilogy seems to me to reside in the middle work, *The Return Home*, which displays all the properties of ritual drama and thus functions as much more than a bridge from one moment of intensity in the cycle to another. The subdued atmosphere that prevails in the play has indeed its own intensity, and seems designed to bring into focus the underlying moral and spiritual stress that the playwright explores through the three plays. After the agitated action of *The Boat* and the meditative cast of this middle play, *Full Circle* can only fulfil our anticipation of a return in the trilogy to a definitive point of stasis.

Coming after the fairly standard format of the first three plays and the grand scale of *Ozidi*, the more withdrawn character of *The Bikoroa Plays* demonstrates the diversity of approach to dramatic writing in Clark-Bekederemo's work. All the plays present a number of problems, inherent in the innovative role they have played in the creation of Nigerian and African dramatic literature in English, which has meant a rethinking of virtually every point of dramatic style. But the principal problem with which the playwright was confronted remains as always that of language, more acute here than in the poems, given the presentational character and function of drama. For Clark-Bekederemo's task in these plays has been to devise in the English language and for immediate utterance a form of speech that is in character with the dispositions and mental universe of the men and women who people his plays.

His choice of verse drama as the formal framework of the first group of plays can be understood in this light, as compelled by the necessity to capture the exact register of indigenous speech in the dramatic situations his plays present. This makes for a distinctive rhetoric, of which the extensive stock of proverbs, with their graphic imagery and terse formulation of thought, constitutes a significant dimension, well reflected in the constant metaphoric turn of the dialogue ascribed to even the most humble characters. That the procedure is well-matched to the context and atmosphere of the plays can be judged from this passage in *The Raft*:

> I have often heard
> It said you could see the street lights of Burutu
> Far, far out from stream. I thought it one

Of their stories—like those about ghosts
Who are never seen but by persons
In distant parts who told it to a friend
Who told it to another and so on till
You feel in the endless coil of the guinea worm.

It is not only that Clark-Bekederemo makes direct use of proverbs in the delineation of his characters in their normal, everyday habits of speech. The language of the plays is permeated by what we may term the proverbial dimension of African modes of discourse. The scene in *Ozidi* where Ewiri brings news to Ofe's compound of the arrival of the young Ozidi at Orua provides an extended example of this characteristic manner of discourse.

It is curious that the playwright makes sparing use of outright transliterations; expressions like "Where God in heaven touches the ground," or "That's the bitter Ijaw truth," taken straight from the Ijaw language, occur only occasionally. This indicates that his interest lay not in a mannered recasting of English but in exploiting its resources to convey the structure and tonality of indigenous speech. In the first series of plays, the use of blank verse enables him to approximate in English the peculiar cadences of his native Ijaw, bringing the pressures of this highly musical language to bear on his adopted medium of expression. Clark-Bekederemo's debt to the great master of English speech is in evidence here. Consider for example the Shakespearean accent of this extract from *The Masquerade*:

Salt and sting, salt and sting, it's surfeit
Of both that has ruined us. But look, there comes
Umuko, a craft with none at the helm.

If the eloquence of the passage sounds too close to the original source, it demonstrates how the same accent can produce the right dramatic effect, as in this simple but memorable passage from *Song of a Goat*:

There will never be light again in this
House, child, this is the night of our race,
The fall of all that ever reared up head
Or crest.

English blank verse was admirably suited to Clark-Bekederemo's purpose, for its peculiar combination of strength and suppleness provided him with an expressive instrument he was able to manipulate for shaping the language of his characters. It enabled him to infuse much of the dramatic language in his plays with the contained power demonstrated by these lines spoken by the dimwitted Temugedege in his single moment of insight in *Ozidi*:

> But here is a boy, full grown, brought to me
> By mother of the wife who fled
> The homestead when lightning struck
> In broad sunshine. Did the bolt that splintered
> Our cornerstone till the soil as well,
> Engendering by that one stroke the seed
> That sprung this stem?

Finally, we might note the transposition in these plays into the register of English of the sheer delight in language that is a constant feature of indigenous modes of linguistic interaction, and which is made evident in the dialogue of the characters. No better example can perhaps be found than in this strikingly visual presentment of swallows in *The Raft*, a passage remarkable for its subtle play of alliterations:

> They are swarming all over the place. Look,
> They dive as if to plunge headlong into the swell,
> But even as their feet graze the wave crest, they
> Have swept steep back into the skies.

It is in the felicity of such passages that we observe the way in which the poet joins hands with the playwright in crafting the language of these plays.

A survey of the kind I've attempted to provide here necessarily involves an evaluation, and I have said enough to suggest that if, as we consider Clark-Bekederemo's work in its totality, we observe the inevitable losses, we can have no doubt that the gains outstrip them decisively. This work is large enough to present a dominant outline on the landscape of modern African literature. But it remains to point out his principal achievement, which for me consists in the signal contribution he has made to the development of a poetics appropriate to the requirements of a new mode of African imaginative expression. To stress this aspect of Clark-Bekederemo's achievement is to draw attention to two fundamental considerations prompted by the development of his work.

The first is in direct line with the formal implications of my remark and is inherent in the elementary fact that the foundation of all literary expression is the structure of words from which it rises. This implies that the writer's first duty is to attend to the particular quality of his expression, matching that expression to the context of his enunciations: text and context thus stand in a dynamic relation to each other. This seems a simple requirement, but it is one that has posed problems not only of an aesthetic but also of an ideological order to the African writer who has to employ a European language. Although Clark-Bekederemo has not involved himself in any elaborate theoretical formulations, his work demonstrates, in the deliberation with which he has worked out his idiom, a thoughtful approach to the solution of the problems of craftsmanship with which the combined pressures of his vocation and his situation confronted him.

The second consideration arises from the tense background of history from which all modern African expression issues, and in particular the role of literature in the reconstruction of African consciousness. The Nigerian context of his work gives a special relief to Clark-Bekederemo's achievement in this regard. His work belongs to a stellar constellation that includes Christopher Okigbo, Gabriel Okara, Chinua Achebe, Wole Soyinka, and Amos Tutuola, who have planted the seeds of what has grown visibly into a national literature. The wholehearted involvement of this literature in the evolving destiny of the national community it represents gives it a social dimension, a live significance, in the difficult quest for cohesion in which that community has been engaged.

The personal role of Clark-Bekederemo in the genesis of this national literature has been remarked upon. The precedent set by his early work was decisive in opening the way to much that is valuable today in Nigerian, and by extension, African poetry and drama, and his later work has been influential in the orientation of literary consciousness and creation on the continent. His poetry in particular has provided the sounding board against which the new generation of Nigerian writers who came after him, especially those who have emerged since the Civil War, have sounded their voices and thus found the confidence of their own expression. For even where no conscious debt to him can be traced in the work of younger poets such as Odia Ofeimun, Niyi Osundare, Harry Garuba, Tanure Ojaide, and Femi Osofisan, they have had of necessity to look to the foreground of Nigerian literature occupied by Clark-Bekederemo and other major writers in order to find their own space. And it is no exaggeration to say that it is largely his legacy that they are in the process of consolidating, in the tumultous climate of a society that has possibly the strongest claim to being considered the most exciting area of creative endeavor in Africa today.

Abiola Irele
Columbus, Ohio
April 1991.

Three Plays

Song of a Goat

PERSONS

Zifa a fisherman and part-time ship pilot at one of the Niger estuaries

Tonye his younger brother and assistant

The Masseur crippled and itinerant, he is to many the family doctor, the confessor and the oracle

Ebiere Zifa's wife
Orukorere his half-possessed aunt
Dode his child
Neighbors as chorus

FIRST MOVEMENT

In a half-lit room Ebiere is lying face up on a mat. The Masseur, seated on a stool by her side and with hands arrested on her bare belly, has just made a discovery.

Masseur: Your womb
  Is open and warm as a room:
  It ought to accommodate many.
Ebiere: Well, it seems like staying empty.
Masseur: An empty house, my daughter, is a thing
  Of danger. If men will not live in it
  Bats or grass will, and that is enough
  Signal for worse things to come in.

3

Ebiere: It is not my fault. I keep my house
   Open by night and day
   But my lord will not come in.
Masseur: Why? Who bars him?
Ebiere: I do not hinder him.
Masseur: My feet drag, but not so my wits;
   They are nimble as the lamb.
Ebiere: My house has its door open I said.
Masseur: I can see that. Too open I rather
   Fear. Draught may set in any time
   Now. Let the man enter and bring in his warmth.
Ebiere: Of course, I want his warmth.
Masseur: Then it is his fault?
Ebiere: Ask him, please, perhaps he will tell.
Masseur: Has he a house elsewhere?
Ebiere: No.
Masseur: Well, he is not crippled in any way?
   So you turn your face to the wall. That is
   The sign of death, my daughter.
Ebiere: Oh, how I wish I'd die, to end all
   This shame, all this showing of neighbors my
   Fatness when my flesh is famished!
Masseur: This is terrible, my daughter, nobody
   Must hear of it. To think that a stout staff
   Is there for you to hold to for support.
Ebiere: It isn't there, it isn't there at all
   For all its stoutness and size.
   There isn't just a pith to the stout staff.
Masseur: When did you discover it lacked the
   Miracle to bring forth green leaves and fruits?
Ebiere: After my first and only issue in his house.
Masseur: And since then you have done nothing?
Ebiere: What could I? I thought it was all in
   Consideration for me. You see I had a
   Difficult time bringing forth my son.
Masseur: I see. Well, your gates are intact
   As their keeper cannot even touch them.
   Someone has to go in or they will take rust.
Ebiere: Oh, no, no, not that!
Masseur: Well, yes, so I fear. Do your parents know
   About this?

Ebiere: No,
  I do not want to hurt him, he is very
  Good to me, besides how will both his people and
  Mine take it?
Masseur: That is true, my child, but
  All the same you ought to have let your people know.
  There's no shame in that. Worse things
  Have been seen before. Why, even leopards go lame.
  And let me tell you, my child, for
  Every ailment in man there is
  A leaf in the forest. If both families
  Cherish each other so much, a good proposition
  Would be for your husband to make you over
  To another in his family.
Ebiere: How can you say a thing like that?
Masseur: I know
  Such a prospect did not open out to you.
  It is understandable.
  After all, you are just stepping out
  On the morning dew of life with mist all prostrate
  On the ground before you. But when the sun is up
  You'll see better. He should make you over
  To his younger brother. That'll be a retying
  Of knots, not a breaking or loosening
  Of them.
Ebiere: That will be an act of death,
  It is what the dead forbid you speak of.
Masseur: I understand
  Your feelings, understand them very well. But
  You are young still as I say, and do not
  Know the ways of our land. Blood of goat
  So large a cowrie may pass thro' its nose,
  A big gourd of palm wine and three heads of
  Kola-nut split before the dead of
  The land, and the deed is done.
Ebiere: Leave me, I say,
  Take your crooked hands off me. I'll not
  Stay here any longer to hear this kind of talk.
  If you see me at your threshold again, call me
  As big a fool as Zifa who sent me to you
  For a cure he knew was unnecessary.

Here is
Your one and six pence. Now let me pass.
Masseur: Do not take it so ill, child, I mean my
    Proposition, you may do worse.
    [*She goes out and another comes in in haste.*]
Zifa: Ebiere,
    She was here just now. I heard her skirt flutter
    In the wind as I came in but even as I called
    Her footsteps died out on the grass.
Masseur: My son, are you the husband of her who ran
    Out now? You have allowed the piece of fertile
    Ground made over to you to run fallow
    With elephant grass.
Zifa: What do you mean?
Masseur: Anyone can see the ears and tassels of
    The grass from afar off.
Zifa: Has she told you something?
Masseur: Here, son, the woman has told nothing.
    Don't you see the entire grass is gone
    Overlush, and with the harmattan may
    Catch fire though you spread over it
    Your cloak of dew?
Zifa: I am not such a child as to set fire
    To my land for fowls of the air to scratch
    And pick up grubs.
Masseur: You have, for no fault of your own,
    But you ought to have called for help.
Zifa: You talk of help. What help can one expect
    That is placed where I stand? People
    Will only be too pleased to pick at me
    As birds at worm squirming in the mud. What,
    Shall I show myself a pond drained dry
    Of water so their laughter will crack up the floor
    Of my being?
Masseur: All this is folly, Zifa. No
    Man ever built a house or cleared
    A piece of ground all by himself. You ought to have
    Asked for help in your plight.
Zifa: This is a plight
    That allows for no help.
    And I will not be the man

To open myself for others to trample on.
Masseur: So it is the woman who must suffer
  Neglect and waste?
Zifa: The woman must wait. The thing
  May come back any day, who knows? The rains
  Come when they will.
Masseur: She has waited too long already,
  Too long in harmattan. The rains
  Are here once more and the forest getting
  Moist. Soon the earth will put on her green
  Skirt, the wind fanning her cheeks flushed
  From the new dawn. Will you let the woman
  Wait still when all the world is astir
  With seed and heady from flow of sap?
Zifa: I know
  All that. And because of that I try to sharpen
  My cutlass on flint to clear the land. Is it my
  Fault I cannot lift up my lifeless hand?
Masseur: This is the third flood of your hoping.
Zifa: Yes, yes, that is very true,
  I admit it's been so these several falls
  Of the flood though as another rose my heart has risen
  With it only to be left aground once more.
Masseur: How much longer will hope hold out?
Zifa: I will not give up my piece of land!
Masseur: One learns to do without the masks he can
  No longer wear. They pass on to those behind.
Zifa: What is your meaning? I cannot
  Follow the drift of your talk.
Masseur: In a situation
  Like yours one may be content to drift as do
  The weeds of the stream. But that carries very
  Little, because the tide always turns
  Back on one.
Zifa: What have you been telling my
  Wife, man? I sent her on to you to
  Rub, not to turn against her man.
Masseur: So you beat your ears, young man. If your wife has
  Been faithful to the point of folly, that
  Is your business and hers. But why must you
  Send her on to me to take the birth cure

When the fault is not with her. Others
May have taken your fees and agreed to help
You keep up appearances. I will not be
One of them. What, are people to understand she failed
To respond even to the touch of my fingers?
Think,
Man, it is three floods now as you yourself said.
Zifa: Others have had to wait more. Why, Ogun's
  Wife has been known to wait seven years
  To bring forth fruit. Meanwhile I may
  Regain my power.
Masseur: No, it is there I fear
  You do wrong by her. Ogun was consistent
  With his cultivation of the land which
  Was his. Only in his case the land would not
  Yield of its own. Why, I remember the case
  Very well as I had to be called in
  To break the curse upon it. This
  I traced to the foot of a tree on
  The other side of the evil grove and there
  The burden was voided and buried
  In the crook of twin buttress roots.
Zifa: Don't I remember it!
  All the town followed as she danced her way
  To the root of her trouble. She kept us men
  On the drums all day, she did. But in the end
  She brought forth a child.
Masseur: And a very healthy seed
  It turned out to be. It was worth waiting
  Many moons for. Every season, they still
  Bring me gifts of yam and fish.
Zifa: Oh, why is such a cure not open to us
  Men? I'd give the gods and my fathers
  The fattest bull in the land to retrace
  My course and cast off this curse.
  I want my son to have brothers and
  Sisters. It isn't that I do not care.
Masseur: I can see you care very much. Everyone
  Can see that. You buy your wife the truest
  Madras, beat for her the best gold and
  Anyone can see she is very well-fed.

But we fatten our maidens to prepare for fruition,
Not to thwart them.
Zifa: I do not thwart her;
It is I who am thwarted.
Masseur: What then do you propose to do?
Zifa: I have been to all experts between swamp and
Sand. What has any of the lot been able
To do but suggest I adjust myself to my curse.
Curse! My father who they dared
Not spit at when he lived is dead
And lying in the evil grove. Was that
Not enough penalty?
Of course, I have recalled
Him into town so at times of festival he can
Have sacrifice.
Masseur: I think of the man's start, his end,
And my head fills out. I knew him well.
Why, if ever there was a killer of
Fish and another of crabs, we were
That pair. Ask anyone in all
The seven rivers.
Zifa: And am I to blame
If all was fish that came to his net?
Masseur: Of course not. You did what every
Dutiful son would do when you brought
Him back home among his people.
It may have been a little bit early
For one who died of the white taint.
Zifa: And for that they have picked my flesh
To the bones like fish a floating corpse.
Others grumble it was in time
Of flood. They will all be too ready now
To smirk if they hear I am become
Drained of my manhood.
Masseur: God made the tree
Apah straight and erect.
Zifa: I have heard
All that talk before. What I want is
A way out, a way to lead me
Out of this burnt patch of earth.
Masseur: There is a way out I spoke to your wife

And only a little while ago.
But you yourself saw even now how the hen
All but blew down the house with the flutter
Of her wings. With the cock himself, the walls
May well give in and I am too old
To start raising green thatch for my grey hair.
Zifa: Let me hear it.
Masseur: No, better go in
   To her first and do not rear too high
   Your crest. The poor woman is in a state for brooding.
Zifa: I cannot look her in the face now our
   Secret is out.
Masseur: Your secret is not
   Out and will remain safe.
Zifa: Next everybody would be saying, there
   Goes the cock with the flaming red crest
   But touch the thing and you'll find it
   Colder than a dog's nose.
Masseur: There is no need
   To whip yourself into this frenzy, Zifa.
   Now I know you, I may as well tell you
   I massaged your own father when we were
   Both supple and strong together and could
   Throw any challenger on the wrestling
   Ground. In all that time I have not shared
   A man's secret with another. Why should I
   With you whom I helped to bring into this world
   And whose fortunes I should love to watch
   As a father his son's?
Zifa: Forgive me, father,
   It is the thought of so many things makes
   Me mad. I will not be separated from
   My wife. She herself will not agree to it.
Masseur: How do you know that?
   Have you ever considered another should
   Take over the tilling of the fertile
   Soil, and had wet mud flung back at you?
Zifa: You lame thing, you crawling piece
   Of withered flesh with the soul of a serpent,
   Shall I crush you between my palms and wipe
   Your face on the ground, you weaker

Than a fowl of the earth that wipes
His beak in dust after meal. Shall I wring
Your neck of fiber? How dare you suggest
A thing like that to me? I am strong and
Alive still and dare you open your filthy
Mouth to suggest I pawn my land?

Masseur: You are eaten up with anger but although
You crush me, a cripple, between your strong
Hands, it will not solve your problem. What I
Suggest our fathers did not forbid even in days
Of old. Why, the hippopotamus wants
A canoe, it also wants paddles.

Zifa: Dirt, dung and drippings at dark! I am
That hippopotamus. I spit but it falls
On my head.

Masseur: No, the gods forbid. I know
You are over-wrought, my son, but that is
Because you have this curse upon your head.
Really, you must go now and sit
On what I suggest. The soil is sacred
And no one man may dispose of it. Both
Your families will have to sit together and
Talk the matter over.

Zifa: And is that all
The help you can offer? They say the crooked
Wood tells the expert carver.

Masseur: Not when the tree
Is blasted, my son.

Zifa: Oh, Ebiere,
My wife, my wife, has it come to this?
And what is to become of me?
Of course, they will have to kill me first.

Masseur: Do not
Think it that way, my son. Some till, but others
Must catch bird or fish. Each is a lot
With its own song.

Zifa: I will die first.

Masseur: No, that is a child's talk. Even I,
That am cripple in more ways than one, live
And hope to some purpose for my people.
Why should you talk then of dying? One must

First lay out all things to talk of going
Home. So go home now and to your wife
And act on these things.
Zifa: For her and for everything I salute
You. Now I go.
Masseur: Go well then, son, and the gods
And dead protect you.
Zifa: Stay well, father, and do not forget me as
You make them offerings of sacrifice.
Masseur: I'll surely not forget you in my prayers.
Well, there goes a man deep and furious as
A river underground. I hope he keeps
The lid down on his wife for I fear
She is fretting already. Oh you dead
And gone, take your fat and flesh
But leave us our skin and bones.

SECOND MOVEMENT

Out in the concession. Dusk is thickening.

Orukorere: Woo-oo-oo-oo-oo-oo-oo-oo-oo-oo-oo
Woo-oo-oo-oo-oo-oo-oo-oo-oo-oo-oo-oo
All you people run this way!!
Zifa: Who is that crying for help?
Tonye: It's she, our father's sister.
Orukorere: I say come out here, all you people.
A goat, a goat, I hear the cry of a goat.
Zifa: Will you keep quiet!
Tonye: Somebody's been giving her drinks again.
Orukorere: A goat, a he-goat, don't you hear
Him crying? Wo—oo—oo—oo!!
Will you come out all you people?
First Neighbor: What's the matter now?
Second Neighbor: Is anyone dying?
Third Neighbor: Has your house caught fire? In this
Weather of high wind, the fish rack
Must be well above fire.

Zifa: There, will you keep quiet, Mother!

Tonye: Now she's roused the whole town again.

Zifa: Oh, keep quiet, Mother!

Orukorere: I won't, I won't, I hear a goat crying
   Out for help and you say I should keep quiet.

First Neighbor: Oh, it is the woman again!

Third Neighbor: What does she say?

Second Neighbor: There is so much snuff in her mouth it
   Is impossible to hear what she says.

Orukorere: I must find him, the he-goat;
   His cry is everywhere, don't you hear it?
   It is all over the house: I say, can't
   You hear the poor billy bleating.
   It's bleeding to death.

First Neighbor: I don't hear anything.

Third Neighbor: This is strange.

Second Neighbor: Well, how are the goats around here?

Zifa: They are all turned in for the night.

Tonye: All are squatting behind chewing the cud
   Till the moon is up.

Orukorere: There goes the cry again! I am sure
   A leopard has the poor thing in his grip.
   We must save the poor brute.

Second Neighbor: What is this she is saying?

Third Neighbor: If there is a leopard here, then this is
   No place to stay.

First Neighbor: Did she say a leopard, get a lantern then.

Zifa: Will you stop that nonsense!

Tonye: Please, you know how it is with her,
   How then can you take her seriously?

First Neighbor: It should be easy to see a leopard
   If he were here. His eyes should be
   Blazing forth in the dark.

Third Neighbor: So I hear. I have heard them likened
   To the lighthouse out on the bar.

Second Neighbor: And its motion is silent as that big house.
   We must be careful.

Orukorere: Of course,
   You do not hear him bleating, the goat,
   How could you? The ram does not cry
   Out for help although led into captivity.

Zifa: Orukorere, will you stop this nonsense?
Orukorere: There goes the cry again.
   [*She makes off.*]
First Neighbor: Stop her, we must stop her.
Second Neighbor: She will do herself harm if she goes on like this.
Third Neighbor: She may have seen something for
   All we know.
Orukorere: Don't you hear it?
   Don't you deaf of this world?
   Are your ears so sealed and congealed
   With pulp of plantain, you do not hear him?
Zifa: I told you people none must pour
   Her wine any longer. Must I beat it
   On calabash back before you heed me?
First Neighbor: Surely no one has given her drinks.
Second Neighbor: Orukorere doesn't need anybody's drink.
Third Neighbor: It's hard getting a bottle even for
   Sacrifice these days.
Orukorere: Do not hold me!
Zifa: Leave her alone there, Tonye.
Tonye: People will say now she is mad.
Orukorere: I must find him, the leopard
   That will devour my goat, I must
   Find him. Surely his footsteps will show
   Upon the mud? Surely, those claws bloody
   From hunt of antelopes in the forest
   Will show in the sand? Or has the wind
   Swept them off before housewives come
   Upon them with brooms at break of day?
   Or sports him no spoors?
First Neighbor: Follow her, let's follow her.
Third Neighbor: The woman may have double vision after all.
Second Neighbor: There she is again. She has torn through
   The plantains behind.
Orukorere: A true leopard flings out his specks even
   At dark, they will spark forth to tell
   The king of the forest is out stalking. And
   He throws his catch up over the roof
   Thatch, however high, to catch it on
   The lee before the quarry falls;
   Else he is no true hunter. We must halt

Him, put a stop to this fault.
Tonye: She has fallen, she has fallen!
Third Neighbor: This is strange.
First Neighbor: More than strange.
Second Neighbor: Zifa, you really must do something.
Zifa: Do what? Put her in a room with goats
    And tie her to a log. Isn't
    That what you will have me do?
Second Neighbor: Nobody said you should shut her up.
Third Neighbor: No, not with goats among their slime and
    Dung.
First Neighbor: Nor tethered to a log with chains.
Zifa: Then what will you have me do, you sane souls
    Of Deinogbo? Or do you think I have
    Not heard your laughter cackle in the playhouse when
    She passed all smeared with ash and dust?
Tonye: Leave them, they are not worth your anger. I
    Should take them up myself if
    I thought it worth while.
First Neighbor: We did not come to make trouble.
Second Neighbor: It was her cry brought me out of my house.
Third Neighbor: If eyes do not see, lips will not cry.
Zifa: Go away to your houses then
    And tomorrow if any of you finds
    Nothing to cry about in his house
    Let him come to me and I'll dance
    With him even to the market place.
Third Neighbor: We are sorry to see you so.
Second Neighbor: See to her, the woman, your aunt.
First Neighbor: She is foaming in the mouth which is bad.
Zifa: Go away, I said. Tonye, let's take her in.
Tonye: Yes: oh, see how she shudders.
Second Neighbor: That's a queer family.
Third Neighbor: A curse lies heavy on it.
First Neighbor: Of the woman there can be little doubt.
Second Neighbor: And to think she was one time
    The sweetest maid in all the creeks.
Third Neighbor: She will have no man for husband.
    Why, young men came from all over the land
    To ask her hand of her father.
Second Neighbor: They all got it from him, you cannot

Doubt that. He would as easy kill inside the
Clan as outside it.
First Neighbor: Remember how the people of the sea
Chose her for their handmaiden.
Second Neighbor: Sure, but then she was so proud she would
Not listen to what the oracle said.
Third Neighbor: As a result, they have put this spell on
Her. But although she has this double vision
Nobody believes a word she says, even
Outside of the gourd.
First Neighbor: Then, you think there is something
To this her raving?
Third Neighbor: Do not ask me. In
A family like that there always will spring
Up leopards. But that they have goats
In their midst one may as well go
And seek eggs among cocks.
Second Neighbor: Yet she cried a goat. I really can
Not understand them of that family.
First Neighbor: There, let us be off. I can see
His wife is coming.
Second Neighbor: She is grown very queer of late too.
See how she carries her wood?
Third Neighbor: Bring up a chicken among hawks
And if she is not eaten she will eat.
First Neighbor: She certainly looks stiff for all her fatness.
Third Neighbor: It is the wrong type what with that
Her clay color.
Second Neighbor: They say he doesn't go in
To her any more, but I wouldn't discuss that.
Ebiere: Who can those be skulking away
Like goats before ants?
Dode: Mother, mother!
Ebiere: Here's a dragonfly I caught you on the way.
Dode: O oo! how bright his colors! But Ebiere,
Mother, mother, she's been—
Ebiere: All right, all right, Dode, I quite follow.
Your mother's been drunk again and
Seeing visions of houses burning.
Dode: No, it was a goat this time. It was crying
Because a leopard had it in its claws.

Ebiere: And so your father and Tonye have taken
   Her in to sleep it out.
Dode: Yes, they have. But, what is a leopard? Is it
   Big as a cow?
Ebiere: Leave leopards alone to the elders
   Of the family. Your father is honored
   For collecting their scalps but everybody
   Discredits your mother who only sees
   Them in visions. Well, was everybody
   Waiting for me to come back and put
   On the lamp?
Tonye: Careful, Ebiere, she has vomited all
   Over the floor.
Ebiere: Thank you, but I can find my way.
Zifa: You are back from the bush, I am
   Glad of that. We were about coming out
   To you when she started seeing
   Things once more.
Tonye: It is so embarrassing,
   Everybody has been here to see her.
Ebiere: I saw them going out as I came in.
   They didn't even stop to greet me.
Tonye: Zifa drove them off the place.
Zifa: I had to. Now, do you think you could clean
   This up?
Ebiere: Of course, I will. Let me get some
   Piece of cloth to mop it up. The woman
   Is almost a child once more.
Tonye: A child?
Ebiere: Why, yes. Anyone can see that from how
   She behaves. And for that alone I get
   Rather fond of her.
Tonye: That is a foolish thing to say.
Zifa: No, Tonye, no.
   She knows what she is talking.
Ebiere: Really, I wasn't trying to be awkward. Of that
   You will agree we have enough
   Already. Well, I thought you said you put
   Her to bed to sleep it off?
Tonye: So we did.
Zifa: Yes, we did.

Dode: She is singing, she is up and singing.

Ebiere: You hear her, too, Dode, don't you? Listen!

Tonye: She is coming out.

Orukorere: The leopard, I have missed the leopard
    That will despoil the prime goat of our yard
    But I do not hear the victor's cry.

Dode: Nor I, Mother.

Ebiere: Keep quiet, Dode; will you?

Zifa: There is nothing like that here.

Tonye: We looked everywhere while you slept.

Orukorere: So I slept? And you didn't find
    Him? I knew it was no proper leopard.
    There, I see it sports the long slide
    Of the earth one. You know it is the dumbest
    Of all beasts whether in town or bush, yes,
    Even as the beast strikes you dead on the sand.

Zifa: So from leopard it is become a snake?

Orukorere: How should I tell? I must go out first
    And find him.

Zifa: No, you must not.

Tonye: She is going to start all over again.

Orukorere: I feel so dry. Zifa, will you give
    Me some coins out of the pot you buried
    Under your bedstead?

Tonye: Give her, if that will make her quiet.

Zifa: I gave you some yesterday, didn't I?
    It's what you have spent drinking all day?

Orukorere: Money is sweet yet it doesn't bubble fat.

Dode: Please, give it her, father.

Orukorere: No, he won't, my son; although he ate
    Yesterday. Therefore he will not eat today!
    Well, let us sing, boy, oh let's
    Sing of souls tied down with ropes
    Of piassava so strong they break!
    "Bailing out to Accra! It's
    To Accra I must bail,
    This cooking of gin, it's
    Killed me, Oh, it has!"

Ebiere: Now you two, do leave her alone
    I'll go and get food for each one.

THIRD MOVEMENT

Late afternoon. Ebiere is bathing Dode on the verandah. A little away sits Tonye, working on floats for nets and hooklines.

Ebiere: A grown-up fellow like you, strappling as
    A banana sucker, you still do not
    Know how to wash your body properly.
    There, steady! Let me bathe you. You have all
    The time only been rubbing the water on
    Your belly, and a big pot you have. Of course
    You call for farina before the cock calls
    Forth the day. When dawn breaks, mouth opens and
    With you it stays so till dusk closes in.
    Now what are you yelling for? Anybody
    Would think you were being circumcised all
    Over again or that you have yaws on
    You. Take that! And that! Now you can holla
    All day just as you please. I suppose your
    Race can boast of that.
Tonye: What are you
    Smacking the boy for, Ebiere?
Ebiere: Better be
    About what you are going. Don't splash
    Me with water I told you, you scamp!
Tonye: That's enough; we don't allow our children
    To be knocked on the head like that.
Ebiere: Don't you lecture me on how to beat my child.
    What do you know of child-rearing anyway?
Tonye: Enough to know that knocking a child on
    The head like that makes him prone
    To attacks from smallpox. We simply forbid
    It in the family. You may smack
    Him on the backside if you please
    But do not beat the boy on the head.
Ebiere: I can well see you people care for children
    A great deal.
Tonye: Yes, we do. Here, Dode, come
    This way and I will carve you a fine canoe out

Of this cork-wood and bamboo. I have enough
Floats already to fence off the bar.
Dode: Will I be able to go to sea like you
And father?
Tonye: Even so. Witches sail
In groundnut husks; and this boat I shall carve
You is many, many times fitter than any
[*She hisses.*]
Witch's craft. Why, what do you make that sound for?
Ebiere: Does it give you pain?
Tonye: From a snake such a sound is only to be
Expected; it is the signal of spite and
Sinister motives. But coming out of a woman
Like you with all the things a wife would want
In the world I do not know what to make of it.
Ebiere: Poor, poor, father-of-my-marriage, what
Can you or anybody in this house do
About anything? At least, one has first to know
The roots to be able to gather the leaves.
Tonye: Ebiere, yes, I confess I do not know
Much. Both of you, you and Zifa, say very little.
But I do know that you have gradually
Become bitter over the months. Why, look
At how you cuffed the little boy just now.
Anybody seeing you would think you were his
Step-mother.
Ebiere: And he not my only child.
Tonye: I wasn't thinking of that.
Ebiere: You ought to have
Been, yes, long before now, since you are
So solicitous about my well-being.
Tonye: Everybody wants children of course.
Ebiere: Thus the elders pray: Only one seed
The elephant brings forth at a time until
The house is full, yes, until the house be
Full even if this takes ten falls of the flood.
Tonye: Ebiere, you are bitter as bile. Lots
Of people there are who want children but
Have not been blessed with a fine one as you have.
Ebiere: That is bad, isn't it? Especially
As custom dictates those who die childless

Be cast out of the company of the fruitful whose
Special grace is interment in the township.
Tonye: The Witch of Nine Plumes has your stomach
For her cauldron.
Ebiere: She is a good cook, she
Must be, to have boiled me dry of all content.
Tonye: I do not mean that, I mean you ought
To be contented and not be so short
Of temper with everyone. You cuff the child
On the skull, and have taken to scolding and nagging
All day. Have you cooked in time today for my
Brother's home coming? Many times
These past market days it has been so.
Why, what is become of you? A man
After long stay at sea deserves a proper and
Regular dish when he arrives home. I wonder
Zifa is so given to your new
Irregular ways.
Ebiere: Don't talk to me about
Your brother or about my irregular ways,
I tell you, don't talk to me of them.
Irregular ways! What do you know about
Irregularities, anyway? If food was
Not ready by noontide, that would be
Irregular, wouldn't it? If I saw
My period and stayed indoors and cooked
For you and your big brother, that would
Be irregular by all standards
And practice, wouldn't it—you that are so correct
And proper you know all these things?
Tonye: Don't you clap your hands in my face, woman!
If my brother takes all this from you, I
Certainly won't, do you hear me? I will
Not have it.
Ebiere: You talk of your brother
And of his patience as if patience were
His alone and he alone has suffered.
Tonye: Surely, he has suffered much abuse
From you lately.
Why, the whole village is talking.
Ebiere: Talking, are they? Like you are doing now

About his forbearance and his
Sufferings. What do they know about suffering and
Patience? And you, what do you know about them?
Of course, it is the woman who is in the wrong
Always—I who have suffered neglect and
Gathered mold like a thing of sacrifice
Left out in sun and rain at the crossroads.
You talk to me of my short temper; what
Short temper have I when it is pulled and
Tugged at daily like a hook-line?

Tonye: You certainly are showing it today,
And nobody has baited you.

Dode: Mother, Mother don't!

Ebiere: Stand aside, child. Flesh with thorn
In it must bud pus.

Tonye: Nobody stuck
Thorns in your flesh; why should you smart so.

Ebiere: You are a greater fool than the idiot
In the market-place to ask a question like that.

Tonye: I said, Ebiere, I'm not your husband.

Ebiere: Well, aren't you? Since you know his duties better
Than he does, why don't you take them up? If you
Don't, I should laugh your whole race to scorn.

Tonye: What you want is a good cry. Now will
You take your hands off me?

Ebiere: Do it, do it now
And show you are strong.

Tonye: I do not have to
With you to show I have one bone. Many who
Doubted have felt its weight in the wrestling pit.

Ebiere: Well, fell me down then; it would be so much
Easier for you to do, I being no cow.

Tonye: I say take your hands off me. Ebiere,
You certainly are desperate for danger.
See how like waters whipped by the wind you
Have run amok. Take your hands off.

Ebiere: No, no, show your powers, I say,
Floor me, march on me, strike me down as
You did Benikpanra the Bull to show
You are the strong man of the family.

Tonye: Why, Ebiere, you are mad, so gone far

Leaves-gathering, and you are hot all
Over, oh so shuddering, shuddering
So, you want to pull me down which is
A thing forbidden, now take that then, and that—Oh my father!
Ebiere: So I am crazed, completely gone leaves-plucking,
And you? Aren't you shuddering too, Oh,
So shuddering in your heat of manhood you
Have thrown me? Now, hold me, do hold on and
Fight, for it is a thing not forbidden!
[*Cock crows beyond.*]
Dode: Help, help! My mother, my mother! Tonye
Is wrestling on
The floor with my mother!
Orukorere: What is it, child, what is the matter? Can't
I have a little sleep but one
Of you in this house must kick me up?
Dode: There, there, look there, they have rolled
And dragged each other over the doorstep,
And now the door is slammed behind them.
Orukorere: Why, boy, these are no leopard and goat
Interlocked between life and death, but
Two dogs at play. Poor child, let me close the door.
Dode: Will you leave them to fight there? My
Uncle is the strongest man in all
The creeks. He will kill my mother.
Orukorere: He will not, my son, rather it is she
Who may kill your uncle. Oh, my son,
My son, I have seen a sight this dusk to make
The eagle blind. I heard the cock crow
As I woke up from sleep. That was sign
Of omen enough but little did I know
It was this great betrayal of our race.
Dode: You won't separate them then?
Orukorere: Only the gods and the dead may separate
Them now, child. And what is your poor father
To do should he hear that the liana has
Entwined his tree of life? I said there was
A serpent in the house but nobody as usual
Will take me seriously. Yet the hiss of the creature
Was up among the eaves, down under the
Stool. Last night I cried it had coiled itself

Into a pad to pillow my head but the house
Was full of snoring sound and as usual
Everybody snorted. Well, come on,
Son, and I'll get you some snuff.

FINAL MOVEMENT

*Day is breaking, and the tall stem of the sky-god set up in the frontyard and
is lost in the slowly lifting light.*

Zifa: I cannot believe it, I just cannot;
    Eyes may as well see ears and night, day. My
    Own brother whom I have looked after
    As a son, if it is true, I'll cut off his
    Neck with my cutlass. Yet there he was sprawled on
    My bed when I thought he was still out
    Inspecting hooks in the bush.
    And when I would call up the boy,
    She comes between us holding my hand
    With the injunction, oh let the man sleep
    He is tired and mustn't be woken up at
    This dead of night. The man!
    When did he become man to her?
    With her he was always the bad boy to
    Be bullied and scolded: "No sense in Tonye,"
    "Tonye has ruined this again," from cock's
    Crow till the cuckoo's song. Now she stands
    Guard over him in my bed against me.
    I'll kill them both if it is true.
    It cannot be true: only last night they
    Had one of their fights but my aunt, she was so
    Much in grip of drink she could not separate
    Them
    Nor call in help. So they struggled like
    Two iguanas till outspent, they stopped
    Of their own. Her account was too garbled for
    Anyone to gather anything.
Orukorere: It is market day

Awake, awake all of you!
Hello, my son who delights me, who never
Lets me touch mud, is that you?
Zifa: I kneel to you, mother, although the
Sun has gone to sea.
Orukorere: Has it? Well, has it? I thought it all night.
But rise my son. You were not made
For mud. But you are up early which is
A thing very good for that means you
Are offering the gods sacrifice today.
One cannot tell how always watchful they
Stand warding evil spirits away from
The gates until misfortune enters the house.
Zifa: Misfortune has been my guest these many floods.
Orukorere: My son, are they still at the gate, the
Housewives who deserted the hearth?
Zifa: A guest after being fed looks up
At the sun. But these many years I have been host
To a guest that will not return.
Orukorere: Oh, he must! He will sometime, but shall we
Pass today, a day dedicated to the dead
And to all gods, is it to be spoilt
With such bitterness of heart?
Zifa: It is others who have spoilt my day.
Orukorere: You must not say a thing like that.
Zifa: Why shouldn't I when my bed is barred from me
For my brother to sleep on?
Orukorere: Is it even so? The world must not hear of it.
Zifa: The world will, even today. Yesterday you
Said they had a fight, is that true?
Orukorere: A goat and a leopard may as well wrestle.
Zifa: Now, look here, mother, I am tired of
Being in the toil of parables.
Orukorere: No, not so strong, these hands you seek
To break have held you to my breast.
Zifa: God knows I will not be violent
With you. But why will you not tell
All that you know? The very trees in my
Grove are being
Felled level with the ground, you yourself say
You hear them crashing one upon another,

And yet you do nothing to stop them.
Orukorere: Indeed, I am doing all I can to arrest
  Their fall, but which of you has shown a
  Heart to give me a helping hand?
Zifa: Save me, Mother, save me from this
  Disaster, I fear has befallen me.
Orukorere: Of course, I will. There, my child, rest
  Your head on my shoulders shrunken up
  With age. But they still can give my son support.
  Who knows how milk enters the coconut?
  Now, don't sob, oh my son, my son, do
  Not cry! Only the goat may cry
  When the leopard has him in his toils,
  And I'm sure my son is no goat.
Zifa: It is, it is so degrading.
Orukorere: I know. But there, I think your brother is
  Coming this way.
Zifa: He must not see my tears.
Orukorere: That's my boy. The strong weep only at dead
  of night.
Tonye: So the adder
  Has risen, Mother? I did
  Not see you, Zifa.
Orukorere: The puffadder may
  Rise late, but it must not be caught asleep
  Else it will stir in the pot.
Zifa: Where is Ebiere?
Tonye: At the waterside to fetch water. Today
  You very well know is the start of market-
  Tide and she's hurrying to cross over
  With your last night's catch which by the way
  Was no larger than a kite's haul.
Zifa: She is not going to market this tide.
Tonye: Well, is anything the matter here?
  She's all set to go.
Zifa: Shut your mouth, will you? I say
  She will not go to market today.
Tonye: There is little starch or farina left
  In the house; she has to go
  And barter the fish for these.

Orukorere: Now, Tonye, do not cross your elder
  Brother. Go in and look for the he-goat,
  The one that is for sacrifice.
Tonye: I go, mother. The poor thing cried all
  Night and all thro' today; perhaps it knows
  Its day is near night.
Zifa: You see how things are
  Between the two? Ebiere now consults him
  Even in matters of household. What further
  Proof do I want now?
Orukorere: Proofs are
  A thing for the blind. Here, you see this
  Calabash? I have laid fern fronds
  Over it, and the white soil of Edo
  Has turned to mere in it already.
Zifa: I do not need cleansing: perhaps others do.
Orukorere: You will stand where you are and let me
  Begin with you, being head of this house.
Zifa: Indeed, am I head still?
Orukorere: Of course. Only one elder there is to a house
  And the young are water. One head and a
  Long tail, that is our one prayer in life.
  How many times do I have to tell you that?
Zifa: All right, Mother, cut the circles under your
  Heel. I am going in for a little while
  But will be back before the seven are
  Complete in front of the shrine.
Orukorere: I shall be waiting for you. My poor poor
  Child, he has blundered upon the beast that
  Is preying upon him. But what is to become
  Of us in this house?
  We have slept with wives who should
  Be outdoors, have eaten of the meals they prepared
  In their corruption, and passed under lines on which
  They hung their underclothes. In such
  Circumstances, what help what quest
  But to look up to the dead. Ah, my brother, it
  Was good you were called home early to our fathers
  Else you would now see your sons like bad
  Fish eating one another. That goat

Again! I cannot bear its cry. I must go
And find me a live chicken to carry
Out this ritual.

Ebiere: [*Singing*] What do you want with the goat?
One would
Think you were a boy still, and not man.

Tonye: We must be careful, Ebiere. My
Brother and aunt, they were here
Together just now.

Ebiere: What about that? They know nothing.

Tonye: We cannot be too sure. They asked me
To fetch the goat for sacrifice and
Should be back here any time. Ts, ts,
The goat is drinking the water.

Ebiere: Let it be. I am so happy today. I think what I
Told you is true. Come and feel it.

Tonye: No, no, we must not do that here under
Light of day.

Ebiere: It is there,
All right, I know it, and it is for you. Oh,
I am so happy. Tonye, let's fly
And set up house in another creek. You'll
Cast your net and I'll hold the stern until
We have our child.

Tonye: You are mad, Ebiere,
Here, step back and pick up your pot. My
Brother
Is querulous as things are.
He says you must not
Go to market today.

Ebiere: Then we shall be
Together this night. Another of his ships
Comes in tonight, doesn't it? What shall I cook
For you? You know we must fly before
He comes back at dawn.

Tonye: Oh, I think you are gone crazy too,
Everybody in this house. I'll tell him,
Yes, I will. Now, pick up the pot and
Go in, Ebiere.

Zifa: Let the pot be.

Tonye: Oh, I can hardly stay on my feet.

Ebiere: It is as well. The thorn in the flesh
  Will draw pus.
Zifa: I said let the pot be.
  Mother, come out here quick.
Orukorere: Here I am. Now, what does this mean?
Ebiere: Ask him, he should be able to tell
  Begin in such frenzy.
Tonye: Keep quiet, Ebiere. You must not speak
  Like that of my brother.
Zifa: Thank you, my good brother, but I
  Think I can well fend for myself.
Orukorere: Will someone tell an old woman what is
  Happening in this house?
Zifa: I'll tell you, mother, soon enough; you
  Said I should make sacrifice to the gods.
  These past several years we have none of us
  Followed your word. Being the elder,
  I agree, I am to blame for this. But now
  I obey you and will make instant
  Sacrifice to the gods.
Orukorere: But you are
  As yet not cleansed, and for that matter all
  The concession is reeking with rot and
  Corruption.
Zifa: In that case, it needs drastic
  Cleansing which is what we shall now all perform.
Orukorere: Be careful, Son, and do nothing that is
  Rash. When the gods ask for blood it is
  Foolish to offer them oil.
Zifa: You shall
  Be satisfied with all that I do today,
  Mother. Here, Tonye, hold the goat by
  The feet and I will by the horns. And you,
  My wife, see how with one stroke of my knife
  I sever the head from the trunk.
Orukorere: A brave stroke, my boy, a brave stroke!
  There was only one man in all the creeks
  Who could do it like that, but he died many
  Years ago.
Zifa: See how erect
  The blood spurts! It should cleanse the compound

Of all corruption today. But hold on,
One little detail more and we shall begin
In real earnest.

Tonye: What is that?

Ebiere: The blood, it has soiled my clothes.

Zifa: Well, never mind that. A little soap soon
  Washes that off. Here, Tonye, hold forth
  The head with all its horns.

Tonye: There!

Zifa: Good. Now, put it inside the pot.

Orukorere: What is that you ask of the boy?

Ebiere: The man is mad!

Tonye: Why, the thing is impossible.

Zifa: It is not. I said put the head in the pot.

Tonye: I will if you so desire.

Zifa: Yes, I not only desire it, I demand
  It. That's right, just like that.

Tonye: It won't go in any further.

Zifa: Who told you? There, push, Brother, push
  Oh push with all your might!

Tonye: The pot will break if I push harder.

Zifa: So you know that? But never mind. Push
  I say, till the head enters in, horns
  And ears, all of them.

Orukorere: The woman has fainted!

Zifa: Has she? Let her then, and you my
  Brother, you see how the pot is broken!

Tonye: This was a trap, a trap, and you think
  You have caught some grass-cutters.

Zifa: Haven't I? You just wait and see.

Orukorere: I said the woman has fainted and nobody
  Listens! Why, what are you about?
  Run, Tonye, run, your brother has picked up
  His cutlass and will kill you!

Zifa: He is running, the coward, he is
  Running and will save his neck.

Orukorere: Kill me first then.

Zifa: No, do not cross me. It is none of your
  Fault but I'll get at him, I say
  Do not cross me. Don't you see they admit
  Their guilt? One falls fainting and the other

Flees. Now, he's fled in and barred the door.
I shall not let him escape me. I will
Break open the door, break it and get at
This monster. Now, will you come out, thief,
Noon-day thief.

Tonye: I am no noon-day thief!
If you leave your piece of cloth in the open
At night, what becomes of it?

Orukorere: Help, oh help,
You people, my sons, my sons, they have both
Turned beasts and will devour each other.

Zifa: So that is your answer, thief? Well, open
And I'll tell you the sun although
It dries the cloth, never assumes it. But
You have, you have, and left me naked
Before our enemies.

First Neighbor: Why, what is the matter here?

Second Neighbor: Has anyone fainted?

Third Neighbor: Is it fire upon the fish rack?

Orukorere: Oh, no, it is no common fire has
Consumed us. There, go to him before
He breaks down the door and does his brother
Harm. And this woman here, she is dying.

Third Neighbor: What can be happening here?

First Neighbor: There, bring some water. Some of you, go
And hold the man.

Second Neighbor: Thrust hand in her mouth
Till she retches. No, not so, take hold
Of her jaws and keep them open else they'll lock.

Zifa: Keep clear, all of you if you like the taste
Of soup. Now, open up, I say!
Or must I break down the door?

Second Neighbor: He has a cutlass!

Third Neighbor: He'll kill everybody!

First Neighbor: What may have caused this madness?

Orukorere: Do not ask, do not, but each will eat
Each although the soup be sour in the mouth.
Will no one go to him? Then I will. But
Good people take away the woman and
Bring her back to life.

Third Neighbor: Yes, We will

Do that, we will do that. What a day!
Second Neighbor: So the thing is true,
   That Tonye sleeps with the woman, his brother's wife?
First Neighbor: That is bad.
Second Neighbor: This is no place to talk. Take her up!
First Neighbor: Yes, better remove her quick. He will
   Surely kill her also, if he comes back.
Third Neighbor: You cannot store up fire in the pot;
   It will blow up and fill the place with rot.
Orukorere: There he has broken in, he has broken
   Down the door while we babble here
   Like hens among corn.
   I'll not let him
   Damn his soul, I'll not.
   Zifa, Zifa,
   Listen to a poor woman, listen, Zifa!
   He's gone in, gone in and now
   We shall see what is not seen.
Zifa: Tonye, Tonye, where will you run now?
   I have got you caged in—even like
   A fish in a trap.
   [*He breaks open the door, the others close behind.*]
First Neighbor: Ah! What have we here?
   Tonye has hanged himself on the loft!
Orukorere: Did I hear the fellow right?
Third Neighbor: Too well, I fear, too well.
First Neighbor: There the boy hangs dangling in the air.
Second Neighbor: He did it with his loin-cloth, standing
   On the mortar upturned.
   [*Orukorere falls down.*]
Zifa: Do not run, oh do not run away you
   People. You see the wretch has gone and
   Hanged himself on the loft. But it is I
   Indeed have killed the boy—my brother,
   Poor, poor brother, do you hang aloft
   There smiling in my face? I sought to kill
   You but in that office you have again
   Performed my part.
   You veer away from me, why should you
   Not avoid me as one with smallpox when
   I have taken my brother's life? For though

You see me bloodless it is this arm
Did this deed and this cutlass you see dry
Is flowing even now with the red blood
Of my brother, the brother, the boy born after me
To look after but who now has twice taught me
My duty. Here I break my matchet upon
My head and may everything fly apart
Even as I throw these iron bits asunder.
The poor, brave boy has truly done for me.
Good people, I hope you understand. It
Is not that I desired to drink out
Of his scalp which is unnatural, but that boy,
He went in to my wife, my wife who
Although under my roof for five years
I could not possess, for you see
I am powerless between my thighs. Was
That not a brotherly act? He sought to keep
What his brother was powerless to keep
In the house. My house, it has collapsed
In season that is calm to others. My fathers
Built it before my time that my children
And theirs to come may find a roof above
Their heads. And now what have I done
With it? In my hands it falls into a state
Of disrepair and now is fallen,
Fallen. Nothing stands; I will go
And find a new place to rest.

Third Neighbor: Where is the man going that has brought
　this ruin
　On his head?

Second Neighbor: There follow him quick,
　He is making for the beach as one in sleep.

First Neighbor: And what is to happen to this poor woman
　Now a bundle of rags on the ground?

Orukorere: Let me be, oh, do not try to lift me
　Up but let me lie in the ruins they have
　Wrought between them.

Second Neighbor: Let us follow the man.

First Neighbor: Shut the door, keep it shut. There comes his son.

Third Neighbor: Indeed, that is no sight for women or
　Children to see.

Dode: Mother, where is Ebiere?
  I heard my father's voice—who is he
  Angry with? Not with Tonye or Ebiere?
Orukorere: Cast your catch aside there and come over
  Here and sit between my knees.
Dode: I'll put them in first. Isn't there a lamp
  In this house?
Orukorere: There will never be light again in this
  House, child, this is the night of our race,
  The fall of all that ever reared up head
  Or crest.
Dode: Mother, what are you saying?
Orukorere: How should I know, son? I looked for a staff
  Long enough to kill a serpent I knew
  Was strangling my goat. In my search is my defeat.
Dode: So you had a sacrifice! Why, you didn't
  Tell me, I could have brought along
  My playmates. I wanted so much to hold
  The hindlegs while father struck.
Fourth Neighbor: Is anyone here in this house? Ebiere—
  She is coming to, but I fear
  The woman has had a miscarriage.
Dode: What's that she says about my mother?
  Oh where is she?
Orukorere: There, another blow
  Has been dealt the tree of our house, and see
  How the sap pours out to spread our death. I
  Believe it, now I believe it. White ants
  Have passed their dung on our rooftop.
  Like a tree rotten in the rain, it
  Topples. What totem is there left now
  For the tribe to hold on to for support?
Dode: My mother, I want my mother!
Orukorere: Do not seek to stop him. Let the antelope
  Run before the hunters arrive.
Third Neighbor: Madam, madam, why should it be my lot
  To bring you this?
Orukorere: Speak up, man, what effect
  Can the words you bring have now? Don't you
  See it is raining over the sea tonight?
  On the sands sprawling out to dazzle

Point till eyes are scales
This outpouring should be impression
Indeed. Here only waves pour out
On waves, only dunes upon dunes.
Third Neighbor: Then you give me some relief where there
    Is much grief. The sea has submerged
    Us; because we are all thereunder I can
    Deliver my burden with little cry.
Orukorere: What is the drift of your tongue? Say, has
    Lightning struck him down that walked
    Into the storm, his head covered with basin?
    I heard the roll of thunder out to sea.
Second Neighbor: That was no roll of thunder you heard, madam,
    But the lowing of a ship coming in.
Orukorere: Oh, I see. So they have come and taken
    Him to the other shore before me?
First Neighbor: Even so, madam. How did you know?
Orukorere: Never mind, tell the manner of my son's
    Going forth.
Third Neighbor: Well, you saw how he
    Went out of here as one in sleep. He said
    Nothing more and so, silent we followed
    On his heels. It was a heavy walk, the fishing
    Baskets scattered all about, the new canoes
    Carving on the shore. And the grass was wet
    On our feet. Presently, fording the sands,
    We saw him reach the water's edge. Just then
    That noise you said you heard as distant
    Thunder rolled out to where we stood. It was
    A steamer calling out for a pilot
    To pass beyond the bar. At the sound of it,
    Zifa seemed to start out of his sleep: Blow,
    Blow, sirens, blow he bellowed as in reply,
    And blow till your hooting drown
    The moaning of the sea. No blow
    Will be stronger. The owls, he said, that should
    Hoot at night have this afternoon blown down
    His house as they have the ancestral hall
    Open in the market place. And the stalls there
    That should crowd with voices are filled now
    Not even with the buzz of houseflies. All

    Are fled, fled, and left behind
    Bats to show their beards by day.
Orukorere: And what did you, you men of Deinogbo?
Third Neighbor: What could we? The thing was so like
    A dream at flood time it was
    Impossible to hold at anything.
Orukorere: Go on, who am I to question you? I heard
    The goat crying all the while and thought
    It a leopard stalking.
Second Neighbor: Just then,
    Madam, the ship blew its siren
    A second time. You may blow and hoot, Zifa
    Answered back, from here to the other shore
    But I will not come to you today.
    Your throat may be iron, your flesh
    Iron. But that is not it, he said,
    And with that waded into the deep
    As one again in sleep.
Orukorere: Umaloku, Umaloku, three times
    I call upon you, look to my boy! But
    What boy? Oh, what boy? Inside there
    One hangs dangling like a fruit full
    Before its time. Who will pluck it?
    And out there you have brought tidings
    Of another who walked of his
    Own will into the dusk. On whom then
    Should I call? Houseflies are not
    Known to answer a call at night,
    So on whom then shall I call?
Third Neighbor: Do not cry, do not cry!
First Neighbor: Come in out of the heavy dew.
Second Neighbor: Here is lamp to light you in.
Orukorere: Take away
    The light. Will you take away your lamp?
    What, am I become so like a statue
    That discovered among ruins in
    The sunset day, you wonder at
    Yet will not bow down to? I know
    I have lost both my face and limbs.
    Recognition therefore's become a thing
    For houseflies and bats, has it? I say

Let there be no light again in this house,
[*She snatches the oil lamp and dashes it to the ground.*]
Let there be none! But good people,
Bear with me, you will bear with me, won't
You? You see, black birds whose immortal
Knot both my sons have tied and slung
Have gathered the loot, all the loot,
And left behind not one seed of my fruit.
First Neighbor: Come away, we understand.
Third Neighbor: It is late, come away.
Second Neighbor: Come away, tomorrow is a heavier day.

The End

ALTERNATIVE CLOSE

In place of the last three lines for those who want the Masseur back!

A Voice From Without: Who is that crying in the dark?
Neighbors: He comes, oh, he comes!
Orukorere: Who comes? So it is you, manipulator
   Of broken bones and flesh torn out of joint?
Masseur: Daughter of Umaloku, the delight
   Of God and pride of unguents,
   Who the merpeople desire, I come
   Ahead of the snail and tortoise.
Orukorere: Then you come with your house
   Entire above your head. Yet I see
   No plumes of smoke.
Masseur: Rain made a pond
   Of my hearth several floods ago.
   But need we recall that?
Orukorere: I recall nothing. Why,
   In my head there breeds a consort
   Of frogs, and they sing so many
   Songs I cannot in the market murmur
   Tell one season from the other.
Masseur: True, true; one might as well number

Raindrops on roof thatch.
Orukorere: Oh, thatch! Everywhere
  They either spring leak or catch fire.
Masseur: It is their way. But although
  The iroko is our burden, we have
  For staff the silk cotton tree.
Orukorere: Have they left us any
  To hold on to for support or cover?
  All around, I smell only grass
  Running to flames, sand to water.
Masseur: Naked then we stand as before. But if
  We shiver, what will children out
  In their first rain?
Orukorere: Dode, now the rain
  Has caught him too. Elder mine,
  I thought at first to rebuke
  You for coming when the market
  Is over. Others have made off
  With the wares you put a price
  On. But now all that is over and
  Only the laughter of wind fills out
  In my ears. I will go and see
  To the chicken wet in the rain.
Masseur: Go, good woman. And you people
  Of Deinogbo, let me tell you, rain
  Or sun, it has been a clean fire. No doubt
  There are some, as she said, among you
  Who will say it is I started it all.
Second Neighbor: You started it?
First Neighbor: How? Do tell us that, old man.
Third Neighbor: What of the young woman
  Taken from another clan?
Masseur: This was no fire begun
  By ordinary hand. All fire comes
  From God, else why the thunder?
  The young woman, being tinder,
  Caught it first, consuming farmer
  And helpmate in the process. I sought
  To bring them water but all
  I had was a basket. Now, see
  How burnt to charcoal the land

Lies, even to the shrubs on the hedge.
Third Neighbor: I said you cannot contain fire
    In a pot. It will blow forth.
First Neighbor: Before we knew it, the blaze was beyond
    Control, its wild multiple tongues
    Licking raw heaven's hooded face.
Second Neighbor: And although we fought
    With all breath and brine, the noise
    From those bamboo rafts aloft
    Smothered us in the face.
Masseur: You may well cry. But this is nothing
    To beat your breast. It was how
    We all began and will end. A child,
    Once out of the womb, will shout,
    Even like the chick or seedling
    Out of its shell. And whether
    For pain, for laugh, who can tell? But now you
    Have lived to this day, perhaps you are ripe
    To hazard a crack at life's nut. Still,
    Do not, my people, venture overmuch
    Else in unraveling the knot, you
    Entangle yourselves. It is enough
    You know now that each day we live
    Hints at why we cried out at birth.
First Neighbor: Come away, now we understand.
Third Neighbor: My heart cuts, and it is dark still all over the land.
Second Neighbor: So dark, we must be away.
Masseur: Home or on the strand,
    Tomorrow for you spells another day
    And the strain, the strength of the band.

The End

The Masquerade

PERSONS

Tufa

Titi his bride

Diribi her father

Umuko her mother

Neighbors, Women
of the House,
Priests,
Others

Drama of one night
somewhere in the Niger Delta of Nigeria

SITUATION ONE

Early evening. On the beach.

First Neighbor: How high the tide! And it seems
It's rising still.
Second Neighbor: Twice already within this one tide
I've been forced to move boat
And post farther ashore
For safe tethering but each time
The river refusing confinement like
Goats to a hearthstead, has moved up
Its shore line. See, I'm wet to my thighs.
First Neighbor: Anyone would think it was
The annual flood already.
Second Neighbor: Look up, and see! The moon's fresh bowl

Is quite upturned. It is clearly
Spilling over towards my left.
First Neighbor: Yes, that's right; the tilt is prominent.
   It is never so but there is disaster
   General down the whole delta. Keep your ears
   Close to the ground.
Second Neighbor: I have never seen the moon so before.
   Why, it is almost tilting over!
First Neighbor: Last time it was so was several floods
   Ago. That year the earth-one was all over
   The place, land and water (I lift my behind
   Up for him) he occupied them all. I
   Was but a child then, just overgrown
   The wetting habit (Oh, didn't mother use
   To nag about the mats falling to pieces!)
   But I clearly remember there was a high
   Tide on then, and a terrible toll
   That was, it took with it. The great Yekpe
   Was on it.
Second Neighbor: Who is there? Oh! It is Ogoun.
   Well, how has it been out there
   Today?
Third Neighbor: Not a bite.
First Neighbor: Undoubtedly it must be this
   High tide. Either the waters have grown
   Too heavy for baits to have the right hang
   Or the fish,
   Taking after the current, steer a through course
   And will not be distracted like dogs
   To stop for a bite.
Second Neighbor: So how are we for market tomorrow?
Third Neighbor: Well, dried out, as you can see, like a fish
   Basket visited overnight by rats.
Second Neighbor: Hunger and worse, that's what
   We are in for. When I came up to the beach
   A second time to find the boat was adrift
   Once more that I had taken great care
   To move up, I knew the tide was driving up
   To something.
First Neighbor: Even a women pregnant is something full
   Of mystery. You can never know what will come

Forth—male, female, or worse delivery.

Second Neighbor: Surely, there must be explanation
For this unnatural phenomenon. One tide
Holding out almost as long as it normally
Takes to rise and fall. It's foreboding enough,
But conjoined with a new moon that has sprung
Such a list, there must be a terrible leak somewhere.

First Neighbor: As far as I know no feast has been left out
That calls for celebration. Indeed, right now
There is great merriment uptown, although
Of private character.

Third Neighbor: You mean the dance is on still
At Diribi's?

First Neighbor: You spend too much time on the streams, and miss
Several things ashore. As Grandfather
Is my witness, I think more than a cask of wine
Has been consumed there today alone.
Think of that! One cask a day and you thirsty
On the stream, and no catch either!

Third Neighbor: Some people I know are without cork
To their behinds. Little wonder so much wine
Is going down their throats.

First Neighbor: Oh, only a slender gourd now and again
Between bite of pepper and kola nut.
I cannot refuse a kind offer
When others seem so free with it. Not even
An Oba does that.

Third Neighbor: You are right, old man, but I must
Get home now, and remove these wet clothes.

First Neighbor: Good. By all means, do so. And don't forget
It is tomorrow the young dashing stranger
Carries the girl off to other creeks. Such
A mermaid of a girl. Now, I get it!
It's on account of her abandoning us
Heaven and sea have put up this show
Of anger.

Second Neighbor: If it ends there, we should all bless
The marriage—but who are those two
Running each other down? I hope there are
No pigs at the hedge. Well, look now if it isn't
The stranger and our maid desperate for each other!

Third Neighbor: Let's keep out of sight and see.
Titi: Oh, what magic moonlight! Look at the sands,
   They are like a silver spawn
   In their first outing with the tide.
   And see how they glide to meet the moon!
Tufa: As I to you! Your flesh under flush
   Of cam flashes many times lovelier than gold
   Or pearls washed up by the streams. And
   The fire in your eyes is
   Several suns by the moon. Let me feel
   The unguent flow of your flesh, and I've drunk
   For life.
Titi: Oh, so the bull can sing!
   But see the fireflies. How
   Like torches at festival time they break
   And shine forth. They put the stars
   Themselves to shame who either in fear
   Or sport tonight stay behind
   Their shutters. I cannot catch any
   For their sheer glimmer, and they flitter so! In
   The dew pods they touch up among
   A thousand, drooping wings of grass
   I see a simple watermaid, and a wicked
   Wicked traveller between her and home.
Tufa: I am that traveller and whatever
   Is changed tonight, does so to flash
   Forth the beauty of the maid. For this is
   The night of our festival, giddy
   But completely uncloyed as when
   Oyin made the world and gave to each his talents.
   Shall the traveller long
   Taunted, dart out now like a spear
   To possess the goal?
Titi: Who stopped him all the while
   With shield? He is no true hunter
   If wattle or wood proved such barrier!
Tufa: No, it was more one girl's coyness
   Than customs of the clan whose tenuous web flies
   May dart through. Titi, let me hold you
   A little, and my heart may stand mute.
Titi: You are hot, young man. Really you are

Restless as the stars that forever
Are flying and rushing although footless.
Take a look at those tireless beings some
Of whom are now beginning to peer down
At us, and learn something of their coolness.
Tufa: I run my course, and leave
The stars to run theirs.
Titi: Oh, you men! Will you never
Understand? Don't you see the bright-eyed
Creatures are the brides of the night!
And aren't they shy! Tears
Dazzle-blink in their eyes. Now, just look
At a whole fresh group of them come out. They are
Peeping from behind clumps of clothes, just
Like those the children and I must take
To the stream tomorrow, after
My final progress to market. I
Wonder what the stars think of us.
Tufa: Simple. That you should come down and nestle
In my arms.
Titi: A safe strong place that! But look,
What rainbow pathways the stars
Throw out on the bay! I should love
To walk down their arrow flight. What worlds
Do you think lie beyond them?
Tufa: Shall I tell you? The doorways
Through which I shall take my wife
Lead to a greater world.
Titi: I should like to see it!
Tufa: Tomorrow when the passage is complete and
Of course if your father agrees to release
The bird.
Titi: You are unkind to my father
Who is himself a great hunter. He hates
Playing the keeper. It was the bird
Herself that chose indoors. She flies out now
To test if the hunter can jump bramble
And brook. Or is he tripping up as did
The rest?
Tufa: Now, haven't I caught her?
Titi: Not quite yet, try again! Well, come catch the dragonfly

First, will you? After, you may tie to her wings
   The stoutest string at hand.
Tufa: I shall certainly hold to the leash so fast, there
   Will be no snapping of string across hedge or ditch.
Titi: And what if some wild wind sweep the prize
   Out of reach, or the loops tangle among
   The woods?
Tufa: Never: As a boy,
   I learned to sail my kites right up the beard
   Of the wildest wind, and I always brought my kite back
   To earth intact except for one rare day
   When lightning set fire to it. I never flew
   A kite after that.
Titi: And did you cry much?
Tufa: No; just felt limp, like the shadow
   Of string left truncated in my hand.
Titi: And who picked up both pieces, and
   Put them together again, mother, of course?
Tufa: No; I never knew my mother. In fact,
   My coming was her undoing, at least
   So my aunt who brought me up, poor woman,
   She died last year, told me the few
   Occasions she would talk. You see,
   Titi—
Titi: All right, all right, enough about others
   Of whom I know we are an extension. But
   Tonight tell me about yourself as man, about
   Your trading ventures up the long river
   To Onitsha, Lokoja, about—
Tufa: There, aren't you in my arms at last!
Titi: Brute, you brute. Oh, my father!
[*She breaks loose and runs into the dark, the man after her.*]
First Neighbor: Well, you saw them?
Third Neighbor: A real dance of
   The dragonflies, if you ask me: A pause
   Here and there to touch wings and tickle
   Feelers, and then a running duel sparking fire
   Left and right, and yet none seemed scorched
   For it.
Second Neighbor: Where did the young man grow his tongue of
   sugar?

Third Neighbor: It's certainly not of these parts. Too many
    Mudskippers around, and of course, there is
    That sweat, fume and brine too
    Crippling for excellence.
First Neighbor: You should have seen their first meeting. It was
    In the marketplace. Nine maids all aglow
    With cam fresh from stem formed her vanguard train.
    Another four of a bigger blossom,
    All of them wearing skirts trimmed with cowrie
    And coins, mounted props for a canopy
    Of pure scarlet and lace, and cool under it
    Walked Titi, in fact some said afloat, doing the last
    Of her pageants. How can I describe
    The bride? Oh, you should have been there!
    Her head high in that silver tiara so
    Brilliant it was blindness trying to tell
    Its characters of leaves and birds, and
    The ivory stick between her lips, the rings,
    The necklaces especially fashioned by a goldsmith
    All the way from Yoruba country, and
    Then those bangles, those beads of coral! But
    What is this I'm saying? The bride herself
    Beat this treasury flung so lavishly
    Upon the world.
Second Neighbor: I hear the thousands massed
    Together there about their several ways,
    Yam seller and silk buyer, all started up
    As to one pair of feet at her arrival.
First Neighbor: Yes, news of her progress had taken tongue
    Instant above the commingled
    Murmur of market and sea. Like sparks of fire
    On grass at harmattan, it bounced off
    One lip to another and knew no break
    Till it had burnt itself out with feeding on its source
    The girl in glory. The gifts they showered on
    Her then quite dammed her path.
Third Neighbor: How did the stranger get to her? That's
    What I keep asking!
First Neighbor: No two tongues will tally
    On the details, but I was there and saw

It all. Why, until then nobody knew
Of the man's existence. It seems he had stopped
At a stall to pick some fabric when
Like others he looked up, and saw the sun
In the girl or her stepping out of that
Orb, I don't know which now, and was struck
To the heart. Next, before the stall-owner and
Others around knew what was happening,
The stranger had tossed every piece of silk
And damask on display as tributary
At her feet, and himself last on the heap.
Third Neighbor: So that was how it happened!
First Neighbor: And more, my good
    Fellow. In that instant with each
    Shouting and shoving the other
    To see clearer, everybody knew
    Titi's long waiting for her man was over.
Second Neighbor: Old as I am, I would sooner myself fall
    For such a lover, than stay
    At home cracking kernels made available
    By other people's husbands.
    Such wooing was never of these parts.
First Neighbor: Reports have it in the market he is
    Somewhere from the creeks about Deinogbo,
    Oloibiri, or is it Odi? I am not quite
    Certain now, but we could find out. For come
    To think of it, none has told us exactly
    Who the young man is that is bearing
    Off our mermaid.
    [*Loud flourish of drums and voices from uptown.*]
Third Neighbor: What now?
First Neighbor: It must be bride and groom back in
    The yard, fresh and aflush from their dance
    Of the dragonflies. Come on, folks, that means
    The pots are topped again, and barrels
    And casks flowing. Come on!

(Curtain)

SITUATION TWO

Later the same evening. Before the courtyard; feasting within; and tapers burning on the lawn.

Diribi: Enough, enough, young man, or
  Shall I believe the stories you are
  In competition with us?
Tufa: How is that, Father?
Diribi: You are too precipitate with your
  Distribution of bounty. Boy, with right and
  Left palm you toss out money and gifts
  Among spectators and dancers in more times
  Than I have done a single round.
Tufa: That's just not true, Father, the story
  That I seek to rival you. It is just
  That my heart opens into one expanse
  Of chalk tonight. Any convoys willing now
  Can find passage through it to Ado.
Diribi: Even the overripe orange tree in grip
  Of wind will not shower forth fruit the way
  You are going. Take it softly, my son,
  Take it softly. If
  You don't know it already, let me tell
  You, my boy, you will need some reserve
  For your wife's upkeep, oh yes, you shall need
  It: All women are expensive to possess.
Tufa: I swear to you again I will not
  Transplant Titi from her life in this teeming
  Household of her father to that of a hall
  Cold with goat's discharge. With your blessing
  We can hardly wait to light the first fire
  In our hearth.
Diribi: Tomorrow
  The ceremonies close to the public
  Although our gates of course stay open
  Always to anyone not tired of rejoicing
  With us. After tomorrow then if you aren't,
  My son, to return home with hands leaky,
  We can think about granting to you loan

Of the pet we have all her life held
  To breast.
Tufa: If I could tear time
  Between my hands right now to have tomorrow!
Diribi: There you go, young man—
  As ever precipitate,
  A real fire to the flesh! They say
  I am too possessive with my daughter
  Titi to grant her hand all this time
  To a husband. But now I begin
  To wonder if by marrying you
  She is not exchanging the pipe for the ladle!
Tufa: She will be soup and wine to me while we live,
  I promise you, Father.
Diribi: Keep your breath
  To earth, my son. Woman is a cow or,
  If you will, a calabash; all placid,
  Beautiful and smooth outside, you can
  Hardly rule out roughness within, or shake
  It, and escape rattle.
  [*A group of neighbors tumbles in, eating, drinking, laughing, one of them
  singing.*]
First Neighbor: Ogomugoro, Ogomugoro,
  Young woman, take a man!!!
  No, I won't: She ran.
  Morning she got the blade
  Between her laps, Oh with her shriek
  And a pinch from her brother,
  A real ostrich with head in sand she made!
Third Neighbor: More joints to the song, Oh, more joints
  To it! Especially that about the gorgeous
  Fellow she at last fell for in the market
  Place!
Second Neighbor: Oh, wasn't that splendid, the glorious man
  Who on the way home was set
  Upon by hill, figtree and others, and before
  Bride could regain breath, her sun-figure
  Had turned scarecrow!
Third Neighbor: Not so! The transformation
  Was into a python later shot down
  By one who had loved her all her virgin

Life. Oh, toss up the song!
   A jolly old song, oh!
Diribi: No; no more of this! What is
   This song you croak within my yard? What
   Indeed is the shadow to it?
Second Neighbor and Third Neighbor: No harm meant!
   It's but an old song!
Diribi: After meal guests look up
   At the sun. What, can this be fruit
   Of over-feeding? If you are drunk
   And cannot join in proper dance and
   Song, get out of here, and don't stay to spread
   Your filth.
First Neighbor: Sweet groom, sweet groom that will now share
   The other side of the mat from Titi,
   Oh, sweet, sweet groom, give us some money.
Diribi: Don't give him a penny!
First Neighbor: Why? I hear the stranger has it like sand
   And water.
Diribi: What is that to you?
Third Neighbor and Second Neighbor: Come on. It seems now we are
   The strangers in Ebiama!
   So it seems. Only dogs will go where
   They aren't wanted.
Tufa: Let me see; do you want some money really?
Diribi: I said give none here a penny! Don't
   You see what they have they turn to vomit?
First Neighbor: Just a small sum of money or some present
   To remember the smashing stranger
   Who carried off our sweetest girl, that's all
   I ask. Is that too much when others have each
   Something? You people, you be the judge,
   Is that too much to ask of an in-law?
Diribi: Now get out: Get out, I say! Or shall I
   Send for maids to chase you out with broom?
Second Neighbor: Come, come. Let's go!
Third Neighbor: We are being thrown out like goats.
Fourth Neighbor: And what cassava, safely stacked by housewives
   In baskets, have we nibbled to merit
   This ejection?
First Neighbor: As I am my father's true son, have

I lived till now to be scorned and lashed out
Of sight to please a stranger nobody
Knows his source?

Diribi: Say that again!!!
Young man, have you not mouth to throw
This sow's dung and grunting in his teeth?

First Neighbor: So I am a sow, am I? And what are some
Folks, I should like to know? Oh, so I am
A sow—ha, ha, ha, ha!

Diribi: This is too much!
[*He strikes him.*]

First Neighbor: Go on, beat me, Diribi, oh, beat
Me dead, if that will give your son-in-law
His tongue back to tell the tale now abroad.

Diribi: What tale? What tale? You dog with tail between
Thighs, whining with nose in the sand from one
Place of discharge to another, what
Peelings and scraps have you raked up
Between your teeth to litter those of better blood
And stock than you? Cough out quick your rheum
Before I choke it out! Or has some bone
Stuck in your throat?

Second Neighbor: Let me go!

Third Neighbor: You'll throttle him!

Tufa: What stories?
Now what stories, old man?

Diribi: So you now find your voice! Have the fellows
Of dark at last released the strings
To your tongue? I thought
You were quick as squirrel, lightning like
The cobra when it strikes. But I have just seen
How swift you are with defence for the nuts
Others will stow off and despoil, how void
Your much-vaunted hood is of venom.

Tufa: Wait, Father, wait—I thought the man was drunk—

Diribi: He is drunk; so what? Don't you know in wine
There is triple sight? The man is drunk! Is
That why you could not tell this beast
Out of the bush who your father is, who
Your mother, indeed your family
To their last root? Now will you

Let me pass before all offerings
Turn offal?
[*He goes in.*]

Tufa: I do not know who you are in this town
Or whether indeed you have drunk too much,
And do not in your heart intend to cause
Me harm. But speak up. What is this tale
You say is abroad? What has it to do with me?
Oh, speak up the slander!

Third Neighbor: Do not speak more! But come with us!

Second Neighbor: Indeed, let's be away before worse
Follows us. As it is, enough bramble
Has been scattered about and Diribi
Is not one to spare the prick.

Tufa: Come, old man
I know the wine is hot in the blood
Of everybody here. I know very
Little, but speak up and if I can
I will try correction.

First Neighbor: Don't touch me! You go
To the marketplace if you are so desirous
To hear. Ha, ha, ha, ha! Come, come away!
The stranger wants to hear what all ears
Prickle at, what the whirlwind has picked up
In the marketplace and even now
Is spilling around to poison the air.
[*They laugh their way out.*]

[*Quick Curtain*]

SITUATION THREE A

About midnight. In the bridal room with a special bedstead of wicker and wood woven all the way to the ceiling.

Titi: When first I brought him hand
In hand to you, then was the correct occasion
To question who the stranger was I had

Chosen for husband. But you not only failed
To find what his name was, you actually
Went the length of showering on him fresh, bright
Ones of your own making. More,
Right there in the presence of all friends and
The family gathered around, you
Invited us in with open arms and eyes
Full of dance. No, Father, do not break in
On me. Not only that. Before the dead
And living of the land, you asked us to kneel
At your paternal feet, and there in words
I have come to carry close
To heart as a newborn child
You called all the clan to witness
A union you said the soil herself must welcome
To sweet fruition. Shall I forget it,
Father, the warm trembling hand
You placed on both our brows,
The lotion you rubbed on his and mine
Forehead, yes, and between my beating breast
Out of the altar you had just poured libation,
Invoking, as if it were possible right there and
Then, the instant issue to us of a child,
Your grandchild, for you to dangle
Between your knees.

Diribi: Titi, don't go dangling in my face the dagger
That in my ignorance and overflow
Of spirits I accepted as a fan of fine
Feathers.

Umuko: Had you not kept us waiting
Longer than was natural? Had all
Your comrades not begun mating many floods
And become already loving mothers while you
Preferred to have everybody guessing?

Titi: So that was why you little cared
Who at last I favored? Was that why
Father was so instant with his approval,
Waiving all talk of dowry? I
Rather half feared that moment it was
A refusal of me, this great delight and
Haste to endorse the man of my choice.

Diribi: You know very well I never
   Would deny you, you of all my children. It was
   The sudden way you burst in on me.
   We were right in the thick of your happy rites,
   And someone, if I remembered well, yes, I think
   It was your Aunt Toro who then was saying
   We must find you a man quick, now beauty
   Was complete between your thighs, before
   You accomplish the maternal feat without
   Helpmate, when, lo, like a couple joined
   Together out of this world, you walked in
   With the man. You were such a match.
Titi: Now we do not match anymore?
Umuko: Listen to what your own father has to tell
   You, stubborn girl!
Diribi: Now will you keep out of this, woman? Hear
   Me out, Titi; he is not for you, not after
   What we know.
Titi: And what is this terrible
   Discovery you have made and on account
   Of which bands already tied and blessed
   Must now be broken?
Diribi: Listen, my daughter, this man's
   Mother died bearing him.
Titi: He has told me this himself.
Diribi: Has he? Did he tell you also his father
   Usurped the bed of his elder brother, yes,
   Brazenly in his lifetime, and for shame
   Of it after hanged himself in broad daylight
   While this unfortunate abused husband
   Walked of his own will into the sea?
Titi: Well, is the seed to be crushed and cast
   Away because of aberration
   And blunder by those who laid out
   The field?
Umuko: Young woman, who taught you this—to speak
   Like this to your father? Not me, as God
   Is my witness, not me!
Titi: Mother, you will let me speak
   The way I know how. It will not be long

Before you have me outside your house. That is
What you have always desired.
Diribi: Shall I send you out, Umuko, or are
You going to leave me the ground
I need to pursue this?
Umuko: All right, all right, it is a matter
Touching the Diribi race, and of course
Only those that belong may open mouth.
Diribi: Come this way, my daughter, come sit
By me. I can still carry my child on my laps,
Can't I? There, don't laugh, or do
You honestly think my loins have got the rheums?
Now, that's better. Are you going to listen
To what Father says now? I know you
Have set your heart on this man. Even
The way you met at the marketplace
For the first time has in it
The very pulse and touch
Of miracle: eyes saw, and arms opened out
Into each other like tendril. But consider the taint,
The bad sap that must flow out
Of one bough into the other, no, pollute
The one stem that really is standing
To bear the graft, what will become
Of us all?
Titi: My sisters before me, none of
Them married a prince.
Diribi: I know that; but none presented me
With this prospect of pollution.
Titi: It's my misfortune then.
Diribi: No, not your lot, my child. Look, cast off
This fellow, who all the world knows has been
A haphazard choice and if you wish
It, I will take boat with you myself, sail all
The creeks, beat virgin paths on land
And sea to find my daughter the best man.
Titi: I will not be put on sale
Like fish or fowl rejected by the meanest
Household.
Diribi: Where sugar is there teem the flies.

No, my child, it is the men-folk
Who will troop after us and seek fight
With one another for your hand and all
My store of coral and gold shall be
Yours to command for dowry.

Umuko: Your store of coral and gold! There, Titi,
Accept, accept! All that coral and gold
To come into this house!

Titi: I said I will not be sold
For any price!

Umuko: Ungrateful child, so hard to please, how is
It you came into my womb?
Was it to wreck my craft of life?

Titi: Father, have you closed your offer? Why don't
You turn into a girl once more and be put
On a platter for hawking?

Diribi: Like hen, like chick. When both your feathers
Have stopped bristling and one of you
Has plucked out the other's eye, then let me
Know what you decide between you. The corn
And pebbles are there scattered at your feet
To heart's content, and
You, Umuko, that are the mother, teach
Your foolish daughter well.
[*He goes out.*]

Umuko: Now you have thrown away
A fortune no bride ever had.

Titi: Leave me in peace, will you? I
Want to go to bed.
[*She begins to climb into the bridal bed.*]

Umuko: Are you so bent on being the ruin
Of us all? Who is that? Can that be
[*A knock at the door.*]
Your father coming back so quick?

Titi: What are you doing here
By this time? I thought
You had your hands full with preparing
For your return home?

Tufa: I must see you now, right now.
Are you there, Mother, I kneel
To you.

Umuko: Young man, after what we know,
   Do you dare still step across this threshold?
Tufa: So you know already?
Titi: Yes, everything, and now you need
   Not begin walking in the vomit.
Tufa: I am ruined.
Umuko: So you should be. Now get out
   Of my house, you masquerader.
Titi: Mother, I will not have you talk like that
   To my husband.
Umuko: Your husband! [*She spits.*] The gods
   And dead do not hear such talk! The man is
   No more your husband now happily
   His past and back are in full view.
Titi: We are man
   And wife already. Who can separate us?
Umuko: Your father and I and all the family
   In the name of all that is divine and decent
   Have dissolved it. Indeed it
   Never was a marriage.
Titi: How dare you? How dare
   You? No bride price was taken on me
   By anyone I know of.
   Who dare then
   Among you make claims over me? What
   Debt is owed that you fear to pay?
Umuko: There, there, you don't know what you say,
   My child. Only a girl born of slaves
   Or found without her flower may go
   Such ways, and night and day I shall remain
   On my knees to the dead and gone of this land
   They have preserved my daughter from both
   Misfortunes.
Titi: Oh, oh, why has this fallen
   My lot! Oh, why? Why? Do you mean till now you haven't
   Found the correct story to wither
   All their tongues? Oh! Oh! I'm undone.
   [*She breaks down sobbing against the wickerwork of her bed.*]
Tufa: You still will have me, Titi, won't you? Oh,
   I am not a masquerader as they seek
   To paint me! You believe me, don't

You, Titi? This evening on the beach
You remember I tried to tell
You of my family—although not
This terrible story which you must
Believe me, like you all, I am tonight
Privy of for the first time.
Umuko: A likely story that. Stranger, aren't
You capable of shame?
Tufa: Woman, it is not your fault.
Umuko: Of course it is not! Do you think people just
Live on good looks and smart display?
Where, if you had succeeded in your scheme
Would you have taken your bride? My daughter
Was brought up on a sound family
Structure, the most solid in all the Delta.
Pray, what mother have you
To fan her welcome, sing her beauties? Indeed
Have you the mother or sister to
Offer her home for the triple moon
Before the bride moves to her own household?
And what father-in-law had you in store
To shower my daughter with gifts that are
More than her due, the piece of land to farm,
Not to talk of the umbrella for wife
And grandchildren to take shelter in,
When owls beat the air? Yes,
Tell me, young husband without a broom
To his stock!
[*She claps hands in his face.*]
Titi: No, no. I will not have any more
Of this. I'm going out of here right now
If you are not.
[*She runs out into the dark, Tufa, baffled, fumbles, but Umuko
is on him instantly, clapping hands in his face, and so forcing
him out.*]
Umuko: Leave my daughter alone, I tell you, leave
Us in these parts alone, and go your curse-laden way!

[*Curtain*]

SITUATION THREE B

In the courtyard before Orise, the Sky-God. Cock has crowed a third time.

Diribi: Yet in what way have I done wrong
    Except that the one whom I took for my heart
    Has turned out worse than a harlot. I have
    Fathered maidens as well as male—all
    By the labor of my loin—so that
    The river that took root at the earth's
    Deep center, come drought, come disease, may never
    Run out. In all that course have I not shed
    My own self to several distributaries
    And seen to it each, wayward or weakling,
    Has a firm foot, a full mouth past heart's
    Common content? But Titi, Titi I loved
    To think sat innocent between my laps and
    Whom I have hugged to myself as
    A river laps an island, now seeks
    To dam my path, even as I answer
    The unavoidable call to sea. Look at
    It, fathers and mothers already arrived
    Home, look at it close, what single harm
    Have I done that this poison more catching
    Than fruit from the piassava palm should
    At this late tide be bailed into the stream
    Of my blood?
Women of the House: One mother–salt does not season the stream,
    One crook of the valley does not trip up
    The river, and the turn up of one
    Water lettuce need not mean the flood
    Is close on the swimmer's heels, and the terrible
    Pilgrimage year after year begun.
Diribi: No, no, they have not done right by me. No
    Festival has passed but I have been
    On both my knees at their feet. What man
    Has offered fatter sacrifice? Yam tubers
    As high as thigh, fish enough to beat
    A wrestler's span? All this and more
    I render to them below and above without

Stint or stop. Now they let this bilge
Come into my blood. No, no, they have done
Hard by me.
Women of the House: A dip in bilge, especially if it is,
As the elders say, out of a craft
Too tardy to put to stream, may remove
From the eye pus or sand too malignant
For leaf or root. But brother, oh,
Our brother, what proof have we
Of the damnifying act you speak of?
Diribi: The bitch was not in her bed, do you
Get that? She is even now not asleep
In the bridal bed I myself built for her before
That mongrel ran in, tongues down, to foul us all.
Umuko: It cannot be! Tell him he does his daughter
Wrong! Titi cannot be far out of here.
It is true we had some quarrel over
That man. After which they went out together.
Diribi: Woman, where is she then? Tell these good people
Where your virgin daughter is now, but
Somewhere mating, already stuck hind to hind
With that cur without pedigree.
Women of the House: Master, you are lashed by forces fit
To confound forests. But you are no simple
Reed, and therefore should ride this tide.
Take the woman's word for it her daughter
Has simply stepped out and will return to bed
Intact.
Umuko: Indeed, she will, she
Will, I swear it by all her forebears
And father's hand-gods who, I believe,
Will surely see their child safe home.
Diribi: Must I kill her, too, this witch and bitch
Who has quite infected her breed and
Now makes corruption of all that is
Sacred?
Umuko: It is true I was given gifts of buba,
Tobacco, gin and such other things, but
As God is my witness: The young
Man chose, Titi accepted, and her father
Approved the match. Now I'm fed on
The brunt. I knew it was coming. Why,

Only this morning I opened my fishbasket
To have stock for our pepper soup; but
What was it I told you I found in there?
A python, coil after coil, had engirdled
It close, and poor old man, he was fast
Asleep. Now I know his burden.
[*She goes.*]
Women of the House: Go in, woman, go in and see to it
The young ones sleep well and that no owls or bats
Hover where they lie. And you, our brother,
Come with us if we must start a search
For her you say is lost.
Diribi: Let her be lost! I will not look
For her; but I will cleanse
The stream of corruption.
[*He goes in.*]
Women of the House: It is the time
Of night. There is a catch in the air
Will not hold. Not a rustle of leaves,
Not a cry of bird, nor the sudden charge
Of sheep or goats between whom and sleep
The moon takes a surprise interception; only
The leaden drop of dew in monotone
Down cheeks and limbs of the plantain
To where the bahama creeps; and far off,
Indeterminate rumors and beat
Of frightened feet or drums still finding
Direction. This is no time to be
Out. Let us look for the young wife as yet
Not arrived home.

[*Curtain*]

SITUATION FOUR

Late morning after. In the marketplace before the ancestral hall.

First Priest: Has it come yet?
Second Priest: No, not a sound. Not even
Of sheep or goat bleating except

For the leaves crackling in the sun.

First Priest: Then they have not met.

Second Priest: You don't believe each will carry out his threat
　　At the encounter?

First Priest: 　　　　　　Certainly as night
　　Tracks down day, as hammer makes
　　Anvil wince. Man, when boa
　　Constrictors grow too tall for palm trees,
　　They take to the stream and try out size,
　　Curve for curve.

Third Priest: Some say Diribi has taken to the bush. So
　　Overcome is he now by this terrible
　　Act.

First Priest: Not he if I know him well. He is
　　Not the type to seek comfort among dwellers
　　Of the forest. He hunts them all down. What
　　Will he be doing among monkeys, who
　　Single-handed has scalped several leopards?

Second Priest: He certainly has made many kills. Why,
　　To kill his own daughter, and a bride all aglow
　　With the cam too.
　　She always was the free bird with her ways. Set
　　Her among a grove of a thousand, thousand
　　Interlocked trees, and she will not knock
　　Her beautiful head against a twig—

Third Priest: Until today. Now she lies squashed
　　Like a lizard in the sand.

Second Priest: Oh, she ought to have listened to her father when
　　The awful discovery was made. What did
　　She want remaining fast to a mongrel
　　Whose race fed upon itself?

First Priest: You had to see the market break
　　Loose like scared colts at news
　　Of her end. Look at all they have left
　　Behind. At other times these should be enough
　　Bounty to keep a man at home for a whole
　　Tide. But up, up with the screens quick. Let not
　　A breath of these tidings get past the gates
　　Else rank corruption overflows us all.
　　[*Tufa staggers in.*]

Tufa: Is the murderer here, the botcher of his own

Blood, has any of you seen his face?
Second Priest: No, not here.
Third Priest: You look in the wrong place, young man.
First Priest: Unhappy man, why don't you look
    For a safe place to hide? They say he is
    Hot after you.
Tufa: So am I! I am after him too.
Third Priest: With empty hands like this?
Tufa: Yes, with bare arms.
    Will no one tell where he lurks? I have looked
    For the murderer in streets and homestead, but
    Everywhere the women herd in
    Their children as if I'm a black kite come among
    Chickens and the dogs come barking at my heels.
    Is it I who have taken life
    Or he whom I find and must kill?
First Priest: It is not still too late. The tide
    Is high and shows no sign of turning.
    If you will only take up paddle
    And baggage, you ought to be safe
    In your craft and upstream before anyone
    Knows.
Tufa: I am a stranger. That is why
    None of you offers help except one to parcel
    Me out of town. Have I got the smallpox?
    Indeed, have I, you people? A girl, my wife,
    My bride has been shot to death right here
    In your midst while foolishly I sought messengers
    To calm a man mad for thinking me
    Fell contamination. Last night she cried,
    Called me all the cruel names I know I more
    Than deserve for being born the way the world
    Now knows with relish. But
    She called herself my wife, my bride ready to go with me
    In spite of my shame.
First Priest: That was time to bear her off
    If you asked me. Elopement has its own
    Color sometimes more crimson than cam.
Tufa: I did, I begged, I raged she come
    With me at once last night, but she would have
    Her pageant through first.

Third Priest: Prospect of cam under greater flush
  Of the sun, and all the world
  Her lover—that is the dream of all girls,
  Born or gone, and Titi was no
  Exception.
Second Priest: Truly, she kept the prow till the end.
Tufa: Did you see her final passage?
  Do tell me about it. What, do you balk at
  Unfolding the shroud when the body lies
  A burden on your soil? I have seen
  Her; yet cannot stand the sight. Oh, my wife,
  My wife, what messengers of ill have come
  Adamant between us?
  [*He beats at one of the pillars of the temple.*]
Second Priest: The moon that threw wide
  Her arms has brought both palms to the full
  And now, even in daylight,
  Smiles at the wreck below.
First Priest: Rise, rise, man! What, would the young woman
  Despatched with fatal fire by her father
  Not spit in disgust to see the man she called
  Husband display this dissolution
  Of spirit?
Third Priest: Indeed, see with what heart she took
  Her terrible fate when at last she knew
  Her father would give in to nothing. Even
  The trout that takes the bait more than often leads
  The angler out of step. And when it does
  In the long run swallow the worm, dies shining
  In her slime. But what could this gazelle of a girl, so
  Abruptly invested with the weed of death,
  Just when she was gathering her skirt of cam
  To mount her bridal bed?
Tufa: Was there none to stop my sunbird slipping?
Third Priest: One might as well have plastered up
  Baskets with leaves to make water stay.
  You know how a smiling sky will sometime
  Assume a sudden terrible scowl, and
  Before you can lift up head, is snarling and spitting fire and
  Torrent about you. This was like that; only worse:
  It has left all wet and scalded.

Tufa: Go on! Shake out the trunk all eaten up
  By termites! How else can fowls feed their fill?
Third Priest: The bride who was deep in the marble game
  With her maids, had Umuko's new boy
  Across her laps, when the storm burst: With a bound
  She was up running, kneeling, presenting the baby
  As a shield although clutching it back
  From harm and all this in one motion—
  Do forgive my running nose.
Second Priest: It was a terrible sight.
First Priest: She tried tears, tried prayers and like some bird
  Already struck, but still struggling
  For sunlight, skipped from one twig
  To another, but leaves and boughs shrunk in her path
  And none could offer her closet.
  Meanwhile, her father with that fowl piece
  In hand—
Tufa: Oh, it was the double-barrelled piece I myself
  Brought him as gift from son to father!
First Priest: With it he chased her like a new-spawned chick to the
      wall
  Oh, is it not indeed a strange tide when cocks
  Turn hawk on their own brood? But there she was,
  Visibly strung to a thread which the man
  Seemed only too daggers-glad to snap
  That instant, and break it he did with one burst
  Of his gun.
Third Priest: In that flash when
  All spirits fled their bodies, when tongue
  Clung to palate, only the girl retained her sense:
  Unable to break the leash which undoubtedly
  Tied her down, she cast off the child to safety
  Even as the blast went off.
Tufa: Put out the nets, oh, put them out
  To dry! And may the wild wind and sun crackle and tangle
  Them, float, lead and thread, till tide's end.
  The season is out. Because the tide
  Has all of a sudden turned on us while
  Others stayed out of sea, the nets we cast
  With pride over shoals sure as shallows
  Have had the floors cut from under them, and

The prime shark we set out to catch has got
Clean away, filtered right through and left
Us dangling adrift like starfish all
Superfluous of feet. So up we come without
A shrimp-drop of fat to stop hobs at home
From crack.

Second Priest: Salt and sting, salt and sting, it's surfeit
Of both that has ruined us. But look, there comes
Umuko, a craft with none at the helm.

[*She comes rocking a cat she addresses as a child.*]

Umuko: Oh my child, oh my child, my child who
Delights me more than stars
The skies, who won't let me drag
In mud, who will give me burial
Home, oh my child, my peerless child, let
Me set the cap proper on your brow. This way,
Not far back! but so, yes, so: now
It's good, very good: but has
The foul wind howling on the beach
Touched your cheeks with his damp
Hand, oh my son, has he indeed?
Let me carry you at my back, tie about
You the calico of my brood, and we shall
Make its knots so blind no shuttle
However sharp may see through. There,
There, let heart speak to heart, breast beat
On breast, flesh breathe upon flesh, and may
The crawling shadow over the earth never sweep near
Where my infant champion sleeps—

[*She breaks into song.*]

And there was a tree,
It grew so tall,
It shook hands with the stars:
So broad it covered all
Air, land and sea:
Out of eyes of fish at fall
Of flood sown by bastard
Babies in sand sprang this tree
With roots so deep the highway
Of all the world lay

In its bowels. And from its shoot
Came a shower of fresh fruit—
Fresh fish at tuppence
Who'll buy fresh, oh,
Fresh fish at just tuppence.
[*She goes out.*]
Tufa: Was that Umuko?
First Priest:　　　　　　Indeed, it was
She, now a house without a roof and therefore
Hard to know. Since eagle ate their kind
None has been able to follow the drift
Of her tongue.
Tufa: Then the man really has killed her?
First Priest: Who? You mean the daughter? Tongue
Cannot tell what eyes saw, what heart rejects
But hands cannot shake off. It's a serpent
Twined down the spine and will suck. But run! Let's pluck
Leaves to cover you up, for there comes the man.
Look, he still has his gun and
Has vowed to blast your tree of life.
Tufa: Then let him finish the meal
He began.
First Priest: Young man, give in to us! Are you mad?
[*He turns to Second Priest.*]
Will you tackle the other?
Second Priest: Yes, I will—
First Priest: Are you so determined to destroy all?
Second Priest: You have done it again! You who alone
Have fought with crocodiles in wild waters
Out of depth for tail or feet, and yet on
Each occasion forced the grand mistress
Of the streams to take your bit of bamboo!
Oh, you who cripple leopards and single-handed scalp
Them! Gloriously do these acts and others too
Many for catalogue win you rights to drink
Of your left hand with gorillas! Who
Endowed with seven crowns disputes them? Now
Let me lead you to your well-won place
Of rest—but first, let me have your arms,
Do let me.

[*Diribi, apparently in a daze, does not heed him.*]

Diribi: These hands you see are two streams
   And through several distributaries
   Have drained me to waste. For, you see,
   I have burst open my heart who was
   My daughter. Now who is man enough
   To take me to him at Forcados? They say
   He has stitches so strong
   They still and staunch the worst breach
   In the dam. But first sling about me
   The chains: So! Oh, how soothing their chime!
   Now pull tighter till trap come up
   With fish and nuts. But I will talk
   No more, no, no more till
   Skies crack open and soil thunders back.
   [*In this wise, still holding his gun which seems now just another part of
   him and is therefore unnoticed, he sits down outside the temple, and all he
   does now and after is grind aloud his teeth.*]

Tufa: I thought you said
   He nourishes a deep parch for my blood?

Second Priest: So he swore:
   Now it appears the leopard is too drunk
   With blood and cannot tell his spoor.

Tufa: Then I will, I will! Oh, do not hold me!
   [*He breaks away, falls upon the other who refuses to wrestle,
   but they roll on the ground all the same.*]

Second and First Priests: Help, help! The two have met—and now
   All that was given the host, the evil ones
   Have refused! Oh, help, help!

Third Priest: They all come home
   To roost! But what a race, what a manner
   To end! Will you two stop your toil?
   [*A shot is heard above the confusion.*]

Tufa: The great hunter has made another kill!
   What, aren't you giving the great yell for a quarry
   Harried home? Your very last who should have been the first!
   For I am that unmentionable beast
   Born of woman to brother and for whom brother
   Drove brother to terrible death. That's not
   All. My mother who they say engendered

The seed, on expulsion of it, withered
In the act, and it was left an old woman
Without wit to pick me up and take
Into another country. Why did she do it? Oh,
Why did she escape their strangling me at first cry?
Others for no reason but that they prefer
To travel double, or too impatient, fail
To collect their kits complete,
Get instant snuffing out or
Are tossed among reeds to rot away
Far from contamination of the stream.
But I whose coming, right from conception
To this apparent deception, has
Been the draining of all that was pure and
Lovely, how is it they left me loose
To litter such destruction? Mud oozes out
Of me, see it flowing hot and thick down my side! I must go
Before I smear more with it. Make way
There. Ah, Titi! So you
Wait for me for us to set out together—my bride, my wife—now
The purging is, yes, almost—
[*He staggers forth out of reach.*]
First Priest: One of you, follow him quick and hold
His hand, before he ends like a fowl. By
This account he rendered, we cannot
Deny him so small a rite. Who knows? Who
The gods love they visit with calamity.
Third Priest: And what about him? For all
We know he may still turn out full of danger
And portent for us all. Shall we not put
Him in chains at once?
First Priest: What chains? For a cripple?
Why, look at him who was so tall and strong
Before. Nobody knew him shave his head
As tributary to the flood. Now at one stroke
See him splintered to the ground.
The hand of thunder, so sudden not even
The double-visioned saw it, has battered
Him down, boughs, bole and straight past pith.
Let us help to pick up his scattered

Scotched pieces, and oh, hurry, hurry
For before the tide turns again we must
For Forcados.
[*He leads the way out behind the tall mat screens now completely offering
cover to the ancestral hall and shrine away from the deeds of men.*]

The End

The Raft

PERSONS

Olotu, Kengide, Ogro, Ibobo—All
  lumbermen taking a raft down
  the Niger

ONE: TIDE-WASH

*Night on a creek in the Niger Delta. In the milky light the shadow of a
cabin is squatting on a raft (which may as well be the board or stage itself).
Through the near end of the cabin showing a cross-section like a pyramid
and a shade darker, one or two figures can be seen lying about, half asleep
and with yet an inner shade of dark to them. Above them flickers a lamp.
Outside is the shadow of a man shuffling and mumbling something to
himself. The others would like him to stop but he seems altogether lost in
some discovery known only to him.*

Kengide: Rise, man, if you will, and stop
  Harassing others in their sleep.
Olotu: Who's it?
Kengide: That blundering bullock again.
Olotu: Can't you leave the fellow alone? He must
  Be having one of his nightmares.
Kengide: Most likely. And this time it might be
  A whole crowd of bush cows are crashing headlong
  After him among cassava plants,

71

And he unable to make away because
He's running on his head. The bastard,
I can't hear what he's mumbling in his depths.
Olotu: Oh, you stop it yourself, you will? It's you
Who'll not let anybody sleep now.
Kengide: This accursed raft—you can't
Turn over once on your side
But some crocodile-baiting wretch
Is hurling stones in the pond of your sleep.
Umph, there he goes still.
Olotu: He got it off his mother.
The fellow has told you himself. So how
Can he stop it?
Kengide: People learn to shed
Their umbilical cords in the dust
Under baobab trees although it was
What tied them center to center to their mothers
For nine blind moons. Oh please, Ogro, will
You let others sleep!
Olotu: Harrumph. Not all
The bulls roaring and glowering
In the skies will touch your man. His roots
Go deep, and now I'd try and sleep
If I were you.
Kengide: His roots must go deep
Indeed for the overgrown bole above
To keep its limbs and locks unbroken
In the wind. The bastard, I could wring his neck
For his endless grunting.
[*Outside the muttering and pottering continue. Now a fourth figure has come up from the other end, and he, too, is querulous.*]
Ibobo: You are walking
In your sleep again, Ogro.
You certainly will
Fall over one day and get drowned.
Ogro: I'm not asleep, nor have done
What you say for a long time now.
Ibobo: Surely you lose track of events as swiftly
As the tide washes off all floatings. Was
It not only a market or two since, yes, it was
The night we lost the boat, well, weren't you up

In your sleep that night, pottering about
With pole erect in your hands, like a girl
Doing the lost fertility dance?
Ogro: Maybe, but look—
Ibobo: And when you were seen in time
And asked whatever ritual you were up to, didn't
You say you were simply sounding the stream—and
In that stagnant dark too!
Ogro: Now listen to me. I think we
Are adrift.
Ibobo: How do you know?
Ogro: Why, look about you.
[*Ibobo does so, then goes down the raft and is back shortly.*]
Ibobo: Yes, you are right. The moorings
Up there are all
Loose. How's it I didn't know?
Let's see the others.
Ogro: No use. I have inspected
Them all. None is intact.
Ibobo: Olotu, Kengide, are you asleep
Still? Wake up quick! We are adrift.
Kengide: No-o!
Olotu: Adrift, you say?
Ibobo: Yes, no doubt about that.
Ogro found it out.
Olotu: Have you tried the moorings?
Ibobo: We have already.
Ogro: Yes, we have.
Kengide: All of them?
Olotu: How come all the knottings are
Unfastened at once?
Who did them anyway?
Ibobo: Why, all of us. I'm sure the two
I tied were fast.
Ogro: And mine. Not even a buffalo
Could have got out of them.
Olotu: It's not stories
About sinews of strength we are after. How
Is it we have gone adrift like this?
I definitely said in the evening
It was unwise tethering the raft

With loops of reeds, but Kengide
Will not let me talk because I am
A townsman.

Kengide: Nonsense, township talk
  Had no bearings with this. I simply
  Explained that in rivers with muddy floors
  And swamp banks like this one, it is
  Not always safe to make boats fast
  To a post, worst of all, a raft. To an arm
  Of the trees huddling close to the waters perhaps,
  But the danger there is the possible
  Visits from snakes and monkeys or worse.

Olotu: Well, see where the use of rush
  Has led us.

Kengide: It is not the first we've used them.

Ibobo: What I can't understand is how all
  The seven gave way.

Ogro: I don't think they gave
  Way of their own. Look here, this leftover
  Dragging in the stream seems smooth
  To the touch at both ends.

Olotu: You don't mean some madman
  Came aboard and cut us loose?

Ibobo: Some ghost or evil god,
  You mean? There's not a single fishing post
  Around here. The nearest town is Letugbene
  Which is several days' sailing.

Kengide: What will anybody want
  With that, anyway? It doesn't seem he made off
  With any of our rags and pans, or has he?

Ibobo: I rather fear it's sea cows. We may
  Have, without knowing, planted ourselves
  Right in the field of their grazing, and now
  They have come and eaten us out of our roots.

Olotu: It's very possible. I almost said
  Last evening this was as large an expanse
  Of grass as any I have seen up in the land
  Of the Fulani and Hausa.

Ogro: Will anyone tell where we are?

Olotu: Yes, where exactly are we going now?

Ibobo: I can't see through the grey baft spread

Of the night. The moon has long turned in, and not
A single star in the skies. Why doesn't
Someone turn up the lamp?

Kengide: No, that will only serve to create
A pale of light. From inside that pool even
A dog will not see.

Ogro: I think I can just see to my right
There trees on the bank drifting past.

Kengide: Don't be an idiot; it's we
Who are doing the drifting.

Ogro: Yes, I see the outline
Of their heads, with plumes flying like clouds.

Olotu: We can at least try shoving the raft
Towards them.

Kengide: I don't like it. We might run ourselves
Into some sand bank. And you know
As well as I do that treacherous
Baskets and stakes for catching shrimps lie scattered
About these rivers.

Olotu: So what will you have us do, Kengide?

Kengide: Young man, don't
You shout my name in this dark!

Olotu: What if I did?

Kengide: I am the elder of your older brother
And have seen more life than you.

Olotu: You forget he who walks sees more
Than who just grows old.

Kengide: And you have been to Lagos, Kano,
Onitsha or whatever other foul dens
You say you have tenanted, while I have
Been just a wall-gecko gone grey at home,
Is it not so? I don't see the great wealth
All this travelling abroad has brought, though.

Olotu: Enough to have had you hired
On this raft.

Kengide: Slime and entrails! You and I
And every fool that ever set foot on this raft
Are on the same payroll, and the man
With the purse is up wining away at Warri.

Ogro: Will you two stop your endless quarrels? Are
You wives to one man?

Ibobo: Anyone would think they were hens, the silly way
  They show the wind their behinds.
Kengide: It's too belly-galling; he just picks
  At me like pilot-fish at a corpse
  Drifting unclaimed.
Ibobo: Now that's enough!
Olotu: I don't pick at you; it is you
  Who always put your nose in the air, saying
  You smell some washback from the gutters
  Of Lagos.
Kengide: You think my mind all evil, don't
  You? Just now when I warned about shoals
  And shrimp traps, it was the safety of the raft
  I had in mind, but no doubt you saw otherwise.
Ogro: Whenever we are at the crossroads, Kengide
  Takes one road, and Olotu rushes up
  Another, but here we're at the fork still,
  And not one of you can tell the forces
  To get us out.
Ibobo: Which way is the tide going?
Ogro: How should I know?
Kengide: Someone get a paddle and place
  It flat on the stream by the raft. By the drift
  Of it we should know where we're going.
Ogro: A bowl would be best
  For that, don't you think? It's so
  Much whiter, and therefore easier to see
  In this dark.
Olotu: Well, get one then!
Ibobo: Here's a pan; I don't think it was washed
  After we ate last evening.
Kengide: It'll do. Now, can you see which way
  It is going?
Ibobo: Yes; to our right.
Kengide: It means ebb tide
  And that we are heading to sea.
Olotu: That tells nothing. What if the raft
  Had swung completely round while we slept?
  It then would mean we are moving inland—
  In the direction of Odi!
Kengide: Odi is not in any direction here.

Ogro: There they go again!

Ibobo: We should be able to tell. Olotu, is that watch
   Of yours working still?

Kengide: What a question. Has paralysis
   Ever left the limbs of that creature alone?

Olotu: I'll prove to you that there at least you are
   A liar.
   [*Runs inside the cabin.*]

Ibobo: You'll break each other's skull before
   We are through.

Ogro: That wouldn't be bad if it yields us as much
   As would a coconut.

Kengide: Pig.

Olotu: Here we are!

Ibobo: Strike a match for him.

Ogro: Look, he has to shake the thing against his ear
   To see if, like the coconut, it has
   Its contents complete.

Olotu: There, read for yourselves whoever can.
   It's several minutes past five.

Ibobo: That means almost day.

Kengide: Not necessarily.
   Only that the brat
   Of a machine has probably been at work without
   Stop, and so outstepped the old woman in the moon.

Ogro: I wish there were some village
   About. It would have some cock whose greeting
   Of the rising sun all the world can recognize.

Olotu: Why can't you rely on my watch? I bought
   It in Lagos—at the Kingsway Stores, in fact.

Kengide: As if it is not common knowledge
   Hausa men hawk the best of them in the streets
   And will barter them for a pair
   Of tattered trousers.

Ibobo: Now, who was it wanted some sign
   In the sky?

Ogro: I said I want to hear the crowing
   Of a cockerel, welcoming in the dawn
   Of another day.

Ibobo: Well, how about that?

Olotu: What now?

Ibobo: Listen. Don't you hear
  The a-moo, a-moo of monkeys calling on
  Their womenfolk to get up and start housework?
Kengide: Yes, there it comes—to the left
  There—several of them—now hear their booming voice
  Again. Is it not amazing such a big manly voice
  should belong to a scraggy,
  Scruffy creature all flaming behind?
Ogro: If we had a gun, we could at coming of day
  Shoot down several and so never peel
  Our palms to eat.
Olotu: Talk of food, and forget
  You are adrift. I really don't know how
  Oyin molded you of this part of the earth.
Ogro: [*Breaks into song.*]
  "Good for nothing craft
  Hee, hee!
  Good for nothing craft
  Hee, hee!
  Just take me to port
  Safely!"
Olotu: You beast of the bush without sex
  Or name, how can you find voice to sing
  At this time?
Ogro: Why not? When flood has inherited all
  The earth, don't the frogs sing?
Kengide: Ogro, were you nearer me, I would touch
  Noses with you.
Ogro: You keep your funnel of a nose to yourself!
  [*He begins singing again.*]
  "Board a boat, board a boat!
  Where's the boat to board?
  Board a boat, board a boat!
  Where's the boat to board?
  My boat's gone wide adrift—
  Where's the boat then to board?"
Kengide: This millipede, he always blunders
  Into the truth, doesn't he?
Ibobo: I don't call that anything; Ogro simply
  Croaks; that's all.

Olotu: He can croak
    For all I care, and as for Kengide
    He just sits there like some foul-smelling
    He-goat at the fireside mauling away
    At the world between his teeth, while you Ibobo
    Babble about who's a canary and who's not.
    But in the meantime, what happens to the raft? Or
    Is it because none of you has a single log
    In it that your heart cuts very little?

Ibobo: Olotu!

Ogro: Did I hear the man right? I have more
    To lose than some people whose tongues are smarting
    With sting. Upon the safe arrival of this raft,
    Hasn't the old chief himself promised to assign
    Me his fairest daughter? Who else has built
    So much on this raft?

Kengide: All who have claims have now made
    Them, but let's not go into the toils
    Of all that. Here, if you'll like to know, come
    And see the bowl. I put it back on the water
    A little while ago when the call of those monkeys
    First came across. I wanted to test if that meant
    The tide was turning—you know they always
    Do that when it's rising—

Ibobo: The bowl is spinning.

Kengide: Yes, that's
    What I thought I should tell you.

Olotu: And what may that mean?

Ogro: My God, my God! It's spinning
    Like a top.

Kengide: I have no pipe to smoke; so you cannot
    Accuse me of regarding the smoke-cloud
    From it so close, others fall asleep.

Olotu: What does the spinning mean I asked.

Ogro: My God! My God!

Ibobo: I promised you a goat
    At the next festival, my great-grandmother. Now
    How have you led us into this?

Olotu: Speak, speak up, before I go wild
    Like all of you!

Kengide: It means we are in the arms
  Of the great Osikoboro whirlpool
  Itself, you fool!
Ibobo: Right in the pit—
Ogro: And we may never find release
  From its vise!
Olotu: Is that all? I think
  You are all gone soft and possessed. Even
  Kengide's head seems to have filled out
  In fear of some undiscovered merpeople
  Supposed to inhibit the place. But you wait
  And see: we'll row ourselves out of here
  Quick enough, will punt the raft free as sure as the sun
  Sucks up the morning mist—yes, you wait
  And see!
Kengide: Now I see why we of the Delta
  Never will make good. You believe all
  The tales tampering with the stars
  That are told you abroad, but never any one
  At home about your own rivers. Truly
  We are a castaway people.
  [*Olotu has already whipped out a bamboo pole and is all set to punt.*]
Olotu: Ogro, will you add your hand? And
  You, Ibobo, if that man over there will not.
Ibobo: Stop! You stir up more trouble.
Ogro: Oh, doesn't he know? Ten such poles,
  Tied end to end, will not plumb the floors
  Of Osikoboro!
  [*Olotu flounders on with the plumbing, all the others looking on, each in his own shade of shock.*]

TWO: WIND-LASH

Late morning. Bright sun shuttered now and again behind clouds. The raft with its rough, low cabin of bamboo and mat lumbers in the whirlpool. In front in the open the men are rising up from a meal—one or two wash hands, mouth, and plates over the side of the logs, and the others do some desultory packing up of the cooking kit and try settling down to wait.

Ogro: On behalf of everybody on board this raft
   I greet you, Kengide, for a soup
   Most full of season.
Kengide: I accept your greetings but the meal
   May well be our last.
Ogro: Now, you aren't playing the tortoise, are you?
Olotu: No: it is the bile bitter Ijaw
   Story the man has told you. Our stock
   Of food is out, completely out.
Ogro: Why weren't we told this before now?
Ibobo: Don't be a baby. We all know there has been no
   Replenishing of stock since we lost the boat.
Ogro: Still we ought to have been told without
   Water in the mouth.
Kengide: So you could turn into a black-kite and run
   A carrier service between here
   And the wilderness around?
Ogro: I don't believe it, there must be
   Some garri or plantain left on this raft.
Kengide: Here, look at this bag, and at this one full
   Of holes—I wonder how they ever got there
   Except rats have swum on board again
   These sodden logs since I hunted down the last
   Of their clan. See? The bags are all emptied
   Of their sweet content just like the dried-out
   Dugs of the witch of Okoloba.
Ogro: Human rats—that's what you speak of
   If there isn't even garri left to eat.
Olotu: Who soaks more garri, drinks more on this raft?
   And who fed on the farina at every landing
   Of pilot fish at our feet?
Ibobo: A bowl of garri is cooling
   In the sun; it sinks right down into the flesh
   And bones. That was the song then.
Kengide: It will be good to remember. The eba
   You have just swallowed whole happened to be
   Our last pan.
Ogro: And we are waterlogged here
   In Osikoboro—the confluence of all
   The creeks!
Olotu: The drain pit of all the earth,

　　　Or are you too caught by fear to say it?
Ibobo: Hold your tongue!
Kengide: With the swift ebb tide coming
　　　And some better lot, we ought to get out
　　　Before the sun goes down.
Ogro: Won't that take us to sea?
Kengide: Not if we court and hug the tide. We need
　　　Not stay on its breast after our release.
Ibobo: It calls for careful navigation.
Olotu: What, to swing from one tide
　　　Into another? Or isn't that what you people
　　　Are saying? I don't see why unless you really
　　　Want to stay here.
Ibobo: It's not as if a monkey were swinging
　　　From one tree to another. Eight rivers empty
　　　Themselves into the Ramos here. It seems
　　　To me if their combined current can sweep
　　　Us out here, it will not stop till we are
　　　Past Age and right in the ocean.
Kengide: You two apply more water than is necessary
　　　To float a ship. Only five of them carry all
　　　The force, since these two flow a parallel course
　　　While the drain-back goes into this—which is
　　　Where we are going, if we must get to Burutu.
　　　To ride one into the other and so skirt
　　　Into our creek without being swept off
　　　In the central on-rush of the Ramos,
　　　That certainly will need great care and skill.
Ogro: Another question. What do we live on
　　　Now—leeches and crabs clinging to the logs?
Ibobo: Tack more lines, my friend, and bring out the spears!
Kengide: You can't catch fish without bait. No boat
　　　To go ashore for worms, and even
　　　The pilot fish now smell rot among
　　　The logs: they don't jump on board anymore.
Olotu: The ghost smell is more on some people
　　　Than on the logs.
Ibobo: Ogro, remove your leg out of water quick. Do
　　　You want some shark or crocodile to snatch at it?
Kengide: Fine bait it will make, dangling under there.
Ogro: Now I have it! We can catch a lot of fish.

Olotu: How? Have you been deep in water
  All this while?
Ogro: Anybody has an empty tin or can close by?
Olotu: Here's one you may take; it puts me
  In mind of cigarettes.
Kengide: What is he about now?
Ogro: [*Running into the cabin.*] You wait and see.
Kengide: I sometimes wonder what unattended dead
  Or god is inside the fellow.
Ibobo: Think of him going about believing the old chief
  Will give him that daughter of his to marry—ha,
  Ha, a proper fool!
Olotu: And not a penny to his purse.
Kengide: Perhaps his parents at home
  Have a pot buried under their bedstead.
Ibobo: No. Ogro does not even believe dowry
  Is necessary. The mermaid shall come
  To him as bounty for his sweat and service
  Before the great shrine.
Kengide: What a fool! The old chiefs who would hand out
  The best of their daughters like that died
  Out generations ago. Nowadays, they drain
  The Delta of all that's in it, and not
  A shrimp slips past their fat fingers.
Olotu: Well, there tears in the bull.
Ogro: Here, here, who will take
  The first peep? Ibobo? Olotu? Kengide?
Ibobo: Come on, what is all the mystery?
Kengide: What mystery? Even the night masquerade
  So full of the lion's roar and the jackal's howl
  Is but sharpened bamboo shafts swinging about
  The heads of boys proclaiming their puberty.
Ogro: Ha, ha! Go tell that to the girls
  In town and see whether they don't take you
  For a plucker of leaves! But seriously,
  As I am Ogrope, born in the laps
  Of the nine rivers and still suckling
  On their breast, which of you shall have
  The first look and so live again?
Kengide: Keep me out of it.
Ogro: Here are three groundnut shells. I'll cast

Them right here on the mat
And if it's a single one that falls
On its back, then you are in for it first, hear
That? Here goes. Ah, the first
Is yours after all!

Kengide: I said keep me out of it.

Olotu: All right. Give it to me and I'll look in. [*He takes the cup, opens it, and flings it out to stream without stop.*] Now, take that! [*He lunges at Ogro.*]

Ogro: What's the matter?

Olotu: Your Oguberi lash you to death!

Ibobo: What was in it?

Kengide: Honey in the hive, probably.

Olotu: Oh! The smell's more
Than an old woman's backyard.

Ogro: That may be so, considering Kengide
Has been our best cook here. Why, see all
The pepper he pours into his soup. But that's
No reason to throw away the best bait
You can get.

Kengide: There at least he is right. See how already
A few fish have fastened their gills to the filth
Bobbing there among the waves.

Ogro: At home when the rains are torrents, before
The flood is among the reeds on the bank,
The boys build themselves special fishtraps
To sail down the tide which at this time
Of year sticks to one course.

Olotu: And they use excrement for bait?

Ogro: Of course yes; and before you sail
The length of town three times, your keel
Is threshing with all kinds of fish.

Olotu: Now I understand why in all the creeks
You Okrika people are called bad names.

Kengide: At least, they throw nothing away as good
Housekeepers and seekers after copper, you will
Admit that. However, Ogro's is not
The only fruitful, if somewhat unfamiliar
Manner of fishing. I once went fishing
Myself with a friend many floods back.
It was a terrible tide for fishing, but

We were young and hungry enough to think
We could break fresh seasons. So down the stream
We sallied, deploying ourselves far apart
So our lines didn't tangle in the fever
To entice some fish. There were a few dips
Of the float, but when you jerked out your hook, thinking
You'd made a catch at last, only the water
Dripped down your line, like bright beads, and
The tide was quick to wash off your bait. I
Became firm then about returning home,
Even as we had climbed the bank that morning,
That is, bare of hand.
The mad woman of the market herself knows
It is a bad tide, I said, so why smart
With shame? To my surprise, my friend
Counselled patience. But just as my parched lips
Opened to call out to him for the last time,
He shouted over to me with great excitement.
"What is it?" I asked. "Oko" (that's how
We called each other) "Oko," he shouted,
"I have caught a chicken!" Of course I didn't
Quite trust my ears in that heat of day. But
Unable to resist an old joke, I tried
To meet my friend halfway. So I asked: "You mean
A snakebird? They take long dives in these
Waters, you know." "You idiot!" he shouted
In anger: "Whoever thought of eating
A snakebird?" "But a chicken? Can one fish
A chicken?" I protested. "Yes, a real
Soil and roof chicken," he affirmed. "And portent
Or omen, when I get home, I'll cook myself
A good meal," he closed the matter. And there
Actually dangling from his rod was a flesh
And feather catch. I didn't ask
More questions; that would have kept
Me outside the feast.
Ogro: Your friend was a real fisherman; he ought
    To be fishing for men next.
Ibobo: Now you are talking like the wandering
    Father of Gbekebo who spoke of nothing
    But carpenters and fishermen all day.

Ogro: Tell me, what happened to that fellow? There was
  No creek into which he did not make incursion.
  Not even the mosquitoes could keep him and his band
  Of paddlers out.

Kengide: He chose poor building ground though. Today
  Not one beam of his house stands. What the flood
  Didn't sweep away, the elephant grass
  Has overgrown. Worse, the net he cast out
  Attracted many, but could not retain
  A single fish. It had too many loopholes.
  There never was a worse fisherman afloat
  In all the rivers.

Olotu: Your stories may serve as wine
  To your spirits, but have you forgotten we are stuck
  In a worse plight here?

Ogro: What can we?

Ibobo: We are in the hands of Osikoboro.

Kengide: Wait for the tide, I say.

Olotu: It's one o'clock; so it ought to be here now.

Ogro: One o'clock? I thought you told us
  It was eleven while we were eating?

Olotu: So I did, and I repeat it's one now.

Ogro: Well, I'm not the man to run down
  The white folks who made your watch there and several
  Other things they have no use for, but what
  Is this idea of counting backwards, when
  The natural thing is a straight count
  From sunrise to its setting. Even the cuckoo
  Knows that.

Olotu: A pure bull that's what you are.

Ogro: Maybe. Now is that any reason
  For hitting me on the ear?

Olotu: Nobody hit you.

Ogro: As my name is Ogrope, one of you here did.

Ibobo: Look at what probably hit him.

Ogro: A bat? On the river and at daytime? Now,
  What evil errand does it run?

Olotu: The salt in the wind must be affecting
  Your sight too. Don't you see it is
  A swift bird?

Kengide: Swallows, I think.

Ibobo: They are swarming all over the place. Look,
   They dive as if to plunge headlong into the swell,
   But even as their feet graze the wave crest, they
   Have swung steep back into the skies.
Kengide: A storm is here, that must be their one message. See,
   There flies off somebody's hat!
Olotu: Gather up the baskets then, and roll up
   The mats. A wet bed we can at least save ourselves.
Ibobo: Bundling up mats like this always puts
   Me in mind of a corpse ready for the castoff.
Olotu: You ought to have been cast off, all
   Of you, a long time ago.
Ogro: Stop, stop—don't roll them up!
Ibobo: So the storm can soak and swell them up?
Olotu: Will you step off the mats: they must all
   Be rolled up.
Ogro: Don't, I say. Don't you see you can string
   Them into sails and so pull out of this tangle?
Kengide: Indeed, man is better than goat!
   Why, with this wind fit to take any iroko
   By the hair and lift it clean off its feet,
   We should be out of here in a moment.
Olotu: There, take the lamp off that post; it will serve
   Us for a mast! Strange I didn't think
   Of it before. Now, we don't have to wait
   For the tide's coming. A mast! A mast, boys!
Ogro: Don't you want ropes to string the sail? Take
   This cane left over from repairing the cabin.
Ibobo: And here are bamboos for as many cross bars
   As we want.
Olotu: Oh, quick, quick, before the gust caves in.
Kengide: It's moving! It really is moving!
Ogro: Now give a loud shout, boys. Our raft
   Is moving again—behind a big bellyful
   Of tornado—Oh, shout for joy!
   [*At this point, a loud creak, then a brief cracking sound, and the raft
   breaks in two, the portion with the billowing sail pulling furiously away.
   On it is Olotu.*]
Ibobo: [*Picking himself up.*] What happened?
Ogro: Has a manatee struck us?
Kengide: No, it is just that your rotten raft

Can't take a little strain, and now one end
Of it is sailing our captain to sea.

Ibobo: Jump, jump, Olotu! Oh, the hippo,
It's too late now.

Ogro: Now he'll have to swim for it! Jump,
Olotu, jump!

Olotu: Help, help, I can't leave the logs!

Kengide: Mark me, the truth
Is that he can't swim. Which of you has seen
Him bathe without his clinging to the raft
Like a snail.

Ibobo: Oh, how do we come together? At this rate
He'll soon be at sea.

Ogro: I'll swim out to him, and take
With me a tow-rope.

Kengide: You young fool, don't you see a school
Of sharks prowling the place? Let the man
Lower the sail.

Ibobo: Lower the sail, Olotu!
Lower the sail! Oh, the wind is too loud,
But don't they teach these people
Anything practical at school?

Ogro: Still, I can make it! Honestly, I can.

Kengide: [*Holding the other back.*] And lose a limb in the jaws of some
shark?

Ibobo: You are a greater monster!

Kengide: Why don't you yourself take the plunge? As for you,
Ogrope,
I'm sure you want the old chief's daughter still.

Ogro: Lord, Lord, he's adrift and lost!

Kengide: We are all adrift
And lost, Ogrope, we are all adrift and lost.
[*All this while Olotu, now swept completely out of sight, has not stopped
crying: "Help, help, I can't leave the logs!"*]

THREE: IRON AND FIRE

Late afternoon; low slants the sun, and the raft drifts on.

Ogro: [*Singing to his instrument.*]
  "All this ululation in town,
  Tell me, to what end?
  Oh, all this ululation,
  Will you tell to what end,
  You of seven crowns,
  My one and only son!"
Ibobo: Do they ever sing to laugh in your part
  Of the country?
Ogro: No, each day some poor fellow is either
  Going out with a hiss or making his brief
  Entrance with a howl, and the women wail
  Going to bed and wake up wailing, for their seeds
  Are eaten up by the black beetle.
Ibobo: Forgive me, Ogro, in my place, too, plants
  Wilt and die, wilt and die, but all
  The same, we have our happy seasons.
Kengide: That is because, like the very creeks
  You live on, your ways meander like the pythons
  You worship. Thus you drink where you
  Defecate, and will have others believe
  It's living water.
Ibobo: And your people have pure wells and sweet springs!
Kengide: No, water swirling with mud. But we
  Upriver people are more upright. Anyway,
  Who wants water, when the palm is pouring
  With wine? Now, that's what I miss on these logs sodden
  As one with dropsy.
Ogro: [*Goes on singing.*]
  "Death that has nothing to do
  With God is what has struck;
  Death that has nothing to do
  With God is what has struck;
  It's Ozidi, the all-strong,
  Who's come to strike down man."
Kengide: Don't dwell on that theme for too long; it is

Mere mud. So you turn your broad back
Upon me and will continue with your sob-songs?
All right then, dwell on the one theme of mud
And sink therein.

Ogro: Oguberi strike you dead! [*He gathers up his instrument and goes beyond the cabin to the far end of raft.*]

Ibobo: What do you gain falling like an evil tree
Across the path of people?

Kengide: I do not stand between anybody and his heart's
Desire—between them and deceit perhaps;
Yes, I may admit to that.

Ibobo: At least you did this morning. You stood
Between him and his destiny.

Kengide: Bile and bladder, I stood between the man
And certain doom.

Ibobo: Not many will believe that when the story
Is told. And you know as well as I do
That an Ijawman's death, especially by water,
Drags like ivy.

Kengide: I don't doubt that; it is the way the world's tide
Flows. They forget a drowning man is like a starfish,
Soft and flailing, but his embrace sucks
Life out of whoever comes within it.

Ibobo: Poor Olotu, he must be washed out somewhere by now!

Kengide: Such fears for a calabash on water!
I tell you the rascal on his own
Bit of raft is much safer than us here.

Ibobo: You don't believe that really. We are in normal
Waters here, going down the Inekorogha
River, and he alone in the wild open.

Kengide: If he was fool enough to leave the sail
On, he still will in all likelihood hit the bar
Before wind or tide carries him out. I tell
You he's already been picked up by fishermen
From the settlement of Age which is right
On the sea's brink.

Ibobo: Let his ancestors help to make matters so!

Kengide: Your man is singing again. [*Both listen, and the words come clear from Ogro over his instrument.*]

Ogro: "Sign on the line, Oh
Please sign on the line:

Whoever wrestles with me
Must first sign his will."
Ibobo: I wonder where he picks up his terrible tunes.
Kengide: You ought to know that piece; it's famous
   Down all Bulutoro River. Some fellow who took
   Our own gin into Lagos threw
   A police sergeant that challenge, after
   His arrest and sentence to a six-months' diet
   On beans and garri.
Ibobo: Did the cudgel-carrying man accept it?
Kengide: The questions you sometimes ask. Do you suppose
   They are jungle people up there in Lagos? They just
   Shaved off his hair and turned him over
   To the sewage people.
Ibobo: Listen to Ogro—he's yelling something.
Ogro: Come out here, Ibobo, come out here quick!
Ibobo: What is the matter now?
Kengide: Is a python crossing the stream? Please
   Whatever you do, don't seek to rouse him!
Ibobo: Now, what is it?
Ogro: A ship; I think it's a ship chopping up
   Our rear.
Kengide: That's unlikely; all ships to Burutu
   And Warri ply the Forcados River.
   What's there to gather in this waste except
   Of course, you mean the ADO's out again
   Wringing dry the tear ducts of the people.
Ibobo: Come over, Kengide. There surely is smoke
   Belching out of something somewhere behind
   The bend. It can't be the ADO from Agoro. He rides
   In motor-boats.
Ogro: It's a Niger Company boat—the *Naraguta*
   In fact—I am certain of it.
Ibobo: How can you be so sure?
Ogro: Of course I am; I know every single craft
   Sailing between Burutu, Warri
   And Lokoja as well as Makurdi
   Or Yola—the red-funnel boats of John Holt,
   The coal-dirty fleet of the Niger Company
   And the slow tugs of the French line gargling like
   A bottle filling under water—I know

All their individual engine sounds. Listen
To this one:
   "Lokoja's too far,
    Lokoja's too far.
    But over there lie riches"
Don't you hear the tune? There, it's blowing
Its horn, blowing that all canoes and offals
Floating get out of its way.

Kengide: Yes; a lumbering ship, all right. We'll have
To coax our raft to the bank bulging to our left,
As the steel fellow is sure to hug
The other side where the river runs deepest.

Ibobo: Oh, if we were the heaviest Hausa craft
Now, the captain will tow us to port
For a mere fee of five bob, and so be
In port long before dark. But this wretched raft!

Kengide: I say, take up oars and lug the thing clear
Before that crazy ship runs over us all.
   [*Meanwhile Ogro has taken to waving his tattered shirt to the ship.*]

Ogro: Captain slow, captain slow! Slow down, captain!

Ibobo: Do you think he'll stop for you? Even for canoes
Full-laden with woman and children they don't
Often limber on the waves stirred up in their wake.

Kengide: You fool, here, add your oar to the job
On hand, will you? Really, what type of game
Do you suppose you are playing out there?

Ogro: Back in my home town, the boys all swim
Far out to stream to board the boats as they pass
By, and the good people on deck help to haul
Us up the bows. Oh it's fun to jump overboard
And climb on again, out and in, out
And in, to the loud cheers of the sailors till
The last puff of smoke is out among the clouds
Above the trees many bends away. Then
And only then is it time to take the final plunge,
Your arms full of gifts from the kind captain
And his men. And there is no need then to give
A stroke because you are lying tired on your back
And your soft, cool bed, the stream itself, bearing
You back into town, smoothly, softly, and safely.
   [*More hooting from the ship which is passing quite close by now.*]

Hold on, hold on, oh!
I'm coming, coming out to you my captain!
Kengide: Ogro, what are you doing—Ogro? Come back!
Ibobo: Ogro, Ogro, are you mad? Oh what uncalled
    Home dead has come into him?
    [*Ogro has already flung down his instrument and plunged overboard.*]
Kengide: He's a strong swimmer at any rate;
    He will surely not drown.
Ibobo: But can he make the ship? We are all three
    Of us breast to breast now.
Kengide: Yes; he ought to have jumped much earlier on
    To be planted in the path of the ship,
    But I think he'll make it.
Ibobo: Isn't he a real fish? Now he has ducked under.
    It seems those on board don't quite know
    What is happening, and now one or two
    Are looking over the gunnel. There,
    He has surfaced, right against the ship's flank.
    What, don't they want him aboard?
Kengide: Probably they are scared to death seeing
    A full naked, brown bull like that spring
    Suddenly out of the deep.
Ibobo: Stop, stop! You can't do that! Oh
    The brutes! I can't look any more!
Kengide: Poor, poor otter.
Ibobo: Have they stopped stoning him with coals,
    Beating off his hands with bars of iron? Oh,
    He's tired out now and slumped back into the deep.
    But they are mistaken if they expect
    He'll drown in their wake.
Kengide: No; no; Ogrope won't drown now; I think
    He has got caught in the mortal arms
    Of that stern-wheeling engine.
Ibobo: Ogro, Ogro!

FOUR: CALL OF LAND

Day is almost gone and the raft makes for port.

Ibobo: Now we are two. I said it is left
   Us two now whereas only this morning
   We were four out of a happy gang that started out
   Seven strong. I hope we make port safely.
Kengide: Look, my dear man, do you see
   These five fellows here? How did they get staggered out
   As they are today?
Ibobo: How should I know?
Kengide: [*Ticking off the fingers of his left hand.*]
   It began like this. The small fellow right outside
   Here happened one day to cry hunger. "Let's
   Go out and grab ourselves something," suggested
   His closest friend, a real tortoise
   Of a fellow. "What if we are caught
   In the act?" this tall, gawky overgrown
   Creature you see here in the middle queried.
   "Easy," counselled this short chap, "We'll just take
   Off the earth on our feet." But here this slow
   Burly being who all the time was drowsing
   In the corner, rolled over farther still
   Saying: "Count me out!" And that's why even now
   You see him standing apart from the group. So what's
   So new about our position, young man?
Ibobo: Sometimes I want to knock you overboard!
   You sit there, your breast unbeating, while Olotu
   Is swept out to sea and Ogro, like an animal
   For sacrifice, is chopped to pieces by
   That terrible stern-wheeler.
Kengide: Had I not allowed that man's sweet tongue to lick me
     round with all his talk
   About the quick money there is to make
   In this log business, I should be safe at home
   Today happily collapsed over my calabash
   Of palm wine. But I let
   That weakling of a wash-back from Lagos
   Fool me into joining his lumber gang, and here

We are tied to a raft of logs whose sole owner
Is miles away rolling on laps
Of his innumerable wives.

Ibobo: So it's true! You did it out of burst bile
When this morning you stopped poor Ogro
From trying a rescue?

Kengide: Gall and entrails, you don't drink soup
The way you will water. The young whelp
I tell you is probably only too glad
That he has been left with his own share
Of the timber. The rogue waiting down
At Warri wasn't going to pay him much anyway.

Ibobo: You take great delight damaging trees!

Kengide: Yes; I burn them down so I don't lack
The charcoal to smear innocent faces.

Ibobo: None will nibble at the other, that's what
I'm telling you!

Kengide: Who told you so? In this game
Of getting rich, it is eat me or I eat
You, and no man wants to stew in the pot,
Not if he can help it.

Ibobo: All the logs bear their owner's name and besides
They have all been stamped by the forest-guard.

Kengide: As if characters however strange ever
Stopped adzes and axes from carving afresh! And those
Forest fellows, you know them as you do
Your loincloth, don't you? A straight
Bribe of five shillings on every twelve
And the most erect of them in all
The forest will as easy erase as imprint
With that almightly hammer of theirs. Oh, yes.
In a case like Olotu's, both thieves
Will certainly be content to settle
For an even split.

Ibobo: Now my eyes are somewhat open. Do
You know I have often wondered at the rate
Those forest-guard fellows put up buildings at Warri.
Surely, Government couldn't be paying them more
Than it does its clerks.

Kengide: There you are right. For all their stiff khaki
And sashes, your green folk don't get paid

One bag of money a month. But who will arrest
Their sway? The police who should apply the rope
Are themselves feeding so fat, their belts and barracks
No longer can hedge in the smallest
Weed. And so with the courts. Man, it is
We ordinary grass and shrubs who get crushed
As the mahoganies fall.

Ibobo: Poor Ogro! He plunged to his death, festering
  Like a sore open to flies because he thought
  It was another who needed saving.

Kengide: There, there, keep her alongside
  The tide. Yes, that's better. I think we'll make
  A smooth slide off those stumps ahead.

Ibobo: Yes, we should now. This was just
  The type of job Ogro was best at. A raft
  Of more than two hundred logs
  Could be heading straight into a beachhead
  Like a herd of cattle lashed by driver-ants,
  But with a slight flick of his wrist when you
  Thought all was lost, and the mighty raft is
  Back on the breast of the tide, clean away
  From crash.

Kengide: He was an idiot all the same.

Ibobo: You will come to no good end
  Yourself, the evil you speak of the dead.

Kengide: Off to the bad bush or under the eaves,
  It is all one burial place to me. Boy, whether
  You die of tuberculosis or
  Of a cold and at a ripe old age with many
  Behind to wail your end, the fruit is fallen
  Anyway. And the family will not wait till
  The next market day before they gather it up
  For the sharing out. Accordingly, your loss
  Is their gain. But that young man was a fool anyway.
  Look at how he rushed forth like a beast
  Long held up for slaughter.

Ibobo: He was a good swimmer, and made the target
  As he knew he would. The brutes balked
  Him. I wish I were near enough to crack
  Their skulls.

Kengide: Ease your gorilla fists, man. There are

Three types of characters the world will not
Accommodate: the mad, the drunk, and the naturally
Foolish. Take all the three to a pit
And see what happens. The mad very likely
Will skirt as he does in his mind, the drunk
Has already got himself into worse
Anyway, but the idiot, he'll break his neck
Therein and still wonder why nobody
Has rushed after his heels in loud cheer.

Ibobo: I want to be in port, I want
  To be in port—now, now!

Kengide: Come, you are tired at the till. Let me
  Take over. This oar is worn already to breaking
  By continuous grip.

Ibobo: I try to shut my eyes, gateways to my head
  Which is one great cage where misfortune,
  Like an alligator trussed within, batters
  At my temples, forehead and back.

Kengide: Don't try to shut your eyes then.
  You don't want the bamboo bars to break.

Ibobo: Even now I can hear Ogro being cut
  And chopped to pieces in the rapids
  Of that stern-wheeler.

Kengide: That tells you he was no crocodile.

Ibobo: Stop knocking the dead, will you, stop it, before
  I batter your skull to pulp!

Kengide: All right; now my mouth's shut don't tower
  Above me. As it is, there are enough shadows
  Creeping around. Now do you think your fingers
  Are steady enough to strike a match
  For the lantern?

Ibobo: My hands are not trembling.

Kengide: I can well see that. Well, never mind. The tide
  Is going to sea pretty fast and we are
  On her breast, and so somewhat dizzy,
  That is, as much as a canoe with more
  Than twenty casks in its hold.

Ibobo: I see lights—Oh, we are almost there!

Kengide: Surely not at this distance.

Ibobo: It's true, right over the mangrove trees:
  There, look and you'll see them dancing

To the fall of night.

Kengide: I really must be getting old. I still
    Cannot see anything except the waters
    And the mangrove trees rushing by on either side.

Ibobo: You will see the lights soon—when it is
    Darker. There, I know we'll make it. Oh,
    My grandfather and your gods on land
    And sea, just see us safely make port
    And I'll slaughter that goat long since assigned
    For your sacrifice. I have often heard
    It said you could see the street lights of Burutu
    Far, far out from stream. I thought it one
    Of their stories—like those about ghosts
    Who are never seen but by some person
    In distant parts who told it to a friend
    Who told it to another and so on till
    You feel in the endless coils of the guinea-worm.
    But now I have seen it myself.

Kengide: If you are right, and now I think you are,
    For what I see blinking there couldn't
    Be one star, and there is no lighthouse anywhere
    In these swamps and creeks, then we can't be
    More than eight bends of the river from port.

Ibobo: They are lights, yes, they are! Come over here,
    You'll see several more breaks above the trees.

Kengide: Don't fall over into the waters in
    Your excitement. Indeed, cataract or no
    Cataract in my eyes, badly battered by wind
    And salt, they have all swum into full sight;
    Yes, they are street lamps or lookout lanterns
    On ship masts at Burutu.

Ibobo: Oh the tall lampposts you see in townships
    And the lovers in each other's arms bathing
    In their glow.

Kengide: You should see crabs out of their holes
    In the peat and swamp, making splendid
    Salutations with hairy forearms under those
    Same lamps. And the scorpions never stop
    Stalking below the windows aglow with light.

Ibobo: A sting by one of them might drive
    Out some of the poison in you.

Kengide: The gods protect you for that happy
  Prayer. Now set that lamp up before you
  Shatter it.
Ibobo: There I hang it up burning bright
  Even as my heart, and may never wind
  Or water, however wayward, put it out
  This night.
Kengide: Boy, boy, you place surely is
  By the shrine. Who put the axe between
  Your palms?
Ibobo: We shall be in port before the town goes
  To sleep, shan't we?
Kengide: Towns don't go to sleep, young man.
Ibobo: What do you mean?
Kengide: If they did, those who run them
  Will have little time to plot their pleasure
  And plunder.
Ibobo: Plunder or pleasure, I shall be in port
  At last and sound in some proper bed.
Kengide: With some woman, you mean. Admit it.
Ibobo: Yes, I should love to sleep with a woman tonight.
Kengide: You have been dying to wreck your wretched self
  At the feet of some woman these several
  Market tides past.
Ibobo: Seven market tides adrift
  On a raft,
  Watching over wood going to rot. I almost
  Forgot my manhood except for those brief periods
  I had to pass water.
Kengide: Surely, you add much water to wine.
  Three weeks without a woman is not such
  A terrible feat. Why, my sister's son
  At college tells me six white men somewhere
  Almost crossed an ocean on a raft no larger
  Than that of our Olotu. And they were
  On it and all alone more than three months
  Together.
Ibobo: I don't believe it. What will anyone
  Do a thing like that for?
Kengide: To prove a point.
Ibobo: I don't get it.

Kengide: Well, that's where they get
   You and me. Now, where is my pouch of kola?
   Yes, here it is under the mat.
Ibobo: You eat too much kola; it will cut your bowels.
Kengide: At least it's not as bitter as life. But
   If what you say were true, all emirs
   From Idah to Gongola would be
   Sheer ribbons today. But coming back to what
   We were saying, how would you like to take
   A pot shot at this nut if placed on top
   Of that lamp you likened to your heart?
Ibobo: To what end?
Kengide: To prove a point.
Ibobo: I would think you are about to take
   To the forest. After all, a roasted kola, they say,
   Pulls out the tongue from its roots.
Kengide: Nonsense. Some white folk, and here again
   I draw on my sister's son at college, for I myself
   Never went to school, well, some white man
   Has done worse.
Ibobo: How?
Kengide: He shot through an orange planted right
   On the head of his only son.
Ibobo: With a gun? and the boy did not die?
Kengide: No, with his bow and arrow.
Ibobo: Come, Kengide, you think you are pulling
   My leg, but I'm tortoise
   Myself and must tell you it's the prop-root
   Of the mangrove you have in your hands, not my leg.
   White men don't use bows and arrows.
Kengide: Oh, they used to. Now to prove their point
   They use something which my sister's son at college
   Says can turn the whole world into one pot
   Of mushroom soup—yes, even as you snap
   Your fingers.
Ibobo: All the same, I want to be in port tonight
   And in bed with some decent girl.
Kengide: There you go again. But I don't
   Blame you; you are not as resourceful
   As others.
Ibobo: What has being resourceful got to do with it?

Kengide: A lot. Didn't you know one white man
    Will go to bed with another—even
    In preference to a woman?
Ibobo: That's beastly. Even the goat that does
    It with its mother will not take another
    He-goat from behind.
Kengide: Now the boy from the bush full of taboos
    Is talking! How do you think they keep sane
    In their great barracks and boarding schools? Why,
    ADO's and holy fathers do it on their boys.
    But seriously, don't you think we ought
    To pull up for the night? It's dangerous sailing
    A raft down the creeks at night.
Ibobo: On a clear night like this—and when
    With a little more height we already spot
    The lights of Burutu smiling
    Us welcome? It cannot be dangerous. Indeed
    It is not at all dark. Look at the moon
    Tearing right over our heads. Before
    It is several clouds to our right hand, it should
    Be journey's end for everybody. Oh, it isn't
    Night at all but some leftover afternoon,
    When the sun, ready to turn in after long
    Travelling, stops short at the threshold,
    And casting his piercing eyes left and right,
    Holds up his lamp for a little longer until
    Three maidens late in the farm come back safe home.
Kengide: You certainly want to sleep
    In a regular bed tonight!
Ibobo: Yes, a regular bed, soft and warm,
    And not this rubbish of mats, strung over
    Bamboo and logs swimming with bugs.
Kengide: That reminds me, how many did
    You capture today?
Ibobo: In the midst of all we have gone through
    Since sunrise, what words you let spring from your tongue!
Kengide: I got mine all the same.
Ibobo: Well, I don't want to hear about it.
Kengide: I am not laughing, Ibobo. Here, look
    In this cigarette tin, and you'll see.
    You people stub yours out, but I hoard

Mine in here, the blood suckers—like merchants
Whose mascot they are, bedbugs must not be let off
Lightly. You can shake the tin for yourself. Hear
Their scraping sound? They are all crawling
In there—little, little pots reared on stilts!

Ibobo: I think your people ought
  To have taken you a long time ago
  To the oracle.

Kengide: How do you know they didn't? Believe
  Me, there are more places to go to to get worse
  Pronouncements, and you don't have to pay.
  Look, in the thick of all we have been through
  Today, to be able to collect
  The regular quota of the enemy that sucks
  You pale and leprous—as a matter of fact,
  I think I even topped the target today—fifty-five
  To be exact—which is more than anybody
  Has ever done, I think I deserve a medal,
  A regular medal, like those
  The ex-servicemen brought from Burma
  And India, and now aren't worth a penny.

Ibobo: I spit at all you say, and see
  How I squash you and your creatures under heel.

Kengide: My poor, poor pets. Let me put you
  To bed. I see you and I are out of favor
  Tonight. Now, Ibobo, open your ears. You say
  You want a woman. Not all the bedbugs
  In this world can suck as one woman
  Sharing with you a bed.

Ibobo: Are you an unwashed dog forever picking and
  Biting at its own tick? I said I don't want
  To hear any more! [*He goes briefly into the cabin.*]

Kengide: The woman I ever called mine own lived in
  This very port of Burutu now bursting upon
  Us in the distance like bells on
  The staff to Tamara. Oh, she was one
  For frying sweet things in the kitchen
  All day, and although she never had a cold
  All her life, you always heard
  Her sniff-sniffing to herself as you came
  In—it was more than any appetizer

Could arouse, and at night she would dance you till
You went dizzy and drunk like a child
Rocked to rest.
Ibobo: [*From inside and above the noise of his search for something.*]
    I suppose you couldn't keep pace—now
Where's that bit of mirror—so you lost your post.
Kengide: What a breast-sucker you still are! Ibobo,
    Women are three types. Some are like log,
Solid and unshakable, after
You've sweated all day lugging them into position.
Take my word for it, run clear of wherever such
Lie fallen. Then there are those who, like the stream
About us now, are placid and spacious. It takes
An unusual storm to stir them, and no passion
However strong, can guarantee that. So you
Just swim every market tide. And then there
Are those who are pure billows; on them you rise
And sink, rise and sink, and like
The water-lettuce, you don't have to do anything.
The woman I lost was the very crest of them.
Ibobo: [*Who has come out with a broken piece of mirror in hand and has
been engrossed in a kind of toilet.*]
    Did she die giving birth to your baby?
Kengide: Bear me fruit? No! The plant
    Of poison. She just went blossoming. It was
In the furious forties—at the time of the Great
Strike. Now, you didn't know I worked
For the Niger Company at one time, did you? Always
Making money for some man other
Than myself, that has been my fortune. Well,
You didn't possess a wife as mine and forget
About finding some extra funds. That was how,
Personally, I got in the strike deep to my neck.
But you know how like the waters at Bussa
The whole thing went. The politicians
And papers who had promised Jericho itself,
By their own divisions, caused a breach
In the wall we workers had at their incitement staked
All to build. So, Government or Niger
Company, two faces to one counterfeit coin,
As usual won the field. Not only that,

They went on to raise taxes and prices on
Everything money could buy in the shop—from buckets
To umbrellas—they raised them all, while lowering
Those on our crops.
Ibobo: What of her?
Kengide: Even in the heat of the row, she was
Already dancing the jig with another—one of those
Who broke our pickets.
Ibobo: A real whore!
Kengide: A reed in the tide, you mean. God made
The dancer, and he gets her who plays best.
Ibobo: When this trip is over, I want to go home
And pick me a decent girl to marry.
Kengide: Oh, happy traveller just starting out!
And may I ask if the bride price
Is all settled?
Ibobo: No, why? Mother will see to that. Without
Her all the rivers will go dry of starch
And farina, and but for her taking canoes
Of fish upcountry, folks there
Will be mere goats feeding on their cassava.
Kengide: So mother is going to set you up
Her vagabond son? I expected it will
Be that way. Why, all the wages that rogue
Will ever pay you for our days in the wilderness
Will not survive the emptying at a woman's feet—especially
The kind you want to have tonight—[*Breaks into a caper and sing-
song tone.*]
Two shillings for make water
An' one a'sissy for look—
Your brother nor tell you dat?
Oh, boy, go on, wash yourself clean, comb your hair
Tough like wire so she can thumb you fine.
Ibobo: Stop babbling! Suddenly,
I can't tell where we are.
Kengide: Well, let's see. We ought to have sighted the first buoys
By now. But where are you?
Ibobo: Here, by the cabin. I have been viewing
My wreck in the mirror. What is happening?
Suddenly, I can't see you either. Aren't
You saying a word?

Kengide: It's the fog; fog has come upon us.
Ibobo: Fog? I saw lights only a wink ago
 In that direction. Now I can't even see
 The mirror in my hand!
Kengide: Where, where is it? Your hand I mean—there
 Give me your hand—Oh this basket of plates—
 Who placed it here so I'll bruise my toes
 On it—but your hand—Good, I have got it. Now hold tight.
Ibobo: What shall we do? Now, what shall
 We do? Burutu is over there,
 I know it—I smell it and we are going past
 Like this, unable to stop, seeing
 Nothing—oh hear the hooting of owls!
Kengide: I hear them—they are horns
 Blowing in concert—the fog
 Is everywhere.
Ibobo: Burutu is there floating past—I hear
 Voices of people as in a market,
 And the beating of drums, the smell of food
 In the air, and we are drifitng past—I
 Shall jump and swim!
Kengide: No, Ibobo, no, not when you yourself
 Say you cannot see your own hand! Why, here
 We are, holding hands, but can you see me?
 Fog has stuffed its soot and
 Smoke in our eyes, has shut up the world
 Like a bat its wings. Don't you see?
 All is blindness and scales! Besides,
 These waters teem with sharks and starfish
 And there must be barges, tugs and ocean liners
 Lumbering about—
Ibobo: You can't stop me—no, you can't,
 You can't! Oh, let me go!
Kengide: Go on! Jump and take me with you!
Ibobo: Let me go! Let me go—will you? [*He hits him.*] Or are
 You afraid to be alone?
Kengide: Aren't you, too, Ibobo,
 Aren't you afraid to be left alone
 In this world, aren't you?
Ibobo: No! No! Let me go!
Kengide: Then why want to jump blindfold

Into a well full of snakes and stakes? Why want to
If you aren't afraid to be alone?
Ibobo: Oh, Mother, my mother, won't I give
You burial home?
Kengide: Shout, shout, Ibobo, let's shout
To the world—we woodsmen lost in the bush.
Ibobo: We're adrift, adrift and lost! Ee-ee-eee!
Kengide: Shout, Ibobo, shout!

[*Both together hand in hand, one holding the flickering lamp, the other cupping his mouth, shout together into the night, into the fog, over the waters, that long squeal as used when women go woods-gathering and by nightfall have still not found their way home: Ee-ee—ee—ee!!! At the same time and above all there is the long hooting of horns and of men crying and calling out to one another in fear and in the distance and rush.*]

(Lights!)

Ozidi

A Play

Ozidi

PERSONS   (in order of appearance)

The Storyteller
Seven Virgins
The Group of Players and Chorus of
   Dancers
The State Council of Orua
Old Woman
Woman with gourd
Ofe the Short
An elder
Azezabife the Skeleton Man
Oguaran the Giant
Agbogidi the Nude
Ozidi the father
Temugedege his idiot brother who
   becomes King
Citizens
Bebeareowei or State Crier
People of Orua
Orea wife of Ozidi
Messengers
Orua Host
Another Old Woman
Boys of Ododama
The Boy son of Orea
Oreame his grandmother
Bouakarakarabiri or Tebekawene
   the Old Man of the Forest

Ozidi who was the boy before
Blacksmith
An Apprentice
Ozidi's Hornblower
Ozidi's Sword bearer
Ozidi's Drummer
Other Attendants
Ewiri the Amananaowei of Orua
Ofe's wife ⎫ the
Azezabife's wife ⎬ three
Oguaran's wife ⎭ marketwomen
Badoba the Tree Man
Sigirisi the Net Man
Tebesonoma of the Seven Crowns
Woman with child, his sister
Her brother-in-law
Neighbors
Woman Odogu's wife, captured by
   Ozidi
Odogu the Ugly
Azema or Agonodi of the sky-
   face, his mother
Engarando the Smallpox King
The Smallpox King's attendants of
   Cold, Headache, Cough, Spots,
   Fever, and his brothers Egirigiri
   and Okrikpakpa.

The orchestra:
a master drummer, three side drummers, one horn blower.

ACT I

Scene 1

As spectators are settling down all around, a man walks into the open area of play. He is dressed in a white flowing skirt and tunic and appears to be in some difficulty. Nevertheless a natural inclination to laughter is shown by his eyes, one of which has about it a halo painted in Benin chalk. First, he clears his throat to attract attention. He has little success and so claps his hands nervously, speaking louder at the same time.

Storyteller: Attention please, all you who have come to see our show, will you please give me your ears? I am afraid there's a hitch. Look, don't let that turn your bowels sore; we are first to admit this a most shaky thing to happen with old hands. However, it is a hitch, one out of which we hope you can help us. You see, our cast is incomplete. We need seven young women right now. Seven young women, and whatever for? I can see some of you raising eyebrows. I hasten to assure you we intend nothing dishonorable! Trouble is that, before we can perform for your pleasure and benefit tonight, we must first have a sacrifice to placate our hosts from the sea. Oh, yes, there are special spectators streaming all around you right now, even though you may not see or touch them. And the seven girls we ask of you, all virgins mind you, alone can bear offerings to our guests from the sea, and so establish between us a bridge. Perhaps, you think this a quaint custom, that we are propping up cobwebs that with broom and brush we ought to sweep clean out of the house. Well, that is your own opinion and you are quite entitled to hold it; for aren't we living in a free, democractic country? But you may as well know that opinion expressed by our principal player; he will not put up appearance in any show that looks down on tradition. You see, the oracle has warned him of a swift finish to the act if the program is not followed properly, and he's nothing if not pious. I know him well; why, I am the fellow himself when I am not the plain narrator of our story; in the actual drama I play brother to the king as well as father to, and in fact your hero himself. Quite some intricate and interesting relationship that, isn't it? But wait until you see the whole epic; that is, on the condition that you grant us our seven virgins. There, I see a number of fair hands

shooting up already; yes, all three of you there please come up this
way. That's not all; oh, yes, you are coming along, too, are you?
Good show, and you beautiful girl over there, let not the forest
cover up your head of fountain. No more willing maids for us?
Now, come, come, only two more now, and we shall be satisfied.
And here they come—I knew they would—two springs tripping
in the sun. Well, this really is most generous of you! Here we are,
our glass already flowing over the brim before we have even
opened mouth to drink. Now, who was it said our country lacks
the fertile soil to produce sweet innocent flowers? Let him come
and view these sprigs to the garland we have gathered in one spot,
all of them undefiled still by bird or wind.

[*While he is speaking, the orchestra and chorus of actors and dancers
gradually emerge behind and swirl around him, singing the solemn,
processional song* Beni yo yo, beni yo yo. *As a group, they are all
dressed up as our first man, although running in the general wash of white
is a dash of black, indigo and scarlet. At their sudden appearance, the
storyteller starts in great excitement, and turns to the seven virgins now
also clustered about him, all in mixed emotions of expectation.*]

Here, to your right you see seven rich dishes all set in readiness.
They are not for you to eat, you understand? For that, you will
have to wait till you get to the fattening house. Now, each of you
take one and step out this way one after the other to the stream.
All others will follow.

[*To the spectators at large, his finger to his lips.*]

Hush, please, hush, or don't you people kneel to any god?

[*Meanwhile the procession to the stream has begun. The virgins, each
holding out her dish of offerings, are led in front by a man; then close
behind him the whole group of actors and dancers. The orchestra, of a
master drummer and three side drummers, remains stationary to the left at
the back. The procession moves slowly round the open place of play, and
then towards its far end where nobody sits all through the performance. At
this stage the chorus of actors and dancers open out to either side of the
storyteller, who stands a little out of line at the head of the seven virgins.
Close by, an assistant steps forward and directs the girls when to give and
take back their dishes of offerings from the storyteller, who now assumes the
powers and posture of priest. When he begins his prayer and invocation,
all the singing and music come to a stop.*]

Storyteller: People of the sea, people of the sea,
Two times, three times I call upon you.
Members of our community, in all their numbers

And from all quarters, sinking here their quarrels
And washing themselves of all colors and taint tonight,
Bring to you in all belly sweetness seven huge pots
Of food, each properly brought to you by a girl still
Untouched by man.
[*He takes from each her dish and makes a motion of dipping it in water.*]
Here's biscuit, here's sugar, here's wine,
All that is sweet to you.
And now that you have taken of
Our food and of our drinks,
Please give us good wives,
Give us good children, and give us good money, too.
After all, in Lagos, Benin, Ibadan, Enugu and
Kaduna we hear people are now running into streams of riches
     right up to
Their necks. Men that yesterday were only teachers,
Depending on schoolboy collections and firewood,
Or shoemakers peeling their own soles to eat
Are today ministers of state riding in cars as big as ships.
Towns, that in our fathers' time were no more than markets for
     cattle
And slaves, are today before our very eyes cleaving
The skies with houses of mirrors. Is it that
You think we of this community do not relish
Long cars to cruise in and palaces to live in?
After all, it is from you water people the wealth
Of the whole world flows. Indeed, why do you cut us off,
Yours sons, with leftovers and offal? See,
This festival in honor of you has not been celebrated
For long, how long now I cannot count on
The fingers of my two hands. Do you think
If we had money, we would not celebrate? So grant
Us good money, good children, good women,
That having all these, we your people, from those
Who stay at home like the wall-gecko to those who like
The black-kite go abroad, come next season,
May at the fall of every flood feast here with you.
[*Now the orchestra and chorus break into song—the fast jogging air of*
Beni owou mu ne yo, *the group forming again in the same order as*
before. They do a recession round the open area of play one or two times

as with the procession. The seven virgins, now relieved of their burden,
retire among the audience. At the same time, the chorus of actors and
dancers fall apart, flanking their leader who is cheered on now by the
master-drummer. The song-leader immediately raises the group praise song
Owa-ama ye ma. *As members of the group take it up, they sink down*
and sit about the principal player who remains standing and anxious to get
on with the business on hand. Meanwhile, two women come in, one
bringing a pot of palm wine along with calabash cups, and the other
holding a broom. The singing grows softer and softer, so that the second
woman can be heard clearly when she starts sweeping the floor to a chant.]
Old Woman: [*performing motions of sweeping the floor.*]
　There are some that are sour all day
　Give them sugar and they see ants
　Give them salt and they smart
　Thrush by the corners of their mouths. There's
　No sacrifice will sweeten them. They have ears
　But their drums beat back words of prayer,
　Bounce back sound of music. They may possess
　Double sight, but they will dart
　Daggers even at a bridal procession.
　If there are any here so
　Disposed, let them go off now
　Let them go off at once
　In great speed, yes, in great speed
　For we do not seek to please them.
　[*She repeats her lines as she does a second round of the floor. She is about*
　to start a third when the storyteller, calabash of wine in hand, stops her
　and shoos her out.]
Storyteller: Tut, tut, tut, woman, now you buzz off yourself! We men
　have important affairs of state to consider right now.
　[*He comes back, takes his seat in the circle of dancers and players around*
　whom the wine is passing freely and all at once, the entire group and
　chorus become the Council of State of Orua. Ozidi is played by the story-
　teller; other prominent people are Ofe the Short, Azezabife the Skeleton
　Man, Agbogidi the Nude and Oguaran the Giant.]
Ofe: A king, a king, time we had a new king
　In this city!
An Elder: Another one
　So soon! We have hardly finished burying
　The last one.

Azezabife: More cause why one must be elected
　　Immediately. This state needs a head to put
　　It on its feet.
Elder: I was not aware we were lying down.
Ofe: You were never one to care in what position
　　You stood in the eye of the public.
　　Right now, if I may tell you, Orua
　　Is like a tree fallen in the open.
Elder: Let it lie there then for a while; a little
　　Respite should do our body politic some good.
Azezabife: How you talk, old man! A tree fallen is free booty for all.
　　Women in long skirts
　　May even walk over it, that is, if they
　　Don't cart it off for firewood right away.
Elder: I still think we should go easy with electing another king.
　　Within the past four floods how many have sat on the royal seat of
　　　　Orua?
　　Six in all, it requires
　　No elephant to remember: six kings in all.
　　In that first year alone we buried
　　Three kings. The rest fared no better;
　　Each rose with the river only to fall with it.
　　Man, none of these men was common yam we
　　Buried with prospects of further yield.
　　Therefore, instead of choosing another
　　And having him planted long before his harvest, why don't we
　　Go and find how we may wash
　　Ourselves completely clean and so dislodge death that
　　Now
　　Sits the permanent occupant of our throne?
Oguaran: Good talk, old man! I always said you have
　　The gift of the squirrel.
Azezabife: Yes; the squirrel playing oracle
　　To the snake! As I am son to my father,
　　The man's plucking leaves to cover somebody.
Ofe: Now wait; if we followed the trail of his talk,
　　We should still all arrive at one place; prompt election
　　Of a new king.
Elder: How come?
Ofe: We require a king to pour
　　Our fathers' libation to wash ourselves clean.

Elder: True enough, but Ewiri as Amanana-owei,
　　Or any elder for that matter, can offer
　　The same sacrifice in our name. Our gods and
　　Ancestors will not refuse offering of food from
　　Our hands if these are clean.
Ofe: What talk is this? We have been to Benin
　　Already, in fact gone as far
　　As Ife to the feet of Ifa; and some of us
　　There are who have followed the sun to where
　　It rises and walked below the roaring
　　River of Arochukwu. On each mission,
　　What message was brought back to Orua except that
　　We have enslaved too many,
　　Ravished too many lands? It is not as if Orua
　　Were the first eagle ever to spread abroad
　　The shadow of its wings.
Azezabife: Nor if you asked me are we likely
　　Going to be last. There are always some people
　　Of this earth living in darkness, and
　　It's only fair one took them light.
Agbogidi: So let's go ahead and choose ourselves
　　A new head.
Oguaran: Yes, a new king, let's
　　Have one right now!
Ofe: And we know
　　Who should be king.
The Other Three: (*together*)
　　Yes, yes, we all know who should
　　Be king here.
Ofe: Ozidi, aren't you going to speak?
Azezabife: Let's hear him!
Oguaran: Ozidi, let's hear what's from your lips!
Agbogidi: [*laughing loudly.*] Don't say all you can do is fight!
Ozidi: [*rises.*] Ofe, your praise name?
Ofe: [*beating his chest.*] I am Ofe-begbulumane, Ofe
　　The Short, so they call me.
Ozidi: Ofe the Short, I greet you.
Ofe: That is my name. And yours?
Ozidi: Ozidi.
Ofe: Ozidi, then I greet you too.
Ozidi: Thank you. Azezabife, your own?

Azezabife: I am the Skeleton Man—
   Azezabife—that's the name
   In full.
Ozidi: Azezabife, our Skeleton Man,
   I salute you.
Azezabife: I greet you also. And your own?
Ozidi: Ozidi.
   Now, you Oguaran, how shall I greet
   You in this august gathering?
Oguaran: Oguaran buo-asi bra-asi, of course.
   That means a man possessed of twenty toes,
   Twenty fingers. Call me that!
Ozidi: Man of Twenty Toes
   And Twenty Fingers, I greet you then.
Oguaran: I give you back your greetings, Ozidi.
   You are a great man though one often
   Frothing over like the palm-wine. Now,
   Pour me more drink!
Ozidi: And you Agbogidi, your name?
Agobogidi: Agbogidi patu-patu, that is,
   The Warrior in the Nude, you fellow. And yours
   Is Ozidi, the latest born in town knows that.
Ozidi: [*pacing up and down.*] I greet you all, I greet
   You all of the Council of Orua. Now,
   Which way shall my tongue turn without
   One of you here putting an ugly tack to it?
   This matter of choosing a king, I recognize
   You have all provided candidates from
   Your different districts. I recognize also
   That now it is the turn of my family. But
   Which of you here does not know how many
   Make up this family? Of a quarter
   Teeming before as a market in session,
   Death has left just me and my brother
   Temugedege, except of course
   You count slaves. Now, you all realize how
   My brother is: he is in no shape for a role
   Like that. Nor can I while he is elder
   To me and living.
Azezabife: Others have had their turn
   On the throne.

Ofe: Is the great Ozidi telling us
   The throne of Orua is not big enough for the buttock
   Of some people?
Ozidi: That's a wicked twist of word
   Coming out of a crooked mouth. Another
   Like that and I'll knock it straight for you.
Azezabife: We have not come here to wrestle!
Agbogidi: What we want is a king!
Ofe: And Ozidi knows who should be king!
Oguaran: Perhaps, the two brothers
   Have locked horns like two rams!
Ozidi: That again is a lie! I decline to be king,
   And so does my brother Temugedege!
Temugedege: [*staggering in to the surpise of all; he is dribbling
   with drink.*] There, there, you speak for yourself, my young
   And strong one. So is this why you locked me in
   With chicken? You see, good people, this is how
   Your champion treats his own elder brother
   Born of the same vagina. Now, turning
   To this business of king, who is
   Temugedege to refuse the offer of royalty
   If Orua wishes it? Of course, Temugedege
   Agrees to sit on the royal throne if only
   For a day!
   [*General acclamation, after the intiial shock and pause for breath and
   relief by all assembled. Only Ozidi, his terrible energy completely gone
   out of him, sinks back into his seat. At the same time, the drums and
   horn strike up the tune of* Temugedege ebu gha, *the whole group
   dancing to it, first up and down the area of play, and then out to the right
   with the new king of Orua, Temugedege, carried aloft.*]

Scene 2

*Late morning, five days later. Temugedege, all alone, sits in state in his room
in the house of Ozidi. In his mouth he has a long chewing stick at which he
is working very self-consciously as he talks to himself.*

Temugedege: Now am I king,
   King Temugedege of Orua, terror of all our
   Territories beyond these creeks and

Keeper of our common store of wealth.
That doesn't sound bad at all, no not at all.
I Temugedege a king! No longer shall I be
Harried to sea; no longer into the forest.
Stacks of fish shall be brought to me daily; bundles of
Fire-wood to keep the fire warming our backside
Now I am king.

Ozidi: [*coming upon him.*] Temugedege, what are you doing with
a chewing-stick in your mouth at this time of day?

Temugedege: [*starts but recovers himself quickly.*] You forget yourself,
young man. I am
King now, you know. So learn not to talk to me
As you have done in the past. I am King
Of Orua now.

Ozidi: And have any of your subjects come to salute
You yet?

Temugedege: Subjects, oh no, come to think of it.

Ozidi: Nor even those councilors who
Proclaimed you king?

Temugedege: You mean our old council of state? Now,
I always thought that body was too infested by
That dwarf Ofe and his infernal gang.
They say a state without a head is like a snake decapitated.
I say, with those men in lead, Orua has been like
A man with multiple heads. And that is
A monster, I tell you. I wonder you suffered
A phenomenon like that all this period, you
With all your gifts of the leopard.

Ozidi: And how do you intend to cope with them,
O king?

Temugedege: You wait and see. The Council of State
Shall be dissolved forthwith by royal command.
In place of those conspiratorial characters, I shall myself
Select a caretaker committee of seven virgin girls who will
whisper
Appropriate words into our ears. Do you
Hear that? One shall fetch me my royal chewing-stick, another my
goblet
Of morning glory, three shall pick the grey hair
And lice on our sacred head, and any climbing up
Our arm-pits; all this as we recline

Basking in the evening glow of our life,
Two shall pare our finger and toe nails, and one
Shall scratch our tender back although we both know
The itch in the flesh is far down elsewhere.

Ozidi: Your royal list is one
Too many already.

Temugedege: Does that matter at all? I am king, and
Shall pack my court according to my royal will
And pleasure.

Ozidi: One small matter though,
My good king. Are you expecting gifts and tributes
At all?

Temugedege: If you are my true brother, you will
Take care of all that. Why, we expect
Canoe-loads of yam all the way from Lokoja and
Abakaliki, a hundred barrels of pure palm oil
From our Isoko and Aboh tenants,
Bales of handwoven cloths direct from the Yoruba,
And if you love me as one brother another,
You will see to it that we have a river of gin
Flowing steadily all the way from Calabar
To wash our throat.

Ozidi: [*going in anger.*] They say man is better than goat,
But having you for brother I can now see
The curse upon our house.

Temugedege: [*running after him.*] I warn you, mind what you say
As from now, young man, I'll have you
Arrested for treasonable felony, my good fellow,
For treason even, and not remember for one moment
You are my brother and one that is principal
Architect of this great nation.
[*Returning to throne he rocks himself asleep.*]
I am King of Orua, King of Orua!

Scene 3

*In the plaza at Orua, which runs the whole length of the city and along the
stream. Ozidi, who has come direct from his idiot brother, is angry with the
people of Orua for failing to bring tribute to the king they acclaimed five
days before.*

Ozidi: You elected my brother king. You knew
　　He was soft in the head. But you placed upon him
　　The supreme burden, knowing well he lacks
　　The pad to bear the weight. It is now
　　The fifth day of his ascension. Or have
　　You already forgotten you have a new king?
　　Has the beetle made empty craters of your barns,
　　And cockroaches invested your fish-baskets
　　That none of you has brought tributes
　　To your new king my brother? When Alale
　　Was king, although for three moons only, did I not lead
　　A raid among the Urhobo that returned with several slaves
　　To build your state? When Zitare
　　Was chosen king of all Kolobiri and
　　He passed out with the going of the flood,
　　Did I not spread wild-fire among the Itsekiri
　　And ravish all their territory? But enough!
　　I see, when the crown comes the way of my family, service
　　Becomes crippled at once, and lions that should be out
　　Prowling are purring by the fireside like cats in
　　Laps of women without seed. Now hear
　　Me, people of Orua: may you all
　　Be matcheted piecemeal a thousand times and left
　　Over to rot by the wayside. Your flesh is
　　Not fit for the fish in the stream to feed on;
　　Your bones are no good for beasts of the bush to maul
　　At. Nor will fowls of the air peck at your entrails.
　　As a body corporate, you are one carcass
　　Filled to bursting with excrement and stench.
　　Is there any among you so deaf
　　He cannot catch in the basin of his ears
　　My curses pouring upon you?
　　If there is any hiding behind empty
　　Covers, I shall call the crier now and have him beat
　　My message to you on the back
　　Of the calabash. And should one of you,
　　Hearing me, go sour in his bowels
　　Or feel like spitting in my face,
　　Let him step out now; I am all set
　　To wrestle with him, but if he prefers the spear
　　Or sword, I should be glad to meet him
　　At the marketplace.

[*While Ozidi rages, there is only grunting of disbelief and suppressed
anger from neighbors too scared to show their faces. Now as he moves
forward down the plaza still challenging all, a number of citizens come
out of their houses and places of hiding. They follow him with eyes some
way out in shocked silence, then, as his voice rises again in anger in the
distance, they turn upon one another, all speaking at once.*]

First Citizen: You heard him?

Second Citizen: He poured excrement upon our heads!

Third Citizen: My ears ring aloud still from his blast.

Fourth Citizen: The man will kill us all; smoke us with pepper
    Out of our houses like rabbits.

First Citizen: He may be the strongest man in town
    But that's no reason for insulting
    And wishing everybody dead.

Fifth Citizen: By and large, the man was right, but then
    He will not be Ozidi except
    He went into excess.

Second Citizen: I fail to see where lies
    His right; he rained curses on us all.

Fifth Citizen: You chose his brother king
    Against his wish.

Third Citizen: Why, should we have elected him instead?

Fourth Citizen: We did not choose Temugedege; it was
    The turn of their house.

Fifth Citizen: The idiot is king now
    And wants his gifts.

First Citizen: Gifts for that fool? Surely, you jest.

Fifth Citizen: I have no water in my mouth as I stand
    Here speaking. You all know a god is
    A god once you make him so. After
    The ceremony, he ceases to be mere wood. Give him
    Palm oil then, and he'll insist on blood.

Second Citizen: Nobody is going to serve
    Temugedege; he is an idiot.

Fifth Citizen: Well, he is secure on the throne
    Now, and until you bring him cowries and cows
    We shall not sleep in this city.

Second Citizen: That's true; Ozidi will hound us
    To death and haunt us thereafter.

Third Citizen: We took part in a children's play electing
    That idiot king, for although his is
    A withered hand, we are going to feel as from now

The terrible weight of his brother's arm.

First Citizen: How shall we stop the leopard's left paw
  From falling on our necks?

Second Citizen: He'll tear us to pieces
  Like mere goats unless we do something at once.

Fourth Citizen: Here comes Ofe, a man more resourceful than
  The tortoise itself. Between him and
  Ozidi there is not much love lost.

Ofe: Have you risen, good people of Orua? I see
  You are sweating. Have you seen Osuosala
  The stick-insect?

First Citizen: Did you not run into Ozidi? He went
  Your way raging against the state.

Ofe: Oh yes, I heard him going downstream
  As I came up. Because he roars all the time
  It was like filtering a torrent
  Trying to catch all he said in one basket.

Second Citizen: He said enough to kill off all fish
  In the river.

Ofe: So I heard, some evil spirit must
  Have entered into his head.

First Citizen: How shall we dam his rush?

Ofe: Why, by doing to his idiot brother what
  The man expects of us.

First Citizen: You mean not to contain him?

Fourth Citizen: On the contrary, it seems
  He wants us to take that idiot tributes, our heads
  Rolling like dogs chastised.

Ofe: Oh yes; we shall even exceed the man's
  Expectations. Not just gifts of domestic kind
  But we shall bring his idiot brother
  The ultimate tribute.

First Citizen: Ofe, are you seriously suggesting
  We pay the ultimate tribute to a king
  No child will accept?

Third Citizen: The coils of the python certainly
  Are growing thick and fast about our necks!

Fifth Citizen: And where, if I may ask, shall we collect
  That human head to pay our ultimate tribute?

Ofe: Good citizens of Orua, will you
  Please hear me through before you place stakes on

My path? You'll admit this has been
A surprise leap on our persons. Now what foil
I have to get us out of the leopard's spoor
We walked in of our own will I cannot in
The open street unfold to the full.
First Citizen: Anyway, we have to mount an expedition
At once, that's what you mean.
Ofe: You get me right, but we do not have far
To go to find our particular head. It'll all
Surprise you, I am sure, if you knew our plan.
But first, let's to the Bebeareowei,
Our town crier so he can spread the word like game meat
For all to eat.
First Citizen: We are right behind you, Ofe.
Fourth Citizen: Just show us the way.
Second Citizen: Any path to lead the leopard out of town
Before he despoils our goats.
Ofe: Come then, friends; I see you will be saved.
[*They troop out after him.*]

Scene 4

The scene is the same. The Bebearewei of Orua, that is the state crier, at the head of an assorted group, is making an important announcement to the beating of an empty calabash.

Bebeareowei: Orua people, Orua people, I ask
You for your ears. Please place them on the ground,
Even as the calabash plant throws itself
Upon the good earth, so that you may catch the words
Falling from my lips and be wise. You know we have now
A new king; truly, a new king sits upon the throne
Of Orua today. And he wants gifts,
He wants tributes that are prerogative
To the throne of your fathers, the throne before which all men
Turn blind. Tomorrow, therefore, at the third crow
Of the cock, let every man who has a beard on
His chin, a wrapper about his loins, leap from
His bed. Even though he may be breaching a wall
To his wife for the first time, let him

Leap up at the first stroke of the master-drum,
And make at once for the marketplace, before
Our ancestral hall where Okorie, our god
And father sits in state. Now, if such a man has a cutlass,
Let him put it to hand; if he has a sword
Or spear, let him whip the same out
Of its scabbard; if he has a firing-piece, let him cork
It well; if he has a bow, let him draw
The string well and bring his arrows
Out of the poison pot. And need I add that
If he has special amulets, girdles
And bangles that charm away the unexpected
Violent finish to life, let him don
His apparel well before he comes forth to the square. There
He will find all his comrades ready for a chase
With a prize far beyond the lion's head. Now, what
I have spoken to you with voice of the hyrax, have you all heard
It with ears open as the calabash?
People of Orua: We have heard oh!
[*The state crier, followed by an assorted group which grows bigger by the moment, moves on. After a short while, the calabash again sounds in the distance followed by the voice of the crier, all trailing away to an echo.*]

Scene 5

In the front yard of Ozidi's house. His shrine stands a little to the front, a mere shadow in the early morning light. He is moving towards it when his young wife, Orea, holding up a lamp, calls to him from the door-step. All through the scene, there is the muffled rhythm of drums in the distance. From time to time the sound of a horn comes across. Drums and horn are summoning, by dialogue and signals, the male population of Orua to gather in the square and set out from there on the raid.

Orea: Ozidi, do not go into the night.
Ozidi: It is not night when you hold before me
    Your lamp.
Orea: I smell a foul wind blowing from the swamp that may
    Put out the light.
Ozidi: Then we will rekindle our lamp and carry
    On with the journey.

Orea: Ozidi, I still do not think
  You should go on today's raid.
Ozidi: Be not afraid, my bride. The hawking-tray
  Roves and roves but it returns home all the same.
Orea: I have an evil vein tugging at my side; here,
  Come and feel it for yourself.
Ozidi: [*half severely.*] One hand on atalaye, the other on
  The cassava-grater; little wonder if you have pulled
  A muscle. You should see the masseur today
  Before I come back.
Orea: [*she slips out of his arms angry.*] You make light of whatever I
    say.
Ozidi: Well, aren't you the sunbird of
  Our world, scattering laughter like light
  About us?
Orea: [*piqued.*] Leave me, and go your way.
Ozidi: [*growing playful.*] Oh, come, come now, little woman that
    plays upon
  Our heart as a drum. Your body is warm and soft
  Like clay firing afresh.
Orea: [*petulantly.*] And yet you leap from my side
  By first crow of the cock?
Ozidi: [*softening.*] We will go back to bed and promise
  You shall make us a present.
Orea: A son, that's what I am dying to bear you,
  All your gods willing.
Ozidi: They will, of course, they will.
  [*He picks her up. At the same time a cock crows at close quarters, and he
  drops her trembling.*]
  I cannot, Orea! It's the third crowing of
  The cock and I have delayed too long already.
  [*He dashes across the yard, parts his way through the raffia-screened
  doorway of the shrine, and bounces out almost immediately.*]
Ozidi: Hello, what have we here, Orea? Bring
  The lantern quick!
Orea: [*who has picked up her lamp again and remains standing on the
  verandah with hands across her breast.*] No use; I have seen it already:
    it is
  A lizard scampering out of your shrine.
Ozidi: I cannot believe it.
Orea: Well, there is the creature

Coming back; perhaps, to convince
You of the fact.
[*She runs down to him and holds him by the knees.*]
Oh, my husband, I have hardly
Had you one day all to myself, please stay
Away from the raid. Let others go today;
You alone have led several raids before.
Today stay home; I'll go and tell them
You have a cold.
[*Ozidi, his hands limp on her head, stands silent and still. Meanwhile,
the drums and horn in the square draw to a crescendo.*]

Ozidi: No, I must go, Orea, I really must.
I called this tune and now they are
Playing it, do you say I may not dance?
It is my brother they seek to decorate,
Remember that, Orea! Am I to forfeit
My brother and king his prerogative
To tributaries?

Orea: But the lizard, my husband, the lizard
Ran ahead of you! And what use
Will tributes be to anybody if you trip?
[*Drums and horn come closer still, and strains of the song* Puba erein *fill
the morning sky.*]

Ozidi: Let go, Orea, let go at once.
You are asking me to eat my words like sand.
Tell me,
Where have you heard it said
The lizard tripped up a leopard in the fight?
There, hold on,
My comrades, I am coming direct
To you, I am coming!
[*He breaks off, tears into the shrine and in less than a minute is back
dressed as for battle: a brief white skirt mounted with bells and cowries, a
cap flying seven feathers of the eagle and in his right hand a huge sword.
He throws his wife one last look and rushes off to join in the raid.*]

Orea: [*still on her knees, looking crushed.*] I have not been in his house
    for one year,
Tamara.
Let him not go now and get killed
And leave me without child,
For then his people will say, when he was

Single, he fought all our several battles and
Returned home unhurt, but now he's gone
And married the daughter of that witch
Oreame, see what befalls him
In the first fight after. So
You will save him for me, won't you Tamara?
And you city ancestors and gods, it is for
Your glory he's gone now as in the past.
Therefore let no evil eye
See him, let no evil hand touch him, this
I beg of you, humbly beg of you.

Scene 6

In an outlying district, the Orua host has stopped to deploy itself effectively before the enemy. Ofe, Oguaran, Azezabife, and Agbogidi, prominent among the generals, are giving their men last directives and instructions.

Ofe: [*to Oguaran.*] You lead your men off to the right flank,
   And Azezabife will take care of the left, his men
   Behind him. Agbogidi will give you close
   Cover at the rear. As soon as he
   Steps out, Oguaran, you file up
   Behind him while Azezabife cuts him off in front.
   Thus encircled close before
   He makes out who and on what side you are,
   Do not stop to parley with him but hit him
   Hard and home until he falls down,
   And even then, do not hold your hand till you have
   Beaten him dumb and dead.
   That is the one way open to get rid of him.
   For remember that bullets
   In contact with the man turn to water, spears
   Splinter off him; and do not let it
   Stick in your eyes that not only
   Do blades go blunt on his skin but arrows
   Bounce off his body.
Oguaran: That is all well said and set out,
   But when we have killed the man, how do we
   Explain the deed when we return home?

Ofe: If your heart misses a beat, better pack
   Your bags now and go back home.
   Others with the heart of men will move on.
Oguaran: That's no way to talk to me, Ofe!
Azezabife: [*stepping between both men.*] Is it here we are going to fall
      out
   Among ourselves? Indeed, are we houseflies
   That cannot assemble a session of court?
   They say whatever their crowd, those creatures cannot knock over
   A cow. We have agreed upon the act
   That will make or mar our joint canoe
   Of life. Must we ourselves now capsize
   The craft? As for your question,
   Oguaran, look at it, is
   There anybody to ask for or avenge
   Our great champion once he is dead? His brother
   Who would be king and demands his honors, carries upon
   His shoulders bent with age
   The mere head of an infant. Who else has
   He then? Is it his young wife Orea? She will
   As soon run off to sleep with another man
   As his slaves would welcome the word
   To go and serve another master. So who
   Is going to ask after him and seek vengeance?
   Honestly, I do not see what holds up the venture
   Except our own hands going heavy on the paddles.
Agbogidi: Hush, here he comes!
      [*Ozidi sweeps in in great style and the effect upon the men is of wind on
      rushes. But only momentarily, for, before he can open his mouth in
      greeting and recognition, they have rallied and fallen upon him with
      sticks and fists.*]
Ozidi: [*turning here and there in shock.*] What is this, people of Orua?
      I am
   Ozidi! I am Ozidi! Don't
   You know me? [*They go on beating him.*] It is no error then, but do
   You in fact lift hands
   Against me? Then strike home,
   All you from Orua!
   There,
   I throw away my sword! Now beat me, oh
   Beat me dead, oh my people!

[*They do not stop beating him but continue pell-mell, eventually knocking the champion down and out.*]

Ofe: Now, let him be, let him
    Be, I say, or will you
    Turn him into pulp of plantain?
    [*They fall back, and in the center of their circle lies Ozidi, spreadeagled, bruised and bleeding. Ofe steps up to where he lies face down, and turns him round for all to see.*]

Ofe: He is dead past dumbness.

Azezabife: After the flowers, falls the fruit.

Agbogidi: I fear this fall will echo down
    Rivers like thunderbolt underground.

Oguaran: What do we do now?
    Carry him
    Entire into town?

Ofe: Certainly not. It's here we sever
    His neck to serve his brother
    The tribute he so much desires.

Agbogidi: You forget no cutlass
    Can cut through the man whether dead or alive.

Ofe: Thank you for remembering that.

Oguaran: So what do we do, I ask
    A second time? Carry the corpse home,
    Shedding tears of cunning?

Azezabife: That's a sure way of turning the people
    Soft on his side. Let's find a way
    Of cutting his neck here and now.

Ofe: I have it, now I have it!
    Two of you there, run off to town at a
    Pace faster than dog and announce to the woman
    Orea her husband has suffered
    A sudden injury, and as such requires
    Special and instant remedy. That should loosen her
    Tongue if her man passed her any secret.
    So, run, run at once to Orea!
    [*The messengers set off and their masters pace about each trying hard to keep calm.*]

Scene 7

In the house of Ozidi, Orea seated on the veranda, is mending a fishtrap and singing the song Tebe kana when the messengers burst in upon her. She starts.

Orea: Tell me, is Ozidi dead? Oh, do not say
  You have come to tell me he is dead!
First Messenger: The gods forbid! Now, what foolishness
  You speak?
Second Messenger: How did an evil thought like that come
  Into your head? Ozidi is safe
  And sound in the bush.
Orea: [*falls on her knees with hands and face uplifted.*] Tamara, I thank
    you then.
First Messenger: As a matter of fact, Ozidi performed
  Single-handed so many feats today
  The other generals in admiration
  Will in triumphant march carry him home
  On their shoulders.
Orea: What? Can't he walk on his own feet?
Second Messenger: He has a small wound we told you.
Orea: Say that again! Did you say he has
  Suffered a small wound?
First Messenger: Of course that's only
  To be expected; in war it is give and take,
  You know.
Orea: I do not like it at all; I do not like it.
  Now you are sure Ozidi is safe?
First Messenger: What stupid questions you ask!
Second Messenger: Your man is all right. All he asks
  Is that you send some medicine down to staunch
  A small sore on his foot.
Orea: Go back from where you came. Whoever sent you
  Certainly is not my husband. Of that
  I am sure.
Second Messenger: But the medicine, woman. All Orua is waiting.
First Messenger: Shall we have the medicine or do you want
  Your limbs broken joint from joint?
Orea: Yes, of course, you may have it. You will tell the
  Whole story if I gave you? There, do not

Lose face. You are only heralds of fortune,
And a messenger's mission, they say, should not
Mean his own death. Of course, I shall tell you
His secret, for how else can we save his corpse
From vultures and hyenas if eyes have seen ears?
As you turn back to return to your masters,
Stop on your way and pluck seven leaves
Of the coco-yam. When you have covered up
Ozidi's face completely with them, then
You may again try cutting his neck.

First Messenger: Nobody's going to cut your husband's neck, don't
You understand a word we say? But thanks
All the same.

Second Messenger: Yes, thank you, Orea. By this you have done the state
Good service. You'll be convinced when [*They run for it.*] Ozidi returns
At the head of Orua in triumph.

Orea: [*hands over head, she paces about her yard hoping and despairing at the same time.*] They have killed him, I fear
They have killed him, and there's not one person
I can run to for help.
[*She wanders off to the tune of* Tebe ka na.]

Scene 8

The messengers have returned to the conspirators in the bush. Ozidi has been decapitated. His body lies covered on one side, while on the other his head lies wrapped in coco-yam leaves.

Ofe: Now, who will carry the crown and
So drink from it?

All Together: I Azezabife! I Agbogidi! I Oguaran!

Ofe: And so I Ofe, but the field is all
Yours, friends.
[*First, Azezabife, to his theme of the skeleton song and dance, tries to lift up Ozidi's head but, failing, falls aside in much discomfiture. Agbogidi and Oguaran also try, each to his own special tune and dance. Finally, Ofe, strutting on the outskirt moves in to loud cheers and cries of "Make way for Ofe! Make way for him! Who stands in his path kicks a stump!"*

Ofe does his own special dance and song three times round the fallen Ozidi. Then swiftly he stoops down and, although staggering like the others, successfully lifts up Ozidi's head, carrying it aloft for all to see. There is a great burst of applause, and all the Orua host take up the theme song of their newfound leader. A procession forms, led by Ofe who is now possessed.]

Scene 9

In Ozidi's yard Temugedege has again seated himself in state, this time on the porch for all to see. He wears a dirty brown long tunic over a cloth, and about his brow is a garland which has withered in the course of the day. His left hand is on his left knee. In his right hand is a tall staff as of office.

Temugedege: You woman, we command you to stop worrying
    Our peace.
Orea: The fowls are turning in already and
    Ozidi has not returned.
Temugedege: And the entire host of Orua,
    Have they arrived home from hunt for their king?
    Shame on you, woman! Would you make of your man
    A hen fleeing before black-kites?
Orea: I told you they sent two men with word
    Your brother has suffered some injury.
    That, to my mind, confirms the worst.
Temugedege: Take off your silly fainting self out of our sight
    Before we strike you down. Like your mother Oreame,
    You may have become a witch and will suck your own kind.
    Out, out of here before we do you harm.
    My brother has led
    An expedition out to provide me royal tributes.
    In one hand he will bring me sweet maidens,
    In the other slaves when he comes home.
Orea: [*holding her ears.*] Listen, listen, Temugedege,
    There's loud flourish outside. It must be
    They have come.
    [*Great indeterminate noise outside.*]
Temugedege: [*rises and stalks about the place.*] Oh, my brother, oh my
        people, have you
    Returned from the raid? Who said you will not do your

Duty by your king?
[*He suddenly pulls himself up and returns to his seat, collecting his clothes
about him with scrupulous care.*]
Yes, I must not be seen
Ruffled so. Only the foolish hen shows
The wind her behind.
[*Orea on her side is rushing out to see for herself when Ofe, still carrying
his burden aloft and now completely possessed, leads in the procession
singing the song* Oyei, oyei yo yo.]
Orea: My husband, my husband, where is my husband?
  What have you done with him?
  I do not see him?
  [*The procession sweeps past her, moves directly to where Temugedege sits
  in state and deposits at his feet the head of Ozidi all wrapped up in coco-
  yam leaves.*]
All: [*with one voice.*] Here is our tribute to you, King Temugedege,
    take it and rejoice!!!
  [*Temugedege with a fixed stupid smile on his face, steps down and opens
  the parcel dumped at his feet. He shrieks at the sight, tottering back in a
  fit.*]
Orea: [*tearing past everybody.*] It is Ozidi, it is Ozidi
  My husband, they have gone
  And killed and brought back
  As tribute to his brother, is it not?
  [*Orea rushes up to where the head of her husband lies on the ground. She
  falls down and wails. The people begin to fall back. Temugedege, with
  finger in mouth, cries his way into the house. By the end of her lament
  Orea is left all alone. The solitary woman gathers the head of her
  husband, and sitting herself down on the ground, cradles it in her lap.*]
Orea: Let me blow the flies from off your face
  Before they pass worms upon it.
  So they have killed you dumb, my husband,
  Before I bore you a son? This morning
  I said do not go to the raid. The lizard said
  Do not go to the raid. But you would not
  Listen, you would not hear us, stubborn man.
  Last night my body was your bed. Sleep on, I said,
  But the cocks woke you up, the drums summoned you
  Forth into the night. So it was to death!
  After how many fights? After how many
  Victories? The enemies of Orua could not

Kill you; therefore Orua people themselves
Did it, Eh, Ozidi, my man,
My man! My man who saw the lizard crawl,
And leapt forward still as a leopard after
His kill: My man who stood on the bow to every
Boat of war, never giving the enemy
His back: my man, the champion, now gone across
The stream before the ferryman heard his coming call.
Ah, Oreame, come over quick and see
What woe they you gave your daughter in marriage
Have done by her. And women of Orua
Your men have gone today and carved up
My man as meat for his brother to eat of.
Today you look wide at me with eyes
Dry as wells in time of drought.
Not one of you is there who is mother, sister,
And wife enough to weep with a wretched woman
Made widow by men of Orua.
Oh, as I wail alone today, like a bird
That has wandered far out of flock and clime
So may you wail, so may you wail, and falling
Asleep, wake up again wailing
As truly, the moon at every fresh tide shall spill
Her bowl full over your house, full over your head.
[*In the meantime Temugedege comes out of the house. He carries his staff now over his shoulder as a yoke, and from it he slings a bundle containing his clothes and other personal possessions he has hastily packed together. Moaning still, he looks up at Orea.*]

Temugedege: Come Orea, let us run for it
Before they do us in as well. I cannot
Fight; nor can you. But we can survive
In the bush. I see you won't come with me
Temugedege? Don't
Blame you at all. Have always known myself
Temugedege is no good, no good at all to himself or anybody.
Oh my brother, brother, brother that blade
Could not touch, bullet could not hit,
Arrow or spear could not pierce,
With sticks they beat you to pulp, my brother,
Oh
My brother!

[*He breaks into the song* Temugedege ebugha *and dodders his way out of sight. Orea turns away from him.*]

Orea: If being female, I cannot stay behind
And fight your battle, surely I can come and keep
You company, carrying your kit
Across the river?
[*She gets up, sets the head of her husband down carefully and, loosening the short upper wrapper which is tied about her waist like a belt, she mounts Temugedege's chair and begins to fasten a noose for suicide. At this point, when Orea thinks she is all alone, an old woman steals up on her and stops her in the act.*]

Old Woman: So you want to tie
The immortal knot of bats? That is no solution,
Daughter of Oreame. Of course,
You do not know I am of the same club as
Your mother Oreame who's our president.
Do not wail more; do not seek to take
Your life. Or don't you know you are heavy with
Another life, yes, a son who Oyin Almighty
Herself is sending forth to put to right
This terrible wrong done to his father? Come on,
For once the idiot Temugedege spoke well.
Come, I must spirit you home to your mother before
Ofe and his gang come for you.
[*She leads Orea out to the strains of* Ba were mune yo.]

ACT II

Storyteller: In the seventh month of Orea seeing
Her belly, she bore the dead Ozidi
A son safe away in her mother's town
Ododama. That day it rained barrels
Of water through a sieve of sunshine. You
Could say of the storm that a giant wind
Had taken the sea as an orange by the mouth
And sucking it, had spat in face of the sun
Who winced lightning, and then hurled it all back
At earth as rain and bolts of thunder. Observing

The phenomenon, men said a leopard
Had generated in the forest.
Now let us see how the cub, fatherless before
Birth, grew under the wings of his grandmother
Oreame, a witch of no hidden
Knowledge from Ododama to Orua.

Scene 1

In the public square of Ododama. A game of kolo is drawing to a close for a group of boys of about the age of seven to ten. In the game of kolo a circle of competing archers try to hit a moving target in the form of a plantain stalk, tied to a string. A neutral, or most heavily defeated boy, swings this above his head in the center of the group. The whirling motion gets so fast on this occasion only one boy hits it successfully. This instantly makes him a target for attack by all the others.

First Boy: Some people
   Never fail to hit the mark.
Second Boy: Invisible hands
   Guide their missiles to the target.
Third Boy: Just as they help
   Trip up opponents when the wrestling gets
   Too awkward for the champion.
Fourth Boy: I hope it is not me you speak of.
Second Boy: I did not call anybody by name.
First Boy: Did he hear his name mentioned?
Third Boy: Has he got a name anyway?
Fourth Boy: Of course I have!
Third Boy: Tell us what it is.
Second Boy: So, you can't after all!
First Boy: Boy, oh Boy, is that a name to call
   Any grown up person by?
Third Boy: Who is it you are calling a grown-up?
   At home his mother still scrubs his face for him.
Fifth Boy: And do you know
   It is the hag that mends his bow?
Fourth Boy: It's your mother that's a hag!
The Group: [*in one voice.*] Are you abusing our parents?
   It's our parents he's abusing! Your mother and father then.

Fourth Boy: [*defensively.*] You abused my mother first.
Third Boy: Some people don't even know
  Who their father is.
Fourth Boy: Who told you I don't know my father?
First Boy: Well, tell us his name!
Fifth Boy: And where does he live if we may know?
Second Boy: You see he can't.
Third Boy: I told you some people are liars.
First Boy: What do you expect of them
  Living among women?
Fourth Boy: I'll crack your head for that.
  [*He reaches wildly for the others. They scatter, hooting at him, and he
  chases them, first one way, and then the other and right off the square.*]

Scene 2

*Before a house at the outskirt of Ododama. Orea, now a widow of about
thirty, sits by the doorway cracking palm kernels between a piece of iron in
her hand and a block of stone on the ground by her knees. Beside her on a
carved stool sits her mother Oreame, smoking a clay-pipe.*

Orea: [*throwing kernels in a basket at her elbow.*] That boy should be
  back now.
Oreame: Let him play
  For as long as he likes.
Orea: My heart cuts more and more that
  I let him out of sight.
Oreame: [*spitting.*] Shame! Will you tie him
  To the heart like a goat—my boy
  That is a leopard and must prowl?
Orea: It's you that spoil him, mother, filling
  Him with talks of hunt and kill. I have lived
  One life like that before—with his father.
  I don't want to again with the son.
Oreame: Say what you will, my leopard boy shall pounce
  Upon them all and tear each limb to limb.
Orea: Much limb he has broken already.
  Now is there any day passes without
  Some angry parent coming to refuse
  At my feet a child crippled by your boy?

Oreame: Wait till he rips open their bowels and
   Drinks up their blood before their limbs
   Stop beating the ground.
Orea: If he goes on like this, they will certainly
   Ask us out of town soon.
Oreame: That day, night will collide with day.
   [*The voice of the boy is heard outside calling his mother in a worried tone.*]
Orea: [*rising in panic.*] Now, what incident is it today?
Oreame: [*jumps up defiant.*] Who is chasing you? Who is chasing you?
   Here I am, my Boy! Speak up quick
   And I'll deal with the fellow, be he
   A monster.
   [*The Boy rushes in raining angry questions at both women.*]
Boy: What is my name? Where is my father?
   Why haven't I got any?
   [*Mother and daughter look at each other and then back to the boy.*]
Oreame: [*going up to him.*] Of course you've got a name, Boy.
Boy: [*moving away.*] That's a name
   For three-month-olds. Now why haven't
   I a proper one? Are you going to tell me
   Who my father is?
Orea: [*with tears in her voice.*] Why! has anybody been taunting you?
Boy: [*stamps his feet impatiently.*] Yes, my playmates. Every time
   I beat them at wrestling, top or kolo,
   They set upon me like flies.
Oreame: You are a cow
   And a whole clan of those flies should not
   Push you over.
Boy: [*sullen still but now weakening to his grandmother.*] But who is my
      father?
Oreame: [*holding him to herself.*] Of course your father is a man
      famous
   All through the rivers.
Boy: Then why haven't I met him?
Oreame: That's because he is held up
   By events in a town far away.
Boy: How far away?
Oreame: Oh, let's see, several days
   Hard paddling from here, I should think,
   In the city they call Orua.

Boy: And shall we go up there some day?
Oreame: Soon, yes, very soon,
    When we are prepared for the journey,
    Is it not so, Orea?
    [*She leads the boy indoors past Orea who throws up her hands in a gesture that means: "You leave me out of it; that is a matter between you two."*]

Scene 3

A bush path outside Ododama. Oreame carries a big basket on her head. The Boy walks in front of her.

The Boy: Mother, is our farm still far from here?
Oreame: No, my son, not very far off now.
The Boy: Where then is it?
Oreame: Don't say your legs are flagging already!
The Boy: [*he makes a great effort to run.*] Who said so? There, mother,
    look at me striding out.
    I still can do another twenty kusu.
Oreame: That's my boy. Let him fall lame who stops
    You striding out with pride.
    [*They keep up the brisk pace for a while but the Boy soon tires again.*]
The Boy: Does our farm lie where God in heaven
    Touches the ground?
Oreame: Oh no, my son, only the rainbow
    Strides out there.
The Boy: I want to walk down the rainbow.
Oreame: You will yet, oh, you will yet. But first,
    Let's plant our feet firm in the earth. Here, will
    You wait for me while I step aside to shit?
The Boy: Go on in and be back soon, mother.
Oreame: You won't be afraid?
The Boy: [*beating his chest.*] There's nothing can scare me in this
    world.
Oreame: Good boy,
    Good boy, brave as the big gorilla!
    [*She steps into the bush and the boy unconsciously wheels round to look about him, half curious, half afraid. Meanwhile, Oreame smartly comes back dressed up as the "hill masquerade," taking up the whole road.*

Consequently, when the Boy faces round again, there is this huge "hill" planted direct in front where there was none before. The sight makes him jump.]

The Boy: Mother, oh Mother, I am dead, I am dead!

Oreame: [*issuing from cover of the "hill" which she has made collapse deftly and thrown back into her basket.*] What is it, child? Now, what's the matter?

The Boy: The hill, look, there was a hill here just now.
I could swear it by Tarakiriye.

Oreame: It must be a phantom hill
For I can't see any around.

The Boy: I could swear it.

Oreame: All right, all right, my son,
What about letting me go back to passing
The water you cut short?

The Boy: It really was here, exactly at this spot,
And it completely blocked all the path.
[*Oreame, by now, has retired into the undergrowth, and again it is the signal for the Boy to begin looking about him in great panic in an effort to keep all directions in view at one and the same time. Then there comes a sudden cry of alarm from his grandmother which sends him running for safety.*]

Oreame: [*behind the bush.*] Help! A leopard is attacking me, oh help!

The Boy: A leopard, did you say, mother? Then
I must run at once for help from town.

Oreame: Oh, it has mauled me, quite killed me!

The Boy: Hold on! I said I'm going for help!
[*He runs a few steps and finds the leopard has cut him off in front. He falls back shrieking, while the leopard crouches over him growling and pawing at his cowering form. Then to his shock the leopard figure falls apart, and out of it comes his grandmother Oreame full of disapproval.*]

Oreame: [*bent and bitter as she packs up her kit.*] Pity a poor woman,
pity any woman who has
A coward for a son. He sees
The moving shadow of a hill and runs
For shelter. A leopard preys on
His aged mother and he pleads for time
To go into town for help.

The Boy: [*regaining control of himself.*] Wait, mother, wait, You weren't
Expecting I would take on the brute

Bare-handed, were you? Give me a cutlass
Next time, and see whether or not
I don't quarry down that hill for you.
And as for that great cat you call leopard, I will
So cut it up next time with my matchete,
You will not see his spots from the scars.
Oreame: [*leading the way out.*] Hear him! Oh, Tamara, who you give
    A coward for child has no child at all.

Scene 4

Some time later. Behind a mat screen, Orea is rubbing down Oreame with hot water. She sits on a small stool, groaning with pain.

Orea: Where else is the pain?
Oreame: Here, here, and there. Oh, not
    So hard, Orea, I told you the fellow
    Bruised me all over.
Orea: [*hardly hiding a smile.*] In what shape did you tempt him this
        time?
Oreame: Not so hard, I said. Oh, yes, first
    As a pretty maid who had lost her way
    To market. All done up, I confronted him
    At the crossroads and cried for help from him.
    Oh, gently, Orea, gently. Very gallant
    He was, saying I was the sister his mother
    Did not give him. "But sister," he says then,
    "You know you ought to have washed your face;
    You cannot show up at market like this." And
    With that he led me, most reluctant, you
    Can guess, to a nearby pond. There he washed
    The grease and paint off my face, revealing
    My true facescape. Next, very methodical
    And full of style I must say of the Boy,
    He plucked first the wig, then my eye-lashes
    And wait, finally my false buttercups
    Off me. And fancy what question he asked after.
Orea: What if you tell us, mother?
Oreame: Of course, you have no
    Imagination. Well, this was what the brat

Asked me, understand, his own grandmother:
"Now, what was that act in aid of—to captivate
Or scare away men?"
[*Orea, now laughing aloud and freely, drops her compress cloth.*]
Oreame: You have very white teeth; so you
   Can laugh jolly well. But it isn't anything
   To laugh about, I tell you, setting a trap
   And getting caught in it.
Orea: How came he beat you so stiff?
Oreame: That was when I put on the python act.
   Orea, the water is going cold, and
   There's mud in the cloth. So will
   You hurry? You see, I yelled to the whelp
   A python had struck me down in his coils.
   I expected he would run off again and not look back.
   But oh no, there he was promptly upon me like a spear,
   Pummeling, grappling, and shouting it was no use running
   First for a club long enough before one beat
   A snake to death. Oh,
   That boy almost killed me, I tell you.
[*She rises up painfully, holding her stiff waist. At the same time Orea,
laughing yet more, throws away the water in the basin and begins
wringing dry her compress-cloth. Then suddenly there is a loud noise of
something heavy falling with a crash outside which shakes both women
where they stand.*]
Oreame: [*straightening up.*] Is anyone felling a tree outside?
Orea: No one that I know of.
   [*The voice of the boy shouting "Make way, make way!" outside cuts them
   short. It comes to them, accompanied by a heavy creaking noise. Soon the
   boy comes into view rolling a huge log before him.*]
Orea: [*severely.*] What's the game?
Oreame: [*coaxing.*] Don't tell me you want to carve yourself
   A canoe already?
The Boy: [*grimy and sweating.*] Not yet, mother, I just want to split
   You some wood for the fire. After those games
   Today in the forest, I thought I should bring you
   Some present home. And like thing done
   By Tamara, there was standing on my way
   This dead iriko which I knocked over
   And carried here on my shoulders. Now,
   Where's the axe? I want to break you

Some wood so you two will know
There's a man about the house.
[*He rushes in, leaving both women looking at each other in disbelief and concern.*]
Orea: [*anxious.*] Now you see what he's turning
Into—a real gorilla!
Oreame: [*infected by her anxiety.*] Don't let your heart cut, Orea
I'll seek protection for him before
He comes to harm, I will instantly.

Scene 5

In a clearing in the forest. Straggling overhanging foliage forms a gauze through which is seen a great deal of the action. To one end of the clearing stands a huge mortar and leaning against it is a tall pestle. A little away are seven pots cooking on seven hobs set out in a row. Watching over them from the other end of the clearing is Bouakarakarabiri, the old man of the forest. He is a half-human character who can walk on his head, and in his hand lie the secrets of all life and leaves in the forest. Standing on his head, his feet in the air, he has dozed off, reclining against a tree, and is snoring quietly and at uneven intervals in his corner. Over this the voice of the Boy outside somewhere comes clear and near, calling impatiently for his grandmother Oreame.

The Boy: Are you coming, Mother, or have you
Begun setting traps again to catch me?
Oreame: Coming now, my strappling hare; I am only a few loops
behind your shadow.
The Boy: Better hurry up, tortoise, or I
Shall leave you behind.
Oreame: Go on, my hare, I know you'd leave me if
You knew the goal.
The Boy: Well, I can't dawdle any longer.
[*He comes upon the clearing and sees the strange household.*]
Come and see
A great spectacle, Mother! A mortar
And pestle, carved straight out of tree trunks,
All set up in the forest! And look,
Pots and pots on the boil, seven in all
By count of my ten fingers! Whoever runs

This place must have some appetite! Perhaps,
He's feasting all the famished tenants
Of the forest—the lion and the antelope dipping
Their paws in the same pot! Now on whose flesh
Will they be feeding, I wonder?
[*He is still laughing at his own cleverness when he observes the old man of
the forest snoring in his uncommon sleeping posture. The boy starts but
recovers himself quickly, walking across to inspect the strange old man just
as he looked at the objects of his household.*]
Hello, old man, you have fallen asleep in the sun
Watching your pots on the boil! But what manner
Of going to sleep is this, planting your head
On the ground like this, your anus in the sky?
No wonder one is bald and the other
All infested with flies.
[*He tries to tilt the old magician and wizard back on to his feet but
succeeds only in waking him up. Next at one somersault, the old man has
caught him by the neck between the vise of his feet, throttling and making
him shout in pain and panic.*]
Hey, take your hands, I mean, your legs
Off my neck! Or do you want to kill me?
Old Man: That's the bitter Ijaw truth. Those seven pots
Have been on the boil for you for as many days.
The Boy: You aren't a cannibal then, are you?
Old Man: Twice today have I refilled these pots
With water. And what sizzling and hissing
They did because I rushed them back from point
Of cracking? You can see there's pepper in those pots
Already. And salt has dissolved long ago
In them. Only this morning I sliced up
Some more plantain to fill those pots; at last
There's meat to cook the meal.
The Boy: Let go your legs, let go, I say! This is
A civilized country, and I won't let you
Feed on me like a chicken!
Old Man: So that's what you say? Soon, we'll see
How tough your bones are between our teeth.
There, I forgot we have none like
The chicken. That tells how long ago
We had our last meal! Well, let's see, let's see!
[*At each pause for breath the old wizard tightens his grip on the boy now
speechless and beginning to dribble in the mouth and show his tongue.*

Oreame arrives at this critical point, sizes up the situation at once, and takes immediate action.]

Oreame: Bouakarakarabiri, may your feet
Plummet back to earth, and stay there transfixed
Till the chameleon's cry!
[*The old wizard's feet promptly fall off the boy's neck, and he stands rooted to one spot shaking in anger. The boy staggers to one side nursing his neck.*]

Old Man: There's only one creature in all the bush
Can carry off this trick, and not die
For it!

Oreame: [*looks over the boy.*] Yes, it's me, Oreame!

Old Man: Will you ever play fair in your life?

Oreame: Did you play fair trying to murder
My son before my eyes?

Old Man: How was I to know the young man is your son?
The filth he heaped on my bald head and bottom!
Better tie his tongue up before it runs
Him into a pit.

Oreame: It is for that we have come.
Make for my son the mortar and pestle charm.

Old Man: Why, you have yourself full possession
Of the recipe.

Oreame: They say the housewife often has
No stomach for her own broth. Now show me
What physician can cure himself. Indeed, I would
Another served my child the fare before he takes on
His father's foes.

Old Man: Your son-in-law showed too strong a taste
For blood, though that was terrible service they did
By him. I had no idea your daughter bore
For him fruit.

Oreame: If the boy is not his father's son then
My daughter shared her husband's bed with another.

Old Man: As a girl you always would twist my tongue
The wrong way round, Oreame. Now I see
You have not changed at all with the years. I did not say
Your daughter took pleasure of the fruit the dead forbid.

Oreame: My daughter had a son for Ozidi after
His death, it is what I am telling you.
Now that issue must go forth and scatter death among
His father's enemies.

Old Man: It's a good son; for how else can
His father come home from company of the castaway?
Oreame: So first we must invest him
With the mortar and pestle charm!
Old Man: [*scampering with excitement.*] Yes, that we shall give the boy
at once! [*Turning to the boy.*] Now, young man, you go over to the
mortar and prepare yourself to pound without stop. I warn you,
boy, that what you have on hand is no new yam or corn of the
season but live ingredients I shall conjure into the mortar fresh
from the forest. Now, you must pound each on the head on its
onrush, else all we shall have is matter all dead asleep as fufu.
[*Here the old wizard takes up his theme song* Tebekawene yo baa wene
wene yo. *Meanwhile, the boy picks up the pestle and positions himself in
readiness. Oreame retires to right, and the old wizard, still singing,
assumes command at center within the fringe of foliage. First, he steps this
way and then that way in a kind of dance, returning to the center each
time with both hands clutching at leaves he has snatched from sides of the
clearing. These he dumps into the seven pots, stoking the fire burning
underneath them. Then, throwing up his arms and beckoning wildly, he
breaks into an invocation summoning all live members of his master charm
into the mortar over which the boy is standing with pestle uplifted in his
hands.*]
Old Man: Come, come, our quests, come our way
I beseech, beseech you; come at once
To us, I beseech you three times:
Who holds you by the tail
Has his roots deep in the sky;
Who seeks to yoke you down
Grinds his head upon flint.
So come, come this instant to us,
Come quick over stump and stone:
When was it heard a bird in flight
Broke any bone in the bush?
[*There is a flurry in the forest at his finish of the chant. As he takes it up
again, a huge lizard scrambles out of the thick foliage into the open
clearing. It pulls up halfway and, raising itself up on both its front feet,
regards him with a nodding gesture. The old wizard, pretending not to
see his first visitor has already arrived, goes on chanting till the flurry in
the forest gathers fury. Out flies an eagle hornbill, its huge wings beating
increasingly loud among the foliage overhead. Again the old wizard
appears not to notice, and his chant and the flurry in the forest soon rise to*

a crescendo together, summoning to the scene an oversize male monkey.
The monkey immediately falls into a dance with the wizard and, for a
short while, man and monkey mix it in the middle of the clearing.]
Old Man: [*gaining ground on the monkey.*] It is a full ripe banana you
 want, is
It not so, my fine fellow? Or is it
A partner for another kind of dance? Well,
It's spring tide, you know, and all the womenfolk
Have gone fishing on the river. But there's sap flowing
In that mortar over there, oh yes. Will
You like a look for yourself? This way then,
That's fine of you.
[*Turning to the eagle hornbill beating wildly above.*]
And you up there who are so importunate
For entry, we have heard you knocking, and
Now stop it! Indeed, what's your intention—to pull
The sky down over our heads? In folly
The fowls of the earth show the wind their skirts.
But you from high up on the hill look down on them
Pulling apart their own feathers. This way
To your nest! After flight over seven seas,
The royal adventurer requires rest
At last, and your rest is here, here in this nest!
[*Then he wheels upon the lizard now nodding fiercely on the ground.*]
Now, do not strike, do not strike the ground
With your head of hammer, my good guest, as though
We forgot you. Well, did your cousin the chameleon
Not tell you the earth is fledgling still, and
As yet not set and firm underfoot? If you
Will follow us, yes, this way, this way,
We will show you what object, already gone
Solid, you may shatter by one blow of your head.
[*In this manner, the old wizard attracts all his three guests into the*
mortar. At the same time he gestures the boy on.]
Your pestle, boy, put to each head
Your pestle, and pound as if it were rock
Of Abeokuta, pound till every bone
Crack as egg of hen!
[*The boy pounds away. Meanwhile, the old man breaks into his theme*
song and, between strokes of the pestle, feeds the mortar with ingredients
from the pots. When at last the guests are all dead and fully pounded, the

*old man stops the boy peremptorily with one lift of his hand, gesturing to
him to drop the pestle. Then he slaps him smartly across the mouth as he
speaks his next lines.*]

Old Man: May your mouth unlock its gate from ear
    To ear like the hippos that swallow
    Up boats and paddles!
    [*He serves the boy from the mortar.*]
    Now, open up,
    Open up, boy, and swallow the morsel
    Of your life!
    [*He makes the boy swallow all at a gulp.*]
    And this
    Your bowels shall throw up boiling as did
    The cauldrons each time
    Another is thirsty enough for death
    He rouses you to the pit of your belly.
    [*As the boy swallows and the old man steps back, a great and unusual
noise swells and fills the place. It is like the cries of each of the three live
ingredients of the charm in the mortar mixed with the sound of several pots
boiling over. It came from the bowels of the boy, now thrashing about like
somebody seized with colic. The cauldron music should be playing all this
time.*]

Old Man: [*regarding the boy with satisfaction.*] That's as it should be,
    that's as it
    Should be with pot of palm-wine: so the spirit
    Will issue forth. Now, you may go home, Boy.

Oreame: [*holding him back.*] No, not yet, Bouakarakarabiri!

Old Man: What more do you want, woman?

Oreame: Tebekawene, when a man has eaten
    A rare repast, may he not drink some water?

Old Man: I have served your son the meal
    You asked for.

Oreame: So I see. But what
    Will people say if he walked out now, one side
    Of him clothed and the other exposed?

Old Man: You are too insistent, woman. One
    Of these days you will pull a frog into a snake.

Oreame: When we are both snakes sitting on
    Our eggs, why try to hatch for me a toad?

Old Man: So what am I supposed to do next
    Which I have not done? No, tell me,
    Since you know all.

Oreame: Not so, Tebekawene. Take
   The boy into your shrine so, like his late father,
   No sword wielded by man may cut through
   His skin nor any spear or bullet wound pass
   Beyond a bump.
Old Man: Shall we go in
   Then, Oreame? And you come on, boy.
   One thing though: it was no pretense
   Or malice on my side, you must understand. You see,
   I have gone so bald with age you can sharpen
   Your cutlass on my head.
Oreame: You aren't that gone yet!
Old Man: I am, oh,
   I am by the look of the setting sun.
   My brain has frozen within the skull; it now
   Knocks like a dry nut in its shell.
   [*The two old people support each other out; the boy, still dazed, following
   close behind.*]

Scene 6

*In the compound of Oreame in the city of Ododama. Oreame is sitting out
on the verandah grinding tobacco into snuff on an open earthen tray. Voices
reach her from outside and she looks up.*

Orea: [*coming in from outside.*] Change your ways, change
   Your ways, I say, if you don't want to dig
   A grave for me before my time.
   [*The boy comes in driven by his mother Orea from behind. She holds a
   broken piece of stick which her son has apparently made useless in her
   hands.*]
   Cover me up, cover
   Me up with leaves, I say day and night. Has some
   Uncelebrated spirit come into you that
   Your mother's words do not enter your ears?
   [*The boy sullen and silent, allows himself to be prodded on.*]
Oreame: What's the matter now, what's
   The matter between my little hen and her cock?
Orea: Your cock has again been pecking at
   People's children.
The Boy: That's not true; it's they

Who have been pecking at me!

Orea: Was that why you almost twisted
   Okoro's neck so his parents will come
   And break mine?

The Boy: He called me a beast without
   Name or father.

Oreame: If people will insist on
   Pelting the cock with corn, do you say
   He should not stop and eat?

Orea: I have only this one child and I do
   All I can to keep him under cover of
   My roof. But you always incite him to fly out
   Among black-kites. Is it not enough that I'm turned
   Into wood for fire in my time of flower?
   Do you want me to fall down fruitless as well?

The Boy: Hold it, Mother. So my father is dead
   Then? Is that the story you two have kept
   From me all my life?

Oreame: [*ignoring the boy and turning to his mother.*] You that allow
     every breath of wind to blow out
   Your feathers like a foolish hen,
   Just let any hawk snatch at the boy and you will see
   Whether or not he is a chick. Now, go and
   Roast me more leaves of tobacco.
   [*Orea throws down her stick and goes off to the kitchen with one head of
   tobacco. Oreame turns upon the boy.*]
   And look
   Here, young man, you are a child no longer.
   Whether or not you have a father and he is
   Above or below the earth, it is for you
   To fly out and find the fact of the matter.

The Boy: I have always wanted to but which of you
   Has as much as shown me the way? Or
   Am I to fly out like a kite without tail?
   Sometimes I do believe those boys outside
   When they say I may be a falcon but one that
   You have tied to a rope tight in your hand.

Oreame: So that's what they say and you believe them, did you say?
   All right then, go there into the house
   And fetch me the bowl with potassium salt
   In it, and I'll tell you a secret.

[*The boy though reluctant is curious; he goes in to fetch the bowl. He crosses the veranda into the house which, like many Ijaw buildings, has a living room opening out direct and down its entire length into the veranda. The boy can therefore be seen clearly all the way in and back. On entering the house, he trips on the floor which he does not know has been highly polished with a special preparation by the witch. As the boy moves farther on to where the bowl of potassium stands on a rack against the back wall, the passage for him becomes one of progressively tripping up. Because as a true Ijaw man he regards a fall, even outside the wrestling ground, as a matter of great dishonor to his manhood, the boy though sliding dangerously does all in his power to stay standing in one continuous struggling movement. Meanwhile, his grandmother has jumped up and, prancing about the place, cheers the boy on in his dance on the slippery floor.*]

Oreame: Hold it, hold it, my son, hold it! Has
The back of the cat ever touched mud although
You throw him to the ceiling top? Does the soldier ant
Slip on the field though caught in a stampede?
I say hold it! Will you shame me? Hold it
I say?
[*The cheers bring Orea to the scene and before long she too is cheering and jumping. The boy eventually reaches the rack and, holding out the bowl of potassium salt, returns shouting in a complete state of possession. As he dances his way out, his words become coherent. And hearing them, both women run after him awestruck and dumb.*]

The Boy: I am Ozidi! Ozidi ay!
Ozidi! Who disputes it? Who dares
Dispute it? I am Ozidi!
Ozidi! Ozidi!
[*He rushes out in a frenzy still proclaiming himself, his name echoing into the distance. Still silent, mother and daughter stop at the gates, looking at each other with sighs of relief and expectation.*]

Scene 7

In the forge of a blacksmith. The master is busy hammering out a new sword on the anvil. He is working at a feverish pace. So is his young apprentice at the bellows. Between them, by the blue flames of the fire in the pit, stands a pot of water into which the master blacksmith dips from time to time the emerging sword. Master and apprentice appear intimidated and overawed by the presence of their clients. One is the old woman Oreame sitting to one side on a stool, and the other her grandson, the young Ozidi, pacing up and down in obvious impatience.

Oreame: Man, can you not fashion a straight
    Simple sword?
Blacksmith: It's a straight sword
    All right, madam, but not a simple one
    You'll admit.
Ozidi: And how many years do they say the fellow
    Has been at his trade?
Blacksmith: Thirty, sir, thirty years,
    My young master. And I served my apprenticeship
    Right back at Awka.
Oreame: [*spitting.*] You may have learnt your trade
    Right at the feet of Ogun for all we care.
    Look at the piece you claim to have forged
    For my son.
Blacksmith: It was of true steel, madam.
Ozidi: But only once I waved it above
    My head, and see the stump of it lying at your feet.
    I suppose the broken pieces are flying like hail
    Outside.
Blacksmith: [*spitting into his palm.*] Oh dear, oh dear, there are
        children
    Playing out there. I sincerely hope
    None are hurt by those flying pellets.
Ozidi: [*walking up to him.*] Shall I tell you a sure target
    If your second blade break in my hand?
Blacksmith: If you want to, sir, but I certainly hope
    And promise you this second sword will not break.
Ozidi: It had better not, for it's in your head
    I shall bury the blade should it break
    In the wielding.
Blacksmith: Oh, no sir, you wouldn't do
    A thing like that would you?
    I am a stranger
    In your country and crave protection.
    [*He dips the finished sword into the pot of water and brings it out for Ozidi to inspect.*]
    Now, look at this, is it not

A beautiful work of art?

Ozidi: [*taking over the sword.*] Let's see whether or not it proves
Useful as well.
[*He wields it several times over his head and then out in his front till the
sword snaps in two. The blacksmith and his boy jump to a safe distance.
Ozidi, too angry for words, pursues the blacksmith to the other end of the
forge and catching up with him buffets him hard with the flat side of the
stump left in his hand.*]

Blacksmith: Oh, no, don't, don't; I will fashion
Another for you now, and if on
The third attempt I am unsuccessful, then
You may beat me, take the skin off my bottom.

Ozidi: You podgy little pig forever foraging
The earth for dirt; if you have buried
Your stock and bag of true steel and tricks in some ground,
Better go out now and dig it up by your snout
Before I bash in your teeth filed to points
From eating flesh of human beings.

Blacksmith: [*cringing and crying.*] One time more, only one time more
     and by
My hammer and anvil you shall have a sword
Not seen before by eyes of man.

Oreame: Let the rat be, Ozidi; allow him
A third attempt, and he shall not escape if he fails.
[*Ozidi throws down the broken sword, the sound and violence of it make
the blacksmith quail on one side.*]
There, look at the fellow crumbling down
Like a stick eaten up by white ants. Get up, man, and set
About your work fast. If it was silver brooches
And bangles for some country bride
You expect extra favors from, you would be
All over the place by leap and bound like the toad you are.
[*The blacksmith goes to the far corner on the right; out of several bars of
iron stacked up there he selects one and returns to his anvil and bellows.*]

Blacksmith: Fire, boy, fire from those bellows if you want
A first class diploma from me.
[*The boy blows hard at the bellows, while the blacksmith picks himself a
fresh hammer and pair of pincers. Oreame returns to her stool and Ozidi
to his impatient pacing. There is dead silence, then the metallic sound of
one blow after another as the blacksmith resumes work.*]

Blacksmith: I have always returned home to Awka

For the great annual festival of our cult. There's not
A single collection and contribution
Levied by the union that I have not paid. Indeed,
This year, I propose to kill a cow to assume
The title that is my due. But shall it be said
Onitshamaka was commissioned
By Oreame to fashion a sword for her offspring
Ozidi, and he presented her
With a blade of clay? The cult certainly
Will throw me out as a scrap piece of iron.
After that, there is none in the whole clan
Of Awka and public will pick me up again.
And outside, God knows how other peoples
Already curse us Igbo. So save me
From odium of the dumping place; save me from folding
Up and going to rust as a bad piece of iron;
Save me, I beg of you my anvil, I beg of you
My hammer and hand!
[*The blacksmith delivers three more strokes and straightens up stiff and
tired. Without another word, he hands the piece he has just forged to the
anxious Ozidi. It is seven-pronged and so striking and strange that
Oreame herself rises and goes over to look at it. Not one of them speaks.
Then there is the noise as of a "night masquerade" while Ozidi wields
and waves the sword in all directions. The roaring, like that of a lion,
moves to a climax as Ozidi swings the sword faster and faster until it
grows almost out of sight in one huge whirlwind. When at last Ozidi lets
go, the sword is discovered to have wrapped itself seven times round his
hand. All give a great shout of cheer.*]

ACT III

Scene 1

The whole group of players does the war canoe dance, that is amoo *or*
Ogbo aro, *three times round the area of play. A smaller party consisting of
Ozidi, Oreame and Orea together with a personal slave, a sword bearer, one
horn blower and several drummers as attendants then disengages itself as new
arrivals going ashore on an undeveloped piece of land outside Orua.*

Ozidi: [*stopping and looking about him.*] The city is still to our right.
  So what
  Are we stopping here for, Mother?
Orea: [*with a catch in her voice.*] To call
  On your father.
Ozidi: Surely, my father did not dwell
  In a place like this?
Oreame: This was where
  Your mother left him twenty years ago.
  And since then we have had no news the family
  Has moved house to another district.
Ozidi: Really, did you say, mother, this is
  The homestead of my father, of Ozidi
  You told me held in one fist
  Of his hand more strength than is packed
  In seven wrestlers put together? I see
  No house here except broken pillars there all trampled
  Underfoot by a herd of elephant grass.
  What that host has not completely
  Invested clumps of canna lilies
  Have claimed as squatters. And are those plantains
  The human beings I must hug to myself?
Oreame: Your old idiot uncle Temugedege,
  If he is not dead by now, from all accounts
  Should be around somewhere to give you welcome home.
  [*She begins to beat a path for the party through the overgrowth.*]
Ozidi: [*joining her.*] What cans of oil
  You pour on the bonfire consuming me!
Orea: [*sniffing.*] This stretch of land more than twenty years ago
  Was a whole section of the city you see
  To our right. Full many families
  Of your father's line lived here in great measure.
  As a matter of fact, there was none among them
  So poor he had not a household of slaves to do
  Him grace. But by one stroke of the smallpox king
  This whole place, constituting
  The seventh district of the city
  Of Orua, was in one season
  Of no rain burnt to the ground. Only
  Your father and uncle were individual trees
  Spared from the general wildfire that like

A dragon licked your homestead to charcoal.

Ozidi: Why did you not tell me all this before?

Oreame: My son, you do not rub charcoal over
   Your body and sit idle at home.

Ozidi: You go out to do battle.

Oreame: Truly, you have ears, my son, and hear
   The voices in the wind.

Ozidi: If my father was not called
   To join the royal barge that bore off all
   His relatives, then how did he go?

Oreame: The wake to that you must discover yourself.

Ozidi: And you say I have an uncle who lives
   Out here in this wilderness?

Oreame: [*pointing ahead.*] Yes, there he is—under the umbrella tree.
   [*The party has now beaten a way within a few yards of the umbrella tree.
   Beneath it is a small clearing where a man has set up his keep. Pots,
   pans, and cans, many broken, and brown and black with wear and
   weather, lie scattered about. On three blocks of stone a decrepit and
   unkempt old man is cooking himself a miserable meal over a fire that
   refuses to respond to his weak puffs of breath. When the party descends on
   him, he is in the grip of a fit of asthmatic coughing, and at the sudden
   sight of the strangers he falls back on his haunches in great fear.*]

Temugedege: Hello, hello, who are you people? I am
   Temugedege nobody wants as king,
   And I want nobody as subjects either.
   Here under my umbrella tree I live
   In my own shadow. Has it fallen over
   Any person or possession
   That you cast dark eyes at me
   Like that? Temugedege is all alone in Orua,
   No brother since that terrible tribute,
   No woman in the house to boil me
   Water to bathe, and not a single child
   Around to run errands since that silly girl ran away
   And left me all alone in the crowds of Orua.

Ozidi: This is my uncle?

Oreame: Yes, this wreck in the sun is your uncle.

Temugedege: [*not understanding, blubbers on.*] Please leave me alone,
      leave me
   In my peace; Temugedege asks for nothing
   But to be left in his peace. Under
   This umbrella tree have I found peace. The rains

May soak my skin but I am not salt, and
In the sun I like to bask as a crocodile
On the river bank. I ask for nothing more,
Nothing more I want. Therefore do not take
What I have from me. You will have to kill
Me first, truly, you will have
To kill Temugedege first!

Oreame: Nobody has come to kill you, Temugedege.

Temugedege: Then who are you? I thought you had come
   To sequester my property and drive me
   Off the land of my fathers.

Oreame: Temugedege, are you so old and blind
   You don't know me, Oreame, whose daughter
   Your brother married?

Temugedege: Hey, Oreame! Did you say you are
   Oreame, that supreme witch, I mean
   My good, good mother-in-law? Ay,
   Temugedege is dead and finished
   Indeed not to have known you at once. Hey, and
   There is nothing to eat in the house—what
   Humiliation I am faced with, oh,
   What humiliation!

Oreame: Do not worry, good Temugedege.

Temugedege: And this beautiful woman fair and fat
   As a hillock, is she the sister behind you?

Orea: Look at him! I am Orea her daughter
   You failed to protect in her period of need.

Temugedege: What, Orea? Our Orea herself? And have
   You gone and taken another man? [*Pointing at Ozidi.*] Who is
   The young man at your side?

Oreame: [*laughing.*] Surely, Temugedege, a young woman
   Like that, did you expect she will stay up
   As a plantain stem in the open country
   And no cock coming to top her tassel?

Temugedege: She is our wife, she is our wife still. As
   The eldest of my family, I may not
   Inherit my brother's wife, but she is
   Our wife still. She had no right to run out
   Of the house. Now it is a foolish hen
   That flees her nest.

Orea: [*clapping hands in his face.*] True, true, and how
   Did you defend the hearth she fouled up?

Temugedege: I say you are our wife still and must
    Not cackle where cocks are stalking. After
    All; we still have money on your head. Or
    To whom did you make repayment? Was it to me
    Temugedege—the dead
    Are my witness.
Oreame: Temugedege is on the right there,
    Orea. You must therefore show him respect
    Due to the father-of-your-marriage.
Temugedege: Oh, that female, she never was one for that.
    Even as a mere handmaid in our house,
    She would as soon cuff me with a broom
    As fetch me snuff.
Orea: It is not true, what he is saying
    Is not true at all.
Ozidi: Oh, keep quiet, will you?
Temugedege: For that service alone, you have my lasting
    Salutation, young man. But who are you,
    Coming into a family scene like that?
    The rest, by their standing, I know are slaves
    And servants to our beloved mother-in-law,
    But who you are she has not told
    Temugedege.
Oreame: Shall I tell you?
Temugedege: Go on, you women have this terrible habit
    Of roasting a man over fire as if
    He still were an infant in state of convulsion.
Oreame: The young man you see there,
    Temugedege, is the son
    Of your brother Ozidi.
Temugedege: Now you've come to laugh at Temugedege
    Afresh. My brother had no issue before
    His death.
Oreame: After long seasons of tears,
    Temugedege, I have not come all this way
    From Ododama to deliver you a parcel
    With dung for its center.
Temugedege: [*advancing upon Ozidi.*] Let me see him then, let me see
    The boy at once.
    [*He takes the face of Ozidi between his palms, closely looking at all his
    features from behind watery eyes. Then, very agitated, he feels the young*

man all over from head to feet, talking to himself all the time.]
If some Itsekiri woman
Had come and made this presentation, I would
Have thought twice about the matter. The man
Liked raiding in that territory and
The girls there I hear are no game at running.
In fact, from all stories reaching our ears
They seem all sure sirens instigating
Their own captivity. And for a man
Who always was fighting one battle or
Another no place for rest could be better
Than the full double pillow held in front
By virgin girls. Never mind if by that
The conquered had the last laugh on us victors.
But here is a boy, full grown, brought to me
By mother of the wife who fled
The homestead when lightning struck
In broad sunshine. Did the bolt that splintered
Our cornerstone till the soil as well,
Engendering by that one stroke the seed
That sprung this stem? These are the feet
Of my brother, show them, not so flat were
His heels, yes, they are my late brother's,
And these calves bulging
Through wrappers, these strong arms
Tapering to fingers of tendril that hold
With grip of iron. Now, I believe it,
Deep in your eyes I see your dead father
Rising above me your ruin—ah!
Do you come to scold me
A scarecrow? It was not my fault,
Oh my brother, my brother, it was not
My fault, I tell you, or don't
You hear me, don't you? don't you?
[*He falls down a bundle of rags at the feet of Ozidi.*]
Oreame: There, you see, Ozidi, it is not
The family house alone requiring
Prompt repairs.
Ozidi: [*picking up the old idiot and addressing his men.*] Start clearing
the bush; on this spot
Let us raise again the compound of my fathers.

Scene 2

*In the compound of Ofe at Orua. A group of prominent citizens are
drinking and laughing in the living-room. With the host there are present,
among others, Ofe's good friends and companions Oguaran, Azezabife, and
Agbogidi.*

Ewiri: [*ambling in.*] Ofe, listen, Ofe, and you Azezabife
    Of half flank, I know the whole gang of you
    Is there gathered, you'd better all listen to me.
    Are you sitting there drinking palm-wine when pepper
    Has fallen in the fire before you?
    [*From his own appearance when he walks in it does not seem he has
    himself been far from reach of the gourd. The group seize upon that
    immediately all speaking at the same time.*]
Azezabife: What wasp is there in your bag today, gossip?
Oguaran: And what have you yourself been doing?
Ofe: Come, tell us about this pepper
    That has fallen in the fire.
Agbogidi: Pepper in the fire? But is anybody
    Smoking out rabbits in some hole?
Ewiri: You wait till you begin coughing aloud
    Seeds of the fruit.
Agbogidi: But I am not coughing yet, am I, Ofe?
    [*He hiccups aloud.*]
Ofe: Now, you take it gently, Ewiri, tell us the news.
Ewiri: Not until I have had a cup myself.
    [*He takes a seat and is promptly served. He drinks self-consciously,
    increasing suspense among the others.*]
Ofe: Now out with it, man.
Azezabife: The fellow's in labor and must take
    His time with the delivery.
Agbogidi: Perhaps he needs inducement! Another cup?
Ewiri: I am not in labor and need no inducement
    To deliver my piece of news but all
    The same, I take your kind offer.
    [*He takes another drink and Ofe, waking to the tricks of his new guest,
    tries flattery and blandishment in place of open pressure and impatience.*]
Ofe: Ewiri, twice our Amananaowei
    By general acclamation, the man
    Who lets cutlass cut through pots, our own tortoise

That beats the dog to every bone, who but
You gets the secret information far
Ahead of the wind?

Ewiri: That's me Ewiri, that's me
All right, Ofe. I like you Ofe; you are not
Like others who think all talents are there
To be gathered only in the field of war. Some sit
At home and still find their fortune—

Azezabife: And of that set
You certainly sit on the stool!

Ewiri: [*cutting him dead.*] Simply told, my good friend Ofe, the story
is this.
Many many years ago several
Of you here present planted a champion yam.
Well, that yam you sowed several seasons gone by,
Has now grown beyond arm's span.

Oguaran: Away with your riddles, man! We are not
Children gathered under a mango tree.

Agbogidi: Besides, it is not moonlight! That reminds
Me, who has seen the new moon? Which way does
It tilt its tray—over our heads, or
Our neighbors?

Ofe: Will you shut your mouths? Please continue,
Ewiri.

Ewiri: May I first wash down the dirt thrown up by
Those two?

Ofe: Certainly. Here.

Ewiri: Well, before the flow of my tongue
Was suddenly diverted and dammed by hands
Not fit to bail bilge out of my canoe, I
Was saying to you for all your good here, Ofe,
That harvest-time has at last come.

Azezabife: Look at him! Like the idiot
Temugedege, the man never goes
To fish or farm. Now overnight
He is weaving baskets all over
The place.

Ofe: I thank you, Ewiri; the nut
You have cast is fast between my teeth.

Ewiri: I knew you would crack our little conundrum
If you tried enough. But for the benefit

Of those who are toothless, and we must admit
They abound in this city of ours, here's
The kernel inside for you to chew
Between your empty gums: Ozidi
Has a son.
All Four Together: What? You jest!
The man had none!
Did you say the cock laid an egg?
Ozidi has a son, you say?
Ewiri: What's more the young cockerel has just
Flown home.
Azezabife: I do not believe the man.
Oguaran: Now I remember! It came to my ears
Not long ago that a party of strangers
Arrived in town early today.
Ewiri: You are more deaf than
The iguana, Oguaran, but this time
You heard well. Ozidi's son has returned home,
His mother and grandmother at his tail.
Azezabife: What, that witch Oreame? We must not
Let her sleep one night in this city.
Ofe: She will only fly back as a bat or
Owl. But this is strange.
Agbogidi: Whoever thought the cock had a chick?
Oguaran: What shall we do before he flies forth.
Azezabife: Seek to contain him immediately
That's what we must do, for without doubt he
Has come to scratch our eyes out.
Ewiri: That's right; for even a hen may ruffle
Up the hawk.
Agbogidi: The sacrifice of a son of the soil
To his ancestors is a long rope
Without end, I said at that time.
Ofe: This is no time to wail like women
Who have lost their wares at market. We must
Start work at once. Ewiri, we greet
You for bringing us this warning.
Azezabife, Oguaran,
Agbogidi, up with arms and whatever
To hand, but only in our self-defense,
Remember that. If first we look for a stick

Long enough, we shall never kill the snake
In the house. So rise,
Rise, I say rise at once.

Scene 3

*On the way to the great market situated far out of town and shared by Orua
with others of the neighborhood and beyond. Ozidi, after the long journey
from town, walks up showing signs of fatigue. Following close on his heels is
his personal attendant carrying his kit.*

Attendant: Massa, papa kuku leaf shed for market sef?

Ozidi: None that I know of. The man was no mean
Shopkeeper; war was his business, and that
He always pursued in the interest
Of the state.

Attendant: An' he nor leaf any property at all at all? I day hask sake
of all them big big people way day say dem day sarvice publick
nor day froget for put plenty plenty insi'e dem own pocket. Dem
tyle like de small girl way day give pickin food: dem give baby
small den dey chop the rest.

Ozidi: Well, you saw on our return to Orua what
My father left me by way of an estate.
You and I have had to drive the bush right back
To raise a new roof over our heads. So
The old man does not seem to have turned public
Service to private profit. On the contrary,
He suffered great personal loss—his own
Life and no less.

Attendant: All de tori I don' hear since we come for dis place say your
papa get too much power. Dem say he fit throway seven man for
one time.

Ozidi: And for that they murdered the man
For his brother to feast on. Anyway,
Why all this sudden inquiry, Omoni?

Attendant: Notin, massa. Ah just day wonder sake of why mama
dem send us go for market. Whosa we go know how papa die for
dere. 'E nor tyle like say he leaf any tenant for shed dere way fit
tell us who kill am for die.

Ozidi: Honestly, I too have wondered myself
Why the women will not reveal to me

At home my father's assassins. But
My grandmother in her wisdom says I
Must go to market for that, and to market
We are now going.

Attendant: Look, oh, massa! We don reach place way road broke for
tree: one hand go for right, one go for left' an' [*turning to the
direction from where they have just arrived*] dis one go for tail. Massa,
waytin' we go do now?

Ozidi: Sit till someone of these parts comes and shows
Us the way.

Attendant: Hey, massa, nor si' don for dis kine place, oh! Na for here
spirits day fly. Plenty people way you day see for market na proper
spirit from watah, nor be man-pickin at all at all.

Ozidi: Have you yourself seen one of these spirits?

Attendant: [*he spins his left hand over his head and snaps his fingers,
spitting at the same time.*] Me, massa? God frobid!

Ozidi: Sit down then with me, Omoni, and perhaps
You will today have your first meeting with one.

Attendant: Oh, nor, nor, nor, massa!

Ozidi: Oh, yes, yes, yes, Omoni! Now,
Will you sit down and stop trembling
Like plantain leaves?
[*Omoni, afraid to disobey, puts down his kit and sits by the crossroads at
a respectable distance from his master. By now it is getting dark. Ozidi,
glad of the opportunity for a nap, falls asleep almost immediately, his
body spread-eagled across the road. When he begins to snore, Omoni, still
very much frightened, gets up and looking here and there, tiptoes to a
place of safety in the undergrowth hedging the road on all sides. There is
a short pause during which the snoring of Ozidi is the one strange animal
noise among the natural life of the place. Later, three market-women come
by carrying huge baskets of wares on their heads. In the poor evening
light, made dimmer still by the surrounding thick foliage, the women trip
one after the other over the sleeping Ozidi.*]

First Woman: I have stumbled over something in the dark.

Second Woman: I too stumbled over something.

Third Woman: And so did I. What can it be?

Second Woman: It couldn't be a tree trunk, could it?

Third Woman: No storm has combed through the forest lately.

First Woman: And nobody will dare fell one across
The road to market. The object seemed live
To my feet.

Second Woman: Well, shall we go back and look?

Third Woman: Careful, it could be a python sleeping
  After a huge meal.

First Woman: Python or no python, I am going to look
  For myself.

Second Woman: I'm coming as well.

Third Woman: And who are you two going to leave
  Behind in this place?
  [*She follows the others who have begun skirting the area cautiously. The first trips again and leaps back with a shriek, but her companion holds her back announcing her find.*]

Second Woman: It's only a human being!

Third Woman: Really, I hope it's alive!

First Woman: People in these parts
  Are sure pirates. Perhaps, they have gone
  And waylaid some trader and left
  His dead body on the wayside.

Second Woman: [*she gives Ozidi a kick.*] The fellow is stirring from all
    I can see.
  Come, fellow, wake up, wake up!
  [*Ozidi only rolls over.*]

First Woman: He's fast asleep, the brute.

Third Woman: Look, it's a young man. Yes, it is,
  A young man.

First Woman: He's probably been out drinking more than
  His belly can hold.

Second Woman: It's terrible how
  Some parents bring up their children.

First Woman: Come on, boy, wake up, do you hear, wake up!
  You can't drop off to sleep on the highroad.

Third Woman: And at the crossroads for that matter. There's
  No telling what youth will do these days.

First Woman: Now, will you wake up, young man, I say
  Wake up and come with us for the rest
  Of the way. Men should mount for women
  Escort; now it is the other way round.

Second Woman: Come with us and we'll serve
  You hot pepper soup at our stall.

Attendant: [*coming out of hiding.*] You hear dem, massa, dem go give
  us pepper soup drink for market.

First Woman: Now, who's this fellow?

Third Woman: A common slave by his looks.

Second Woman: And how the wretch made me start.

Attendant: Dis na my massa, na my massa dey sleep here.

Second Woman: Well, let him get up quick if you
   Are coming with us.

   [*Ozidi stirs more in his sleep, kicking the first woman quite viciously on the shin.*]

First Woman: He has kicked me, the brute has kicked
   Me on the shin.

Third Woman: Really, the fellow must be a mad bull!

Second Woman: Truly, as the elders say, go out of your way
   To help a dog and it will bite your finger off.

First Woman: He slept on the crossroad to market
   And when I try to lift up the beast, see how
   He goes and breaks my foot.

Third Woman: The foolhardy fellow, does he know
   Whose wife you are?

Second Woman: Not since that man Ozidi was killed
   Has such effrontery been seen around here.

First Woman: The fellow falls across the road
   Like an evil tree and refuses to get up
   For honest people to pass.

Third Woman: He must be put back in the pit
   Where he belongs. Look here, young man,
   Nobody insults me, the wife of Azezabife,
   And lives to tell the story. When Ozidi
   Took on more feathers than the eagle's
   My husband it was who first plucked off
   His shock of feathers.

Second Woman: Who cut off his neck
   But my man Oguaran?

First Woman: And when it was time to pick up
   His stubborn head and carry it
   Into Orua for his idiot brother to drink from,
   Who did, yes, who did? It was Ofe
   My husband, it was he! And let me tell
   You, foolish boy, my husband suffers no
   Overbearing acts, and will punish you
   For this.

Ozidi: [*springing to his feet.*] Enough!
   Enough now! You have said
   More than I want to hear.

[*To his attendant who all through the confession of the women has been running about mumbling bemusedly to himself: "So na so de tin happ'n!"*]
And you there,
Keep a good grip on your gritty teeth
Before I pluck them out for you.
Attendant: Massa, waytin my eye see today my mouth no fit talk. So na so de tin happ'n. But una country people dey too do wicked oh!
Ozidi: Yes, these good women have here confirmed it.
Second Woman: And who may you be, young man?
First Woman: After what you've done, do you dare
Stand up and look me in the face?
Third Woman: It is like the cobra: he puffs his cheeks
After spitting into your eyes rank venom.
Ozidi: I should gladly offer to carry on my head
Your baskets for you all the way to market,
For it is a big thing you three have done
For me today.
First Woman: Have we rendered you any service?
Third Woman: Is the fellow not a real peacock?
First Woman: Ha, ha, next he will be offering us fees!
Ozidi: No; as for payment, it is I
Shall demand that.
[*With that he starts to pluck from each woman her headtie and upper wrapper. They all shriek in horror, protesting with loud ululations. Ozidi does not heed them, but goes on giving the articles one by one to his slave for safe keeping.*]
First Woman: What, will you strip me naked? No,
Don't, don't!
Third Woman: He's a highway thug,
Surely he is a common highway robber! Leave
My cloth alone, will you?
Second Woman: Let go your hand! I say, don't touch me!
It's rape you are attempting—what, young man,
Will you force me against
My will, and on the wayside too!
[*Ozidi has by now divested all three women of their headties and upper fit. Only when he has finished does he speak.*]
Ozidi: You may call me all the names
You like but the actual one is Ozidi.
Do you hear that? The name is

Ozidi, Ozidi, son of the man
Your husbands butchered from behind. Now,
Go home without crest and cover and tell
Your husbands how like three garrulous hens
I have plucked you clean of your fine plume.
There, go off quickly before I do that
I have no mind to.
[*He pushes out the three women, and returns to his servant.*]
Now, we too are going home. The pot
There on the fire boils over, and
The tortoise in it must die.
[*Master and attendant run out to the strain of the song* Puba erein yo.]

Scene 4

In Azezabife's compound. The divested wives have returned home and told their story of shame to their husbands. Now all three, completely dishevelled, sit down in the sand, their feet stretched out forward and their hands sweeping the ground while they moan and sob in silent grief. In contrast, their husbands Ofe, Azezabife and Oguaran, together with their friend Agbogidi, are strutting about the place, fuming aloud and, as a result, hardly hearing one another speak. A crowd of curious relatives and neighbors has gathered around them.

Ofe: This is too much, too much for belief.
    A young adventurer like that just come
    Into the city, I cannot believe he could be
    So crazy as to insult our wives.
Azezabife: You cut half the matter: he has plucked them
    Naked, and turned them loose for the wind
    Of public laughter to lash at.
Oguaran: In another man
    This would be straight assault with intent
    To have indecent carnal knowledge of our wives.
Ofe: No damage is too big to exact
    From the whelp. Now, how shall we bring him to bay?
Azezabife: I say, deal with him as we did
    With the father before he was born.
Oguaran: We can't all go and attack him
    At once. The fellow is no *iroko* tree

That we have to call together the whole
Community before we cut him down.
The sucker!

Agbogidi: Yes, to meet him as of a body
Would be to award the pulp the title we did
His father. And Oyin knows he deserved it.

Azezabife: Let me tackle him alone then. This day
I shall go and challenge the fellow
To single combat. Be not afriad of the dog
Returning to his kennel with all
His four limbs unbroken.

Oguaran: It is that witch Oreame swells
His heart. Left to the idiot Temugedege,
The yam we buried in his backyard was
As good as eaten by worms and weevils.

Ofe: Now they are asking us to roast it
Afresh for them to eat.

Agbogidi: I here and now offer them
The palm oil for it.

Azezabife: What are we waiting for then? The feast
Is on,
[*They all disperse gesticulating wildly.*]
And you women,
Go home, all of you! Today you have become
Full vessels for our wrath. The cup bubbles over
And, you see, we have sworn to drain it
To the dregs. Come!
[*He scatters the crowd before him and rushes to his shrine in the middle of the compound.*]
Now, who is there? Who is
There to hand? Give me my skirt of seven
Girdles! Give me my amulets, the snake bangles
About my forearm. Ahn! Dada, has your son
Lived to this sunrise to be dipped
In water of cassava by a mere infant?
I must wash off this stain with blood.
Oh, my sword, my sword! I am Azezabife! I
Am Azezabife the Skeleton Man!
[*As he disappears declaiming, the strains of his theme song rise and fill the compound.*]

Scene 5

It is early morning in Ozidi's house. Oreame is rousing up her grandson to get ready for his fight with Azezabife in the marketplace from which direction the orchestra can be heard beating in the event of the day. Oreame is in a brief scarlet skirt and skull-cap, a headtie, folded into a belt, about her breast. In her right hand is a fan.

Wake up, Ozidi, wake up! What, are you
  The puffadder that you stay in bed till noon?
  Housewives already have filled their pots
  From the stream, indeed they have swept
  From outside the excrements of worms and goats,
  And gone out with the sun are farmers and fishermen.
  And, Ozidi, do you snore still?
Ozidi: [*staggering into view and rubbing the sleep off his eyes.*]
  What, Big Mother, has day broken already?
Oreame: Shame! Look at the sky
  Through the eaves, and hear the drums beating
  In the marketplace!
Ozidi: Then Azezabife is there already?
Oreame: No; he's waiting till you
  Get out of bed! Now run, boy, run and bathe
  Yourself from the pots boiling in the shrine.
  Or shall people of Orua say your bottoms
  Suddenly have got stuck to your seat?
  [*She rushes him out into the shrine. Then she falls on her knees in prayer.*]
  Ay, Oyin Tamara, you who are mother
  Of all mankind, molder of earth, sky and sea,
  I beseech you, is my child in the right
  In this matter? Twenty years ago, men of Orua
  Turned upon his father's head the mortar aimed
  At the enemy and pounding the man to pulp, served him
  As a royal dish to his brother. Where has it
  Been heard said a son of the soil was sacrificed to the spirits
  Of his land? Where has it been seen one dog ate
  Another? Only in Orua, only in this city
  Are such abominable things taken in jest.
  The seed you were pleased to grant the man, even
  As he fell splintered in the afternoon like

An oil bean tree, seeks today all agents to that mortar
So that the feast begun before his birth may find
A finish. The boy has no left paw of the leopard;
He is not possessed of the cunning of the cobra.
He is a fledgling eagle flying for the first time
To call home his father forgotten in some dung pit
In the swamp, so he can take the seat among
The worthy dead and have served to him his own dish
At times of sacrifice. And now as after,
He flies forth under the shadow of your great wings.
If I am in the wrong inciting the boy forth,
Sever right now the string that binds him
Firm to my hand, for I do not want him shot down
As a duck. But if it is your wish the falconers
Have long forfeited the hunt, then let
My eagle go, let him go now and pluck out their eyes,
Pick the flesh clean off their bones.
[*A clap of thunder without warning breaks across the clear morning sky.
Hearing it, Oreame touches the ground with her forehead and with
outthrown arms, jumps almost in one act.*]
There, did you hear it? She is with us,
The woman of all the world herself gives the signal
We go forth to the fight, Ozidi. Now, where
Are you, where are you, my eagle?

Temugedege: Come, come, you people, what is all
    This noise about? May I not have a little sleep
    In my own house? Who talks of battle
    Before the ground is dry of dew? Oh!
    It's you again, I see.

Oreame: [*prancing with excitement.*] Give way, in-law, it is the boy's
    first outing.

Temugedege: [*looking at his nephew who has now issued forth in full battle
    dress: a white skirt, vest and skull-cap sporting no eagle feathers.*]
    Have you allowed these women to fool
    You, Ozidi? Your father began and
    Ended in blood. Have you too chosen to go
    That way?

Oreame: Temugedege, make way for the boy! Not all
    Are wall-geckoes forever hugging
    The kitchen wall.

Temugedege: Oh-ho! So is that what you say, woman?

Your silly fearless head! Was this
Why one fine day you flew in with your flock
In full tow? You witch, you of seven feathers
Falling across the sea between Agoro
And Akassa all in one night, was it
So you will pull the thatch off above
Our grey hair? Come and hear, all
You people of Orua!

Oreame: Who sickens at blood must stay on diet
Of palm oil!
[*Turning upon her grandson.*]
And do you stand there turning
On one toe like a whirlpool?
[*She beats him lightly but briskly all over his body with her special fan.*]
Have any spirits
Laid hands on my boy, let them flee, let them flee!
Does any mist swim across your eyes, Ozidi,
Let it dry up as a dew in the sun!
[*As she carries out this ritual, Ozidi wakes up, trembling visibly. His horn blower also begins to call him insistently. Soon there is a rush as of a lizard, the shriek as of an eagle hornbill and the cry as of a male monkey, all against the background of several huge pots boiling over their lids: it is the mortar and pestle charm taking effect as it will on the occasion of every fight to come. And with it Ozidi whips himself up into great frenzy, charging forward to the fight.*]

Ozidi: I am Ozidi ay, Ozidi, Ozidi!
[*Oreame, the horn blower, and the sword bearer all rush after him, sweeping past Temugedege.*]

Temugedege: [*corking his ears and stamping on the ground like a child frustrated.*]
Peace, peace, that is all Temugedege
Asks for, peace to smoke my pipe, peace to drink
My wine under the umbrella tree. Now
They have come and taken all that away.

Scene 6

In the public square of Orua later that morning. Ozidi and Azezabife are locked in a duel to death. Ranged behind each on either side are supporters and friends: Azezabife's is a huge group on the left which includes his principals and partners Ofe the Short, Agbogidi the Nude, Oguaran the Giant, Sigirisi the Net Man and Akpobrisi the Tree Man. To the right is the small family group of Oreame, Ozidi's horn blower and sword bearer. Temugedege is at home as is Orea who is too afraid for the safety of her son to step even out of bed.

The orchestra is behind and to the center. It strikes up the personal tune of either champion whenever he makes a telling stroke. At the opening of scene, there is a catch of breath in the atmosphere with drumsticks left suspended in midair. Both men in the pit strain locked by the other's arm and with head to head like two fighting rams.

Ofe: [*cheering on the line.*] Break, break, man! This is no wrestling match
And don't allow that strippling to draw
You into one!
Oreame: [*dances behind her son.*] Breath pains him now,
Ozidi! One stroke more and he will splinter
Into two like a plam tree!
[*Both men break loose and then close upon each other immediately. Ozidi loses his sword; he is beaten about the ground by Azezabife who bounds about like a football.*]
Oreame: [*retrieving sword.*] Here, have your sword back quick!
Lightning
May furrow the earth but in the free sky
Lies his home.
Azezabife: [*laughing.*] The child you are! The old woman still has to feed
You—ha, ha! But poor boy, her dugs are dry, let me
Tell you, quite sucked dry by the sun! Now look me in
My one eye: standing on one foot as the stock, with one hand
I shall this day clip your thread of life.
[*Incensed afresh, Ozidi drives Azezabife back.*]
Ofe: [*frantic for his friend.*] Hold it, hold it, man!
[*Azezabife retreats still, the blade of Ozidi's sword raining a hail of sparks about him.*]
Oreame: It's no race
Of the antelope Azezabife:
So stand rooted to one spot! Yes, there,
Like the half-splintered tree you are!
[*Following her command, Azezabife suddenly makes a stand. But it is obvious to all now that he is a tired man.*]

Oreame: [*whipping up wind with her fan.*] Cut him down now. Ozidi,
    cut
  Him down! Or woman that I am, shall I come
  And cut him down while you look? That's it,
  That's it, son of mine! Now, he is a tree caught in
  The wind, and see how he snaps and totters,
  Maggots flowing from his pith.
  [*To the lines of his personal theme song* Asaan yo yo *Ozidi strikes down
  Azezabife. A great spontaneous cheer fills the air and the people pour
  into the square cheering and beside themselves with excitement.*]

Scene 7

*In the compound of Ofe after several more fights all won by Ozidi. Now his
remaining enemies, still led by Ofe, debate what next they should do. Beside
Ofe, there is Badoba the Tree Man, and also Sigirisi the Net Man.*

Ofe: [*pacing about.*] Now we are how many left in the chase,
  Badoba? The whole circle of us
  Set out after a quarry we thought was
  A grass cutter: we threw about him our ring;
  With loud taunts and shooing followed
  On his heels till at one stage it was like
  A hurricane raging full above his head.
  But heedless of our horns, with our ring a tightening pit
  About him, the fellow took one leap after
  Another, and here we are knocked off a heap,
  Unable to rise to our feet for the simple
  Shame and shock of our adventure.
Badoba: I suggest a two-pronged attack, undertaken
  By all of us at once, instead of sitting here
  Counting our broken bones.
Ofe: Not so; things are not so bad now
  It is no longer one against one.
Sigirisi: It is this dancing manner of his puts our men out of step.
  Let me hunt the fellow down with my net, and call me the fool
  Who went to the stream with a sieve if I do not
  Return with that butterfly in my bag.
Badoba: I agree we still can dispose of the wretch, and
  Like father like son, there should be no talk
  Of vengeance. Already his uncle Temugedege

Rains curses on him; you should hear the idiot
Struggling with the morning cock for the world's ear.
Ewiri: [*entering with others behind him.*] Ofe, do you hear the sweet
    music outside?
Ofe: No? Who's it rejoicing at this time?
Badoba: [*listening.*] If my ears are not ringing with water, that's
    No sweet music I hear coming outside: it's
    Some ululating.
    [*The noise draws nearer.*]
Ofe: Is some poor fellow dying again? The sun
    Does not rise anymore in this town
    But it is setting on some person.
Ewiri: This time it is Oreame requesting your death.
Ofe: Ewiri, do you have to tell me? Don't
    I know it is my own head she wants to dump in the pot
    Of her shrine? Oh, who knew that woman Orea
    Could bear? Kill her, kill her too, Azezabife said, but
    I was such a fool, believing the catfish cannot come
    Out of a bamboo trap. Now I am pricked on
    All sides by its thorns.
First Citizen [*Stepping forward from behind Ewiri.*] You led the tilling
    of the land.
Second Citizen: Alone you carried the head of the yam
    That you all planted.
Third Citizen: Now it is harvest time, and the yam
    Has thrown such a tuber it taps
    The bowels of the earth.
Fourth Citizen: Above the ground, its leaves and
    Tendrils spread so wide, if you do not shore up
    The plant, it certainly will choke all the land.
First Citizen: So please trim down this blossom.
Second Citizen: Dig up the treasure to its last root.
Third Citizen: A whole season now there has been
    No masquerade.
Fourth Citizen: Nor any offering to the gods and dead; and
    The flood is falling, falling, Ofe.
Ewiri: You must admit there's a list in your craft
    Frightens everybody. Where are today
    All your fine comrades? Azezabife,
    Rotted on one side though he was, offered
    A flank more than enough for any foe.

But he was first to fall by him
You would kill as you did his father. Next
He chopped down Akpobrisi from that
Great height of his, the man going to pieces
In midair like an overripe bunch of palm nuts.
Agbogidi who scared all with his gorilla
Nakedness the young man promptly invested
With a fine cover-cloth, I mean, his shroud.
And what became of Oguaran who went
To the rescue? Alone this man had dug a moat
For our city by merely walking round our walls.
Each footprint he made in that march cut a lake
That knocked one into the other became
Our famous moat. So on the day of the fight
When like an elephant king he tore up
Iroko trees and swept his way to market,
Who thought an army could stop the man in his course?
Well, as you know very well yourself, Ofe,
Young Ozidi not only stopped Oguaran but
Before our very eyes clipped his toes
And fingers, in all their two score, turning
The great giant loose to beg for food
The rest of his normal life. It is not that
The people do not pity you in your plight,
Ofe; they want protection for themselves
Now there can be peace for you no longer.
That then is the message the people say
We must bring you.
[*The ululating now is at the gates.*]
But I see another
Demands entrance through your gates.
Ofe: The witch, tell her I am out.
Ewiri: She will not believe that; you forget
    She sees everything in that mirror of hers.
Ofe: Say I have caught a cold; surely
    She'll take pity on a man sick in bed.
Ewiri: Oh yes; she will herself offer you
    Instant cure, if only to restore you to full health
    For her son to slaughter.
Ofe: Is there no safety then for a law-abiding
    Man in this state?

All Four Citizens: Who made that possible but Ofe and
   His friends? Who gave wings to the foul wind
   That has despoiled Orua these several
   Seasons? Now the center to the whirlwind approaches
   Like an ill-footed top, and you do, Ofe, ask why
   There is turmoil over our land? Go out
   Quick into the field, Ofe, and if you have
   A fan stout enough, knock over the top
   On the head, but whatever you do, do not let it
   Engulf all our people.
Ofe: Good people of Orua, these many years I
   Have stood steadfast as a staff on your behalf.
   Is there a storm has blown over our good state
   But I have met it full face to face? Is there
   A tide of disaster flowing over our city but I
   Have stemmed it with every dam at my disposal?
   [*The ululating swells into the room.*]
Ewiri: There is another now mounting at the gate
   And Orua expects that you shall go
   Out and ride it.
Ofe: Of course if the people so desire, I shall
   Go forth at once.
   [*He runs for the battle dress and charms which are hung up in his
   shrine. Outside, the witch appears against a sky scurrying with
   clouds. Those inside the compound flee at her sight. Similarly,
   Ewiri and members of his delegation rush away as the woman
   ululates more and more. Only Sigirisi makes a stand, reaching for
   his net.*]
Sigirisi: [*casting his net over her.*] This dress I meant for your son.
   Now
   Better still that I capture the mother, the origin
   Of his strength. There, what a catch! Ofe,
   Come out, come out quick and see the old she-goat
   Sweeping the ground with her feet!
   [*He breaks into his theme song* Sigirisi efe. *Ofe runs back to see the
   strange sight, as do all the others: Oreame inside the net of Sigirisi.*]
   You don't believe your eyes, do you? But
   Single-handed I trapped the witch and without
   Help of spirits and charms? How shall
   We hang her, head down or do you think
   That too indecent for the old bat?

Oreame: [*laughs aloud.*] Hardly so, Sigirisi! This dress
    You were good enough to fling me has not
    Much fitting. See how with one shake of
    My shoulders it falls off my back. Quite
    Like water off the duck, is it not so,
    Sigirisi who waxes strong with women?
    But never mind, never mind; it is Ofe
    I have come to call.
Ofe: Tomorrow, Oreame, let it be tomorrow, and
    I shall myself meet your son in the marketplace.
    You err if you expect us to flee this city
    For you to prey on.
Oreame: Tomorrow did you say? All Orua had heard
    You choose a day to fight my son
    Whose father you killed. And tomorrow
    Then it shall be. But let there be no failing
    Tomorrow from rain or cold. I go now to cook
    Your bowels in my cauldrons.
    [*She goes out ululating, breathlessly watched by everybody, her dada hair
    streaming in the wind.*]

Scene 8

*In the marketplace of Orua on the fourth day of the fight between Ozidi and
Ofe. The arrangement of the square remains the same as in the last fight.
One important change however is that the people of Orua are in a neutral
place behind the orchestra at center back.*

Ofe: People of Orua, a terrible thing
    Has befallen me. I have a pot of herb I buried
    In my garden on the day I began service
    In our state. There are several among you
    Here were not born at the time. Now overnight
    Some person has gone and dug up my pot of herbs.
Orua People: Our hands did not touch it; our feet
    Did not carry us there.
Ozidi: Are you holding us swine in the hedge, Ofe?
Ofe: Wild boar though you regard
    Yourself, short is your snout: it is that witch
    Your mother has dug up my pot, do you deny it?

Oreame: Of course not. You expect, Ofe,
  I'll sit on the sideline while you throw
  Into my son's eyes dust you have gathered
  Over the years. Yes, I dug up your treasure
  All right, and now your house is ablaze you can call in
  Black-kites to the rescue.

Ofe: You hear the witch, people of Orua, you
  Hear her? She has been indulged too long in our midst
  She now does her backward dance
  By broad light of day.

Ozidi: [*striking him.*] For that you take this, Ofe, and this!
  [*They fight, the lightning from the clashing of their swords lighting up
  the square of Orua. In fear the people all break into ululation. Ofe
  performs disappearing acts as Ozidi gains ground, making him miss
  widely. A hush descends upon the field as with each stroke Ozidi discovers
  he has either hit a stone, shell, or tree stump. Oreame grows angry.*]

Oreame: Your sword, give me your sword, since I
  An old woman must strike your blows for you.
  [*Ozidi misses his mark even wider still to the great amusement of Ofe
  who keeps popping up at spots where he is least expected.*]

Oreame: I said your bowels are in my cauldrons
  Cooking, Ofe! So what manner of dance
  Is this? Can your feet not stand a little heat?
  Let me put the lid on your head then!
  [*She strikes him with her fan and Ofe stops his disappearing acts. Both
  champions close again, hitting left and right in common fury. Then,
  without warning, Ofe turns on his heels and runs away. He is pursued by
  Ozidi across the arena and disappears into the earth at the foot of a silk
  cotton tree providing shade for much of the marketplace. Ozidi just
  manages to catch him by the feet. And, because Ofe has got his hands
  onto some prop roots inside the hole there is a tug of war between them
  both.*]

Ofe: [*struggling inside the hole.*] Fool, fool, you are pulling at
  The roots of the tree instead of at mine feet!
  [*Ozidi almost lets go, catching at roots in an attempt to grip what he
  thinks are Ofe's feet. At this Ofe gives another mocking scream.*]

Ofe: [*still half-inside the hole.*] Look at the bull with more muscles
  Than sense, he's grabbing at my feet and thinks
  He's uprooting our cotton tree!
  [*Thus taunted, Ozidi pulls up, quite baffled by the true identity of his
  enemy until his grandmother, left behind in the chase, arrives on the spot.*]

Oreame: What is this, Ozidi? Can't you tell
  The man's foot from root of the tree? Is it
  To such low subterfuge you now resort, Ofe?
  Come out quick, will you? Or shall
  We pull those stumpy legs of yours out by
  Their sockets? The man won't let go! Pull then,
  Ozidi, pull at the stumps in your hands!
  [*Ozidi gives a great tug, and Ofe comes scrambling out on all fours. He
  manages to kick Ozidi in the belly, sending him reeling back in sharp
  pain. Ofe looks frantically for his sword to finish off Ozidi, finds it where
  it fell, and rushes at Ozidi. He strikes home.*]
Ozidi: [*reeling before Ofe's onslaught.*] My hand, I feel faint in my
    hand! Oh,
  My hand's falling off!
Ofe: As I killed your father so shall I serve
  You. Now, woman, have I by the same blow
  Cut off your tongue?
  [*Three sharp claps of thunder break suddenly overhead, racing one another
  across the sky. All wince visibly, but the effect upon Oreame is like a bell
  to action.*]
Oreame: [*prancing.*] Agbraragbrururu! Agbraragbrururu!
  Your children are on the ground. There now,
  Ozidi, are you still faint when Tamara
  The Almighty Herself declares you fresh?
  Hold up your sword straight, man not
  Like a paddle in the hands of a landsman!
  [*Turning upon Ofe, she whips a number of articles out of her bag.*]
  And you Ofe, Tamara bids me serve you
  This dish, a dish most sweet to the tongue:
  Head of rat, head of yam you planted in
  Your backyard, and tip of plantain shoot
  Are all in this pot that never passed through
  The kiln. Eat, Ofe, eat of it
  To your fill for the gadfly has today entered into
  Your bowels and will gnaw them to bits.
  [*Ofe, his sword limp in his hand, tries to avoid seeing the fare set before
  him, but with Oreame literally swamping him on all sides, his efforts are
  hopeless, and his hands fall away from his eyes. Meanwhile Ozidi is
  aroused afresh. As he rallies, running Ofe to the ground, the orchestra
  takes up the cauldron music of his bowels.*]

Ofe: [*Ozidi deals him a blow and he falls writhing on the ground.*]
Suddenly, I'm cold, very cold.
My wives, are you there at my side?
I am cold, so cold, bring me hot water, do you hear me?
Bring hot water and bathe my brows running as a molten brook.
Ofe will fight no more,
No, no, not in this cold. . . .
It is in my feet, it fills out in my trunk,
Oh, my head swollen as a cask . . . out of this
Crack in the cask comes this cold . . . let
Me bathe myself in its shower.
[*Ozidi hacks Ofe to death and cuts off his head for the public to view. The sight is too much for the people; they rush away in a rout and Ozidi and Oreame are left alone in the deserted square. The old woman falls on her knees, overwhelmed by events and bewildered by her grandson who is possessed. Silently she watches the horn blower and other personal attendants follow him out, pleading for his return to normal.*]

ACT IV

Scene 1

Some time later in Ozidi's home. The young man is at breakfast. In comes his mother bringing him a small dish of palm oil with which to eat the yam in the soup. She is surprised to find him washing his hands.

Orea: Haven't you begun eating yet?
Ozidi: No: I have finished.
Orea: [*she goes over to look at the pot of food.*] Already? I don't see what
You've eaten: not even a morsel.
Ozidi: Hunger has no hold on me.
Orea: So you said yesterday; and
The day before it was the same story:
Hunger has no hold on you, you said, as
If hunger with death are no longer
Twin rulers of the world. Tell me, does
Your stomach ache?
Ozidi: I have told you, Mother, I have no pain.

Orea: Then why aren't you eating any more? I cooked
　　This pot of ukodo at your special request.
Ozidi: I know, but I find now I cannot eat it.
Orea: Is there not enough salt in it? Or
　　Is the pepper too weak on your tongue?
　　The fish in the soup has much flesh to it,
　　And little bone. It was a perch I bought
　　At great bargain against stiff bidding
　　From others. I didn't mind the money it cost me
　　As long as you ate well.
Ozidi: I am sorry, Mother; my tongue must
　　Be full of soot for everything is
　　Tasteless on its tip.
Orea: If my son will not eat of
　　The food I have cooked, and the other male in
　　The family is an old fool in bed refusing to die
　　So others can have rest,
　　Then I shall call in strangers from outside.
Ozidi: [*rising.*] Now, must you take it that way? Oh, how
　　Can a man go on and on from one day to another
　　With leading a life like this, a life of stone
　　Upon which one drop of rain is a great event.
　　The kingfisher plunges for his catch deep
　　In the riverbed, and only after a royal feed
　　Does he sit on the bough by the bank
　　Nodding welcome and warning to wayfarers, each
　　To his own calling and inclination.
　　I cannot farm or fish; nor as others
　　Exchange fruits from both for profit. I was born
　　With sword to hand, fists clenched firm for fight. This course
　　I have followed without deviation
　　Doing my duty by my dead father. But now
　　Like a river at a whirlpool I am come to
　　A spinning stop. Worse, like a lion plucked clean of
　　His whiskers, I growl now only in my sleep.
Orea: I knew you were hungry all right,
　　But not for common food like other men.
　　It is for more fights you are famished, yes,
　　All Orua knows that, but I am not going
　　To let you feed fat again on such desire.
　　Your father is fully avenged,

And after second burial, sleeps well in company
  Of his compeers.
Ozidi: Yes, my father sleeps well but what
  About me? I only have to step out and children
  Are running to hide their faces in between the feet
  Of their mothers. When I appear on the wrestling ground,
  Even the iguanas that teach them tricks at Tuomo scamper at
      sight.
  Oh yes, my father, all set up now and free from the grove of
      night,
  Sleeps well indeed, while I walk here awake, for
  I have only to close my eyes and heads of those
  I have slaughtered tumble forth, rolling and
  Hopping about my feet like huge jiggers
  Screaming to suck my blood.
  [*Ewiri appears, sums up the scene, and waits outside by the door.*]
Orea: After the purification
  Rites we have done, you still have terrible dreams?
Ozidi: Only last night I had another,
    This time, of Engbesibeoru,
    The great Scrotum King himself. Without warning,
    He rolled up to my doorstep and asked for fire to light
    His pipe and water to wash his throat. These
    I gave him, and when he had finished after much
    Dithering and delay, I said to him which way was
    He going. "Oh, no other place but here,"
    Says he. "As a matter of fact, Ozidi, it is you
    I have come to fetch."
Orea: The gods forbid!
Ozidi: What for? I asked, And
    Says he between puffs of his pipe: "To eat you of course,
    For despoiling the land."
Orea: Ozidi, we must send home for Mother at once.
Ozidi: Laughing a little, I made to pass the old man,
    But there he stood with his great big bag and burden
    Filling the whole doorway, and before I knew what,
    I was on the ground dead drunk from repeated punches
    Over all my body and head delivered
    By Engbesibeoru.
Orea: Did he carry you off? Tell me,
    Did the monster?

Ozidi: As usual, it was our mother saved me.
  I think I must have moaned for her in my helplessness,
  For in she flew just when the Scrotum King,
  Like the irrepressible bundle of rubber he is,
  Was bounding about the whole place,
  Boasting he had left the son of Oreame
  Prostrate as marsh-meat for supper.
  "You lie!" Our mother shut him up that instant,
  And turning to me gave me a bow. With the one arrow to it
  I shot at the great big ball then spinning on
  Rebound in midair, and behold, at its
  Bursting a heavy shower broke loose over the field,
  Flooding the place out. We almost drowned in it.
Orea: [*laughing in spite of all.*] You mean you two were unable to
    swim, just like
  The Urhobo
  Who wax strong only when on land?
Ozidi: [*piqued.*] This was a dream, and we almost drowned in it,
  I tell you, but for our mother raising a chant
  Like this: "A man dead ends up on the earth; a man
  Dead rots on the ground. This break out of water,
  Is it so we may not pass? Here, dry up,
  You stretch of water!" And so where
  She struck with her magic fan a dry causeway
  Rose up like the manatee out of water
  And led us home.
Orea: [*hands folded across her breast.*] A terrible dream, Ozidi. We
  must consult
  The oracle or send for mother.
Ewiri: [*stepping forward.*] Save your money, Orea.
Ozidi and Orea: [*together, and with a start.*] Ewiri!
  When did you come in?
Ewiri: Oh, yes, I walked up while you two
  Were wrapped in talk. I said to myself, now, don't you break in
  On this most domestic scene; it's between
  A dutiful son and a patient mother;
  And there's nothing as sweet and close as that
  In the whole wide world; no, not even the accord
  Between husband and wife, between father and child.
  Only between woman and the issue of her womb

Does there persist such union, one the umbilical
Cord forged. I always say between its cutting at
Delivery and burial under the eaves
There's a great gesture of human denial and
Deceit dogging man all his life.
Orea: Why, Ewiri, would you have it hung out to dry
And then worn about the neck as a string of pearls?
Ewiri: Not a bad thought at all, not a bad one. It
Should teach youth to whom they belong.
Ozidi: That sounds to me
More like a chain tied to a dog's neck. But did
You say you have powers to decipher dreams?
Ewiri: No special powers, boy, no secret
Powers whatsoever. I do not boast of
Strange possessions; such things we leave to your grandmother.
It's common sense alone I wield to effect.
And armed by that I have been
Amananaowei of Orua
How many times now you can ask me and I wouldn't
Be able to tell you.
Ozidi: [*inducing him to get to the point.*] Will you have a drink first?
Orea: Yes, there's
Some wine in the house, freshly tapped.
Ewiri: Is there bark of *ugu* in it?
Ozidi: Yes, plenty of it.
Ewiri: Then I will drink a cup, just one cup, I
Assure you, for I still have not eaten
My morning meal, and it's a fool who feeds drink
First to an empty belly. That reminds me, Orea
Did we hear you say the boy will not eat?
We are a dung pit, you know, and will not refuse
What others throw away, yes,
A veritable beach; we refuse no canoe
Berthing space.
Orea: You want food, Ewiri? Here then, sit down
And eat your fill. I was going to call in strangers
Or give it all to goats in the compound.
Ewiri: [*settling himself down and falling to.*] So we have come in good
    time—have we—
To save the day our warrior there would ruin?

Ozidi: [*serving him drink.*] Just in time, Ewiri.
  We were receiving terrible terms already
  When you came in.
Orea: Look at him; he's not ashamed.
Ewiri: [*stops drinking.*] He is a wonderful boy, a wonderful boy
  Orua is proud of. [*He belches.*] Who said a good wine
  Needs no bush? I say, add one good thing to another
  And you get gold. It is for that we seek
  Our offsprings worthy partners in marriage.
Ozidi: [*getting impatient.*] Now for the meaning of my dream, Ewiri;
      are
  You going to tell us that, or shall we to
  The oracle after all?
Ewiri: But I have told you already!
Ozidi: When was that?
    [*Ewiri winks at Orea who seems to have caught on with him for both
    begin laughing at Ozidi, who is still baffled.*]
Ozidi: It is a riddle then you'll unravel
  My dream with?
Orea: Go on, tell him so he can hear it from mouths
  Other than mine. Tell him, Ewiri what has
  Been talk of the town these many market-tides.
Ewiri: A wife, Ozidi,
  A wife is what you need! So you go gruff
  And glum at that? What else did
  You think your dream of the great Scrotum King
  Meant? All the signs and symptoms are for your taking
  A wife now, Ozidi. When you go out,
  Don't you ever see a girl that catches your eye?
  Don't tell me you don't see them swinging hips
  Whenever you pass by. Why, I have myself seen some
  Lead you on by the length of their budding breasts.
  Are you so blind a cockerel you don't see all those hens
  Preening their beautiful feathers wherever you walk?
  Or shall we believe, like the giant eunuchs that guard
  The Oba of Benin, you are all bulk and no balls
  Between your thighs?
    [*Ozidi dismisses him with a wave of the hand.*]
Orea: There, see him, Ewiri; speak with him
  So he can hear the stories others are carrying
  About him. He will not listen to me.

Ozidi: They can say what they like about me; it is not
   Of things like that I am thinking.
Orea: Of course it is of fights alone you think.
Ewiri: If that's all the obstacle, it should be
   Easy to clear. A little fight now and again
   Does the cub no harm; in fact it's the one thing
   To burnish his mane. And to speak the bitter Ijaw truth,
   I came here to deliver a message of
   Allied interest.
Orea: How's that Ewiri? You aren't
   Seeking to involve him in a fresh fight? Better leave
   My house at once now, now, if that's your intention.
Ozidi: Mother, let the man speak. Your message, Ewiri.
Ewiri: Well, it really is
   From Tebesonoma of the seven heads.
   Just this early morning, I was passing by
   His lonely cottage where his terrible
   Character confines him far out of town,
   When what should come to my ears but commotion as
   A market. First, I thought of a wake of witches,
   Then of spirits in session; but keeping my ears
   Close to the ground and my eyes to the sky, just
   As collectors of nuts look up at the ripening bunch atop
   The palmtree, I discovered that commotion
   Issued from the seven heads of Tebesonoma,
   His multiple hands sweeping the earth like fronds.
Ozidi: And man, what was he saying?
Ewiri: Oh, you know how
   It is with him of the seven heads: some then
   Were shouting, some shooting, some in dialogue,
   Some working, some drinking and eating
   On that figure of his staggered as
   The boughs of the silk cotton tree, at the center of which
   Was one crowing as a cock; while about
   Him were several marketing, some
   Laughing, some fighting, and others singing,
   All giving forth that great commotion I told you of—
Ozidi: And his message, Ewiri,
   The man's message?
Ewiri: He speaks in seven tongues, you must
   Remember. But if my ears caught it all,

The seven had but one message: a fight
With Ozidi to decide the strongest
In town and forest.
Orea: [*clapping hands in Ewiri's face.*] Ozidi will not fight! He'll do no
    such thing!
Now get out of here, get out now
Before I break my broom on your head of farina.
If a man does not grow tall, must his senses
Also be stunted? The dwarf you are, now
Get out of here, I say.
[*She pushes out Ewiri protesting loud into the distance.*]
Ewiri: [*speaking at counterpoint to her.*]
Why, woman, will you kill me a poor messenger
For carrying the word? What will you
With the man contemplating the act?
Your son wants food, and have I done wrong
Showing him prospects of a feast?
People of Orua, you come and be judge!
Ozidi: [*running out after them.*] Wait, Ewiri,
Wait! Take a message back to Tebesonoma—
Tell him on any day that he chooses
Ozidi shall be at hand to crop all
His seven heads to the ground. Any day,
Any place, let him name it.

Scene 2

*In the forest outside Orua. Ozidi, together with his sword bearer and horn
blower, is trussed up and being dragged on the ground by Tebesonoma who
looks more or less as Ewiri described him in the previous scene. The man is
in high spirits having apparently done a good day's job, so that he enters
singing and dancing to his personal tune of Kpare nama yo yo yo. After-
wards, he leaves his captive lying on the ground, strutting round him, teasing
and taunting.*

Tebesonoma: Is this the famous Ozidi stories of whom
    Will not let me sit back on my own buttocks?
    I cannot raise hand to mouth but his stories
    Are spoiling my meal of the day; I cannot lift

A cup to lip but they are spilling my drink with stories of Ozidi.
Most insolent of all, he sends me message
Through that man Ewiri that vegetable man that I am,
Sprouting about branches in one idle spot,
I should dare move one step and he'll clip me
By my several crowns to the ground. Well,
Tell us, boy, who is on the ground now? Who lies
Trussed up like an alligator? With one hand
I took him captive, with the other I swept
His men together as sticks to a broom
And before his mother at market could hear his cry,
I was off on my way to a solid meal. How do
You like that, Ozidi? I am going to eat
You up today, you know that. Your bowels, I hear,
Boil over with power of seven pots, but today
My one pot shall silence all that. And if
As they say you are in the trickster's habit
Of swallowing up your sword, you'd better spring
It out now. I want a decent meal, no pieces of iron grating
Between my teeth, none sticking in our throat. Well aren't
You going to say a word, even by way of
A last request? I might be disposed to grant
A reasonable request, you know. I see,
The man is playing the ram: he's being led
Into captivity; still he refuses to cry for help,
All in stupid belief that one man cannot carry home
Another! Well, see how I do it!
[*He picks up the free end of the rope with which he has bound up Ozidi
and his attendants, and giving them a series of kicks, resumes his march.*]
Ozidi: [*with an involuntary shudder.*] Ay, my mother!
Tebesonoma: Call for her, poor suckling boy, call for
Your mother and let's see whether she can hear
And get you out of this.
[*Before he finishes his lines, there is a noise of an airplane coming in to
land—with a surge and noise so close Tebesonoma drops his load to put
hands to ears.*]
Tebesonoma: [*turning round in one place.*] Now, what strange bird is
this? What bird
Hurtles through our forest?
Oreame: [*touching ground with the air of* Fine yamabo.] It is I! It is I
Oreame!

[*Ozidi's men give her a great shout of welcome and relief, but Tebesonoma is too taken by surprise to speak.*]

Oreame: [*pursuing her advantage home.*] Tebesonoma, because I moved
    to Ododama,
Did you think I have like a lazy nightwatchman
Fallen asleep? There, may your feet turn to roots, and
Your arms droop to earth—yes, like branches of
A tree blasted!
    [*She runs off to where Ozidi lies trussed up.*]

Tebesonoma: [*transfixed to one place.*] Unscrupulous woman, release me
    and
I'll fight your son man to man!

Oreame: [*releasing Ozidi.*] What's this—a pig fattened
And being taken to market for slaughter? Wake up,
Ozidi, wake up! Is this how you fare
Immediately my back is turned?

Tebesonoma: [*trying in vain to free himself.*] He called the fight,
    Oreame.

Ozidi: That's a lie; you called it. Ewiri
Can testify to that.

Tebesonoma: Ewiri? It was he told me
You wanted a fight.

Oreame: He tricked you both, the tortoise!
But better finish off the fight today
Than clash on another: this forest cannot contain
Two champion lions.

Ozidi: [*trembling, his bowels beginning to boil in growing rage.*] He came
    upon me asleep in the sun.

Tebesonoma: Free me, and I'll take your son full awake.

Oreame: [*snapping her fingers and releasing him.*] There!
    [*They fight. Ozidi's cauldron music fills the place. He crops off six heads
    from Tebesonoma, one after the other.*]

Tebesonoma: [*falling on his knees.*] Now Ozidi, don't cut off this one
    head! It's
My one crown left to me. The rest you've struck down
Like pumpkins. So spare me this single piece.
You see me, an old man, on my knees to you; now
Is that not honor enough to you born
Only yesterday?
    [*Ozidi relents.*]

Oreame: Not so, my son! This cannot happen! I
  Was tending at home a client bleeding to death when
  Tebesonoma dragged me forth. And do
  You want to let him go who brought you here,
  Your feet trailing dirt?
Tebesonoma: With my one crown on I still can wrestle
  Your son down, if you'll keep out of matters
  Concerning men.
Oreame: What manner of man are you, falling on
  Your knees in the middle of a fight? Next
  You will be taking to your heels, the cock
  You are!
Tebesonoma: [*leaping to his feet.*] Not I! Now are you coming, boy?
     Your mother
  Refuses to be satisfied until you are killed.
Ozidi: Come on then; it's I will kill you.
  [*They fight afresh. Ozidi weakens Tebesonoma, stalking him on all sides
  with such speed his blows fall in thin air.*]
Oreame: [*angry.*] This cock any housewife can knock out
  With one blow of her kitchen knife—is it
  What throws sand in your eyes, Ozidi?
  [*Turning on Tebesonoma and feeding him with corn from her satchel.*]
  Here's for all fowls of the earth! What fowl
  Ever withstood sight of corn? Eat,
  Eat of our ripe corn scattered free at your feet.
  [*Tebesonoma is distracted. As he bends down trying to pick up the grains
  of corn, Ozidi rallies to his music.*]
Ozidi: [*dealing the man swiping blows.*] Die, die, Tebesonoma!
Tebesonoma: [*in death struggle.*] This is not the end, Ozidi,
  This is not the end. I may die,
  Unfairly killed between you and your witch of a mother,
  But I shall be avenged. In the next town lives a woman
  Just delivered of a son . . . she is my sister
  . . . Take it from me, Ozidi, except you murder them too,
  Twenty years from now, as you did
  With your father's assassins, you shall be called to account,
  Compelled to cross the river against all tide. . . .
Oreame: [*feeding out more grain.*] Eat your corn, eat them whole.
     When a fowl has
  Been wrung by the neck, its wings beat

On ground. But only for a while; they cannot
Gather wind again to smother a fly.
[*Ozidi cuts off the neck of Tebesonoma and leads his party out in a dance
to the tune of* Kpe kpe timi koru we.]

Scene 3

*Ozidi and Oreame, direct from their encounter with Tebesonoma, arrive at
the house of Tebesonoma's sister. Ozidi simulates a running knock on the
open door by both sound of mouth and clap of hands. A woman, of about
forty and of a spread not simply of middle age, emerges from the dark of the
room and receives them.*

Woman: [*surprised at seeing strangers at her door.*] Are you looking for
   some person?
Ozidi: Yes; does
   The sister of Tebesonoma live here?
Woman: That's right; and you don't have to ask
   Another, for I am she.
Ozidi: I see.
Woman: And you are?
Ozidi: Tebesonoma asked us to call.
Woman: You are his friends then? I hope
   He has not been courting trouble again? He's always
   Fighting, you know, that terrible brother of mine.
   But won't you come in, all of you?
Ozidi: Well, yes—
Oreame: [*interrupting him.*] No, I am sorry; we cannot
   Come in.
Woman: My elder, I kneel to you. Do come into
   The house.
Oreame: It's not possible; I am
   Outside bound.
Woman: [*looking at her closely.*] The true Ijaw thing?
Oreame: Young woman, do I look too old to see
   My period?
Ozidi: Mother, the woman was not abusing you.
Woman: I thank you, young man. How can I do
   A thing like that? Everything flows from

The hands of Tamara. Why, look at me here:
After twenty-three years of marriage,
It has just pleased Oyin to grant me my first child,
And for that my belly is full of delight.
Ozidi: We would share your joy with you
But we are in a hurry.
Woman: Oh not in so great a great hurry that
You can't step in for a little while when you
Are friends of my brother. His blame of me
For that will never end. And my husband,
He's just gone into the bush not very far out
To inspect his ponds whether or not the water in them
Has fallen to a level sufficient to bail them for fish.
You must wait for him till he comes home
For he too will not forgive me if he hears you came
And went as the wind.
Ozidi: [*turning to Oreame.*] Well, Mother shall we stop a little?
Woman: Elder mine, stop with us however short, while
We find you something to drink and eat.
Oreame: It is not that I wish to spoil your stomach;
The bitter Ijaw truth is that we have not
Come to be entertained. So leave the gourd where
It is, and cut no plantains for the pot.
Woman: Then what will you have? [*To a young man who has just come in.*]
These are friends of my brother Tebesonoma.
Run off quick like a dog and tell your brother
Guests have descended on us. [*To Ozidi.*] He's my husband's
    younger brother
And therefore father-of-my-marriage.
[*To the young man.*] Now run, and don't stop everywhere like
A dog to pick up bones.
[*Her child begins to cry inside the room and she goes in to tend it.*]
Oreame: [*to Ozidi.*] Are you a dog that you waggle tail
At every fond whistle? Have you no work to do?
Ozidi: [*sullen.*] Did I say I forgot it?
Oreame: [*stamping her feet.*] Then do it.
Woman: [*returning with baby at her breast.*] Naw, naw, naw, my
    schweet schweet lil'le man,
Itsh no good cryin' like thish,

No, itsh not manly at all. And before vishitorz too?
Naw, what do you exshpect them to shay? That men
Of these partsh cry like women?
[*She turns to her guests.*] He's just two market-tides today. That's
why
You successfully got us out at all;
We have been indoors seven whole days. Now isn't
He beautiful?
Ozidi: [*unable to resist approving.*] Yes; very beautiful.
Woman: Wasn't he worth waiting twenty-three years for?
He's the image of his father who should be with us
Any moment now.
Oreame: I told you, young woman,
You must not take the trouble to entertain us.
Woman: [*sweetly.*] Why?
Oreame: Because we have come for
Your son and you.
Woman: [*amazed.*] You've come for my son and me?
Why, I don't understand.
Ozidi: Your brother Tebesonoma has just fought a duel with me.
Look, it was a straight fight between us.
Woman: You fought my brother? Then you are not
His friends? Tell me, was he injured?
Oreame: [*walking off.*] He dropped his breath in the sand.
Woman: Oh, my brother! So you killed him,
And now you have come for my son and me?
Ozidi: [*confused.*] That was what he said
Before he fell by my sword. But be not afraid;
I shall not kill you, nor your son.
Woman: [*increasingly hysterical.*] All you people, come and see my lot!
The stranger says he'll not slay my son, nor me anymore?
Yet he has killed my brother already. Oh, come
And hear my story!
[*Hugging her child to breast, she bursts into the lament and alarm song
Ama me lulou fie me* while neighbors stream in on all sides,
surrounding her and her assailants.*]
Neighbors Together: What's the matter?
Who assails you?
Did you say your brother is killed?
Not your son,
He's not seized by sun ones already, is he?

Oreame: [*furious with Ozidi.*] Fool, fool, see what bees you've
   Plucked about our heads.
Ozidi: Let me be! I don't want to kill anybody again.
Woman: No, no, no, look, the hawks have scattered our brood.
   Oh, they'll even kill him, my child I awaited
   For twenty-three years, they'll as surely kill him
   As they have my brother. Now, is there
   None here will go and call my man? Is there nobody
   Will tie to my back the cloth of my child?
Neighbors: [*closing upon Ozidi and Oreame.*] Is it true what she says?
   What kind of people are you
   Attacking a poor woman?
   She's with child, don't you see that?
   Nobody touches her while we are here!
Oreame: [*holds her fan up.*] There! There!
   [*The neighbors all fall back, dazed and gasping with recognition.*]
Neighbors: It's Oreame! The witch herself! And that's Ozidi her son!
   Between them they've emptied towns untold!
   Now, spare us of this town
   We've done you no wrong!
Oreame: [*laughing.*] You put too much water in the wine.
   [*To Ozidi.*] To work! To work!
   [*She slaps him with the fan thus arousing him.*]
A Neighbor: [*running in.*] A terrible thing has happened! A terrible
    thing!
   Out of the clear sky has fallen a thunderbolt.
   At one stroke, it ploughed a path all the way
   To where Agonosin stood by a pond, mowing him down
   To earth. If you'll come out, all the bush
   Is burning about him, and not the entire town
   Bearing pots of water can put out the fire.
Woman: [*reeling.*] Oh, my husband!
   [*Some of her neighbors run to support her, others turn upon Oreame.*]
The Neighbors Together: There—she did it!
   She flung the bolt on its errand!
   Oh, woman, why destroy a whole house like this?
Woman: [*brushing aside help.*] No help now:
   Our forest lies completely level with the earth at last.
   Come, my boy, let us also die down. What need have
   We to stand up when silk-cotton trees lie prostrate?
   We are reeds only, mere reeds in the storm, and must

Stretch our broken backs on the ground. The good
Mother earth will not deny us.
[*She lays herself down on the ground, her son crying on her breast. She
tries to rock him silently by resuming her lament song. The neighbors all
accompany her, throwing a huge circle about her, Ozidi and Oreame,
which crowds all four of them from sight. Then with one gasp of horror
they break away revealing in the middle mother and son dead on the
ground in the middle. Oreame and Ozidi have vanished.*]

Scene 4

*In a bedroom in Ozidi's compound. It is late at night. From the faint light
of an oil-lamp burning very low at one corner a figure can be seen sleeping
in a bed against the wall to the right. Through a door to the left another
comes in, walking across the floor to the bed, startling its occupant.*]

Figure in Bed: [*a female voice.*] Who is that?
The Other: It's I!
The Woman: Who's I? Has the person no name?
The Other: It's I, Ozidi!
The Woman: What do you want here?
Ozidi: You guess!
The Woman: You have no right to come in here.
  I am another's wife.
Ozidi: Not now: you are mine.
The Woman: You have paid no money on my head.
Ozidi: You are mine by possession.
The Woman: I am no slave
  You bought in the marketplace.
Ozidi: Oh no;
  You are the most beautiful bead of coral man ever set eyes on,
  And I have
  Carried you off from your husband, a creature too
  Ugly to wear you on his chest.
The Woman: How dare you?
  How dare you say such things about Odogu?
  He's my husband, most handsome, and when
  He gets to hear of this, he'll come and
  Set fire to your house, to all your town,

And not a rat out of the whole lot of you shall
Escape death by fire.
Ozidi: Oh, will he? Let the gorilla come then—
After I have eaten of his banana.
[*He touches her breast.*]
The Woman: [*beating his hand off.*] Keep off, keep off! How dare you
touch me?
Now will you keep off? I am another's wife,
Wife to Odogu, I've told you!
[*Ozidi does not listen to her but goes on to fondle her haunches, taking
her into his arms—very clumsily, so that the woman frees herself with
ease in the course of the next lines.*]
Ozidi: [*hardly audible in the state he's in.*] The ropes of man are
tugging at me.
The Woman: Are they? Then pull back at them;
I am another's wife although by you set adrift.
Ozidi: No, not adrift:
You are my boat and I am restless to tether you to my post.
The Woman: [*who has extricated herself.*] Tether me—with those hands
trembling
Like reeds in the tide?
Ozidi: [*angry.*] Are you abusing us?
The Woman: [*collapsing in one corner and bursting into lament.*] I did not
abuse you, Ozidi, I did not.
Oh, poor lost girl caught like a dragonfly by the stream,
Do wail, do wail,
Oh poor lost girl cut adrift like a boat on the stream,
Do wail, do wail,
Wrappers of your man you were washing in a basin by the beach
Do wail, do wail,
The wind among the mangrove woods was in your ears
Do wail, do wail,
And without warning your captor came upon you on your knees
Do wail, do wail,
With one paw of his sealing your lips, he bore you off with the
other,
Do wail, do wail,
Who knew it was to this?
Who knew it was to displace Odogu at your side
—Odogu with eyes bigger than the mud-skippers,

Odogu of shins vast as buttress of the bombax tree,
Oh poor lost girl, do wail, do wail!
Ozidi: [*more in horror than disgust.*] Please put on your dress, and I'll
take you back to your man.
Quick! and stop stirring up the whole town.
All this for a man more forbidding than a god
Carved to keep guard at the gate! No more please;
Dress up and I'll take you back myself, yes, now.
The Woman: See how he'd pack me off like a little dog
To her keeper the moment I cry out! See him,
This man who says he wants me!
Ozidi: I am not kicking you out as a dog,
But I cannot bear you barking.
The Woman: Aren't you such a child! Do you really
Mean you have heard no barking like this before?
Ozidi: I am not a child! I am a man full grown,
One that has performed feats more than your husband.
The Woman: Now, shall we keep your mouth off my husband?
Really, you are a child.
Ozidi: War is no occupation for children:
So stop calling me child.
The Woman: Women after war—is that not the way with men?
Ozidi: Not for me
And will my mother let me forget it!
"Time you took a wife," she wakes me up morning after morning,
And at night it is the same story:
"Take a wife, take a wife, Ozidi." I suppose it was
That pushed me on to swooping down on you at the streamside.
You see, if she could, she would check on
My early morning stirring.
The Woman: Here, come and sit by me;
No, you may on my laps, leaning against me;
Yes, like that, like that! How light you are!
And is this how you tremble before battle!
See, my palm can almost reach round your wrist;
Indeed; you are not at all big of bones, Ozidi.
Ozidi: [*confused.*] Man—he does not depend
Alone on size of body to be strong of bones.
The Woman: And are these the hands have
Plucked down so many trees in the forest?
Ozidi: Not me really, but the storm

They flogged up themselves pulled them down.
And of course my grandmother, she is
The sea that fills my stream.
The Woman: So I have heard it said;
  Stories of her and you have come like
  The river in flood to our part and quite past it.
  And may another not know how you do it,
  How you wash all your opponents
  Like logs and debris downstream?
Ozidi: No, no, not that.
The Woman: Yes, yes, why not? Oh, come now, play with me,
  Or is it the dragonfly shall race its catcher?
Ozidi: Now there isn't much room here to run, is there?
The Woman: Oh my terrible captor, you turn the bed into a field!
Ozidi: Do I, indeed, do I?
The Woman: [*edging away and yet staying in his arms.*] And what you
    promised—are you
  Going to give what you promised?
Ozidi: What is it now I promised? You know there is
  Nothing you want in the world and I will not
  Bring it to your feet.
The Woman: The secret to your success—
Ozidi: [*weakly.*] You want that—whatever for?
The Woman: So now I am your wife I can keep it under lock.
Ozidi: [*drowsily.*] And until we hand over our key
  You'll not lead us through those gates of gold?
The Woman: Nobody spoke of such an exchange. Really, you make
  Everything sound so cheap!
Ozidi: [*jumping to his feet.*] No, I don't; it is you made it so. True,
  I took you captive as I would a canary, but if
  At dawn no song comes out of the cage, I can only
  Coax the bird; I cannot force one from its throat.
  But a tune at a price, that is another thing.
The Woman: [*also getting up.*] Are you calling me a harlot?
Ozidi: Not long ago,
  I said to put on your clothes and go.
  This time, I shall not turn you loose
  To seek more subjects of taboo so you can
  Foul up a stream of men.
The Woman: Suddenly, you've gone strange, Ozidi. What's on your
    mind?

I am the wife of Odogu! Lay your hands on me,
And you are dead underground.
Ozidi: [*seizing her and dragging her out.*] He or I, it will be one of us
    walking there soon;
  But before then I must make
  Sacrifice to my shrine you sought to defile.
The Woman: [*ululating.*] You are not going to kill me, are you?
  Murder, people of Orua, murder in your midst!
  The man will kill me—I am wife to Odogu
  He wanted by force—this man crowing like
  A cock with a crest none ever saw
  Flaming but in fight! He's going to kill me,
  And will nobody come outdoors and stop him?
  [*So, protesting, she is pulled outside by Ozidi into the night. A pause
  during which doors can be heard opening and feet running in a hurry from
  all sides. Later the frantic voice of Orea.*]
Orea: Leave the woman alone, Ozidi!
  Now is there nothing else you can do but kill?
  Oh, no more sleep for us again in this house.

Scene 5

Storyteller: The sun is going down fast, and now
  We are in a field littered with bodies
  Of supporters from both sides in the battle
  Between Odogu the Ugly and
  Ozidi over the woman he abducted.
  Cauldron music to the left, cauldron music
  To the right; for as the bowels of Ozidi
  Boil over in rage from the mortar-and-pestle charm
  So do the bowels of Odogu. Unknown to either,
  The old wizard of the forset Bouakarakarabiri
  Or Tebekawene, as some call him after
  His habit of walking on his head, has invested
  The other with his celebrated master charm,
  Thus creating our deadlock. So for several days
  They buffeted each other without stop: they fought with swords,
  They fought with sticks, they fought with stones, and tiring of
    weapons,
  They grappled with hands: wrestling, rolling times out

Of number from one end of the field to the other
And so back again, till the fire went out of them,
And like two motor vehicles in head-on collision,
One fell in shambles to this side and
The other to that side, both their drivers stepping out
More angry than injured.
[*Suiting mime to words, he falls one way while Odogu who is hovering behind falls to the other. Instantly, two old women spring into sight flying at each other: one is our old friend Oreame, the other Azema, mother of Odogu. Her face perpetually fixed in the sky, she carries a crown of volcano, her teeth dripping with blood of victims she has eaten raw.*]

Oreame: Thief that you are, you stole
My son's master charm to give to yours!

Azema: You lie! It is you have stolen the charm
I bought at the hand of Bouakarakarabiri.

Oreame: So he sold it to you, the double-dealer! But
You wait and I'll show you I am
Oreame of the innumerable plumes.

Azema: Go shake your lice-infested feathers in
The face of some other person.

Oreame: I am Oreame; don't you know that, Azema?
I walk through walls of rock to reach the hearts of men;
Doors barred with locks of steel fly open at
One graze of my back; and in the hollow of my hand lie bolts
I can fling about me on lightning errand.
Now shall I strike you down, shall I
Before my son finally rams yours to death?

Azema: Try it, try it, and you will see there are lots
Of trees in the forest.

Oreame: And I am the tallest, admit it,
The tallest tree in all the forest!
[*The two witches fight. Azema tears at Oreame's hair. She seizes upon her head to bite it off with her cannibal teeth. Oreame cries her off and flies above her head of fire. Oreame turns herself into a tsetsefly, sticking needles and pins at Azema: streams of blood in the air. Azema develops a headache, she flakes Oreame with sparks of fire, Oreame replying with a shower of sand. Both witches are driving themselves to a standstill as did their sons when a loud peal of laughter breaks from the forest. Both witches recognize it immediately as of the old wizard of the forest Bouakarakarabiri, and they break off, listening intently.*]

The Wizard: [*still laughing.*] Two hens fallen out on a field under

Another wing, I am the hornbill,
I am the hornbill in flight.
Where housewives are at fight,
Forgetful of the leaf at the foot of the hill,
There I fly, out there I fly,
Sitting on the hilltop,
Cheering from the hilltop
Not that hen scratching the sand,
But she that finds
And fetches the leaf,
The leaf upon which the hill stands.
[*The witches stare at each other; then without a word they engage
themselves in a race to fetch the magic leaf. A short interval during which
the orchestra plays the tune* Oreame poka poka erema. *On the repeat,
Oreame returns triumphant with a herb between her teeth. This she
squeezes into the eyes of Ozidi still collapsed on one side.*]

Oreame: Now rise, my son, rise and swallow up
This last morsel to our feast!
[*Ozidi rears up in a fresh frenzy and she rushes off to Odogu where he
lies, prodding him up.*]
And you ugly lump in our passage,
Get gone! Roll down the pit! Your mother, unavoidably
Held back at market, bade me deliver you this frog,
This redbreast, this egg knocking at the center.
[*Odogu jumps up incensed, meeting Ozidi halfway. Their bowels in
conflict rage afresh and they fight with great fury.*]

Oreame: [*taunting Odogu more.*] Won't you accept your wares, the
wares
Your mother sent you from market?
[*Turning on her son.*] Let not one morsel defeat you!
[*Ozidi cuts Odogu down, blinded by the herb that gained him
ascendance, he mows down his own grandmother as well. His horn blower
sounds the alarm and disaster, followed by the full orchestra with the tune*
Due-ama me egberi. *Having gone completely berserk, Ozidi staggers
out shouting his name.*]

Oreame: [*crawling dazedly on the ground.*] Oh, what an end! What an
end!
To fall by the hand of my own son here.
I held up a shield for mine and myself
Against all comers, but none for me
Against him—my son, my son!

[*Oreame falls back on her haunches, with one hand trying to stop her scarlet cap of many feathers from falling, the other reaching in vain for her magic fan that has dropped. Dying, she catches a handful of earth and at the same time digs the ground with her left big toe.*]

ACT V

A Twin Scene

The scene should be played on two parallel planes, the movements of one flowing into the other and back again as the action and the occasion demand.

On the left half of the area of play is the waterside and beach of Orua. It is nightfall. A steady drizzle adds a misty screen. Just visible in the wan light to the center is the tall white flag to the sky-god Tamara, wet and limp in a faint wind.

The song Kono kiri yowe yo inyo *floats on the wind above the sound of the waves sucking and licking the keels of the craft. These boats, which are moored to posts, show as interlocking shadows in flight on the beach. The song swells and, in a very short time, comes to flood the place.*

Coming into view at its crest is a party of players in a double dance formation representing the moving barge of Engarando, the Smallpox King. He is an imposing figure in charcoal colors and clothes and is borne shoulder-high in the middle. Among the members of his retinue and crew are Cold, Cough, Headache, Spots, Fever, all led by his younger brothers Egirigiri and Okrikpakpa, one facing forwards and the other looking back. The result is a deliberate revolving dance with the row of men on the left gunwale paddling in one direction and those on the right side in the opposite. Covering the beach of Orua end to end three times, the royal barge of Engarando eventually docks at the section owned by Ozidi. The party then gives forth a great war chant (recording of Orua kile *or praise chant). After this, they relapse into silence, the figures falling into sitting positions, all huddled together and merging into the night and mist.*

To the right at the same time emerges the house of Ozidi. Orea, an old woman now and wearing deep black mourning dress, sits by a low lamp on the verandah, which opens along its full length into the living room. Her cheek is sunk in the palm of her left hand which she holds at the elbow with her other hand lying across drawn-up knees. She is a desolate figure staring anxiously into the dark and drizzle. All about her is quiet except for the

*rain water falling drop by drop from the roof thatch into a basin under the
eaves outside.*

    *A few drops later Ozidi walks in from the night and the rain, his
clothes of mourning bedraggled and dripping and making a distinct swishing
sound. He goes past his mother without a word.*

Orea: [*rising and following him.*] Is it in the rain you have been
    walking, Ozidi?
  Couldn't you take cover in some place until
  It stopped raining?
  [*Ozidi says nothing but walks up the long sitting dais of mud covered
  with a Kano cloth by the wall to the right. He flops down on it without
  first removing his clothes. He puts his head in his hands.*]
Orea: [*coming up to him.*] Did you walk into some spirit or wizard
    out there
  In the dark and rain that you have lost
  Tongue and voice? Tell me, what happened?
Ozidi: Nothing.
Orea: Yes, nothing.
  And where have you been that you are so wet?
Ozidi: Oh, only to the waterside. The rain
  Comes down there as one heavy sheet hung from the sky, and
  The stream is one continuous run to the sea.
Orea: I see. Now what about removing these
  Wet clothes of yours before you catch a cold?
Ozidi: [*struggling to stifle a sneeze.*] A cold? I feel brittle like bone.
  [*He begins to remove his clothes.*]
Orea: [*watching him fumble.*] Here, let me help you. But you are hot,
  Burning hot, Ozidi! Like a child, you stay
  Out in the rain, but a child dances in the shower, you know,
  And in that way scatters the wetness and chill off
  His back, whereas you have done nothing but soak it up.
  Surely, you'll be the death of us all.
Ozidi: [*with a hollow laugh from the folds of his dress.*] There's nothing
    else
  I know how to do, is there?
Orea: What happened has happened as Tamara
  Set it out. So stop twisting my tongue.
  Now what's all this, Ozidi, what's this all
  Over your body?
  [*She goes over to fetch the lamp.*]

Ozidi: What is it you have found? Oh, how
My head echoes me.
Orea: [*looking him over.*] There is a riot of rashes breaking over
Your body I cannot quite make out.
Ozidi: [*shrugging his shoulders.*] Oh, it's nothing.
Orea: [*running her hand over his skin.*] You have eaten no electric fish
lately?
Ozidi: You cook all my meals, Mother.
Orea: And a lot of it you eat. Your rashes,
I think they are of an oncoming cold and should go
When you have had a hot bath. But first
You must have a change of clothes.
[*She calls out to an attendant.*]
Omoni, Omoni! Now, where are all
Your men gone? If it were day I would say
They were deep in a game of draught, boasting, beating
Their breasts like gorillas about brave deeds
Better best forgotten.
Ozidi: The night has a thousand sirens, and if
The master will not answer their calls, why should not
The servants?
[*Orea regards Ozidi without a word, and goes out through a door farther
right at the head of the couch.*]
Ozidi: [*shaking his head.*] My head echoes me with the toll of a
thousand bells,
Perhaps, I should lie down after all, yes,
Lie down here and put my ears down as
Bells placed upon the ground. That should still their tongues,
It should silence them all, really
It should, after all this babble and tug.
[*He slides off the wall against which he has been reclining, scrambles into
the couch, and falls into a dog sleep to the strain of the song
Onumunumu, sung on the beach by boatmen of the royal barge. The
light rises over them, revealing them in the same position they were
before.*]
Cold: I put my wet hand on his shoulders, and
The man welcomed it all the way home.
Headache: Upon his head I have founded a forgery
With enough anvils and hammers to occupy
All hands from Awka.
Spots: I did a leopard daubing of his body.

Each spot thereon carries a nest of wasps,
A hive of bees turning his splendid flesh
Into honeycomb for worms to suckle.
Fever: I breathed my fumes over his face and now
His insides are furnaces all aglow,
Pouring molten lead into his limbs.
[*They all laugh together, a loud, long laugh. The noise of it rolls into the dark, upshore to the yard of Ozidi where we see him struggling in bed as one in a nightmare. At the same time Orea, sleepless and careworn, comes in with lamp in hand, a number of neighbors close behind her.*]
First Neighbor: How long has he been like this?
Orea: Since dusk.
Second Neighbor: I do not like the look of it, Orea.
You must do something.
Orea: When can I alone?
Third Neighbor: Yes; one hand washes the other.
Orea, it's a thorough purification ceremony
You of this house require.
First Neighbor: Not at so early a stage, but without doubt,
The matter is grievous, and demands
A drastic remedy.
Orea: [*leading them to where Ozidi lies.*] Look at him for me first,
    please look at him.
He tosses so I cannot look at him close. Not, that
I have knowledge of these things, for since childhood
He has not fallen ill one day. Only this evening
His body was covered with rashes I thought of
An oncoming cold. Now I cannot tell for certain.
[*All three neighbors go up to where Ozidi lies tossing, take a close look at him, and without saying a word or looking at Orea, tiptoe out one after the other, each with hand to mouth. Orea runs from one to the other in frantic, silent appeal but they all hurry out in great fear. She turns round, runs up to the couch to see for herself, and falls sobbing over her sick son. Then almost immediately she jumps up and enters into feverish activities talking to herself all the time.*]
Orea: No, it cannot be! Tamara—You cannot
Let this happen to me. My mother no longer lives
In this house; so it cannot contain you.
She grew wings, she walked on clouds, trespassed
On sacred grounds, and for that you struck her down
By the hand of one born of her own daughter.

No, I am only a poor hen roosting
Here in a hut by a hearth at which only one chicken
Nestles—my one child bigger than a crowd!
A child sees home his parents in the dusk
Of their lives; so should his in his own turn.
No such duties has my boy done; indeed
He still has not caught yaws. This
He is now doing as every child cuts teeth.
Here's common water then, here's common soap,
And here's sponge crushed from leaves of plantain—
I need nothing more before I scrub dry a mere riot of yaws
Broken over my son. When a guest
Comes on a visit, he goes home after.
Return therefore, our late visitor, taking your flesh
With you, but leave behind for us
Our skin and bones.
[*She assembles all she requires and scrubs Ozidi through her speech,
beginning nervously, but growing more and more gentle and composed as
dawn begins to break outside. Meanwhile out on the beach, the party on
the barge stirs and grows restive. At the same time, Engarandon the
Smallpox King himself, accompanied by both his younger brothers, comes
abroad from what seems an unsuccessful sortie ashore.*]
The Smallpox King: [*in obvious huff.*] She called me Yaws! Look at it,
    all of you,
  The woman mistook us for common Yaws!
Members of the Crew: [*together.*] What, the insolent woman!
  Does that mean her son is paying no tributes?
  How dare they take our king for a commoner?
  You've been too gentle with her; let's go
  Ashore and take the whole town captive.
Egirigiri: [*climbing on board.*] Too late, they have all fled, all
  The townspeople to a man.
Okrikpakpa: [*close behind the other.*] That is, if you count that
    squawker and
  Her chicken of a son. Yes, the whole place is
  Deserted. Not a goat left behind;
  Not a gourd of wine. Phew, a wretched race!
The Smallpox King: [*pacing in anger.*] The mortal wretch called us
    Yaws to our royal face!
  Now hear me all of you: let no member of our train
  Set foot again on this shore where men see

A royal python and call it worm of the earth, where
They hold a goblet of wine between their hands
And think it rainwater. It is a rank
Forsaken land. So push off; push off at once!
Who looks back on this barge will never again see
His front in notice of which
I spit here into the wind three times.
[*As he spits, the barge pulls out in the brisk dance of* Ogele *to the tune of*
Asaba doh. *Later, the dance flows back with the Storyteller as* Ozidi *at
its head. It draws all the players into its wake, so that a long processional
dance finally forms in which all spectators may join.*]

The Bikoroa Plays

The Boat

CHARACTERS

Biowa alias Govena, i.e., Governor
Bradide his elder brother
Peletua his peer, later serving as
  the Onoumbra or Bebeareowei,
  i.e., Spokesman of Town
Kelemere Bradide's young wife
Eseni a peer, later serving as the
  Owubia, a court official
Burubo a cripple and peer
Umuto Diakohwo mother of the
  brothers
Sanfio another peer
Kpuruku a young serving relation
Angalakizide the Amaokosuowei
  or Town Elder
Maika a peer, serving later as
  Amadiowei or Town overseer
Bienware a senior citizen or
  Okosuowei
Ogedegbe a youth

Okoro Yale brother-in-law of
  Biowa and Bradide
Emonemua his wife and sister of
  the brothers
Ambakederemo leader of the
  delegation from Kiagbodo, the
  capital of Ngbilebiri
Uyo leader of the delegation from
  Amatolo, a sister town
Onduku leader of the delegation
  from Ayakoroama, another
  sister town
People of Bikoroa as Neighbors,
  Dumu Okosuowei-ama or Ward
  Elders, *Okosuwei-ama* or Elders
  or Senior Citizens, *Voices from
  Outside and from the Floor, An
  Elder Asleep, a Young Man of
  Wisdom, Children,* and *Others*

ACT I

Scene 1   ARRIVAL

The beach at Bikoroa on the Kiagbodo River in the Western Niger Delta at the turn of the century. It is evening. A boat is coming in to berth among several others already moored on the water's edge. It is bigger than all of them, and it carries a canopy of mat from bow to aft. There is singing within but this is coming to an end above the sound of oars being drawn in on either side. In the glow of lanterns, hung up from the canopy from stern to bow, there is movement of men all ready to go ashore. At the same time, from upshore, a reception party is scrambling down to meet the incoming craft with everybody speaking together, some carrying lanterns before and above their heads, others clapping and cheering.

1st Neighbor: It's Govena!

2nd Neighbor: It's Biowa our Govena!

3rd Neighbor: Govena has come!

4th Neighbor: Our Govena has come!

2nd Neighbor: How long he has been!

4th Neighbor: Where's he? Where's he?

1st Neighbor: We want to see our own Govena! We want to see him!
[*The boat has docked by now, one man at the prow slowing it down with a pole, helped by some of the welcoming party who have waded into the water, wanting to see their man. He emerges from under the canopy on to the bridge, past the man with the pole, and with wide-open arms receives the greetings of the people. He is extravagantly dressed and has a gun slung over his back.*]

Biowa: Here I am, good people, here I come!

1st Neighbor: Why did you delay so long?

3rd Neighbor: Is Lagos such a sweet place as they say?

4th Neighbor: Had you forgotten us in our backwaters?

2nd Neighbor: How long you have been in!

Biowa: Well, here I am, here I am all in one piece! I wouldn't be here had I forgotten you, would I?

All: Welcome home!

Peletua: Odokuku!

Biowa: That's my praise name!

Peletua: Odokuku!

Biowa: Wood though I am, I weigh like iron.

Peletua: Govena the great!

Biowa: That's mine as well!

Peletua: Govena, oh, our Govena!

Biowa: That's me! I am the stranger who came calling and stayed to rule the land!

Peletua: Now come down, come down and let's see you!

1st Neighbor: Let's carry him ashore! His feet must not touch water.

3rd Neighbor: Yes, they must not be wet!

[*Someone offers his back and they carry him shoulder high, still clamoring, clearing for him a passage through the crowd now massing from all sides. He acknowledges the cheers of the people, many of them blinking and laughing behind lanterns in their hands.*]

Biowa: How have you been doing since I was away? Kelemere, you mean you delivered your baby behind my back?

Kelemere: The moon has come and gone since you left.

Biowa: No, have I been away that long? Is it a boy or a girl?

Kelemere: A girl it is.

Biowa: That's splendid; then we shall collect a fat dowry on her. Now, greetings there! Is that Ogedegbe I'm seeing there looking so tall and strong? I shall take you with me in my next voyage.

Ogedegbe: Oh, will you?

Biowa: We shall make a fine oarsman out of you. Greetings there, Eseni. How are the hooks?

Eseni: Not very good waters running now, I'm afraid. I don't have any fine catch to welcome you with. Oh, the shame of it!

Biowa: There, do not worry; there's enough fare in our holds to feed everybody for a month. Sanfio, how are all the birds singing up on the palm tree?

Sanfio: Most precarious still, and no wine running to reward the risk.

Biowa: Never mind; we bring you real stuff to burn a hole in the palate. Here's my hand!

Sanfio: It's soft and oily with wealth.

Biowa: Well, we can't all be carvers of canoes, getting our hands all callused over. No, do I see Burubo here too!

[*It is a crippled neighbor, and Biowa stoops to shake hands with him.*]
You shouldn't have come in the crush.

Burubo: I carry no crutches for anyone to knock down, and I came as fast as any walking.

Biowa: True, true! When has the iguana lost a contest to the gorilla?

Burubo: We're but wall-geckos, Govena, so when adventure like this moves to our very door, who is to stop us scuttling? It is not every day a prince comes home safe from the seas.

Biowa: Thank you, thank you very much. I brought you some fine pairs of shorts. You must come straight away for them. Life's so uncertain these days.

Burubo: Oh, my brother, oh, my kind brother who always remembers me! Long life is not for the stay-at-homes alone. They also die who sleep in their beds.

[*A sprightly old woman now prances in.*]

Umuto: My son, where is my son? My son who never lets me touch mud, my son who delights me, where is he? Where is he? Put him down for me to suckle. My child, here's breast for you. Now put him down and let me back him.

Peletua: Oh, are you going to back him now?

Umuto: Why not? Didn't I when he was a child? Is he so big now you think I can't carry my son? Put him down, now put him down for me and see whether or not he's a burden on my back.

[*They make way for her and set him down. She embraces him and tries to suckle and back him, all at one and the same time.*]

Umuto: There, mount! Mount my back. The milk is not sour yet, yes, it hasn't flown.

Biowa: Gently, gently, mother. Now doesn't she beat the ray fish that ferries ashore the wrecked sailor?

[*The old woman bursts into song.*]

Umuto: Set a cap upon him
  It isn't quite right yet
  Isn't it so?
  It is!
  The way it's sitting
  The way it's sitting
  It isn't quite right yet
  It isn't quite right yet
  Isn't it so?
  It is!
  Isn't it so?
  It is!
  Isn't it so?
  Yes, it is!

[*She has not made much progress trying to bear off her son but all the same there is general ovation.*]

Burubo: Oh, isn't life sweet?

Peletua: Yes, who would want to part with it? It's a great gift from the Almighty.

Eseni: Let's praise her.

Biowa: If after every crossing come such cheers, who will not want to ride the waves, even at Ekremo, when the wind, inflamed by lightning and thunder, drives them over treetops? I have men with me in my boat who have not seen sleep in the last seven nights, toiling at their oars all the way from Lagos past Ejirin, Epe, Atijeren, all Yoruba towns in the route, into our own waters through Arogbo, past Nana's town to Ogidigben, and finally to Izon Oborotu. You will understand therefore, my good people, if they are all tired and dying to come ashore. Still some of them there are who will continue tomorrow on their onward voyage home. To these our brothers of Seinbiri, Tarakiri, Kabo, Kubowei clans and our own towns upstream I say stop with me in our town tonight, and see how we turn strangers into sons of the soil. [*General laughter.*]

Peletua: Yes, let the strangers stay, let them come out and share in our joy. Tonight there are no marital ties!

Biowa: Did you hear that, oh, you sailors come home after long sailing at sea? It's a feast without bars, so come out. Kpuruku, lead them forward. And see to the luggage. Only our boxes are to be off-loaded. Tomorrow, each passenger going upstream can collect his before making his connection home.

Sanfio: Now, for a song, a song, girls, or are you melting already before the boys have even touched you?
[*General laughter, immediately followed by a song started by one of the women, and to its beat the party leads home Biowa, his mother fanning him in front and pouring on him his praise names. Briskly, it moves dancing up the beach, past the main street running alongside the stream, and so into the compound of the brothers.*]

Scene 2 RECEPTION

The same evening, soon after. The living room of Biowa in his part of the compound, settled by him and his elder brother Bradide. To the right is the bedroom, and to the left a room serving as a store, both with beautifully carved doors. A large wooden table in the Sapele style at the turn of the century occupies the center of the room, and around it, against the walls, are several chairs to match. Upon it is a collection of china and lamps left perma-

*nently there on display, leaving just enough room for a fine tray of silver
holding a number of liquor glasses. Up on the walls hang two sets of double-
mounted buffalo horns, between which are a bronze sword, a brass bugle, all
crossed. Also hanging on the wall are two well-framed pictures, one of a
black mermaid in a striped yellow and blue jersey, wrapping round herself a
boa-constrictor, and the other of a white lady looking obviously like Queen
Victoria as Empress of India, etc. There is much movement in the room,
with several people already seated and several more coming in from the crowd
outside to join in what is a reception party for Biowa, but which he himself
appears to be provisioning, much to his pride.*

Biowa: Kpuruku!

Kpuruku: Yes!

Biowa: Is everything stored away?

Kpuruku: Yes.

Biowa: Everything? The bales of cloths, the case of drinks, and the
cartons of food and biscuits?

Kpuruku: Yes!

Eseni: Oh, don't call them out like that. They make my mouth
water so!

Sanfio: When hasn't your mouth dribbled in anticipation of a feast
thrown by another?

Biowa: Be patient; you'll all eat tonight and drink to your hearts' fill.
There, Kpuruku, did you say everything is well stored away?

Kpuruku: Yes.

Biowa: Kpuruku!

Kpuruku: Yes!

Biowa: In that case, you may bring out a bottle of gin.

Kpuruku: Yes.

Biowa: Kpuruku!

Kpuruku: Yes.

Biowa: Also bring out a bottle of whisky.

Kpuruku: Yes.

Biowa: And here, Kpuruku, a bottle of schnapps as well!

Bradide: Why not open one bottle first?

Burubo: O-o-oh! Are you seeking to stop the flow of the river?

Umuto: Let my boy display to the world. Do not stop him. Oh, my
boy!

Bradide: Did I say he shouldn't display?

Angala: Now, don't take it that way.

Bradide: Well, well!

[*Kpuruku, caught between conflicting commands, compromises and brings in two bottles.*]

Biowa: Look, we won't tantalize you longer. The house is full and it seems there are more wanting to come in. Truly we have returned home. To all of you who have come to rejoice with us on our safe return we must say the sight of you fills us with warmth and sweetness. And now here are drinks for you all. There are kola-nuts as well, and other good things besides. Kpuruku, serve everybody within and outside.

Peletua: No, pardon me. A good act must be done properly.

Angala: That's right.

Peletua: The entire town is more or less here represented, and our Amaokosuowei, the eldest himself, is right in our midst. Angalakizide, do you give me mouth to voice what's in our hearts?

Angala: Here I touch the good bottle, and now you may shove out the boat.

Peletua: I kneel, my eldest.

Angala: Rise!

Peletua: Your praise name.

Angala: Ama-mon-koro-ka!

Peletua: Ama-mon-koro-ka!

Angala: A town can't all go hungry at the same time; it must be your host that's stingy. Now your own?

Peletua: Agba!

Angala: Calabash I am; you cannot press me underwater. Now, Eseni, your own?

Eseni: Ere-ma-ebi-ka.

Peletua: Ere-ma-ebi-ka!

Eseni: What a beautiful woman, you cry! Well, marry her first, I say. Your own?

Peletua: Agba, you know it.

Eseni: Agba then I call you.

Peletua: Never will I go under. Sanfio, now your own.

Sanfio: Okinikini.

Peletua: Okinikini!

Sanfio: That's my father's! I eat once in a moon. Who dare come near? Okilolo!

Peletua: That's my father's! There, Burubo, your own.

Burubo: Apiapia.

Peletua: Apiapia!

Burubo: It's from up, up the treetop I watch events.

Peletua: Ogoun!

Bradide: That's my father's! However hard or huge the tree, I hew it down.

Peletua: [*Turning to Biowa.*] Ogoun!

Bradide: How dare you when I am here?

Peletua: A mistake, a most regrettable mistake in my state of happiness.

Angala: It was a slip of tongue: even the cat slips on a roof. Forgive him.

Eseni: Some of these our customs are too discriminatory. Why shouldn't a younger son answer his father's praise name when the heir is present?

Sanfio: You wait until you go among the Urhobo and you can do as your mother's people in all their lack of hierarchy.

Burubo: You misrepresent them. It's so among them even as it is with the Itsekiri.

Angala: Save us all your stories. The matter is forgotten.

Sanfio: On then with the fare.

Peletua: Blessings of Tamara! How could my tongue slip like that?

Sanfio: Go on. You've been forgiven.

Burubo: He won't be satisfied until the thing is bitten off.

Eseni: Time somebody did.

Peletua: Greetings then, greetings all, now I have been well and truly chastised. It is our brother who has returned from the far away place now taken over by the white man. We should be doing him the honor of receiving him with drinks, food, gifts. Instead he it is has brought us all these rich bounties you see spread before us. I see a bottle of pure fire; I also see a bottle of golden water. And I see there are biscuits and canned meat and fish all the way from the white man's land. What hand has so generously offered how can mouth and belly reject it? All we can say is that where these good things have been taken from let many more go in to fill it severalfold. Let the generous lady of the water fill his store with her bounties, good money, good wives, good children, and the long, long life to enjoy them. Biowa, our Govena, all you have given us we accept with open arms. I didn't start the matter. Now it is finished. I won't say any more. The story is finished.

All Together:
Yes!
Yes!
It's finished.
Now let the drinks flow!
How parched my throat!

Biowa: Kpuruku!

Kpuruku: Yes.

Biowa: Don't you hear everyone crying out for a drink?

Kpuruku: That's what I'm trying to get.

Angala: Kpuruku, Kpuruku! You've called the young man how
many times tonight my poor old head is beginning to reel.

Biowa: That's how it is, old man.

Kpuruku: Which shall I open first?

Eseni: The gin!

Sanfio: The whisky!

Biowa: No problem; open them both, Kpuruku, did you hear me?
Open both bottles and serve all within and outdoors.

Burubo: Look at the boy. He's breaking the seal himself.

Eseni: Boys of nowadays no longer respect custom.

Sanfio: They don't know custom it's more like.

Peletua: There, give it to our Amakosuowei.

Burubo: It's the same way he'll force his way to a virgin, watch him
well.

Angala: Oh, it hasn't come to that, has it? There, I've touched it,
now you may serve. They seal them extra fast these days. Is it so
no adulterer will find his way in?

[*General laughter. Kpuruku takes a glass from the silver tray, blows dust
from it, and serves the old man.*]

Not so much to begin with, young man.

[*He takes the half-filled glass and, passing it to his left hand, turns
towards the door.*]

Let no evil spirits drift here to partake of our fare. This is to them
and may they stay outside and keep their own company.

[*He tosses the drink out and hands the empty glass back. He is served
again and empties his glass at a gulp.*]

Aagh! Another, my boy. The hands are beginning to shake.

Bradide: Who said? They will still be wielding the axe, come next
flood.

Angala: Not really. My sun is almost level now with the ground to
our left. But let not the shadow of our days fall on this happy
occasion. Now, give me the kola-nut and I'll split it: may we all
hold together even as its lobes!

[*While he breaks the kola-nut, the drink goes round, served only in one
glass, taken in turn by each with a personal touch, some swilling, others
gurgling and guzzling, and one or two beating their chests and belching
in satisfaction as they each take their share of the kola-nut which now is
also going round.*]

Burubo: This is water flowing from no river!

Peletua: It's fire: see the sparks.

Sanfio: The other is stronger still.

Eseni: That's a lie; this is more powerful.

Burubo: Are you arguing so the other bottle will be opened before you've finished the first? Oh, you of this town really are possessed of long throats.

[*More people come in.*]

1st Neighbor: It hasn't got to me yet.

2nd Neighbor: And me too.

3rd Neighbor: And me. How's he serving the drink all to one side?

Peletua: Don't stampede! There's enough stuff running to fill a barrel.

Biowa: Let them all come in. Don't keep them back. A house is not a boat; it will not capsize.

4th Neighbor: Govena, you really know what stuff to bring home.

1st Neighbor: It was worth waiting for.

2nd Neighbor: Still you were so long away your brother was asking us to start thinking of a search party.

3rd Neighbor: But whether for ship or captain he didn't say.

1st Neighbor: Now, how far could we have gone? It is not exactly like going across the river to fetch some benighted woodcutter.

Burubo: Is it true in Lagos there are houses serving nothing but drinks like this all day to music and dance?

Eseni: I hear the women there pack their power in their bottoms, and they roll the things like barrels in a man's path.

Sanfio: And don't our own women?

Eseni: Here what they lack from birth they make up with bundles of cheap beads. And for that they are ready to sell a man. Some even would make rolls of cast-off rags to gain girth.

Sanfio: How do you know? Have you ever seen a woman naked except the careless bather at the beach?

Eseni: That's an insult; I may not have a wife now, but that does not mean I'm incapable.

Sanfio: All some people can do is talk.

Eseni: This is too much. Come out and I'll show you who can do what.

Burubo: We haven't come here to fight.

Eseni: Do you see him abusing me? I'm the peer of his betters.

Biowa: All right. Let nobody fight tonight. If you must, then it should be in joy over the good things of life. Kpuruku!

Kpuruku: Yes.

Biowa: Get me some more biscuits and sugar.

[*He takes them and, approaching the doorway on the other side of the overladen table, tosses them out to the crowd of young people pressing up to the verandah and front windows. They scramble after the goodies much to the merriment of everybody.*]

[*Enter Umuto, preening.*]

Umuto: Now, who said the rich don't need the poor? Will Govena himself now do his own picking? Aha! Bring out drinks and food for the people, said my son, and somebody wanted to stint.

Bradide: I never said your son should stint on his hospitality.

Biowa: Now, let's not start again, Mother.

[*He takes off his gun and hangs it by the sword and the bugle on the wall.*]

Burubo: Did you find some Yoruba pirates to shoot out there?

Biowa: The Yoruba as a people don't get their feet wet, my friend. The pirates are all our own Ijo people, and they range all the way to Lagos, half-submerged like crocodiles.

Eseni: Did you hear that?

Sanfio: Oh! Let's have more drinks?

Burubo: Now is there none here can laugh without biting his tongue?

Angala: Where are the drums? Boys, what's happening? Time the drums spoke up since men have lost control of their tongues. Sanfio, what's come over you tonight? A song. Now let's have a song and loosen our limbs a bit. Oh! the cramp is come upon us all.

Burubo: Rheumatism you mean!

Angala: Whatever it is, let's dance and be merry. In our time we needed no inducement.

[*Sanfio starts a song; it is taken up by all; a couple of people get up to dance to it, but it does not really go on for long before it dies off.*]

Peletua: It hasn't quite caught fire but still you can see the difference already. Come, let's have another. Or are we going to let the guests in our midst think we are a cheerless clan?

[*Enter Maika.*]

Maika: I am Agbrarara-gbru"ruru! May it not thunder, I say! Now let me have my own share of drinks; yes, I want a drink first.

Sanfio: First will you sit down. You have just come.

Burubo: Now, will someone turn up that lamp? I believe it's running dry of oil.

Biowa: Recharge it then, or put on another.

Bradide: I think all it needs is trimming. Kelemere, come and attend to the lamp.

Umuto: No, let's have more lights on for my son. There hasn't been light in the house since he was away.

Biowa: Oh, Mother!

Angala: Woman, what's the matter?

Bradide: All right, Mother, you may light up the house to the roof top if you like. I am going.

Burubo: Oh don't go.

Peletua: She didn't mean it that way.

Angala: This is the night of your brother's homecoming. Do not spoil the fun.

Bradide: It's not me spoiling anything. Let me go.

Biowa: You better let him before things get worse.

Maika: Yes, differences like this grow worse if you attempt to settle them.

[*Bradide leaves, with several hands trying to hold him back. Somebody tries to start a song, but at this point the lamp sputters and goes out, creating some commotion. Over it can be heard the voice of the host trying to calm everybody and protect his property.*]

Biowa: Careful! Careful! I say careful! You'll break things, you're going to break precious ware here if you move. Just stay where you are and everything will be all right. I said wait! Kpuruku! Light, light, please. Do you hear me? Are you in the store? Let nobody try anything funny there. My eyes can see in the dark. Kpuruku! Kpuruku! Kpuruku!

[*The effect of his appeal is to create further panic, as none there wants to be accused of breaking or stealing some valuable ware.*]

All Together: I'd better be going. I've taken nothing. I've broken nothing. Naked I came, naked I'm going to my poor house. My hand hasn't touched; my foot hasn't either.

Burubo: I'd like to collect my gift when the trunks are opened tomorrow. Now good night. At daybreak we'll be seeing again.

[*They all go out.*]

Biowa: Abaiyo! Let day break and we'll see!

Angala: Now, why are they all rushing out like that? Tomorrow is more fearful than the dark.

Scene 3 HANGOVER

[*The following morning. The family compound. Bradide enters from the beach, calling to his brother.*]

Bradide: Biowa, Biowa! Is Biowa up yet?

Umuto: Let my son sleep. Let him sleep. I tell you!

Bradide: Why, will he sleep like the puffadder till noon? The sun is a quarter way above the earth already.

Umuto: Let him sleep as long as he likes. He's tired after his long voyage. That you should know or are you bent on disturbing his sleep as you tried wrecking his welcome last night?

Bradide: I did not wreck your son's welcome nor . . .

[*Enter Biowa, gathering his wrapper about him.*]

Biowa: Mother, Mother, what's the matter now?

Umuto: There, are you happy you have woken up the boy?

Biowa: It's all right, Mother. Now what is it?

Bradide: How did you arrive?

Biowa: By water of course.

Bradide: I know that. How did you bring that boat home?

Umuto: What do you mean by that?

Bradide: Mother, have you seen the boat?

Umuto: What about it? What about it?

Biowa: I agree it's in a bad shape. We suffered a number of mishaps.

Bradide: The prow is broken.

Biowa: That was when we tried to dock at Ereko. We misjudged our speed combined with that of the ebbing tide.

Bradide: So you rammed her straight into your jetty and broke her nose.

Biowa: I said it was an accident.

Bradide: Accidents don't happen; they are caused.

Biowa: All right, all right!

Bradide: What happened on the port side? The gunnel is split down the side, and half the thwarts are loose at one end.

Biowa: I see you have carried out an inspection tour as would soldiers from a British gun-boat boarding a ship. What else did you find amiss on our boat?

Umuto: Yes, what else did you find?

Bradide: Mother, this is not a matter for women. That boat was badly used.

Biowa: It was not.

Bradide: It was—all the way to the stern where that fancy box you put up as a stoolhouse has spilt its content on the helm.

Biowa: We haven't washed the boat yet, you know that. Part of our luggage is still in its hold, and I'm sure my passengers were still outside asleep, when you carried out your inspection tour.

Bradide: Your passengers not only were up but catching the first connection, have gone home and left their captain sleeping ashore, all of them anxious no doubt to abandon a sinking boat.

Biowa: It was not a sinking boat till you set your hands on it. I sailed it in face of all the freak storms that wake the wanton waves in the lagoon of Lagos, never went aground once on the wide flats that stretch from Leki to Epe, and through the narrow, tortuous passage between Oboto and Gbekebo suffered not a single scratch on an oar.

Umuto: That's my son, a brave pilot. Could you have done as well?

Bradide: There are also freak storms on the Niger, Mother, and at each flooding of the river, the sands wash up to your own waterside.

Umuto: That is nothing for adventure. Are there pirates upstream to dispute your passage?

Bradide: Maybe not quite the regular kind. But the Igbo are on the banks all the way from Aboh.

Umuto: What dish will they make of your dry sinews and bones?

Bradide: I know you care very little what becomes of my poor body.

Umuto: Tut, tut! You are too querulous like a woman wanting attention. Instead of rejoicing your younger brother has returned home safely, you have done nothing but hold an inquest as if some son of the soil has been brought home dead.

Bradide: I rejoice with him so much that I would not let him venture out again on that boat until repairs are carried out.

Biowa: But I have still several days left, and after a little rest would like to take my wares to markets around.

Umuto: Yes, how will he sell his wares and his bales of cloths, his barrels . . .

Bradide: Don't go on, Mother; all the town knows the long catalog of his wealth. Let his customers come to him as they usually do when market is good.

Biowa: Having stayed behind more than usual, I thought I should go out to them.

Bradide: You know you cannot in safety go out again in that boat.

Umuto: It brought him safely home from a seven-day voyage.

[*She sings.*]

Biowa: That will do, Mother. When do you propose dry-docking?

Bradide: Immediately.

Biowa: How long will that take?

Bradide: You know in normal circumstances how long that should take. What damage we see now is all above water. It is not until we bring the boat ashore that we shall see how much of the hull has been eaten up by sea-worms in Lagos.

Umuto: There are also worms in our waters.

Biowa: Let's not go into that. One thing I'm sure of; we didn't have more than the usual amount of bilge to cope with. We kept our normal bailing shifts.

Bradide: We must thank your water-goddess for that. It's quite possible barnacles in their shoals had given you a false keel.

Biowa: We made normal speed, considering our condition.

Bradide: Well, let's take up the boat and see how much marine life we have to scrape off her backside.

Umuto: There, don't let him.

Bradide: What do you mean?

Biowa: What do you mean?

Umuto: Don't you see what he's trying to do? By the time he does his repairs you will have no boat to your name.

Biowa: How?

Umuto: You fool, for then the new moon will be up, and your brother is always quick to spot it.

Biowa: I believe there is still more than a market-tide left for the month to end.

Umuto: Go to the waterside and see the tide. It's beginning to turn already. That means the new moon is on the upsurge.

Bradide: Mother, you are always seeing bad in my actions.

Umuto: Tell me how many days will be left my son to take the boat out?

Bradide: You can count them yourself.

Umuto: [*Clapping hands in his face.*] There, I knew you weren't sincere in your great concern to carry out repairs on the boat. Or will you let your brother take up some of your days?

Bradide: The matter has not come to that yet.

Umuto: Of course, it will be too great a sacrifice for you to make.

Bradide: That's a lie, and may the dead and the gods judge you for it.

Biowa: It's enough!

Bradide: Every time the boat has needed repairs, all of a major kind, and each time upon the return of your son from Lagos, who carried out the repairs, brought the parts from Warri, and sweated in the sun without getting reimbursement or praise?

Umuto: Take that as the elder's duty for eating the head of the fish.

Bradide: Some fish head! It seems I'm always being fed the stock fish.

Biowa: I knew there would soon be a declaration of our debts.

Bradide: You can take the boat out and sink for all I care.

Umuto: Nothing will please you better.

[*Enter Bienware.*]

Bienware: Don't let more water into the boat. And you, woman, stay out of this. Let the men settle the matter. It's quite simple. Bradide will carry out the repairs and if they take him into the new moon, that will be eating into his time also. But why quarrel over a tilt that hasn't come? The moon should shine over everybody.

Biowa: There is a catch somewhere.

Bienware: Come, there is none. When will you not be suspicious in your life? And you, Bradide, don't be angry.

Bradide: I'm no longer angry.

Bienware: That's a good fellow. Come all of you. Let's go and get some breakfast instead of beginning the day with a quarrel. Where are the wives of the house? We want to hear the ukodo pots boiling over, and not angry bowels this morning.

ACT II

Scene 1   GAME

Afternoon, some days after. At the etele or playhouse on stilts by the beach. In the middle of a game of draughts between Biowa and Sanfio. Looking on and making comments are several of their peers. One player is apparently hard pressed.

Sanfio: Chop, man, chop, I say.

Biowa: There, I have, Big Mouth.

Sanfio: Now chop again.

Biowa: Do you dare me?

Sanfio: I do. I said chop and choke.

Maika: Sanfio, do you know what you are doing feeding out all your seeds?

Sanfio: Shut up! And here's another seed for him to chop and fill his belly down to his great umbilical hernia. Well done. Now see what the son born of a man from Okoloba does with your champion. One, two, three—are you looking, all of you of Bikoroa—and four, I take them all, yes, three, seven steps at one move, I take them all like a leopard vaulting a house to catch his prey at the other side of the roof. And now I'm king! Crown me, there, crown the king of all the clans.

Burubo: A brilliant move, Sanfio!

Eseni: A fluke, I say.

Peletua: No, an exceptional stroke, admit the dazzle of gold when you see it.

Biowa: Yes, a brilliant move; I didn't see it at all.

Sanfio: How could you? Who knows how a column of ants files in from the forest? And who knows its length?

Burubo: Hear the braggart of Okoloba! Have you heard the forest is even now reclaiming your famous city?

Sanfio: At least we have never claimed to have left it behind us. You can take some people I know out of the bush, but you can't take the bush out of them. Take our good neighbors, for example. . . .

Biowa: Play, man, and take your mouth off other people's business.

Peletua: Look at his lips sucked in like a kitchen knife eaten almost in two.

Sanfio: That means a life of long service to men. I need an award for that. And now that's for you, it takes care of your queen. No longer can she whirl about in her dirty petticoats. Oh, will you play more? I said I'll wipe the draughts-board dry today with every comer that ever counted out sixteen.

Biowa: Your move.

Sanfio: Great. Now tell me where you can run? Look, all you his backers, his calves have all fled up his buttocks, and all flattened out now is he like a sole served out on a plate.

Biowa: All right, all right, you've won. Another game.

Sanfio: Nine games in a row? No, no, no more. You can carry home the kit: board and seeds, I present them to you. I'm playing no more today. This game takes intellect, admit it, you that are of

direct descent in this town, and after so many games, one begins
to tire, although you may not know it, you who do not brain
work.

Burubo: Boaster! Look at his teeth carved as a cannibal's.

Sanfio: [*breaks into song:*]

> I am eagle, I am eagle
> Across the face of the sun
> Across the seven seas
> I fly, I fly
> Over earth my prey!

Maika: The day you crash, there'll be no rescue boat out to save
you.

Biowa: It's his lucky day. Let him crow.

Sanfio: I do it lots of days. Know that when luck repeats itself so
many times in so many days, a pattern emerges, and that pattern
we call technique. Admit it, men; I have talent, and that's
something you can't buy in the market.

Biowa: What else have you to sell?

Sanfio: Well, what else is left us second sons to do but play? Our
elders if they don't inherit all our fathers' estates, use us as
seconds, and let the joint enterprise but succeed and they assert
again their title. It has always been the tradition since the clan
began at Ugobri.

Biowa: Oh, what a cramping life! I think I'll go and stretch my legs.
The left one has gone asleep. [*He goes out.*]

Burubo: How you play with everything till what was on its feet
before is spinning on its head. Did you have to sail that close?

Sanfio: I meant no harm and mentioned no names. I was only
speaking generally.

Maika: That may be so but that mouth of yours will get you into
rough waters one day.

Eseni: That's as certain as a boat sails on water.

Peletua: Now tradition, if we must talk about it, actually tells us
differently. The second sons were often setting out to found new
settlements.

Maika: Are you saying Govena should give up the boat to Bradide?

Peletua: I made no such suggestion. I said only when there was open
dispute, and always it was over some foreign woman or an
antelope of which the elder had taken possession, did the younger
brothers break away. Oh, why can't we as a people die for some
better cause? Quarrel over mincemeat or fleshpot! And for such

acts and desires brothers roved endless waters to found new dynasties.

Eseni: Our Govena is not about to go into exile.

Sanfio: It wouldn't be a bad idea if he did.

Eseni: Why should he?

Maika: I have always wondered why he doesn't settle in that Lagos of his if the place is that exotic and full of all the good things of life as he tells us.

Sanfio: Bile, man, that's what's eating up you old ones. Head to head we stand on these shores. We don't want the law changed at the mouth of the river.

Eseni: Our doctrine of equal rights didn't say the elder has no special rights.

Maika: Who said it did? Look, let's brush the cobwebs from before our eyes so we can see the matter in hand like a fish in clear water. In this dispute between the brothers our past offers us no precedent. Perhaps, that's why brother has not brought brother to open court.

Peletua: Yes; consider the case: one boat between two brothers, both of them very industrious, and each with equal right to take it to his place of business every other showing of the moon as many times as he can so he falls within the stated tide.

Burubo: A most peculiar arrangement, we all admit.

Sanfio: What else do you expect of a family like that?

Peletua: Well, that's how the pact has worked between them so far, Bradide making a total of five and Govena three, because Lagos, I gather, poses a more tortuous course although with greater reward.

Maika: Why hasn't he bought himself a fine boat en route all this time? I hear the finest craft are carved at Ofinama.

Sanfio: It's the old pull of heirlooms.

Burubo: So which way are things pulling?

Maika: How can anyone say? It's not a game of draughts.

Peletua: The thing to do is watch out for the moon.

Sanfio: Somebody claims to have sighted it already.

Burubo: What? In these skies taken over by clouds? That's like spotting a boat in a bay of many islands.

Sanfio: Still somebody claims to have.

Eseni: I did not; so stop leering at me.

Sanfio: Oh, I thought you said you did yesterday.

Peletua: Probably the turn of tide has touched his head.

Sanfio: [*singing*]
>   An empty skill sailing out to sea.
>   Before tide turn and turn again
>   Seven times, a full moon
>   Will bring you a fortune.

Eseni: Fool!

Burubo: Well, if we aren't sure about what there's above in the skies, we can at least go and see what's on the ground.

Peletua: A good idea. I hear the boat is ready for launching. The man has worked at it like an Itsekiri slave, and now the boat so badly battered by the winds and waves of Lagos is back in trim.

Sanfio: Listen! Our master boatwright is hammering away still on the beach while we play here. Just hear the echo of his blows hop over the stream. There, it is at the other bank already, among the trees; now it's fallen, lost forever like some potsherd cast into a stream, at first playing ducks and drakes, and then is sunk forever.

Burubo: All our best efforts peter out that way. He means to launch out soon.

Eseni: Who?

Burubo: Bradide of course; he is in a hurry to get to Lokoja.

Maika: And our Govena is in a hurry to get back to Lagos.

Eseni: That's stalemate.

Peletua: To speak the hard Ijo truth, I wonder who will use it first.

Eseni: The younger man, if their mother has her way.

Maika: What's the matter with that woman, anyway? She's forever baiting Bradide to please Govena. Look at her the other night.

Sanfio: One brings her gifts of tobacco and gin from Lagos; the other yams and groundnuts from Lokoja.

Eseni: The witch, has she got the teeth to sample anything except the brains of newborn babies?

Peletua: Oh, she is the fierce mother-hen who'll fight owner and hawk alike, protecting her brood, while trampling on the chicks in the process.

Burubo: I hear Bradide was brought into the world as a result of forceful entry by his father. She has never forgiven him for that.

Maika: That was no fault of his.

Sanfio: You are telling me!

Burubo: Well, shall we go and see whether he's finished and ready to launch the boat?

All: Yes, let's go.

Maika: Watch out, the draughts-board. Some people can't see where they are going.

Sanfio: Pick up the seeds, pick them up before they fall between the bamboo, will you?

Peletua: If you tended life with as much care as you give to play you would be as rich today as Ambadederemo of Kiagbodo.

Sanfio: Come, come, let's go. He is a great player himself, they say.

Burubo: Idler!

[*They all scramble down and go out.*]

Scene 2   LAUNCHING

A little later that afternoon. The boat freshly fitted but without canopy and toilet box. Bradide is regarding it with pride, sweat running down his bare torso. The party from the playhouse descend upon him, shouting him greetings and praise names which he returns.

Greetings!

All   Greetings, oh, cooper of Ganagana!
Together: Well done!

So you've put her together already?

Bradide: Yes, I've managed to.

Sanfio: Oh, it's a beautiful job! See how the prow shoots out like the snout of a shark. See how it bodies out from the head on both sides along lines no longer like those of the giant tree out of which it was hewn. And see how, after all this great house it carries as a turtle its carapace, it tapers at the stern into a fin laid flat as a seat for the helmsman. What pilot will not be proud to sit there in the face of any wind inciting the waves?

Bradide: Well, we tried, man; it takes a good eye to see what a good hand has done.

Burubo: It's the eye that's afraid. Once hand sets to it, it's amazing how fast it eats up work.

Sanfio: Take note, you lazy bones!

Eseni: Hear! Hear!

Sanfio: It's a beautiful boat, an extraordinary piece of work. It reminds me of the master mask in any age-grade collection. I wonder whether that wasn't what gave our forefathers the idea of the leading mask—the man, the fish, the vessel, all brought

together in the one act of quest by man for fish over waters
spilling into the sun.

Maika: Go on! Dance off with the thing! Dance, dance, all day
dance, and at night dance of another kind. Is there any other thing
we can do as a people?

Bradide: Oh, come now, Maika, things are not as bad as that. We
can't all be fishing and farming all day. Indeed nothing makes the
farmer and the fisherman work harder than a little dance at the
right time.

Maika: Then let the singer limit his art; let him limit it and learn
some concrete craft instead of playing his days away at dance and
draughts.

Eseni: He's just drubbed us all, Govena included, sucking delight out
of draughtsmen like an orange.

Maika: Must he treat everything as he would a bladder fish—never
to stop blowing into it, until it bursts on all sides?

Sanfio: I came to praise, not to quarrel. I'd love to see the craft on
water. One will hardly touch the other.

Peletua: Yes, it's a beautiful craft; it looks so light though large.

Burubo: Let's launch it then.

Bradide: How many hands have we?

Burubo: As many as we would ever want. Work like this calls up its
own labor.

Bradide: True; let's see what a crew you make. Suddenly, you have
lifted the load of days from off my shoulders. Now we'll see how
the boat rides the waves once more. But first the tools.
[*He leaps in and out over the gunnel, speaking all the time, part issuing
directives, part rushing up and down the length of the craft and around it,
supervising the launching operation.*]
Who will jump in with me and take out all these tools, that pack
of nails, and hammer, the basket of candle, the saw, and those
washers there? Collect them all into this bag. And there's the adze
you must not forget has a keen touch to its thick head. That's
good, very good; gather them all to stow away like a squirrel.
And now, Sanfio, Eseni, Peletua, everybody, look under and make
sure the rollers are firm and all in place. Those three in the
middle, for instance, must be set dead straight, and the four to the
stern, are they right and firm? You remember in this reverse order
they take the full weight of the boat, all the load, when we begin
to pull. That's right now, yes, all fully set and square, and in line
with the thwarts to the boat. There, are you all ready for the great

push forward? This is where the faint of heart fall out. Well, are there such among us here?

Burubo: None, Bradide, none! Not even Sanfio the dancer from Okoloba!

Bradide: Then all hands to the gunnel, each to the nearest thwart. Now, Eseni, you come and man the prow with me, we need strong toughened hands to lift it. Right here, that's it, up, up into the air until the keel begins to shy off the ground at this end and slide down the first rollers, the weight of it running down that incline to the stern now in the lead. That's it, that's it, so here we go over the bank into the river.

[*All except Burubo apply themselves strenuously but the boat seems most reluctant to go. They strain more at it, and time seems to stretch out under the strain, their breath coming out in short, sharp grunts.*]

Sanfio: Phew, we really are a lazy people! We shall never advance.

Burubo: Come, come, it'll go.

Peletua: He's forever giving up before trying. How can anyone make progress that way?

Eseni: Some people are not pulling at all but just pretending.

Maika: Name the persons.

Sanfio: I know I'm pulling as hard as anybody.

Eseni: Hear! hear!

Bradide: Let's not quarrel. Everybody here is doing his best. Perhaps, we should rest our lungs a little.

Burubo: Yes, a good blacksmith whispers to his bellows.

[*Bradide goes round briefly and checks one or two of the rollers.*]

Sanfio: My palms are bruised and bleeding.

Bradide: Not so soon?

Sanfio: See: I'm not playing.

Peletua: White man! Oh, white captain sitting pretty on his poop!

Maika: Right now, I feel like one of them out of their boiler-room, all roasting . . .

Sanfio: Except that unlike them, you aren't glowing like a lobster on the grill.

Maika: Idiot!

Bradide: Shall we try again? Every man to his previous position.

[*Enter Ogedegbe and others.*]

All Together: Hold it, hold it! Are you floating the boat already? Hold it! We are coming! Can we join in?

Bradide: Of course you can, Ogedegbe, and all of you.

Burubo: Didn't I say work calls out the hands it requires?

Eseni: Go on with you.

[*They all take up their positions.*]

Bradide: Now, are we ready? Now, are we ready? There, off we go!

[*Again, though they strain and grunt, the boat does not move, and they lower it a second time.*]

Sanfio: Shall we go and call for more hands?

Maika: We've just had reinforcements.

Burubo: How many are we altogether? Six, seven, eight, and nine, counting my good self. We should be able to launch a boat.

Bradide: Yes, it isn't a ten-puncheon boat.

Maika: Soon, women and children will be laughing at us over their washing.

Sanfio: I say, let's go for more people.

Peletua: No, there isn't enough wine here in the gourd to share with others. Bradide, shall we try a third time?

Bradide: That's my peer! Now, is everybody ready?

All: Yes!

Burubo: [*to Ogedegbe*] Roll up your wrapper, young man, and don't stand there like some chief newly installed.

Bradide: Are we all ready?

All: Yes, we are!

Bradide: Can we float a boat?

All: Yes, we can!

Bradide: Then here we go!

[*Once again they surround the boat and take the strain. It resists . . .*]

Eseni: Does the thing demand sacrifice?

Maika: Nonsense!

Eseni: Why not? The white man breaks a bottle over the bow when launching his big boats. I've seen it done at Burutu and Forcados.

Maika: Keep your adventure stories to yourself.

Peletua: For once what he says is true. We are not alone in worshipping our prows.

Maika: I'm not going home until we've launched this boat. I shan't be able to look my wives in the face.

Burubo: Yes, are we women that we can't float this boat?

Bradide: A song! Let's have a song, Sanfio, and then try again!

Sanfio: So song has some use after all!

Peletua: Too much price and pride put off the buyers, Sanfio. So out with the song or we'll stitch up that wide mouth of yours forever.

[*Sanfio starts a song which all take up as they start pushing again.*

Slowly, the boat begins to move on the wooden rollers laid out for it. The double strain brings more people cheering out on the bank, and now the boat is going at such a speed the men are running with it, some laughing with relief and letting go, others holding on fast, the owner climbing onto the prow as it hits water with a great splash over and above the singing and cheering from the crowd now gathered ashore.]

Scene 3 DEPARTURE

Early morning a few days after. The courtyard in the family compound. Movement of men and women carrying baggage as for a voyage: sleeping kit, kitchen ware, etc. One, carrying oars and punting poles on his shoulders, is challenged by someone just then opening his door. It is Biowa, obviously stirred by all the activity.

Biowa: Who is there?

Kpuruku: It's me.

Biowa: What are you doing with those things on your shoulders?

Kpuruku: Taking them to the boat. Don't you know our brother is off to Lokoja?

Biowa: Lokoja today?

Kpuruku: Yes. He means to sleep at Bomadi today, all going well.

Biowa: I see. Where is our brother?

[*Enter Bradide with paddle and bag.*]

Bradide: Here. What's the matter?

Biowa: Where are you going so early before cock has crowed first time?

Bradide: Cock has crowed thrice already if you must know. Some of us have to wake up early to find our feed.

Biowa: And where are you stealing out now to find your feed?

Bradide: You watch your mouth. I'm not stealing anywhere.

Biowa: You didn't tell me you're sailing today.

Bradide: When did I start reporting my movements to you?

Biowa: So Mother was right.

Bradide: About what?

Biowa: That you mean to cheat me on our arrangement regarding the boat. Don't laugh my brother. The new moon has not come but you say you have seen it, and now you are setting aside my days to go to Lokoja, knowing my wares are stacked still in the house.

Bradide: The new moon is up and I have seen it as have others if you will not believe me. As for your wares, you have only a few left and none of them will perish from long storage.

Biowa: Whereas the beetles will eat up your yams up there in Lokoja?

Bradide: Exactly.

Biowa: Brother, you treat me like a child.

Bradide: I do not.

Biowa: You do, and today we split.

Bradide: As you please. Only tell me how much you want for your share of the boat and I'll make refund on my return.

Biowa: Do you have money?

Bradide: I believe enough to pay you on my return and sale of produce.

Biowa: I will not touch a penny of yours.

Bradide: I thank you then if you will take no money.

[*Enter Umuto from the sideline.*]

Umuto: Shameless man! You are the elder and he should inherit from you, wives, property and all, and not the other way round.

Biowa: Keep out of this, Mother, I said keep out of this, and let me handle it myself.

Bradide: Well, let me go my way while you two settle as you like.

Biowa: No; you are not going.

Bradide: Why, what will you do?

Biowa: I said today we split.

Bradide: And I said I accept, though you still have not told me how, since you refuse payment for your part.

Biowa: You who are clever with the axe should know how to split a boat.

Bradide: Bah! Is that what you mean? You must be mad.

Biowa: I'm not mad. Mother, did you hear him calling me mad?

Bradide: You are. Your mother should have taken you to your goddess at Alota estuary a long time ago to appease her.

Biowa: Now you will see what a man mad can do.

Umuto: There, hold him! Stop him!

Bradide: Leave him! What can he do, the unweaned one?

[*He goes out with Kpuruku and others, as several neighbors enter.*]

1st Neighbor: There, what's the matter?

2nd Neighbor: It's not quite dawn yet.

4th Neighbor: And have you people started again?

3rd Neighbor: What is it this time?

Umuto: Hold them, please hold them! One's rushed indoors, and the other going to the beach. Don't let them ever meet! Oh, my sons! What have I done!

Neighbors together: Who should we hold? Who separate?

[*Enter Biowa, gun in hand.*]

Biowa: Somebody's child will die today.

[*He rushes past his mother and neighbors in the direction of the beach after his brother and party. All rush after him shouting, remonstrating.*]

All Together: It's Biowa! Run! He has his gun!
Don't, Govena, don't!
Oh, run, run!

[*Gun shot heard at close range in the hard morning light.*]

ACT III

Scene 1   SUMMONS

Later the same morning. At Agbodobri, a nearby town. In the living room of Okoro, husband of the only sister of the two brothers. He has heard the news and is pacing up and down, discussing with the person who brought it. The man is seated and rubbing his hands between his knees.

Okoro: This is terrible, terrible.

Sanfio: Yes, most terrible. Language is not adequate to handle it.

Okoro: I knew the arrangement between them would not last. Everybody knew it. But you know how it is with relations-in-law. You see a thing going wrong like an owl flying in broad daylight, but you dare not say it direct for fear of sanctions being applied against you. And of course the old lady was forever adding salt to fresh sores.

Sanfio: She has been their curse all right, and now she is gone distracted knowing she has caused her own injury.

Okoro: I knew one brother would be the death of the other but I didn't know it would be this way round, the favorite son killing the unloved one. How shall we tell my wife? She'll soon be back from the stream, having put out scant nets overnight. Now, how shall we tell her?

Sanfio: In circumstances of normal death, we still would be circum-

spect bringing news to the bereaved abroad. So as people like
Peletua do it so well, we'll begin as usual with spinning sweet
stories of life round the present state of things like a cock
courting. Then we will follow with parallel ones from elsewhere
carrying messages of equal import, the weightier if drawn from as
far as possible across the wider world. Fed upon such parables of
man's lot, all supplemented with actual diet of food and drink, we
can then proceed to delivering the news which we know will come
still as a stunning blow.

Okoro: It will kill her.

Sanfio: Oh, bereavement never killed anybody except by accident; the
taste of food is too strong a counter. But we shall of course
prepare her for the additional blow to come.

Okoro: I don't understand.

Sanfio: Envoys more powerful than me have carried the news to
Kiagbodo, Ayakoroama, Amatolo, and indeed to all settlements in
the clan with messages for all to meet today in open court at
Bikoroa. The trial is immediate.

Okoro: And we must all be there?

Sanfio: Yes, of course. Who will wash the corpse if the bereaved stay
away?

Okoro: True, true; but events are rushing as a torrent.

Sanfio: We cannot leave things for bluebottle flies to discharge upon.
Hush, I see your wife coming.

Okoro: What shall we tell her?

Sanfio: That her mother is taken ill and she summoned home as her
one daughter.

Okoro: Let me do it myself. Emo, welcome!

Emonemua: Haven't you gone yet to work?

Okoro: No. We have a guest here—from home.

Emonemua: Oh, is it you, Sanfio? Don't tell me you've got yourself
some sweetheart here and overstayed the night with her?

Sanfio: No such good fortune. I wouldn't land one so close and not
inform you, my sister. I came to collect a keg of palm wine. How
was the catch?

Emonemua: Empty we went; empty we return. We have lost our
lucky touch.

Sanfio: No; it's the season. The white man with his stern-wheelers is
churning up our waters so much the fish have all gone down to
hide on the riverbed.

Okoro: They come more and more. How shall we stop them?

Sanfio: No way. Iron chops up wood. So will their iron-boats our canoes.

Emonemua: You should hear the tears in your voices! Now, have you had something to drink? Or has he kept you talking all the time? What about breakfast? There's that weave of grub I got yesterday, and I have farina that's white and soft.

Sanfio: No; no breakfast.

Emonemua: A drink then?

Okoro: Emonemua . . .

Emonemua: Yes; is anything the matter? You're sweating all over.

Okoro: Your mother isn't very well, Sanfio was just telling me.

Emonemua: And is that your way of telling me my mother is dead?

Sanfio: The gods forbid! Why do you say things like that?

Emonemua: Well, when a person has reached her point of life, the list of what might happen becomes short. What is wrong with her this time? I hope she hasn't gone and got her head broken trying to stop a fight between her sons that she herself started?

Sanfio: Oh, no, no, blessings of Tamara! I understand she just took suddenly ill. With proper attention which only a good daughter can provide, she should be herself again soon enough.

Emonemua: You mean my two brothers and all their wives cannot attend to one sick woman?

Sanfio: They are not her daughter, all put together. And you know how our wives go off nowadays to their week-long markets in Letugbene and Angala. You can't find them anymore to do anything in the house when you need them.

Emonemua: All right, all right; we'll come. It's great to be missed.

Okoro: I'll come with you.

Emonemua: That should not be necessary. You should stay at home and keep your powder dry for the funeral.

Okoro: Didn't you hear Sanfio say she is not dead? And will you stop your foul humor! Well, I'm coming with you. Even sons-in-law have some rights.

[*She goes out.*]

Sanfio: Well said, man. Let's go. Now I'll have a glass of that gin you offered earlier while she's packing. The mouth needs rinsing of this foul matter.

Okoro: Oh, if one could hold back the motion of days as one dams up the flow of a stream, what wouldn't I do to reverse this day?

Sanfio: No way again, man. The sun is over the trees already.

[*Enter Emonemua.*]

Emonemua: Are you two still there yapping? I thought it was us
  women spent all day packing our kit if we aren't gossiping. See,
  I'm all set to go. I must be homesick after all.

Sanfio: Man, what have you been doing to our sister—beating or
  starving her?

Okoro: We do our best, but as you know the husband is always in
  debt to the other side.

Emonemua: Hear them chattering.

Sanfio: We stand rebuked.

Emonemua: The children are crying to come.

Okoro: Do you think we should take them?

Emonemua: I don't see why not. They haven't seen their granny for
  some time. And they should be additional company for her in her
  condition.

  [*She goes out. Okoro brings out a bottle of drink from a small sideboard.*]

Okoro: There, your drink!

Sanfio: And yours too!

Okoro: What a day!

Sanfio: Yes, what a day! Now, let's go before the news breaks over us
  here and defeats our purpose.

Scene 2   TRIAL

*Afternoon the same day. The town-court or amaogula in the central,
ancestral hall at Bikoroa. Seated upstage in front facing the audience is the
Amaokosuowei or Eldest-Man-in-Town, Angalakizide. The Dumu-
Okosuowei-ama or Ward-Elders (with one sleeping in and out of session) are
grouped behind and around him. Behind them are the Okosuowei-ama or
senior citizens, all more middle-aged than really old. In both these groups
are several characters already familiar from previous scenes. Prominent is
Peletua in his public role of Onoumbra or Bebeareowei, that is, Spokesman
and Prosecutor. He stands to the side in front of the Amaokosuowei. Farther
down the floor, downstage, upon their own stools and mats, sit men and
women of the town, others standing around both outside and inside the hall,
almost mixing with the audience. From among them Voices from Outside
come in occasionally to contribute to the proceedings, one of them that of a
Young Man of Wisdom. And all through, children climb in and out of the
low open windows, playing without much hindrance. This is not to say
Maika, the Amadiowei or Town-overseer, supported by Eseni, the Owubia,
that is the General-factotum of the court, is not doing his best to maintain
law and order.*

Angala: This is terrible, terrible. And to think that this would happen to us, and in my time as head of this town. Who said old age is not a curse? At best, it is a slowing down of all our motions to sleep from which there is no waking, but most of the time, it makes us see what we should not see. We bury the children we bore, and all that we hold dear we see destroyed before our bleary eyes, and our limbs are too infirm to stem the tide of destruction.

Peletua: Try and be calm before the clan descends upon us, and let it be clearly understood they are not coming to hand us ruin. After all, this is not an inquest that they will come raiding livestock and crops to be found anywhere in town. Nobody has committed suicide nor has anybody done an act here for which family or town can be held accountable.

Bienware: I hear drums close by; I think one of the parties has arrived.

Owubia: Silence all!

Angala: Oh, it is terrible! What shall we do? How are we going to feed all these people?

Owubia: Make way! Make way for the party coming in!

Bienware: It is the party from the capital, led by Ambakederemo himself.

Angala: I said we shall be crushed by this affair.

[*Enter Ambakederemo, followed by the Kiagbodo delegation.*]

Peletua: Rain like sea water! Shroud of death! Pit without bottom! Man as good as his word! This way, this way to your seat. Did you have to come yourself?

Ambakederemo: The king himself would have come if he could, but here we are, plucked out of bed by reports you brought us of the events here this morning. I hope we have not kept you waiting.

Angala: Oh, no, no. You have been as prompt to the call as the eagle to a house on fire.

Ambakederemo: I see in fact we have arrived ahead of others. Where is Amatolo? Don't say they are again at their game of diplomacy, saying one thing here and saying another there on one and the same issue.

[*Enter Uyo at the head of the party from Amatolo.*]

Uyo: Ambakederemo, you are always abusing us, though you cannot resist our daughters.

Ambakederemo: I thought since you two stand in such special relationship within the family, you would be here before everybody.

Uyo: We came as fast as we could, almost at your tail in fact. And don't forget we are farther upstream.

Ambakederemo: Welcome then, welcome in spite of all your wily ways.

Peletua: Here, this way, this way.

Uyo: How are you all?

Angala: Terrible, terrible, as you can see. Tell me, brother Uyo, how have we offended that we should be visited with events like this?

Uyo: Nobody is blaming you, nobody can. However deep the river, we have divers here will get to its bed.

Peletua: Ayakoroama is here.

Angala: We didn't hear their drums.

[*Enter Onduku, leading the Ayakoroama delegation.*]

Onduku: Well, here we are.

Ambakederemo: You make speed like a true pirate, Onduku.

Onduku: Ask your white trader friends at Ganagana and they will confirm it if they are not the inveterate fabricators of evidence that they are. With their own guns seized from them I engaged them midstream till they called truce. How can I observe it when my brother went in the encounter?

Ambakederemo: Take care, take care. In Benin they flattened a whole city because of the loss of one man. They called it pacification as indeed they did when they sacked Nana.

Onduku: Let them try, let them try it here. Now, where do we sit, Bienware?

Peletua: Here, this way. Greetings, greetings all.

[*The delegations are now all seated on either side of the Amaokosuowei, separate from the local groups already seated.*]

Peletua: Oh, Mein!

All: Yes!

Peletua: Oh, Mein!

All: Yes!

Peletua: Is there man in Mein?

All: Yes, there is!

Peletua: If you see will you act?

All: Yes, we will!

Ozi Drum: A sword, a sword is the town
                     A flesh-eating sword
                     A fish-eating sword
                     That's our town!

[*All take up the chant.*]

Uyo: Let the man who committed the evil act be now brought before the court of the whole clan assembled.

Onduku: We don't know yet whether he committed an evil act.

Voices from the Floor and Outside: True, true!
But we saw him, we saw him!
He killed his brother, he killed him!

Ambakederemo: That is the fact we are here to establish.

[*Both the Amadiowei and the Owubia bring in the Accused, chained hands and feet, to center stage. A general audible silence sweeps through the court.*]

Ambakederemo: What is the case against this man?

Peletua: Oh, Ngbilebiri all assembled here in open court, the case that it is the unhappy duty of Bikoroa to bring before you today has no parallel in our history, certainly not in any that I can recall within living memory except there is someone among the elders here who wants to correct me.

Onduku: Go on.

Peletua: As cock called dawn today, a quarrel, not an uncommon occurrence among brothers, broke out between the dead man Bradide and his younger brother Biowa, who stands here accused of his murder. The dispute was over the right of the deceased to take to Lokoja the boat they held in common possession while the accused, disputing his brother had seen the new moon in the sky, and recalling the days he had lost while his brother carried out badly needed repairs on the boat, considered his term to it unexpired. When his brother would not yield to his claim, backed as usual by their mother, a proposal even more peculiar than the original arrangement between the brothers was put up by the accused, namely, that they split the boat, not in any sense of metaphor allowing one to put up money for the other to give up his part for sole possession to reside in one brother, but in straight literal sense of splitting the craft from helm to prow.

Uyo: That's a mad proposal, as mad as the entire arrangement.

Onduku: Are you saying brothers must not work and own things together?

Uyo: I don't know about that; but what are we to make of this business of sighting and not sighting the moon like Hausas seeking to end their fast?

Onduku: Tell us a better way of measuring time.

Okosuowei: Yes, as the sun spells the day so the moon the seasons, and tide and annual flood aid them.

Ambakederemo: All right, all right, let's get on with the case, and not
　　prejudge.

Peletua: Well, if I may continue, Bradide too thought it a mad
　　proposal, and proceeded therefore moving with his party to the
　　beach to board the boat. Thereupon Biowa, by now incensed,
　　dashed indoors, came back with his gun and, rushing past
　　everybody after his brother, caught up with him, and shot him
　　direct in his chest. That is the case for Bikoroa against Biowa.
　　Now did I present it correctly?

Bienware: Yes, most correctly—nothing added, nothing removed.

Okosuowei: There were occasions though when I thought you would
　　convulse!

Onduku: Cut that out.

Ambakederemo: Are there witnesses to the act?

Peletua: Yes, several.

Ambakederemo: Shall we first hear the Amadiowei, your town
　　overseer?

Peletua: Certainly.

　　[*Maika steps forward.*]

Peletua: Maika, before Ngbile our father and before Odele his god of
　　justice, tell the court what you know of the case of Bikoroa against
　　the accused.

Maika: Well, it is as our Onoumbra outlined.

Ambakederemo: No; you tell us what you saw.

Maika: Actually I was not present during the quarrel, but on hearing
　　so much noise in the morning, followed by gunshot, I ran with
　　others to the scene of crime and saw there, lying on the ground at
　　the Ogoun waterside, already dead, Bradide. There was confusion
　　all round, what with several trying in vain to revive the dead
　　man, some running for cover, and others accusing Biowa, who
　　was then walking away with gun in hand.

Onduku: Was there no man among you in this town?

Maika: It is easy to say that now the man is in chains and without
　　his gun.

Ambakederemo: Never mind; it is not everybody has taken the title of
　　ogbu as our friend has. Tell the court what you did next.

Maika: Actually, there was not much to do, for Biowa of his own
　　gave up himself and his gun. I led him straightaway to our
　　Amaokosuowei, returning thereafter to have the dead body
　　covered with mats.

Uyo: Where is the corpse now?

Maika: Still at the beach, lying watched over by peers, quite close by where your vessels are moored.

Onduku: And where is the gun?

Maika: Here. It is unloaded now.

Ambakederemo: Good, leave it there. We shall send men to view the corpse later. Call in the other witnesses one at a time.

Peletua: Kpuruku! Call Kpuruku!

Maika Joined
By Several } Kpuruku!
Inside and
Outside

[*Enter Kpuruku.*]

Kpuruku: Here I am.

Peletua: Now before our founding father Ngbile and his god of justice Odele, tell the court what happened in your compound this morning.

Kpuruku: Bradide and Biowa had another of their quarrels over that boat, and Biowa took his gun and shot Bradide.

Uyo: Is that all you have to say?

Onduku: What more do you want of the boy? He went straight as a spear.

Kpuruku: That's what I saw as I helped to carry things to the boat.

Ambakederemo: And that's quite enough. You may go.

[*Kpuruku goes out.*]

Who next?

Peletua: Kelemere. Call in Kelemere.

Maika: Kelemere! Kelemere! Where is she now?

[*Enter Kelemere.*]

Peletua: Kelemere, come here. Look up from your tears, and do not be frightened by the sight of so many important persons present here. They are here to do justice by your house. Now before our founding father and before our god of justice, tell the court all you know of the case.

Kelemere: He killed his senior, he killed him with his gun during their quarrel over their boat. I saw it all.

Peletua: Can you not tell more, give more details?

Ambakederemo: That will not be necessary. You can see the poor girl is shaking all over. Young woman, you may go.

[*Kelemere goes out.*]

Onduku: What about the woman their mother?

Peletua: I am afraid, since the fire she herself helped to start, she has gone somewhat distracted.

Ambakederemo: Then we shall not call her. Shall we consider your case closed?

Peletua: Yes, it is closed, and now we ask for justice.

Ambakederemo: What have you to say that are accused of the crime of killing your brother?

Onduku: Did you hear the question put to you?

Voice from Outside: Before the man answers, I have an observation or rather a question to ask the court.

Uyo: We want no stupid intervention here.

Onduku: Let the man speak.

Ambakederemo: It is a free and open court. Let him speak as a free-born child of the land. Now what do you have to say?

Voice from Outside: The white man I hear has opened a court at Frukama and another at Forcados. Should we then be hearing a case like this, when the directive is for all cases of grave kind in these rivers to go from now on to the white man?

Onduku: Good fellow, shall we also ask the white man permission before we sleep with our wives tonight? No, no, do not laugh. Can we not sneeze again without seeking the permission of some strangers? Oh, tell me how did we live before he came among us? And how shall we live when he leaves us, for leave he must, considering how he yellows all over and dies on our shores like a mango leaf even when not touched by anybody.

Ambakederemo: Do not mind the fellow. As you all know, I have myself invitations to sit on both courts, but I am not on account of that going to leave my bottom behind on their chairs. Now, put the question again to the accused so we can hear his defence.

Peletua: Biowa, you stand here accused of killing your brother with a gun during a quarrel over a boat you both owned. What is the truth to this charge facing you? Speak up so that the whole court and clan can hear you.

Biowa: It is as you have said. I have nothing more to add.

Ambakederemo: Had he too a gun?

Biowa: No.

Ambakederemo: Any kind of weapon at all, say, spear, cutlass or cudgel he was going to strike you with?

Biowa: None.

Onduku: So you did not shoot him in self-defence?

Biowa: No.

Uyo: Were you out of your mind?

Biowa: I am not mad and let no man call me so.

Ambakederemo: You are not mad, and you killed your brother. Then were you angry with him before the quarrel?

Biowa: There would have been no quarrel if there was no anger.

Ambakederemo: Well answered. Are you angry still?

Biowa: I don't know. He tried to overturn our arrangement when I had days still to go.

Ambakederemo: Did you then want to kill him earlier? Did you hear me, Biowa?

Biowa: Who has not thought of killing a brother from the day one is weaned of the breast for the other to suckle?

Voices from Outside: Oh, Biowa, so you have been of such evil heart all this time?

Eseni: Quiet!

Ambakederemo: Biowa, we are not the ones on trial. So do not ask us questions.

Biowa: I know.

Ambakederemo: Do you accept you have done an act forbidden by both the living and the dead?

Biowa: I have done wrong. What more do you want me to say? I didn't see the new moon he said he had seen.

Onduku: The new moon has been up now two, three days, though the clouds have been like smoke from a cannonade.

Uyo: He should see it tonight, clouds or no clouds.

Ambakederemo: Is there anybody here ready to testify on behalf of the accused? Yes?

Voice from Outside: Bradide was always trying to override his brother as the elder. I know their mother encouraged the rivalry between them, taking sides always with the younger, but the senior wasn't an easy man to live with. He always was insistent upon his rights.

Ambakederemo: Was that enough reason for his brother to kill him?

Voices from Outside: No; of course not.

Peletua: Then the case of Bikoroa against Biowa for killing his brother is closed. Perhaps you will want to rise now to consider your decision in conclave?

Okosuowei: [*waking up from sleep*] Oh, have we finished already? The man's guilty I say!

Ambakederemo: You have been asleep through half the proceedings, old man, so go back to your slumber while we retire to reach judgement.
[*All the leaders of the delegations go out together with the Amaokosuowei and the Onoumbra.*]

Okosuowei: I wasn't sleeping; I followed every step of the case as stated.

Young Man: Stay at home but you won't agree. See how you have disgraced yourself.

Okosuowei: You shut your mouth, boy! I haven't disgraced myself. It's your mother and all her foolish, silly people have disgraced themselves, not me. And if you don't all behave in this town, you better pack up your dirty clothes now, and go back to your own place, silly, foolish people, telling one all the time what to do and what not to do. Who gave you that privilege?

Voices from ⎤ It's enough now.
all over ⎬ He meant well.
the Court ⎦ He meant no harm.

Okosuowei: Meant no harm, the foolish, silly scamp who has taken after his mother. Too cheeky all of them of the clan.
[*Pause: Master drum.*]

Eseni: Silence now! They are coming back from the conclave. Silence there! You children, stay by your mothers or I'll throw you out.

Voices from Outside: Have they reached decision already?

Another Voice: What was there to argue about? The case is clear for all to see.
[*The delegations return to their seats.*]

Eseni: Silence, I said!
[*All resume their seats and a dead hush descends upon the hall.*]

Ambakederemo: Biowa, the clan, sitting in open court, after due deliberation, finds you guilty of killing in long festering anger your elder brother Bradide. It has however not agreed on the manner of punishment, splitting down the middle. Do you meanwhile have any special request to make before the court proceeds to determine sentence?

Peletua: Did you hear the verdict? And did you hear the offer?

Biowa: I did.

Peletua: Then speak.

Biowa: I want to see my mother.

Onduku: What, that woman who from all accounts has helped to bring you to your present position?

Ambakederemo: Let him see her. She is still his mother.

Uyo: We made the offer.

Onduku: It is amazing how our wives come as handmaids and then take us over as their puppets.

Uyo: I am no woman's plaything.

Ambakederemo: Call the woman. Let her come before her son in whatever condition she is.

Uyo: Meanwhile, shall we pronounce punishment?

Ambakederemo: You are like the fire in the gun, always jumping ahead of the sound.

Onduku: Yes, we still have to agree on the kind of penalty.

Several Voices from the Floor } Here comes the woman. Most unhappy mother! The witch, she ate up her own eggs.

Eseni: Silence! Clear the way for her!

Ambakederemo: What's her name?

Peletua: Umuto Diakohwo.

Ambakederemo: Umuto Diakohwo, come up this way. Help her up. There, our eyes smart for you.

Umuto: I didn't tell him to kill his brother! I didn't tell him, believe me, believe me!

Onduku: We believe you. There is your remaining son. He wants to see you.

Uyo: There is your mother. Now you may speak to her.

Biowa: I thank you all for your kind consideration. What I have to say is for the ear of my mother alone.

Umuto: Did he say for my ear alone?

Onduku: Yes. Now go to him.

Biowa: Come, Mother, I'd like to tell you something.

Umuto: Oh, my son! [*She rushes to embrace him. He leans over as if to whisper into her ear which he bites off.*]

Umuto: Oh, he's bitten off my ear, bitten off my ear!

The Delegates Together } Stop! Stop him! Take the woman away from him.

[*Eseni takes out Umuto crying.*]

Uyo: Now, why did you do that?

Ambakederemo: Simple to see, I should think. By mouth she fed him on the poison of her pap, and by ear she poured the venom of her tongue against his brother.

Onduku: My father who bore me, an accursed family all right, there is no doubting it.

Uyo: Now shall we decide on the punishment? We have delayed too long, and some of us have far to go.

Ambakederemo: It is a man's life we are dealing with.

Uyo: As we said in conclave, the man has taken life and must pay for it.

Ambakederemo: That it is not that simple a matter you will also recall we discussed at length. Or are you trying to play alien to the public? We all know the past provides us no precedent in this case. The man has not killed in combat an enemy from outside the tribe. If it were so, we would of course be awarding him the title of ogbu as our good friend here Onduku has honorably won for himself and his heirs forever unless they want to renounce it. Nor has he killed a compatriot in combat. If it were so, we would be awarding the bereaved family a virgin for marriage to the nearest of kin and a dowry to go with her. And if the killing was in cold blood and out of malice, we all also know what we would do. By now, the tall pole should be standing by the beach for the hanging, after which the bereaved can take as many shots as they like at the corpse of the hanged man laid out in the square. This, however, is no ordinary killing we have been called here to adjudicate. The killing is not outside the clan, nor outside the town. It is dead within the house—that of a brother by a brother. I do not then see how we can award punishment without raising fresh problems. And there are those who will always say we do not kill a child of the soil as sacrifice to the state.

Uyo: It will be no sacrifice. Far from it! But since we are afraid of shedding further blood, let's sell the man as slave to the Itsekiri, your mother's people. They rise to become kingmakers there, I hear.

Ambakederemo: They even do better among us, let me tell you. Did you not hear King Jaja was a common Igbo slave who supplanted an indolent Ijo heir?

Onduku: Then let us sell him to the white man to take across the seas.

Ambakederemo: That's no use either; the white man will probably send him back to us as a priest or teacher to preach his cause. This is why some of us have refused sending to their schools our sons, and rather than that, send them our house-slaves when they come importuning us.

Voice from Outside: In their book, I hear it is written God exiled the first man to kill his brother and he ended up peopling half the earth. It is true. I heard the preacher tell the story at their new shrine in Warri.

Bienware: Keep your outlandish stories to yourself. We are faced by a grave matter.

Ambakederemo: There, you see, Uyo, you can call the fight between us any other day on any issue you like and I'll come meeting you in the open square.

Angala: Don't be angry, Osuo, don't be angry!

Ambakederemo: My anger is gone.

Bienware: How then shall we settle this grave matter before us?

Onduku: Yes, how shall we settle it?

Young Man of Wisdom: I have a word to say, my elders!

Ambakederemo: Come forward and speak up, young man.

Young Man of Wisdom: Since penalty there has to be, although you still have to decide on the way of doing so, being, as we have been told, the first time this thing is happening among us, should we not, if we are to avoid some of the fresh problems we are being wisely warned against, should we not consult at this point the person who, without having taken any part at any stage in this terrible action, remains probably the most affected, I mean, Emonemua.

Delegates: Who is that?
Who is she?
Who is Emonemua?

Peletua: She is the one sister of the deceased and the accused.

Onduku: Where has she been all the time?

Peletua: At home, recovering from the shock she received on hearing the news.

Ambakederemo: Let her then be brought, if she is in a fit state.

Peletua: Bring in Emonemua, bring her in!

Voices from the Floor: Oh the poor woman!
Look at her husband; he came with her this morning.
She collapsed like a wall when the news broke on her.

[*She is brought in, supported on either side by her husband and Sanfio.*]

Onduku: Find her a seat to sit down.

Emonemua: No; I will not sit down.

Ambakederemo: You know what has brought us here; it is not a happy business for everybody but you must feel it most of all, being their only sister. We shall therefore not prolong the pain of the occasion by engaging in long interrogation. The clan sitting in court has found your brother Biowa guilty of wilfully killing his

brother, Bradide. It has however not been able to agree on whether
or not one brother should be executed for killing another, thereby
doubling what already is a grievous loss to your family.

Uyo: Speak, woman, for it is what you say that the court will do.

Emonemua: You it is who own me, and I speak by your permission.
When I came home with my husband this morning, believing my
mother was ill and needed nursing, I little knew I was walking
into a house of ruin. Had the wreck been by some outside hand,
we who are within would have resisted together and warded it off
as best we could. But the blow, as you see, has been by our own
hand. My brother has killed my brother who was his brother, and
shall I now weep with him and laugh with him later in make-
believe nothing has happened to our house? I do not know what
men will say, but, for me, my choice is clear. If he could kill in a
quarrel my brother who was the head of our house, he would also
kill me, a mere woman, when I as much as arouse his anger which
will be often, as friction is most between those who are closest.
That my brother's orphaned children may not suffer any handicap
beside his own children, and none of us left behind live in
permanent fear of this man who may fall upon any of us any day
and take up again the destruction he began today, I plead with
you, my elders who own me, that you do to him as should be
done to anyone who takes life in this land. It will be easier for me
to live mourning my two brothers than remain with one remem-
bering the other he killed. There is nothing more I have to say.
Thank you all.

[*She turns to go and the court does not stop her, but waits until she has left
the hall which remains in complete silence.*]

Uyo: Well, what are we waiting for? The verdict is death.
Yes, it's death!

All   Yes, it is!

Delegates: Death it is!
Death it is!

Onduku: Then let's be quick! We have the means the occasion itself
calls up! Odokuku trees, cut down odokuku trees, and let's strap
the man to wood that, though frail-looking, will not burn in any
woman's kitchen and will weight him as iron down the riverbed.
For there we must take him, together with their accursed boat,
which today must be split from end to end for him to take his
half, while the other goes with the brother he murdered to his
shallow grave in the evil grove. Come on, are there no men in this

town of Bikoroa or shall we of the clan take over your part?

Angala: The gods will not approve! The dead will not! There, Peletua, Eseni, Maika, Sanfio, Ogedegbe, where is everybody? Let's do what we have to do.

[*They close in upon the Accused and lead him away without resistance amid cries and hisses from the floor, some cursing him aloud, others spitting and waving hands over their heads and snapping their fingers after him.*]

Ambakederemo: Then the court rises.

All: It rises.

Onduku: Oh, Izon!

All: Yes!

Onduku: Oh, Mein!

All: Yes!

Onduku: Oh, Ngbilebiri!

All: Yes!

Onduku: Is there man in Mein?

All: Yes, there is!

Onduku: If you see will you act?

All: Of course we will!

Onduku: Then let's go!

[*They all stream out.*]

Scene 3 AFTERMATH

Later the same day. The living-room of Bradide at the family compound. Emonemua is sitting on the floor with several women surrounding her, all looking exhausted from much weeping. Men form an outer ring, sitting on chairs against the walls. Among them is the Amaokosuowei. Umuto enters, crying with hands over her head.

Emonemua: Sit down in one place, Mother, and let them dress your ear.

Umuto: What do I want with my ear? Oh, what a life I have chosen, to lose in one day my two sons who should see me home in my old age? I made them fight so others will leave them alone.

Bienware: That was a policy full of danger although we won't go into that now. We may weep as the rain and all year long for the dead but that will not bring them back.

[*She goes into a bedroom right.*]

Angala: Yes, we pray let such and such not happen to us; yet it happens. Let's not see such and such a thing; yet we see it. So a house burns down one night or a canoe capsizes and a whole family perishes. Our most fervent prayers fly in our face, as if the gods in hearing us wish ourselves so much happiness take offense or take us for children crying for what they know not may harm or soothe them.

Peletua: The gods know best.

Angala: I wonder. Had I been there when the Almighty was creating the world, I would have given her some good suggestions.

Peletua: And what would you have told her, oh, wise man?

Angala: Just a simple suggestion—that she should have provided a key to the heart of man so that, if anger entered in, you could open it and wash the thing out, and if disease of any kind found its way in, you could open the wretched thing and sweep it out.

Peletua: And what if you lost your key or somebody went off with it one day?

Angala: I've made my suggestion; why don't you young people come up with yours?

Emonemua: You old people can be funny!

Burubo: It seems the other party has come.

Sanfio: Yes, it has come back. Now be strong. I know it is easier said than done. But what else can tongue say or head offer?
[*A party of several men enter the room after washing their feet and hands outside, leaving behind their paddles and cutlasses.*]

All Together: Have you come back?
Greetings! Greetings!
How was it?

[*The newcomers take their seats.*]

Angala: Well, how was it?

Maika: We took him out of here in our boat down the stream to the wide Forcados River where black and white waters meet. There, in the circuitous current of the confluence, we lowered him, tied full-length to those slender boles of the trees he loved to be called by.

Emonemua: And did he not say anything all the time? Did he not curse me his sister who sent him to his death?

Eseni: No, on the contrary, the only time he spoke, and that when we seemed to fumble in the act, was to say with pride you should have been the man in the family, for then you would have shown us how to do our duty.

Emonemua: Oh, my brother, my brothers! I said do not buy one boat together but you would not listen, you would not listen to me, because I am a woman, and a younger sister. Now the canoe you staked your lives on is split down the middle, I am left behind to do salvage work mid-stream. How am I a woman become the diver? I thought they say sisters and brothers have such special claims upon each other not even their own parents can make, sharing in their veins those very properties that the parents bring individually to the union.

Peletua: That is true, very true. It's a claim not even their own children can dispute.

Emonemua: Then why have they treated me like this?

Peletua: We who were their peer feel for them too a special relationship badly betrayed. Springing from the same soil as we did, like seedlings in close seasons, rain or sun, we saw quite a bit of life together, and it cannot be said that the wicked wind that has swept them down today has not left us all splintered and singed, even if in the removal of one trunk from the other we seemed to side with thunder.

Emonemua: Oh, my brothers!

Sanfio: You will have to be strong, be stronger still as you have shown already you can more than anybody in bearing this load.

Angala: Oh, yes, she will have to be. Of course the people will help part of the way part of the time, but soon they will all return to their separate homes, even as our kith and kin from the clan have already done, leaving you, Emonemua, with the full load upon your head.

Emonemua: Oh, my brothers!

Bienware: Yes, it will be left with you as a sick child with her mother to nurse to sleep when everybody has retired to rest. But when you remember you carry the load not for yourself alone but for others as well who must be protected from it, like the children they have left behind for you to look after, and of course there is also your mother, you can see why through all the tears that must be shed in this unhappy business, we pray God and all the dead of our land will give you the back to bear your load.

Emonemua: I cannot cope, I cannot cope with this burden, oh, my brothers gone without burial!

Peletua: They will both be buried some day when the season is right. Now ours is to endure the pain and clear the land. But if the berth refuses the boat after storm, where will it turn?

Burubo: When a canoe capsizes we know the inventory is never again complete but still we try, and the trial finds the champion diver.
[*A child runs in, followed by another and another.*]
Emonemua: Here, here, who is chasing you? Who is chasing you?
1st Child: Tobo!
Emonemua: Why are you chasing him?
2nd Child: Because he abused me.
Emonemua: He abused you? Now why did you abuse him?
3rd Child: Because Tobo won't let him play with his toy.
Emonemua: What toy?
2nd Child: My beautiful boat I made out of a bamboo. He broke it struggling for it with me.
Emonemua: All right, we'll find you another piece of bamboo to carve a boat. Now run off and play.
1st Child: I don't want to play; I'm hungry!
Emonemua: How true! You must all be famished. Kelemere, why haven't the children eaten? Find them some food, all of them, let them have enough to eat. And our guests—have they eaten?
Peletua: No; they are gone.
Angala: A good thing too; they would have eaten us quite bankrupt.
Bienware: You were always tight-fisted.
Angala: One must be frugal with life for it to last, for it to go on.
Sanfio: Oh, yes, it goes on and on for the group, doesn't it? It is the individual who loses out.
Angala: Oh, man is a funny creation! Even as eyes and nostrils dribble, belly will still grumble and before you know it, mouth is beginning to water.
Emonemua: Good people, you must bear with me if I forget myself.
Angala: No criticism was meant. Indeed who can offer any?
Emonemua: Still we must not forget. Kpuruku!
Kpuruku: Yes!
Emonemua: Where do you keep your drinks in this house?
Kpuruku: There are lots at the other place.
Emonemua: Then get the men a bottle. They must all be thirsty after so much unpleasant labor.
[*Kpuruku goes out.*]
Bienware: A drink is welcome any time. It makes all things assume their proper state. Oh, yes, a drink in season softens the hard; strengthens the soft.
Angala: And while we are waiting for the good cheer to come, you may like to know the great Ambakederemo is going to send me

one of his voluptuous girls to marry.

Burubo: Oh, Angalakizide, at your age?

Angala: What age? Does the sap stop running up the iroko tree because it is a hundred years old? Throw me into the river, and leave me there for seven days, and my blood will not stop surging. I am the stream, and mean to go on running until I enter the sea.

Burubo: When was all this arranged?

Angala: Oh, as we saw the parties off to the waterside.

Emonemua: You'll never change! What will the young do when you ancients carry on like this?

[*Kpuruku enters with a bottle of gin and starts to serve all round, beginning with the old man.*]

Angala: Each to his own canoe, I say. If the young will not paddle for themselves, I offer to teach them one or two strokes, but first, they must make over their rights, oh yes, to those fresh delectable wives of theirs with bottoms and bosoms always bobbing up and down in your face.

Peletua: Ama-mon-koro-ka!

Angala: It is your host that lacks means: a town can't all go hungry! Now, isn't this a great drink?

All: Ama-mon-koro-ka!

The End

The Return Home

CHARACTERS

Fregene son of Bradide
Egberibo his first cousin, son of
   Biowa
Maika an elder and friend of the
   family
Tonwe
Apele } all peers of the cousins

Diri
Omonibo
Emonemua aunt of the cousins
A Boy son of Biowa
People of Bikoroa, consisting of
   Elders, Neighbors, etc.

ACT I

Scene 1 SHAPES

Late afternoon at Bikoroa in the Niger Delta toward the end of the twenties. The frontyard of the compound of the brothers Bradide and Biowa, both killed in "The Boat." Fregene, the son of Bradide, is carving a figure in wood for a customer. Sitting with him is an elderly man, Maika, a contemporary of his father, making fun of his art, which he takes in good part.

Maika: Why do you give them such big and pointed parts?
Fregene: Who?
Maika: Go away; you know what I mean. Your men and women, they are forever so well endowed. Look at this figure you're hacking to shape before me. From the bulging top I see there, I can tell right away it is a woman. And if it was male, you and I know what will be sticking out.

Fregene: Well, you have yourself explained the matter.

Maika: How have I explained the matter to myself?

Fregene: That we humble shapers of form pick upon properties that tell one kind immediately from the other.

Maika: I call it falsification; the Almighty herself doesn't make them big and pointed like that; a few perhaps, but it seems to me you people make the exception the rule.

Fregene: Let's say with our little gift from our Almighty Mother we try to make some of man's dreams come true, arresting in fixed form what is passing.

Maika: In wood, and in clay? Bah!

Fregene: Oh, eyes that have not seen, and hands that have not touched!

Maika: Young man, I don't have to take sixty-odd wives like Ambakederemo of Kiagbodo for you to know I broke out of the common mold of men in this town. Foreign wife from Urhobo, I married her; local maid from the next quarters, I married her as well. Tell me any of my peers who has done better.

Fregene: Agbraragbruru!

Maika: May it not thunder! The Almighty's children are here below. Anyway, who are you carving that thing for and for what purpose? Don't you go and lend your hand to some evil plot you don't know of.

Fregene: The gods forbid! You know my policy—the crooked wood tells the expert carver.

Maika: Your client may turn out to be crooked, young man.

Fregene: What he does with his piece, once I have delivered it, is not my responsibility.

Maika: There you are! You people are not consistent in the practice of your profession.

Fregene: Now, what have we done this time?

Maika: Take this business of finding the right shapes for things we were talking about; you don't do with birds and fish what you say you do with the human form. Nor for that matter, do you with your animals, whether you take them from the forest or the homestead. Bird, fish, or beast, you make them all quite natural.

Fregene: I'd say there too we pick upon those properties that reveal the creature, although I'll admit that here we seek the breed as a whole instead of the types that make it up.

Maika: Heads and tails, wings and fins—and, sometimes, limbs and necks are what you traffic in with the lesser breed.

Fregene: Yes; although, as you said yourself, we do not try to improve upon Tamara, the great molder of all things.

[*The singsong voice of a fish-monger hawking fish is heard from outside.*]

Boy: Fish for a penny!
 Fish for a shilling!
 Who will buy
 Fish for a penny,
 Fish for a shilling?

Maika: Who is selling fish at this time of day? They must be pretty rotten by now.

[*The strain comes closer.*]

Maika: Bring and take away, if you won't let one hear.

[*The hawker appears, a young boy of about twelve, with a wide wicker tray displaying his ware on his head.*]

Fregene: Well, it's my own boy, my brother's son.

Maika: So I see. You people are so industrious: one a trader when not making false images for clients he won't disclose, and the other the fisherman-hunter always gambling away his money.

Fregene: When will you see good in us?

Maika: Who said I don't? Come here, boy! Let me see what you have in that tray of yours. I see the waves carried you away and the waves have washed you back.

Boy: I've gone from one end of the town to the other and have not sold everything. Mother will beat me.

Maika: Nonsense, let's see what you've left. Now, where is the head of that one? Who bought it?

Boy: Nobody. It was kept behind for big mother.

Maika: So it's cooking right in there now?

Fregene: You may stay behind to share in the feast. We have to wait for Egberibo to come though.

Maika: That means waiting till night. Your brother won't leave the playhouse until he has cleared everybody out or he has been cleared out by some other adventurer. But, boy, I can't see any portion here to buy. Heads reserved for the big matron of the clan—

Fregene: Don't be envious. There's a fine portion, a right round size, for you to take home to your wives, if you will dip hand into that deep pot of yours buried under your bed.

Maika: A fine portion of the right size, you say? Where's the under-belly then?

Boy: It was sliced off by my father to send to my uncle here.

Maika: I see. So all the delicacies are trimmed away to feed the favorites at home, and it's the rejected parts that are pushed to us of the general public to pay hard cash for? Now, why are hunters, farmers, and fishermen so inconsiderate to the public?

Fregene: Go produce your own, that's what they are saying.

Maika: If everybody becomes a producer, who will be the buyer? It is unfair of the farmer to keep the best yam for himself. And the hunter and fisherman should not keep the better part of the catch for himself. They used to send the town elders the head of whatever was killed before, but now they are so greedy and disrespectful. Head, heart, liver and all those fine innards, ask for them, even when you say you are buying and want to pay cash, and all you hear these days is the part's been kept back at home for private consumption.

Fregene: Agree, Maika, those who hunt by land or water engage in great danger. Let them pamper themselves a bit. And it could be, as you elders say, they want to transfer to themselves some of the properties of what they kill.

Maika: Bah! Who wants to own the heart of a rabbit or grass-cutter?

Boy: May I go now, if you won't even buy a single piece?

Maika: Yes, go boy, go! And may you find some more gullible customer to off-load your rotten ware on.

Boy: Oh, they are still very fresh, sir.

Fregene: I think you better go in now.

Boy: I can still get to the end of town before dark. I'm sure to sell what's left or Mother—

Fregene: All right. You better go then, but make sure you come back home before dark.

[*The boy goes out singing his strain.*]

Maika: What he doesn't sell his mother is sure to put on the rack, and tomorrow what wasn't sold to us today as fresh fish will be touted to us as dry fish from Angala.

Fregene: We throw away nothing that is useful. Give that to us.

Maika: Oh yes, look at the chorus of flies following the boy. There ought to be a law forbidding the sale of fish in that state..

Fregene: Aren't you the people who make the laws? You were town-overseer for many years, in fact; so why are you aching in your belly?

Maika: The white man has taken all our powers away. He now has native courts at local, clan, and district levels, and only those he calls warrant chiefs may with his court-clerks and messengers rule in his name.

Fregene: Oh, surely, that's overstating matters a bit, isn't it? You still decided quite a number of matters.

Maika: Tell me one. Even divorce matters, if either party has the stomach or purse to pursue the matter, now go all the way to some appeal court in Warri, presided over by an Itsekiri man. What does an Itsekiri man know about our laws? Oh, the last time we decided any matter of weight in this land was that case concerning your father—now, forgive me. I should not have said that.

Fregene: Why not? The law took its course.

Maika: I wonder.

Fregene: Anyway, that's a long time ago.

Maika: Yes, a long time ago. You were but a boy then, no bigger than that child hawking fish. And many of us who took part in that case are dead and gone now. Where's Peletua? Where's Sanfio? I never could tell between the two who had the quicker tongue and toes. And where is Burubo who, on his legless stool, heard before anybody all that happened on land and water? Even the great Ambakederemo, who presided over all, went home a flood or so ago, and he took nothing of his great fortunes with him, including his ship, the first by a black man and one as good as any floated by the Royal Niger Company. But see what his children have done, squabbling over how many times the first-born son should run it to Lagos and how many the rest should run it together—they have left the craft grounded with a little leak. Sometimes it is no use having children, certainly not so many by so many women that they fight for what they didn't work for.

Fregene: There can be feud, too, between the few of the same womb, as you saw with my father and his brother.

Maika: That was unusual, for often, when they fought, we left them alone, knowing, as their mother used to say, it was dog falling for dog to keep the cat away. It seems like yesterday, and yet more than twenty years have passed since that terrible event. Now, when are you people going to call home my friends?

Fregene: You know how things affecting several persons go. One may be ready today while the other is not, and when that one is, the other then is not ready. So it goes on until what one man can do on any day he chooses drags on and on and is forgotten by everybody.

Maika: You cannot forget your duty.

Fregene: Why, am I alone to do it? There, I almost cut my hand. It's dark, and I can't see to carve anymore.

Maika: What does it matter? You see most of your shapes in the dark of your dreams, anyway.

Fregene: I'm going in. Come along, if you want some of that fish cooking in the pot.

Maika: Oh, yes, I smell the smell of pepper soup. If I hadn't come, you would have eaten it all by yourselves. Now, when will that brother of yours return from the playhouse?

[He follows the other out.]

Scene 2   STAKES

The playhouse at Bikoroa.
It is almost night, and a game of cowries is coming to an end with Egberibo,
son of Biowa, playing his last hand.

Egberibo: No, no, no; don't rise yet!

Tonwe: What is left? You've lost all you came with. Egberibo, give it up.

Apele: Ah, ah, ah! Give the man a chance. People from Akarakara-biri, you never know what they'll come up with next.

Tonwe: There can't be any trick left. He came with a bag so well stuffed it was standing on its feet. Now the poor thing is lying flat out on the floor.

Diri: Money is a prostitute; it has no permanent place of abode.

Omonibo: That may well be so, but all the money in circulation today happens to have found a home right here.

[He gathers all the cowries to himself and begins to count his money.]

Tonwe: We'll see how long she cohabits with you and brings you happiness. Now, Egberibo, let's go.

Egberibo: Leave me alone, will you, and let me think.

Apele: I said the man from the other place has some surprise in store.

Tonwe: You are the tortoise from Amatolo, always pushing others on, and never risking anything yourself.

Apele: Now, what have I said that I'm being abused so?

Egberibo: I'll go to market again.

Tonwe: Who with?

Egberibo: I said I'm going again to market.

[*He begins to gather the heap of cowries on the floor.*]

Tonwe: Are you mad, Egberibo?

Apele: There, I told you the man has a masterplan to save the day.

Diri: Do not do it, Egberibo.

Omonibo: Well, if he is ready, I am willing to play for as long as he wants.

Egberibo: I want only one game more, only one.

Tonwe: And with what are you playing I asked?

Egberibo: One game if you are ready to stake all your winnings.

Omonibo: All my winnings?

Egberibo: Yes.

Omonibo: You all heard the man. And what's your counter if I agree?

Egberibo: My niece.

[*Amazement all round.*]

Tonwe: No; this is gone too far now. If you are taking the game to this length, then I'll scatter all your seeds.

Apele: You dare not. This is a properly constituted game. We abide by the rules of it, regardless of who is losing.

Omonibo: Yes, there's law and order in this land. You can't just go taking the law into your own hands to protect relations and friends.

Egberibo: I am offering nothing that is not mine. The stake stands.

Tonwe: You fool!

Apele: There is ample precedent to what he's doing. Even Ambake-deremo once staked a niece—Siake, to be precise.

Tonwe: And, Egberibo, do you expect a dramatic turn of fortune, relying on the precedent just cited?

Omonibo: What is your business in this matter anyway? Let the man do what he wants. I accept his challenge and hereby match all my winnings to his niece.

Egberibo: Here, I am going to market. Dare you stop me?

Omonibo: I do.

[*Egberibo throws the cowries and everybody bends down to inspect the seeds and see how many have fallen on their faces and how many on their backs. If the number is even for the latter, then the staker takes all.*]

Apele: One has fallen outside the floor.

Egberibo: Don't tamper with it. Leave it where it has fallen.

Diri: Do we count it as well?

Omonibo: Start counting what's within and stop all these questions.

[*The count begins with Apele picking out the seeds on their backs.*]

Apele: One's fallen on top another—like a man taking a woman.

Tonwe: You idiot! Separate them with care and do not change their positions.

Egberibo: What's the count?

Apele: Here we are!

Omonibo: Let's hear it.

Apele: There are eleven seeds here in my palm.

Egberibo: O, my father!

Omonibo: Hurray! I've won again—this time a wife, or shall I sell her, collect the money, and build myself a house?

Tonwe: Not so fast, man.

Omonibo: What do you mean?

Tonwe: We haven't counted what's outside.

Apele: That's right. The game's not over.

Omonibo: They are forfeit and should not be counted.

Tonwe: You should have raised that objection immediately.

Omonibo: I did, didn't I?

Diri: No; you did not. All you compulsive players always forget it is when dance is sweet that you stop it.

Apele: Where are the seeds, anyway?

Tonwe: Seeds? I thought it was only one that fell outside.

Diri: Now, I am not quite sure myself.

Apele: Here's one. It's lying face up.

Omonibo: No!

Egberibo: Yes! I am saved! And I'm collecting all your money.

Omonibo: No, look again, everybody! There may be another lying face up, in which case I win. Yes, get a lamp. Somebody may be standing on it. This is playing foul.

Tonwe: Are you accusing us of taking sides?

Apele: It's you playing foul. Here, look at me; I've pressed nothing down with my big toe.

Diri: Pay up, man, and obey the rules of the game like a man.

Omonibo: It's he who should pay up.

Egberibo: I?

Omonibo: Yes; you debtor!

Egberibo: Debtor? Whose debtor—when I've won back all my money and more?

Omonibo: Go and ask your father's nephew.

Egberibo: My father's nephew—you mean Fregene?

Omonibo: Ask whichever of your brothers you like. I'm not talking

anymore. And nobody's taking my money.
[*He gets up to go with his winnings and is blocked by Apele.*]
Apele: You aren't going!
Egberibo: No, let him go.
Apele: You aren't letting him go away, telling this tale?
Egberibo: I said let him go. It's my brother I must go and see.
[*He rushes out.*]
Diri: There goes a whirlwind with a lot of dust in its eye.
Tonwe: Let's follow him. We don't know where all this will end.
[*They go out after Egberibo.*]

Scene 3   REPRISE

*Not long after. In the compound of the brothers at Bikoroa. Egberibo rushes
in, followed by some of his playmates, and is met in the courtyard by
Emonemua.*

Emonemua: My son, my son, what's the matter, what's the matter?
   Has someone abused you? Tell me, and if it's a woman of this
   town, I'll go right now and tie one wrapper with her.
Tonwe: Somebody has abused him all right, but it seems the agent is
   here.
Emonemua: In this house? Who?
Fregene: Mother, who's abusing who? And Egberibo, what's
   happened?
Maika: See the adventurer! We've been waiting for you to eat. The
   soup is going cold and must be boiled again.
Egberibo: Dare you stand here asking who's abusing who?
   [*He slaps Fregene.*]
Fregene: [*more dazed than hurt*] What's this?
Egberibo: Today I shall die with you.
   [*Egberibo slaps him a second time.*]
Fregene: Do you see him slapping me?
Emonemua: Why ask? Are you not his senior? Or are you a woman?
   Slap him back.
Egberibo: I'll slap him again, if he has no hands.
   [*He tries to slap him a third time.*]
Fregene: No; this is too much.
   [*Fregene dips into him, tries to carry him bodily on his shoulders and
   throw him, but Egberibo holds tight to his neck and a great Izon*

wrestling match ensues. Attempts are made to separate them but they wrestle on.]

Emonemua: Leave them alone, I say leave them alone and let them fight it out. Why should Egberibo slap his elder, not once but two, three times right before me?

Maika: Oh, you woman, so you have no sense after all? Why are you so quick with your judgment? What, if incited by your example, the younger behind Fregene, I mean Atie, Ofoni and Isoun, join the affray in defense of their brother? Will you be able to contain the fire? Or do you want to burn down the house? Have you not learnt your lesson, sending one brother to death for killing his brother?

Emonemua: Oh, oh, oh, oh! Come, all of you, and see my nakedness, and let nobody hold me! True, I buried both my brothers in one day, giving judgment against one for killing the other, partly so that one set of children may not become slaves to the other, and have I lived so long to see my children about to kill themselves as their fathers did, and I their cheer-leader? Oh, oh, oh, oh! Let nobody hold me in my nakedness. I am going in to hang myself.

Maika: Follow her quick before she carries out her threat. There, you two, are you still fighting when you have a burial on your hands?

[*The two allow themselves to be separated. At the same time, their aunt is led back, shaken and silent.*]

Maika: Now, Egberibo, what's all this about? Will you tell us why you slapped your elder brother?

[*Egberibo moves away, silent.*]

Apele: At the playhouse, Omonibo called him a debtor.

Egberibo: Yes, why should my brother give me money and tell the whole world?

Fregene: I did not.

Egberibo: You did. How else would Omonibo know about money matters between us?

Maika: Now, don't start it all over again. We can hear the whole case later on.

[*Fregene breaks into hard laughter.*]

Fregene: I don't think a trial will be necessary.

Tonwe: Why not?

Fregene: Did you say Omonibo called him debtor?

Apele: Yes; so he did, including you, before all of us.

Fregene: I see, I see.

Maika: Well, tell us, so we can share in the laughter.

Fregene: I think there is a debt. Omonibo called my brother debtor on my account, not because of any story I told him about any money matters in our house.

All Together: How? Tell us! Yes, tell us!

Fregene: Well, you see that figure there I'm carving? It's for Omonibo, and he has already paid me for it while I'm yet to deliver.

Egberibo: That does not make you or me his debtor. How dare he call us debtors? Now I have more than money to collect from him. I shall kill him with my bare hands.

Emonemua: There will be no more killing in this house.

Maika: Nor in this town.

Tonwe: That man was always God's own crooked piece of work.

Maika: Do you see what I see, good people? That cursed carving there. I asked Fregene not quite long ago, whom he was doing it for and what it was meant to be, but he wouldn't tell. There was something about the figure—whether it was to raise a spirit from the sky, land or water—I couldn't quite tell. Well, we won't go deeper into that. I can see other spirits around and they cry for attention as I was telling Fregene earlier. Come, you two, lead your mother in. We need to discuss in more detail what must be done. [*The family party goes in.*]

A Neighbor: And how much, anyway, was the stake on account of which people were going to be killed again?

Tonwe: [*Finger to his lips.*] Hush! Do not say it!

[*They go out severally.*]

ACT II

Scene 1 ABLUTIONS

Early evening. The waterfront at Bikoroa, leading to the compound of the brothers. The family, with the people of Bikoroa, are performing the ceremony of calling home the brothers.

Apele: The thing should be done properly.

Tonwe: Come and do it if you know best.

Fregene: Let's not quarrel now.

Apele: Have I said anything wrong? All I'm saying is that things should be done right.

Maika: It has not been done in years, not so much because there aren't many souls out there waiting to be called home as the high cost of putting it on.

Diri: Who stops to count costs when the dead start playing havoc with the living? Look at those two rams. Together, they could well outweigh a cow from Hausaland.

Apele: Those rams should have been led here to slaughter.

Egberibo: Whoever wanted to see them has seen them slaughtered in the compound, and you saw the dead themselves approved from the way the blood from one jetted across the ground splashing many close by.

Apele: Soaked their clothes well. They crowd round every beast of sacrifice as if wanting to eat it raw.

Maika: Now set down the basin and let's see how much of that blood was collected.

Diri: More than enough to bathe both brothers.

Maika: Yes, it is good. And who is carrying the bowl of cam and bottle of pomade?

Fregene: They are all here with my daughter. And the two figures are with the boy.

Maika: Is that our great hawker himself! Now, let's get the whole thing straight. There are two baths to do and they must not be mixed up.

Apele: We begin with water.

Tonwe: No; with blood, you fool. First you cleanse the dead of their ills and then you decorate them.

Apele: The last time we did it for Diribi, we dipped him in the river first as a newborn baby.

Diri: It wasn't like that at all. How can you forget so soon? This is why the white man writes down everything on paper. So that next time he can read and remember.

Maika: Must you Izon people fight over every matter? No wonder we make no impact at these assemblies of strangers the white man has set up. They take us for dry pepper—all fire and no weight.

Fregene: Everybody is a leader here.

Tonwe: Let's cut out the politics. This is a matter of religion.

Diri: "I see," said the blind man to his deaf daughter as they came upon a cliff.

Egberibo: And what may that mean?

Apele: Don't mind the man—let's get on with the work, although I still think we ought to send for Omonibo.

Egberibo: We don't want him here; we won't invite anybody who doesn't want to celebrate with us.

Maika: This is a day for forgiving and rejoicing, and we welcome everybody.

Emonemua: That is so; that is so.

Fregene: We don't need to quarrel with the man further.

Maika: Yes, we've forgotten all that. There are many things left to do, and the man can join us later. Now, you don't have to belong to a secret society to know the order of things. First we cleanse with blood, then we wash with water and, finally, we rub with cam and pomade before decking them out as newly borns. But first we must call them.

Fregene: And who will do it now? Omonibo has suddenly developed a cold since the last incident. Who will now act?

Tonwe: I will. I have no father nor mother.

Apele: You sold them at your coven a long time ago to get rich.

Diri: I see nothing but rags on the figure.

Emonemua: Will you men ever be serious for once?

Maika: Don't mind these young ones. Do begin, Tonwe.

Apele: Or if he doesn't know how to begin, let him give way to some other person.

Tonwe: I said I will if you will all shut your mouths.

All: All right, go ahead! We take too long doing things. Really, my legs are aching! And the blood is beginning to set in the basin.

Tonwe: Biowa, Biowa—

Maika: No, you call the elder first.

Apele: I told you he'll foul up things.

Tonwe: Was he not the elder?

Apele: Hear him!

Maika: You were but children running all about town without wrapper when the thing happened.

Tonwe: Forgive me. Then I got it wrong.

Emonemua: Bradide was the elder by birth, and in death too he was the elder though they went the same day.

Maika: That's right.

Tonwe: Well, I'm starting all over again.

Maika: That's right.

Apele: And let everybody be silent and listen carefully.

Tonwe: Bradide, Bradide, Bradide! Biowa, Biowa, Biowa! Three times I call upon you in true masculine count.

Apele: That's right!

Tonwe: You were born of the same mother to the same father in the right and proper space of three years as was the practice between couples in days of old.

Apele: That's how it was before the white man came and corrupted the world.

Egberibo: Can we cut out the commentary, and let's make progress?

Tonwe: But all the world knows that counter to the flow of the river, death came and carried you out together to the other shore, while the sun of life shone right over your heads. Disagreement over the management of a property you owned in common was the manifest and immediate cause. Many years have passed since that sad unusual event, so many, children, who were born then, now have their own children. During all that time, you, Bradide, have been lying unburied in the evil grove, exposed to bird and beast, while you, Biowa, have been lying weighted down upon the bed of the white river, washed over by waves, nibbled by varieties of fish.

If men who are no worse than their neighbors suffer penalties such as these for the deviations of one day, what should the habitually bad who foul up life for the fun of it? You did not die of sores nor of swollen parts, and in your lifetime neither of you was accused of practicing crafts that declare a wreck beyond salvage. We must therefore admit that certain duties ought to have been done earlier. But you know the living are often negligent and forgetful by the very business of living, and it is not until unwelcome incidents visit them in a row that they wake up to shut the doors that should have been bolted long before. So it happened this market-tide your two sons, Fregene and Egberibo, nearly repeated your story over the money one loaned the other to trade, and only then did everybody remember you have not been called home. Bradide, Biowa, we are now calling you home. Come now between the feet of your fathers. Come now and take seats in the council of our ancestors. Come now and eat with your peers, and drink again with them in full company of the clean and free. Oh, come now and be guardians to your family so that whatever the differences in future, however high the heat may rise in the heart,

there may be no such events again as you went through more than
twenty years ago. All this we are saying, have you heard it all?

All: Yes, we have heard it all!

Tonwe: Have you heard it all?

All: Oh, yes, we have heard it all!

Tonwe: Then bring forward our sons and let's bathe them!
[*Both figures are brought forward, and ceremoniously he bathes them in
the basin containing the blood of the rams.*]
You are again newly born, truly born again. May you by the grace
of the Almighty grow up into strong upstanding men, blessed
with good wives, good children, good fortunes, and the long life
to enjoy them. May you this time see the evening of your lives.

Maika: There, they are now clean. You may wash them in water.
[*Water is brought in a basin and both figures again are washed in the
course of the lines following.*]

Tonwe: A child newly born gets a good bath after his first gasp for
breath. Here is the other great element of life. May it keep you
clean, cool, and full all the days of your lives.

Apele: Aren't they shining and glowing now?

Tonwe: Cam befits them now! Bring out the cam and pomade that
decorates bride, mother and child. Rub it all over them from their
feet to their heads, shaven clean of hair from the other world. And
now bring out the clothes, full of frills and patterns spectacular,
for our brothers to dress and step out again into the world. To
confirm their birth we call you to witness, oh, you nine founders
this side of the rivers: Mein, Seimbiri, Tarakiri, Kabo, Kunbowei,
Tuomo, Oporomo, Iduwini and Ebeni! Forgive me if I forget your
exact order of seniority. I am only a child and it is with your
authority I proclaim: Bradide is born again! Biowa is born again!

All: Bradide is born again! Bradide is born again!

Emonemua: Oh, my brothers! Oh, my brothers! Have you indeed
come back?

Maika: How beautiful they are!
[*The brothers are carried ashore shoulder high.*]

People of ⎱ Oh, to have children is a great thing!
Bikoroa   ⎰ Life is truly sweet!
Severally

Maika: I didn't know you've become so expert at these things.

Emonemua: So young and already so versed in the lore of the land.

Tonwe: We have merely watched our elders perform.

Maika: No; these gifts are natural. Your performance was as great as any I have seen done at Ugobiri.

Diri: Dare you play with us of Tebegbe, as tiny as we are?

Egberibo: Boasters all, that's what you are.

Apele: Now, let the guns boom out to welcome the travellers home.

Maika: Not so fast, not so fast! We still have to make sure of what
they have brought with them. If they carry with them contraband,
then all we have done is for nothing.

Apele: You Izon are too awkward for words.

Maika: Complex, perhaps, complex, perhaps! How else could we
survive in these hostile surroundings?

[*They go out together.*]

Scene 2   LADDER

*Late evening. In the public square of Bikoroa. Omonibo is standing center
upstage, facing the audience. He is supporting in his right hand a bamboo
pole planted upright in the ground. Facing him, center downstage, are
Tonwe, Apele, Diri, and a fourth man, all carrying on their shoulders a
rectangular bamboo frame with three cross-bars representing a ladder. They
are led by Tonwe at right front. Dangling by him at the corner of the ladder
is a small bundle in leaf wrapping. To their left and right are the family of
the brothers as well as the people of Bikoroa, all of them waiting in silence
for something of mystery to happen, as is the audience.*

Omonibo: Obebe, Obebe, Obebe! You are the ladder of life, the
bridge between earth and sky upon which whatever goes up and
whatever goes down must walk this suspended stretch of breath
called life. Of course you were witness to the story of the
brothers, Bradide and Biowa, sons of Gbogbolagha. One killed
the other over the ownership of a boat, and was in turn killed by
the clan at the plea of their sister. Now a boat is an expensive
property to own. It carries people, it carries goods. It therefore is
an instrument of service, and a symbol of position among a
people. It is however not such a great thing that brother will kill
brother over the ownership. If it was, Bradide and Biowa, for I
now call upon you to mount the ladder, you would both have taken
it with you to the other world. But you did not, as indeed no man
takes away with him any of the many things he seeks to
accumulate in this world of ours. As a matter of fact, the property
you fought and died for had to be split in two and sunk in the

wake of your violent passage. What we would therefore all like to
know, drawn as we are from all quarters of the land, is why it all
happened the way it did. More than twenty years after, we still do
not understand why eyes saw ears of the same face, why noon saw
night!

[*The ladder, led by the carrier in front at the right-hand corner, dips its
head all the way to the ground, and it seems like staying there a long
time.*]

Obebe, do you bow your head all the way to the ground? Is that
because the burden is still too much to carry? Tell us. Or is it the
sheer shame of the event you would rather not remember?

[*The ladder rises back to shoulder height and moves from side to side.*]

So you shake your head and consider that perhaps too impertinent,
too irreverent a question. Let me frame it again then. In the usual
run of life, husband and wife quarrel, parents and children quarrel,
and brothers and sisters quarrel. Indeed the closer people are
together the more likely it is that they will quarrel, sharing things
of various kinds and value. Strangers do not quarrel. What do they
hold in common? Only when there is something between people
that each would love to keep for himself is there quarrel from the
individual to the state. So quarrel among relations and among
friends is a thing natural, and one need not be ashamed of
acknowledging it.

[*The ladder lifts a couple of times upon the shoulders of its carriers.*]

But, Obebe, relations and friends quarrel to reconcile. Indeed, as
all peacemakers know too well, he makes himself the common
enemy of husband and wife who comes between them in time of
quarrel. As soon as the quarrel is over, he becomes the object of
laughter when husband and wife are in bed together.

[*The ladder nods again.*]

Tell us then, Obebe, why this quarrel between brothers did not
end in laughter, why the stream of tears flows still after so many
years.

[*The ladder surges towards the man with the pole and hits it several times
and forcefully.*]

Will you knock over the pole that conducts the dialogue? Tree and
earth are child and mother. Yet when wind blows wild, earth lets
go of the tree. So who knows who betrays one?

[*The ladder charges all round the square in front of the hushed gathering.
Whenever it seems to stop or stall in front of someone, all around shy back
in fear. But scanning all there, it fastens on nobody and comes to a stop*

center stage, backing the polester.]
So there exists no instigator to the act here. Is that what Obebe is
saying, is that what you are saying—that this community here
gathered is composed of men and women not one of whom has
evil in his heart, no malice in his mind—an unusual collection of
human beings, if there is none among it capable of plotting the
downfall of his neighbor to possess his property, to possess his
wife, or the other way round? Shall we then believe that you were
the agent of your own wreck. Shall we? Shall we?
[*The ladder rears violently backwards, swinging from side to side.*]
Well, we knew it could not have been that. You did not kill
yourselves. So who did? Tell us the witch, tell us the wizard who
tied to you a string not seen by the eye but by that very reason
pulls strongest in its hold, turning perfectly normal men into goats
being led without their knowing to slaughter. Specifically, for
Obebe, let's not drink water while trying to speak, was it your
mother, was it your mother who everybody knew fed to one so
much milk that she denied the other, was she?
[*The ladder rocks violently from side to side, almost tilting over on each
occasion.*]
If her hands were clean although there was some folly, who then
was the culprit? Where is he or she to be found if not in the house,
in the family circle?
[*The ladder sways left and right, then rushes forward, past the people
gathered in the area of play and heads straight into the audience.*]
Hold it, hold it! So there is a guilty one after all, and right there
among our guests gathered here, believing they have come to
watch a show about some strange characters, engaged in some
fictitious action in some distant place that they have no connection
with in any way? Well, if a man does not die before his time, he
sees a lot.
        Is the guilty one, seated there in the circle, all dressed up in
keeping with his high estate, when in fact behind all that smooth
surface he is busy orchestrating the most heinous of crimes against
neighbor and state? Look at all seated from row to row, at all the
ladies, past the dazzle of their gold and lace, and tell us. We know
you will do so without fear or favor. He is not there then, the
guilty party, since you shake your head, going from side to side.
[*The ladder moves up.*]
Perhaps the person is deeper down in the gathering, installed
somewhere in the stalls, hoping you will not find a heart missing a

beat behind so many faces smiling out of fear. You cannot be fooled, I know that. But if the quarry is nowhere to be found in the pit, is he up among the gods? If so, go up there and bring down the person, however high his station or her connections. [*The ladder stops halfway up the aisle, again swaying from side to side. Then, turning round, with full upraised hands, it returns at a trot to the area of play. There, in full view of all, it begins whirling round and round in clockwise direction, releasing a great shout of joy from the family of both brothers. The movement is repeated three times after which the carriers deposit the ladder carefully at the feet of the polester who in turn places the pole on top of the ladder. All five men are now in the middle of a jubilating crowd, all talking at the same time.*]

Emonemua: My brothers are clean, clean, clean!

All: All clean! No taint of witchcraft on anybody! No wickedness in the heart of any! Oh, how excellent!

Omonibo: May we drink now? That thing really is heavy!

Maika: Ah, do you know what powers descend on it?

Egberibo: We can now bring out the drinks!

Fregene: Yes, and all the food. Where are the women?

Apele: Let the drums rise and speak out, I say!

Maika: It was fate after all!

Diri: Fate is what we say after the event, not what we see before it.

Apele: The guns can now boom!

Emonemua: Next time my brothers will choose well!

Maika: There is no condition cannot be changed!

Diri: Yes, the problem is finding the means and ways.

Apele: And there is no prophet or priest living can tell for certain!

Omonibo: Oh, let's have the drinks and the food if the women have finished cooking.

Tonwe: There, when did they start? Give the women a chance!

[*They go out severally. Three shots in quick succession are heard offstage, followed by loud cheers and singing.*]

Scene 3   HEIRLOOMS

Night. In an inner room in the compound of the brothers. The Boy is up in the open loft to the back trying to bring down an old iron trunk box. Below, pacing with arms across breast, is Emonemua. Beside her are Egberibo and one or two others, all looking up in various degrees of expectation.

Emonemua: Have thieves also visited Biowa's box as they did
  Bradide's?
Boy: There are signs of the same rats. The chains about the box are
  loose and the locks again have been prised apart. Yes, it is the
  same pattern as in the other place.
Emonemua: Oh, the rats! May Odele set iron traps to catch them by
  their necks. May he set them food that will dissolve their guts
  with gum from the weeping tree. He shall himself be such a
  vulture to them, ripping the flesh off their bones before they are
  dead.
Egberibo: You curse, assuming the rats are from the street or field.
Emonemua: Worse for them if they are of this house, for then I shall
  curse them with my breast and womb, call upon my brothers to
  hunt down the vermin.
Maika: Careful, careful now. We want our brothers home in
  triumph, not to draw more tears.
Emonemua: Again you are right to arrest me there. But what kind of
  man living will steal from the dead?
Maika: The Almightly makes them in all sorts. Now, there comes
  the box.
Emonemua: I cannot believe my eyes. Is that my brother's box of
  treasure, sliding down the wall like a leaky bucket coming up a
  well? Set it down, set it down here gently. Now open it. Yes, the
  locks have been forced. I cannot look. You tell me what the thieves
  have carried off.
Boy: [*Coming down the ladder after the box.*]
  It will be easier to tell what they left behind as at the other place.
  [*The box is now open and they all gasp together.*]
All: What!
Boy: It is almost empty.
Maika: Only one robe left behind—a gorgeous one though.
Egberibo: Why did he leave it behind, taking all the rest?
Boy: There is a straw hat beneath it.
Emonemua: It was my brother's favorite robe. He bought it off a
  British trader plying between Akassa and Calabar. It was the dress
  he wore on that unlucky night he came back from Lagos.
Maika: Yes, I remember. It was probably what scared off the thief.
  He must be old enough to have known it.
Egberibo: Where has he sold all those wrappers and shirts without
  our spotting one of them?
Maika: Far away among the Urhobo and the Itsekiri, I bet. They

don't carry on that kind of trade at their own doorsteps.

Emonemua: And you say I should not curse the persons who have done this?

Egberibo: Will cursing bring back what is stolen?

Emonemua: My brother labored between Bonny and Badagry to fill that box with the finest print and real madras that money could buy.

Maika: We know.

Emonemua: And it always took two men, sitting on the lid, to shut that box.

Maika: Oh, yes, Biowa was a collector, all right. None of us could come near him at festivals. The girls always flocked to him, seeing all those fancy dresses and fineries he brought from Lagos. It was very unfair, I tell you.

Emonemua: Oh, what a waste, what a waste! I stayed so long in my husband's house raising seeds to uphold a home that may not see the end of my days, and all the time, out here in my father's house, white ants were eating their way up the wattle to the roof-top.

Maika: No point crying now. [*To the boy.*] Come, young man, out you go.

[*The boy goes out.*]

Egberibo: We must not let the world know what has happened.

Emonemua: What difference does it make? We've been in deep disgrace all along. How many of our sons going to ask for the hand of a girl in marriage have not been turned back because of the incidents in our family? And how has it been easy for us women? Tell it to the world, oh, tell it to the world. It will be adding water to the sea.

Maika: Nonsense! Come, Egberibo, try on your father's dress.

Egberibo: Right away?

Maika: Yes, of course. And the hat as well; we'll find a walking-stick to match. There must be one around, if not, you can have mine.

Egberibo: It's rather small, isn't it? I thought my father was a tall man.

Maika: You were a child when he died. So he looked almightly huge to you.

Emonemua: My brother was a big handsome man who stood above his peers. It's the robe that must have shrunk.

Maika: Well, in that box and up on the loft in this heat all these years, I wouldn't drag the matter.

Egberibo: Now, how do I look?

Maika: Like an Itsekiri chief going to the regatta for the Governor on tour from Lagos.

Emonemua: But you are not as impressive as your father.

Egberibo: He was your brother.

Emonemua: Of course, yes. That's why he is my kin before yours. The blood is full between us, flowing direct from our parents, but between you and him it is half from another source—diluted.

Maika: Gasigele!

Emonemua: Like the leading masquerade, I cut through all barriers.

Maika: [*Touching foreheads with her.*] That's my girl I should have married many years ago instead of letting her go off with that man to Agbodobri.

Emonemua: You lost your chance, man! But may our foreheads strengthen each other.

Maika: That's our one prayer in life so we can be around long enough to bring up the young to look after us, until we too are ready to join our fathers.

[*A knock on the door, and the boy returns with a message.*]

Boy: They are waiting for you outside. So is my uncle Fregene.

Egberibo: Oh, they can wait.

Maika: Tell them we're coming.

Boy: They say their bottles are empty.

Egberibo: Why don't they go to the other place? They are more numerous there.

Emonemua: Egberibo!

Egberibo: Well, tell your mother to take them one bottle of gin, one of whisky and another of schnapps.

Boy: The leader of the party from Kiagbodo, the one with the blind eye, says they will leave if you don't come immediately.

Egberibo: Shut up! There, run off now, and stop being so forward.

[*The boy runs out again.*]

Emonemua: Now, leave my child alone. What has he done? He was only delivering a message, and the envoy should not suffer for doing his duty.

Maika: True, true. Let's finish with ours before they fish us out and find there is little left in the net.

Egberibo: I'm all set to go.

Maika: You haven't put the hat on yet.

Emonemua: Again it looks a small size.

Maika: Never mind; put it on.

Emonemua: Look at him! He has a head as large as a watermelon and he says it's my brother's hat that's undersize.

Maika: Watch out! It's his hat now he's put it on. So is the robe. Indeed, everything of his father, that he wears to go out tonight, becomes his property from the hat to the walking-stick. That is why the first son, secure in his claim to a third of the estate that is his birthright, makes sure he is on the good side of his uncles and aunts so that, when they come to dress him up in the image and person of his father, they will bring out the very best in the kit. Oh, yes, you should have seen Fuludu when Ambakederemo died. That giant of a man, he could barely walk for the strings of coral beads round his neck, hands and feet. They say it was more than you ever saw on the Oba of Benin.

Egberibo: Those thieves have robbed me of my legacy.

Maika: Let's not wail for what's lost. You may have my walking-stick if that's what you're looking for. We must go, yes, right now before the blind one from Kiagbodo comes for us.

Egberibo: There, lead!

Emonemua: Doesn't he look like his father now! Oh, my brother! oh, oh, Govena, the stranger who came to visit and stayed on to rule! [*They go out singing in procession and are greeted with loud cheering from outside.*]

Scene 4   REPOSE

Early dawn. Before the funeral canopy of mat, richly hung with clothes, in the compound of the brothers Bradide and Biowa. Both are laid out within in effigy, and at their feet sit the heirs, Fregene and Egberibo, each supported by several people in late stages of merriment and in various shapes, cast by the three oil lamps arranged at the head and feet of the brothers. To the right, downstage, there is a wicker-work of bamboo and cane like a coffin to which one or two hands are putting finishing touches.

Apele: There goes the cock.

Tonwe: Don't say day is breaking already.

Apele: Hear it. There it goes again.

Egberibo: It can't be anywhere around here but from across the waters by the shortcut, all the way from Aya—that's where cocks crow out of rhythm.

Diri: Some cocks, like men, dream in their sleep, and moved by the nature of things they see in their heads working overtime, wake up, calling for the sun that is himself deep asleep in the sea.

Apele: If guns have not deafened the ears of some people, they should hear that crowing clear enough. And make no mistake, it's well within rhythm. The tide has turned twice already since we began these merriments for our brothers returned home. Step up to the stream who cares to check it up. I saw it, going there to wash the sleep from my eyes.

Tonwe: You went to check on your fish-traps.

Apele: May Amakore pluck out your tongue for uttering that slander! As Ngbile sees me, I want to wash the sleep off my eyes.

Fregene: Let's have no quarrels. Here, have some of my drink.

[*He pours out libation first and then hands over the drink.*]

Apele: [*Taking the glass.*] Thank you, my peer. If he has had too much to drink, why doesn't he go home to sleep.

Tonwe: Some people don't want an end to the flow of drinks.

Apele: If they can't hear well, let them look up, and there they will see the morning star peering clear and bright out there—above the mango tree to my right.

Diri: Hey, through the mist of your drinks, you say you can see the morning star beyond this great pall drooping over us?

Apele: Come out, you chicken! Come out and play with us children of the hawk and see if you won't be carried off to the top of the silk cotton tree and get torn there limb from limb for breakfast.

Maika: Yes, I can see it, though the eyes are beginning to dim! In days when we went catching the mackerel at Forcados all the way past the bar, it acted for us like a pilot. And Biowa was always, in that flotilla we formed, the first to hail the star as he sat astern, holding the boat against the tide for Bradide to bring aboard the line of nets. You could see from far off the squelching fish, enmeshed there, dazzling like silver coins beneath the star. Day truly is breaking to my right.

Apele: Oh, oh, Izon!

All: Yes!

Apele: Are you strong?

All: Yes!

Apele: If you see, will you act?

All: Yes!

Apele: Then let's get done with this coffin. Day is breaking.

Maika: It was good we decided on one carriage for the two. Do you think we would have finished weaving two coffins at the rate we've been picking bamboo and cane? We did it faster in our time.

Tonwe: It's almost finished as you can see. Bottom and sides are all set, and the top is now ready.

Diri: It's a close weave, fit for a king. Let's drink to it.
[*Enter Omonibo.*]

Omonibo: Will you people drink down the house under pretext of weaving one coffin, while we strong ones are bruising our palms digging graves? There, listen!
[*Strains of the grave-diggers' song float in from upstage.*]

Diri: How many are you digging? We decided on one to take both brothers.

Omonibo: So we did. But we have to dig it wide enough to hold them both. It's no work for rheumatic joints and waists bent with lumbago. I had no idea the ground in this part of town was that hard. You should see the sparks flying as spade hits ground—quite like a cutlass on stone. We shall lay down our tools if we don't get our own share of drinks.

Fregene: Of course, you'll have drinks! What is it the boys want? Is it the usual stuff? Name it, and you shall have it!

Omonibo: That's my kin, that's my kin! Now we shall throw the soft subsoil right up to the roof top.

Apele: You haven't yourself handled a spade, and you are making so much noise like the boiler of a Niger Company boat.

Omonibo: Oh—oh! So you want to leave youth floundering there in the pit? Is that why you have remained glued to your seat all night, not moving your bottom even when mosquitoes are sticking needles in your sides? Someone with experience and knowledge has to be around for the right thing to be done at all times. Look, the boys were going to dig some hole deep only to play tops in when I arrived on the scene.

Egberibo: How far have they got now?

Omonibo: Up to here—right to my waist—as tall as I am. I leapt in, you know, to make sure. We aren't going to have dogs digging up at daybreak what should remain preserved for generations to come.

Tonwe: Whatever you do, don't let them hit water.

Omonibo: Where do you think you are—in the swamp of your fatherland Ayakoroama.

Apele: There they only have to dig ankle-deep, and the grave is flooding with water.

Fregene: Otobo—tebe—ka—bede po!

Omonibo: That's my motherland! It's on top of the head of the hippo we wash our clothes.

Fregene: Now, step out here and let's give you a drink.

[*Gin is poured out for Fregene which he gives his father first by way of libation before handing the glass to his friend, after taking a sip.*]

Dada, take your drink, take your drink! And now good fellow it's all yours.

Omonibo: [*Takes the glass and drains it at one gulp. Then he raises his right hand, fist clenched, and salutes Fregene as his father.*] Ogoun!

Fregene: Kada!

Omonibo: Ogoun!

Fregene: Kada!

Omonibo: Ogoun!

Fregene: Kada!

[*There is a great burst of cheers all round.*]

Omonibo: [*Turning to Egberibo.*] And now give us a drink.

Egberibo: But you've just had one.

Maika: Give it to him, give it to him, and let's all be merry.

[*Drink is poured out for Egberibo which he proceeds to serve his father by way of libation, going through all the motions as Fregene did, after which he hands the glass to Omonibo.*]

Egberibo: [*Gruffly.*] There you are!

[*Again Omonibo gulps the drink, and then gives him the salute three times.*]

Omonibo: Govena!

Egberibo: Kada!

Omonibo: Govena!

Egberibo: Kada!

Omonibo: Govena!

Egberibo: Kada!

[*Another burst of cheers.*]

Omonibo: [*Strutting about the place.*] Now, dare any trifle with us when we are together?

Maika: Boaster! You mainstream people leave your Urhobo and Isoko tenants all the dry land to farm while you sink deeper in your swamps.

Diri: And the tenants make their homes there forever. You know they bury their dead in their bedrooms and parlors.

Tonwe: What a horrid practice!

Apele: I wouldn't sleep in a room like that if you paid me a bag of money.

Maika: Their heirs sleep there, fearing no ghosts; what's more, in complete bliss with the widows they take over.

Diri: Why should anybody fear the dead, when, living, they did no harm?

Fregene: They work ever so hard—those people—men and women, they work all the time like ants.

Apele: And all for how much—a barrel of oil the white man buys for a penny. In no time, they shrivel and die.

[*More strains of the gravediggers' song.*]

Maika: We all shrivel and die in the end, my dear man.

Tonwe: Meanwhile, Omonibo is drinking glass after glass of gin, forgetting the workers he came here to represent.

Omonibo: Who said I have forgotten them? If the baby-nurse does not eat first, how can she see to tend her charge? I tell you, we shall down tools if you deny us our rights.

Fregene: Drinks, drinks! Take drinks to the youths before they throw aside their spades.

Egberibo: Let them come here who want to drink. No drinks should be taken to the graveside. Soon spades will be flying among bottles.

Tonwe: Look who is talking. They better take their drinks out there; we want no muddy feet here.

Apele: So you would rather have broken heads.

Maika: A little knock on the head from time to time keeps the head clear.

Omonibo: There, I go bearing cheer to the weary.

[*He goes out with bottles of drink.*]

Diri: The lamps are burning low.

Apele: No; it's daylight; can't you see?

Tonwe: Still let's have more oil in the lamps. None must go out before we finish.

Diri: That by the headstead still carries a strong flame in the wind. Indeed, the elders say we may all start out at the same time but we don't all finish together.

Apele: [*Going to the rear of the canopy and calling out.*] It's day, it's day, and time to rise, everybody; look at them all wilted there. Why come to a wake if you can't keep awake? Now, let the master-drum speak.

[*Going to the other side of the canopy and calling out again.*]

There, our good master drummer, are you asleep? Wake up! Let's have music for waking! Now, percussions, percussions and side-drums! And where is Omonibo with his young men digging the grave? Are you ready?

[*Enter Omonibo.*]

Omonibo: You vilify us in vain. We've been ready for you a long time.

Maika: Wait, wait, we haven't quite got there yet. We began well and let's finish well.

Apele: What's left now?

Maika: First, the coffin must be taken in for the final rites. Let's not do things as you do at Obotebe.

Apele: Oh—oh! What have we done wrong now, my mother's people?

Maika: Nothing. Just take up the coffin. And you three there, help bring it in.

[*The coffin of bamboo and cane, very closely woven, is laid with calico and mat and carried into the canopy by Tonwe, Diri, Apele and Omonibo, and the effigies of both brothers are laid in it.*]

Who has the finest piece of cloth to present to his father, let that son or daughter step out now to present it, for our good brothers are all dressed up to go out.

[*Relations now file in, bringing their offerings, which they carefully tear up before dropping them on the coffin, each with a prayer and wish.*]

Emonemua: Are you going now, oh, my brothers? In your next cycle of life, may you come again as my brothers! But this I ask of the Almighty with all present as may witness:

May you choose different lots, yes, may you choose different talents that will lead you to the evening of your lives, each weighted like the kola nut tree with wives, children and riches. Oh, may you paddle your different canoes of life, while enriching each other! One hand washes the other, but it is only when it is good for this and good for that that kinship is sweet. You have been called home; you have been washed; you have been robed; you have been feted as princes; how beautiful you are, my brothers, oh my brothers, and now all the state is escorting you to your kindred, oh, my brothers, may you go in peace, may you bring us peace!

[*When the line of mourners part in about a minute or so, the two heirs, each in the outfit of his father, step out in front of the coffin, and together raise up leg and hand, first the right and then the left, in salutation to their fathers. Then they turn round, split, one to the right, the other to the left, and the drums begin to beat the final passage with the leading*] motifs of "*Kon mu dibi! Kon mu dibi!*" and "*Erein sokote! Erein sokote!*" meaning, "*Take up burial! Take up burial!*" and "*Sun is setting! Sun is setting!*" The two, together, dance downstage, back to the canopy, round the area of play, repeating the movement three times. The group now join them with song and cheers in general rejoicing. Finally, the coffin is taken up, carried high by four pallbearers, and led on either side by the two heirs, a procession of song and dance forms, bearing the two brothers round the area of play, out of sight upstage right to their final place of rest. Then there is a cannonade three times—above the song, the orchestra of master drum, side drums and strip-board, followed by loud cheering and wailing, all mingled together.]

The End

Full Circle

CHARACTERS

Ojoboro grandson of Bradide
Kari his brother
Tibo their mother
Apele an elder and relation
Eferemua a cousin

Afokise daughter of Emonemua
and a cousin like an aunt
Brother-in-law
Neighbors and People of Bikoroa

ACT I

Scene 1 ARRIVAL

*In the fifties. The homestead of the brothers Bradide and Biowa at Bikoroa,
in the section built by Ofoni, another son of Bradide, and now inhabited by
his grandson, Ojoboro, and his mother, Tibo. It is night, and the town
almost asleep, when Kari, the younger son, arrives home and knocks on the
door. In the half-light, the room is notable for its assorted furniture and
variety of mirrors hanging on or standing against the walls. Tibo leaves the
household things she is putting away for the night and goes instinctively to
open at right center stage.*

Tibo: Who's it? [*She opens and sees her son.*] It's Kari! Kari is here!
   Oh, Kari's home from Lagos! Come in, come in, my child, and
   let me embrace you!
Kari: I'm on my knees.
Ojoboro: [*Coming in from his bedroom through an inner door.*]

287

Who? Who are you welcoming at this time of night?

Tibo: Rise, my son! Come into my arms.

[*Turning to her first son.*] It's your younger brother, Kari, don't you see, come from Lagos.

Ojoboro: I see. [*To his brother.*] You do travel late.

Kari: Does that make me less welcome?

Ojoboro: Of course not. You are welcome home anytime. You didn't send word you were coming.

Kari: By whom? By telegram?

Tibo: Who was that he called? Was anybody by that name coming this way?

Ojoboro: No, not anybody. It is a message white people send by wire.

Tibo: Does that kind of thing reach here?

Kari: No, Mother; even if it did, I would have got here ahead of it.

Ojoboro: Well, then; where's your luggage? Let's bring it in.

Kari: I don't have any other luggage. I came with this travelling bag only.

Ojoboro: So you aren't staying long then?

Kari: I don't know yet.

Ojoboro: You don't—?

Tibo: Oh, stop asking my boy so many questions. Don't you see he has come a long way and must be hungry and tired? Now, my son, what will you eat? There's no food in the house; we ate it all up this evening. Yes, there's that dry fish. I'll make you floor-pepper with it. Roasted, it should make a sizzling dish, and I'll quickly turn you a round of starch to eat it with. Do you get starch to eat in Lagos? Tomorrow I shall cook you some ukodo with yam and plantain or whichever way you like it—with fish or chicken. Oh, yes, I have quite a brood left from what black-kites and poachers have not taken away.

Kari: Do as you like, Mother.

Tibo: No, not as I like but as you like. Or perhaps you want to wash first. A proper hot bath is what you need to wash the dirt and dust from your body. I hear the red one of Benin clings like jigger and takes some scrubbing to come off the hair. How bushy your hair, my child! You need a haircut. Don't they have barbers in that Lagos of yours?

Ojoboro: Mother, which are you giving him now—food, bath, or haircut?

Tibo: All of them; what's wrong with that?

Kari: I'd like some drink though.

Tibo: Better eat first before you take a drink. I'll see to your food directly.

[*She goes out.*]

Kari: I'd like some now.

Ojoboro: There's no drink in the house unless of course you brought some in your bag.

Kari: No, I didn't. Isn't there any in the house?

[*He goes to the bedroom.*]

Ojoboro: Well, not really; certainly nothing so fancy as the stuff you bring from Lagos.

[*Tibo re-enters the room, a large open earthenware pot in one hand and a ladle in the other.*]

Tibo: Are you still talking about that drink? Send to Atiko for a bottle.

Ojoboro: She must be asleep by now.

Tibo: A shopkeeper does not sleep. She will be too delighted to get up and sell you a bottle. It's genuine stuff from Ogodo.

Apele: [*Heard from outside.*] Who are you entertaining at this time of night?

Tibo: It's Kari my son—you won't believe it—come all the way from Lagos.

Apele: [*entering*] Kari's come home, did you say? When did he arrive?

Tibo: Just now; only just now. [*Turning to her first son.*] Ojoboro, where did you leave the box of matches? The fire's gone out in the kitchen. I know you asked for it to light your cigarette earlier in the evening.

Ojoboro: Under the table; it must be there still. Apele, you are still up at this time?

Apele: The old fear to lie down, my boy.

[*He settles himself down, rubbing both his palms between his knees.*]

Tibo: Are you sending for the drink?

Ojoboro: There's half a bottle somewhere in the house—the one I put some bush in.

[*He goes to the inner room as Kari comes out.*]

Apele: That should do until tomorrow. It's what a child finds he eats in his mother's house.

Tibo: Look at him; doesn't he look good?

[*She goes out.*]

Apele: Why shouldn't he? He is from Lagos, isn't he? Well, Kari, there you are! So you've just arrived from Lagos? Welcome home!

But you enter late in the night like some character we won't mention. There, take my hand.

Kari: I kneel.

Apele: Rise, my boy. How's everybody in Lagos?

Kari: Fine.

Apele: Are they well? Akara, Pide, Oweibi—do you see them? Now, tell me, when did you last see them?

[*Kari looks away into the night, while Ojoboro returns with a bottle which he is shaking between his hands.*]

Ojoboro: Do you think Lagos is a small place where people see each other every day?

Apele: Is it not a town like any other? Why shouldn't people from one place see one another daily?

Ojoboro: End to end, it stretches from here to Warri, and that's a distance of some twenty miles going through Aya.

Apele: All of that built up, and filled by people? I don't believe it.

Kari: [*Walking back and slumping into a seat.*] It's true, and it's expanding every day. You can live there a whole year and not see a relation or friend except you have business doing together.

Apele: I hear there is no poor man in Lagos. That's why everybody is rushing there, although I also hear going to Lagos is not hard but coming home is a great problem. Anyway, what kind of a town is that where brothers don't see one another? Do let me have some of that gin.

[*Ojoboro fetches a glass from a small wooden corner-piece with shelves, hung halfway up the wall in one corner. He blows into it to remove the dust inside and then fills it.*]

Ojoboro: Let me first take out the poison.

[*He drinks and then serves Apele, genuflecting at the same time.*]

Apele: Rise, my boy! What a drink! It's so strong. Where did you get it? Or is it the roots you stuff it with? These days, you can't tell what's in a bottle, you know. It could be water straight from the river.

Ojoboro: Another?

Apele: No; one will do for me now. Now, serve our great guest from Lagos.

Kari: [*rising*] No; I'll serve myself.

Ojoboro: That's all right.

[*He hands bottle and glass to Kari who helps himself, draining two shots one after the other.*]

Apele: Man, drink hunger must have hit you really hard.

Ojoboro: He's been travelling all day, and they don't get water to drink on those roads unless you buy it by the bottle.

Apele: Buy water before you can drink? What wouldn't people sell these days to get rich?

Kari: What root did you say is in this drink?

Apele: That's your brother's secret, but we all know he won't kill a fowl.

Ojoboro: How do you know I haven't got for myself some antidote that you don't know of?

Apele: That's true, that's true; man is so trusting. We jump into a boat every day to go down the river, never stopping to see if it has a leak. And we eat and drink whatever is set before us at home or on the roadside. But, Ojoboro, your heart is too good, too soft to kill anybody.

Kari: Whatever it is, it gives your gin the taste of schnapps while making it look like whisky.

Apele: I hear you have all the brands free on board your ships. Did you bring us a bottle or two? And what about those white girls we hear you have a great time out there entertaining, are you bringing home any for us to see or shall we remain content with photographs?

Kari: I haven't been to sea for some time now.

Apele:
Ojoboro: You haven't been. Has anything happened?

Kari: No; I haven't had a place on a boat for some time, and I'd like to get to the bottom of it.

Ojoboro: I hope those people are not at it again?

Apele: Which people?

Kari: Well, those running the unions say sea-going should not be the preserve of the Izon, but it seems they are now making it exclusive for their own people.
[*He pours himself another drink, sinks into his chair and falls asleep without the others knowing.*]

Ojoboro: Oh, the big ones know how to protect themselves all right; it is us small ones who give ourselves away. That was even the pattern then, when I worked in the docks at Burutu many years ago for the Niger Company.

Apele: I can't follow you people.
[*Tibo enters, carrying food in both hands.*]

Tibo: What can't you follow? I hope you two haven't been asking my son questions as if you were conducting an inquest.

Apele: The gods forbid. There, ask him. Well, what do I see?

Ojoboro: I think he's fallen asleep.

Tibo: How? And I've brought him this nice dish of floor-pepper with dry roasted catfish sizzling in it. Look, it's smoking still— and the starch is straight from the fire.

Apele: I can smell it all, the shrimp ground so fine with the pepper. Kari, wake up, here's fare fit to wake up the dead.

[*Ojoboro tries to wake him, shaking him, but he sinks farther into his seat, snoring without restraint.*]

Ojoboro: He must be very tired, travelling all day in those moving coffins they call taxicabs. Oh, it's so dangerous travelling on these roads.

Apele: Then that drink—he drank quite a bit of it.

Tibo: I said he should eat first before drinking.

Ojoboro: Hey, Mother, wasn't it you who said I should send to Atiko for a bottle for him?

Tibo: Well, not to drink immediately. By the time that bottle was delivered, my boy would have fed and got himself a full belly to take all your drink. Now, I have to go and cover up the food.

Apele: Whoever heard of floor-pepper being left overnight? Let's eat it on his behalf. A good guest attracts company.

Tibo: Keep walking, man; nobody's touching this dish I prepared specially for my son.

[*She goes out with the food.*]

Apele: Ojoboro, is this fair, what your mother is doing, stowing away food right in front of the hungry?

Ojoboro: Oh, you can't really be hungry, Apele; not at this time of night. With a full belly you will roll in bed.

Apele: An empty belly is more likely to make me roll off my bed. All right, let me have another glass then.

[*Ojoboro fetches both bottle and glass from where Kari has left them, and proceeds to serve Apele who is rubbing his shins in anticipation.*]

That's good, that's good. I think I can do with another. Thank you, thank you. There, what about a song?

Ojoboro: A song? At this time—

Apele: You are the bard, you know, and a song or two pouring out of that big voice of yours to tell the town your younger brother is home will not be out of place.

Ojoboro: And when they come, what will they see? A man crumpled like an empty bag of beans in one corner?

Apele: Song and dance certainly should summon him back from wherever he has sunk.

Ojoboro: I think the drink is beginning to have effect upon you as well.

Apele: What's that you are saying? Three common shots knock me out, when you know I can carry a keg?

Ojoboro: Yes, we know but, really, Apele, it is quite late now. And we have to settle Kari in for the night. Come, let me walk you home.

Apele: Oh, no; I can look after myself. Things aren't that bad yet.
[*He gets up, hitches up his wrapper about his waist and across his shoulder toga-wise, looking at the sleeping man and around the room to the travelling bag lying at one corner.*]
So we won't know till tomorrow what he brought us in that bag?

Ojoboro: You see how things are.

Apele: I was hoping he would open it tonight. Kari never fails to bring us nice things. But I suppose we'll have to wait now till tomorrow.

Ojoboro: Yes; till tomorrow.
[*Tibo returns.*]

Tibo: Are you going in now?

Apele: Yes, since you denied us food. We shall see tomorrow.
[*Apele goes out.*]

Tibo: Yes; tomorrow we shall see!
[*Turning to Ojoboro*] How is he—your brother, I mean?

Ojoboro: Sunk into deeper sleep, as you can see.

Tibo: Shall we carry him in? We can't leave him sleeping in a chair.

Ojoboro: How do you carry a full-grown man to bed? The best thing is to leave him alone where he is.

Tibo: He'll get a stiff neck.

Ojoboro: He's not a child anymore, Mother; and stop treating him like one.

Tibo: My boy, my poor boy, no food for his empty stomach, and now he cannot even sleep in his beautiful brass bed on his first night home.

Ojoboro: Is that all that is worrying you, Mother? Have you looked at your son closely since he came? There, look at him slouched there in the chair. Does he look all right to you?

Tibo: Well, I see the dust of the road upon him. That's why I said he should have a bath first, and water is boiling there on the fire for him, if he'll wake up and eat.

Ojoboro: Well, Mother, if you don't see any change in your son, then
I won't say anything.

Tibo: Why, tell me if you know anything. He's your younger
brother. Is he ill? Is he in trouble? You've been talking with him
all the time I was in the kitchen cooking him a meal. What do you
think is the matter?

Ojoboro: I don't know, I don't quite know yet, Mother, but he said
something about being out of work and not knowing whether he's
going back or not. I don't like how he looks.

Tibo: He's all right. Nothing will happen to my child. The dead
will defend him. The Almighty will bless my child. He'll be all
right. Oh, Tamara the Almighty, tie the wrapper of my child
firmly round my back.

Ojoboro: Well, I'm going in to sleep. Whatever is wrong we shall
find out tomorrow. Turn off the light before you go in.

Tibo: I think we better leave it burning. He'll need light when he
wakes up. Anyway, I'm going to sit up and watch over my child.

Ojoboro: All right, Mother, do as you please. Tomorrow we shall see.

Tibo: Yes, tomorrow, my son.

[*He goes in, and she tiptoes up to Kari, looks at him and returns to take
a stool. His snoring gets deeper and deeper, the lamp burns lower and
lower, and soon she too begins to nod.*]

Scene 2   REPLAY

*Morning. The same. The furniture in the room under light of day consists of
wooden folding chairs, locally called "croak-chairs," soft water-cane
armchairs, originally ivory in color but now the gold of grime and old age,
well-worn upholstered single seaters, the small round table weighted with
odds and ends, the wooden open cupboard containing tumblers upon the wall
at the far corner and, gleaming in the bright morning light, the variety of
mirrors. Kari is up and alone, looking at these items many of which he
collected and sent home from abroad. Now that he has taken off his shoes and
the top of his French safari suit and is left only in his singlet and trousers, he
looks haggard and, for all the deep sleep he has had, not fully rested. He
goes to his baggage, opens it, and fetches from under layers of clothes his
toilet bag out of which he takes his toothbrush, toothpaste, and finally his
shaving set. He hesitates briefly between brushing his teeth and shaving his
two-day-old crop of beard, and finding no water immediately within reach,*

decides to fit his shaving set, looking at his wristwatch. At the point, in
comes his mother, still very much the proud mother, ready to please her son
fresh home from the city.

Tibo: Have you risen, my son?

Kari: Yes; and you?

Tibo: I did, at the parting of night from day, and went straight into
town to find some good yam to buy to prepare you ukodo,
knowing you didn't eat last night.

Kari: Did you find any?

Tibo: Oh, yes. That Atiko girl, she has quite a setup. Go there and
ask for anything outside market-day and you'll find it from
groundnut oil to rice to kerosene but, oh, her prices are so high.
Anyway, I bought my yam and it's already cooking on the fire,
ready for you to eat.

Kari: What about Ojoboro? I suppose he woke up with the cock to
go out and see to his many business concerns.

Tibo: Oh, yes, he rose quite early; in fact, a little earlier than usual
so he can do the round of all his traps in the forest and then go
down to the river to inspect both his fish-lines and nets to see if
he can come home with a catch worthy to welcome his younger
brother home.

Kari: That's very good.

Tibo: He should soon be back.

Kari: And all the time I have been asleep in that chair, and left alone
like a child who has been so much in the way everybody is glad
that he has fallen asleep.

Tibo: What a thing to say! We didn't want to disturb you last night,
seeing you were so tired after your long journey. I sat up by you,
although sleep did cross my eyes a number of times.

Kari: And did you talk about me?

Tibo: Well, a little, not much, just that things didn't quite look well
with you.

Kari: You should know.

Tibo: How?

Kari: Do you really want me to tell you?

Tibo: Of course, my child. Is anything wrong? Your brother says
you are out of work. Surely, you will get another. Work is not a
stray dog, and will not run into the bush.

Kari: It's not that easy, Mother. You don't pick up jobs in Lagos like
you pick leaf wrappings in a marketplace. And when there is

work, it seems I'm always among the first to be laid off when there is a crisis.

Tibo: Are things that bad then?

Kari: Don't ask me.

Tibo: Well, I merely asked.

Kari: So I told my brother I have been ashore for some time. Why should he be the one to announce it to you?

Tibo: He did not.

Kari: He did, and with pleasure, I'm sure. He is the man of industry with wives, children and whatever mouth asks for, while I am the wanderer unable to keep a job, unable to raise the money to marry.

Tibo: Of all the numberless people in the world, why do you compete with your own brother, Kari?

Kari: What have I to do with other people? Do they see me naked? Do I eat with them?

Tibo: Your brother cares so much for you. In all your years away in Lagos you cannot say you sent him something to keep for you and he turned it over to his own use. You cannot say he has treated you like those unhappy soldiers who came back from the Hitler War and found the money they sent home to marry and build houses had been spent by their brothers. Look around you. Everything is intact. So you can see he cares very much for you.

Kari: Oh, yes, just as much as you do. Isn't that why I have made so much progress in life, being looked after so well by my mother and brother?

Tibo: Oh, my son!

Kari: Tell me, my mother, why do you shadow me night and day all the way to Lagos, to Liverpool, so that when I believe I've made a strike, and all around me agree it is a catch sufficient to change the course of my life, it slips through my fingers and I am left to drift again from port to port, while my brother puts roots deeper here at home?

Tibo: Oh, my son, are you calling me a witch?

Kari: Aren't you? Aren't you?

Tibo: No; I swear by all the dead, by Udele, by the Almighty who sees me, I have not bought, I have not inherited any craft to harm one child and promote the other.

Kari: Deny, deny as loud as you like, you are a woman of the night.

Tibo: Who told you this lie?

Kari: Several seers I consulted, holy prophets in long cassocks,

ringing bells and burning candles and incense, from Lagos to
Calabar.

Tibo: Then they lie in Lagos, and in Calabar.

Kari: One even put before me a basin of water, and another a magic
mirror, obtained all the way from India, and in each case, when I
looked, I did not see myself or any other face but yours burning all
I do to ashes with your eyes.

Tibo: You saw wrong, my son.

Kari: Yes, I saw wrong, all right, and you were the principal agent.

Tibo: You are sick, Kari.

Kari: That's right; and you made me. Tell me, Mother, how have
you riveted my canoe of life that, when I want to weigh anchor, I
find I'm only circling in one place? Unlock me, unlock me, I say,
so I too can take my ware to market.

Tibo: My son, I have no padlock or chain with which I have locked
you. I am ready to face ordeal by water or fire.

Kari: No; you will not pass. Release me now, woman of the night,
flying as an owl all over the place!
[*She tries to pass but he intercepts her, and seeing how threatening he has
become, she starts to shout for help.*]

Tibo: Help, Bikoroa, help!

Kari: No; this is no matter for all the town.
[*To stop her shouting, he holds her and tries to cover her mouth with one
hand, but she bites at him and he lets her go to look at his hand. Seeing
blood, he goes after her, striking his mother again and again.*]

Tibo: [*Holding onto his legs.*] Beat me then, yes, beat me dead today!
[*Noise of neighbors outside at the door.*]

Neighbors: What's it? What's going on in there? Tibo! Tibo! What's
happening?

Tibo: He'll kill me today, oh, yes, he will today!

Neighbors: Is it Kari? He came home, we heard, last night. What
could have happened? Open the door, will you?

Tibo: You'll kill me today. Beat me dead since that's what you came
from Lagos for; oh, yes, beat me dead today and bury your failure
in me!

Kari: Take your hands and teeth off me, take them, you witch! Or
aren't you satisfied with the blood you've sucked already?
[*The voice of Ojoboro is heard outside above the continuing calls from
outside.*]

Ojoboro: What's going on here? I heard the noise all the way from
the waterside.

Neighbors: It's your mother crying for help. Kari, we think, is
　beating her. We don't know what for, and none will open the door.
Ojoboro: Is that it?

　[*He pushes the door open. Kari is over his mother who is clinging to him,
　still begging to be killed. With a couple of steps, the elder brother is upon
　the younger one, and wrenching him free of their mother, pitches him
　across the room, past the neighbors struggling behind him, and his brother
　lands sprawling on his hands and feet at the doorway. Ojoboro follows
　slowly, dusting his hands in disgust.*]

Ojoboro: There, is he going to get up and fight like a man?
Neighbors: Let nobody hold them. Why should Kari beat his mother?
　Something must be worrying him!

　[*Brother by now is standing over brother with their mother wailing and
　trailing behind, but the one fallen does not get back on his feet to take up
　the fight. Instead, feet, knees and hands give way under him, and before
　all he sinks to the ground.*]

Ojoboro: [*Walking away.*] Well, it seems our champion from Lagos
　isn't going to get up and fight anymore.
Neighbors: Wait, I think he's hurt. It seems he's hurt—quite bad, I
　think. Yes, he's foaming at the mouth.
Tibo: No! What are you saying? What is it you said about my son?
　My son, let me look; let me look at him.

　[*They clear room for her and she falls on her knees beside him as one or
　two hands roll him over on his back. He does not move.*]

Neighbors: He's dying! Yes, he's dying! There, somebody bring
　water quick. Water, water, water! And a ladle or spoon, somebody,
　quick!
Tibo: He can't die! He can't die! My son has just come home. He
　can't die! It was just a quarrel we had—nothing more than you'll
　see between mother and son.
Ojoboro: Let me see. He must have just fainted. Can't you people
　revive a man?
Neighbors: We're trying. We are doing all we can!

　[*They force ladle and spoon between his teeth, walk upon his outstretched
　limbs all the way to his chest, and when water comes in basins and
　buckets, they throw it freely over him, but still he does not respond, and
　slowly it dawns on all that Kari is dead. The mother sinks moaning over
　her son. She appeals in a daze to the neighbors, all equally dazed.*]

Ojoboro: [*Hands over head.*] You all saw it. I didn't fight him. All I
　tried to do was separate him from my mother. I didn't kill him!

Do you hear me? I didn't kill him! My own brother, born after
me, how could I kill him?

Neighbors: Yes, we saw it all. But it's happened again; what's not
seen has happened again in Bikoroa, in the house of Bradide and
Biowa. Can it be a curse? And how far does it go? Oh, what shall
we do? This is a matter that must not be heard abroad. What shall
we do? What shall we do? First, let's take in the body. Then there
is the poor woman; take her in as well. And do not forget the
brother, he must be well looked after. Oh, what shall we do? How
do we handle a case like this? This is a matter that must not be
reported abroad.

[*They lead in the family, and disperse in various directions.*]

Scene 3   SETTLEMENT

*The same—except that the room is now cleared of its center round table, and
all the mirrors are turned round, face to the wall. Seated on the bare floor
and keening intermittently is Tibo, and a little behind her, also on the floor,
is her surviving son Ojoboro. Around them, sitting in conclave, are key
members of the bereaved family among whom may be recognized Apele.
There is also a middle-aged woman, Afokise, daughter of Emonemua and
first cousin removed from the brothers. There is also a brother-in-law, from
the family of Tibo in the neighboring town of Ogodo. All through the
proceedings, mother and son do not speak and are not asked any questions.*

It is late afternoon going to evening.

Apele: That is the story. I did not start it. Now I am cutting it. The
story is finished.

All: Yes, it is finished.

Apele: Now for another story. A hard, unripe fruit, full of poison,
has dropped here right at our feet in the form of a corpse, our
son's corpse, killed in a most lamentable, most unfortunate
accident, which occurred before us all today, as our other son here
tried to save his mother, our wife here, from the hands of his
brother. How shall we handle this terrible fruit fallen fresh from
the branch of a tree whose roots we all know run very deep? This
is the matter we now must settle together.

Afokise: Take it away and bury it at Obibasan.

Eferemua: Just like that?

Afokise: How else? The boy started out on a wrong foot, and should go out the same way. He had no wife, no child; so take him to Obibasan, I say, and let's forget the affair. We have of course precedents. Our fathers, faced with the first fruit, picked it up boldly and disposed of it in a manner now celebrated all over the world.

Eferemua: Did that settle the matter?

Apele: That is true, that is true. Did it? Otherwise, why are we seated here? Terrible though it is to recall, we are faced with the bitter act of eating the same fruit without knowing whether we shall ever contain its seeds, and stop it from sprouting again.

Afokise: Take it away to bury, I say, and let's forget the matter. In his next world, let him pick a better lot from his maker, and then he may come back here and be reborn. It is the one who is dead whose lot is finished.

Apele: There is no dispute about what we do with the dead; it is what we do for the living that must leave no doubt behind. And when we say we have a precedent to guide us, do we in fact have one? The first time we know our fathers dealt with such a matter, it was a clear case of a brother killing a brother in the course of a quarrel over a canoe they held in common title. The second time the incident was almost repeated, it was over some account which got mixed up between cousins, and happily we know that tragedy was not only averted but turned into a great festival of recalling home the brothers. In this third instance of which we are the sad witnesses today, the one element similar to the first is that two brothers are again involved in the process of one death. Otherwise, there is nothing common between these three cases repeated in three generations of one family. No crime has been committed; the motivations did not exist for it; and the act was never carried out. What happened was an accident, an accident which could have happened with any of the several and all of the persons present and ready to stop the affray between mother and son. It so happened that one person among them, though coming late on the scene, had the strength and swiftness to intervene. We cannot therefore draw too close a parallel between the original and—

[*A neighbor enters noisily.*]

Neighbor: What are you people trying to do? So it is true what they are saying outside. A whole human being is dead, and are you people trying to settle the matter between you and behind doors?

Apele: What will you have us do?

Neighbor: Report the matter, of course.

Apele: To whom?

Neighbor: To town and clan, if you will not go direct to the police. This is a world of government.

Apele: We know it is a world of government, and one controlled from abroad. But when did we start reporting deaths and births to government?

Neighbor: Oh-ho! Am I the one to ask that question?

Apele: You should be able to answer, knowing your law so well. What kind of death is this you want us to report abroad?

Neighbor: A sad, unfortunate accident, everybody knows that.

Apele: So why do you break in upon us like some unripe plantain dripping acid?

Neighbor: I spoke wrong.

Apele: You always do, because you speak before you think. There, sit down, if you have anything sensible on your tongue.

Afokise: No; he cannot sit among us. This is a family meeting, not a town or clan assembly.

Eferemua: Let him sit, let him sit. We are all one, after all, all children of Bodakeme.

Neighbor: No; I'll go; I'll not stay where I'm not wanted.

Apele: Sit down, man; and stop behaving like some spoilt housewife wanting to be treated as a bride.

Neighbor: No; I'm going. I've said what was on my mind.

Afokise: Let him go!

[*He goes out.*]

Apele: Whew! Some fire in the roof! Now, as we were saying, we have a totally new situation to deal with, and as we have just seen, it is not one we can take to the police.

Eferemua: Police? Don't think of it for one moment. Who here can face police trouble? In a matter like this, they will come at breakneck speed in their loud vehicles and vessels as if for war, and before you and I know where we are, they will have rounded up all of us adult men in town, while throwing glances at our wives and daughters, who they will insist must cook them all the three huge meals a day that they do not eat at home. Oh, yes, they will insist on eating fried eggs with boiled yam in the morning, and if there are no hens laying in the town, then goodbye to all the brood, to all roosters running around, for they must then be caught, plucked, and cooked for the police to have their breakfast, while we men stand like capons gawking at them from a distance. In the afternoon, what do you think they will ask for? The fattest pig, digging for itself a pond in the marketplace, must be slaughtered, peeled, and turned into pork for the masters to feast on, and what they don't tuck into those potbellies of theirs must be penned or pickled for them to take home. It is the same summary treatment they will administer on the prize goat they want for their dish in the evening, even as their roving eyes are directed at some other kind. Oh, you cannot cope with a visitation by the police. They will eat you out of your house, burn it over your head if you resist arrest, and when they are ready at last to leave town, you can be sure no penny will be left clinking in our private or common purse. Oh, yes, you cannot cope with police palaver and wahala, for after they have stripped you of all you possess, they will drive you like common goats, all manacled and handcuffed, to their station out there in Forcados or Warri. And there begins another story.

Apele: All right now, we'll hear that another day. We are all agreed this is no police case but one to resolve within the family.

Afokise: I have a solution.

Eferemua: Let's hear it.

[*Enter the same Neighbor as before.*]

Neighbor: The sun is going down, and the body is beginning to go stiff.

Afokise: We know.

Neighbor: Then what are you dragging for so long, as if it were some guinea-worm you were extracting from a patient?

[*He goes out in a huff.*]

Apele: There at least he's right. Now, what did you say is your solution?

Afokise: The oracle, let's consult the oracle.

Eferemua: Consultation after the event! What manner of action is that? Think again, madam.

Afokise: What about Obebe? Perhaps, we should take up the ladder and carry out a full inquest.

Eferemua: That's a final solution for us to take later; what we seek now is an interim measure to contain the worm in the seed.

Apele: When a thing is close to the eye, we do not see it clearly, not to talk of seeing other things around. Look at our good brother-in-law from Ogodo, sitting with us here all the time through this painful discussion. We have all agreed no crime has been committed. If there is any, it has been by forces and agents that we do not understand, and it is we who have suffered and are afflicted. However, one thing that we do know, although we have not realized it before now, is that while we have no crime before us to devise punishment, there subsists between us and our brother-in-law a contract that has been partially breached.

Eferemua: How?

Afokise: What do you mean? We don't quite follow your words.

Apele: Well, look at it like this. His family gave us a girl to cultivate as a wife just as a farmer a piece of land he has been given to hold in trust. We on our part have tilled the soil, and the products, until the unseasonal events today, were there for all to see. But without any warning whatsoever, the soil has given rise to a strange worm, despoiling us of our seeds. Since responsibility in the end belongs to him who owns the land in perpetuity, namely, the parents of the mother of our sons who is our wife, a freeborn daughter who must return home one day, is it too much, if we, as the permanent losers in this matter, ask by way of a little repara-tion, no, by way of further fulfilling the contract, a token contribution from our good in-laws at Ogodo so that, sowing again with that much aid, we may all look forward to reaping a normal, if richer harvest in future.

Afokise: That was a mouthful, but you carried it off like a squirrel.

Eferemua: And it is an excellent proposal.

Afokise: What does our brother-in-law say?

Brother-in-Law: An in-law speaks only when spoken to. What can I say? And when fruit is ripe and ready to eat, you do not look around for the sun. This is a sad day for us all. A freak fire has broken upon our land and threatens to burn it down, crop, farmer, landlord and all. Fortunately, we are told we have the means to put out the fire. Tell us, and as heavy as our hearts are, we shall provide.

Apele: That was well spoken, my great in-law; and now, if you will excuse us for just a moment, we would like to consult among ourselves a little.

Brother-in-Law: No problem there; go right on.

[*The family group briefly put heads together at one corner of the room in a consultation done mainly by mime, returning almost immediately to their seats.*]

Brother-in-Law: What is our fine?

Apele: Not a fine, but a small token.

Brother-in-Law: All right, tell us. We said we are ready to pay.

Apele: We don't want to take advantage of you, you must understand.

Afokise: Take advantage of our good, priceless in-laws? When did we become such sharks eating so close to the shore? And remember I come from Agbodobri on my father's side and will not cheat you of Ogodo, our sister town. Yes, I am the daughter of Yale, son of Azana of the royal house of Ogbolu.

Brother-in-Law: So are you going to tell us now?

Apele: All we require is a fee of five shillings.

Brother-in-Law: Is that all?

Afokise: Look at the man! He wants to pay out more. All right, pay us fifty pounds then so we can marry another wife to give your girl competition.

Brother-in-Law: Oh, no, no! You won't; you have been most fair, and we are filled with gratitude at your show of compassion. Here is your fee.

[*He gets up, unties a corner of his wrapper, and counts out the coins.*]

Apele: It is to buy kola-nut with—and a bottle of gin. Just to pray and pour a little libation for now. I did not begin the story. Now I'm cutting it. The story is finished.

All: Yes; it is finished!

[*Enter the Neighbor a third time.*]

Neighbor: So you have finished at last!

All: Yes; we have.

Neighbor: Then let those who are men come with us, for we are now taking our brother to Obibasan. And let nobody cry!

[*As he turns round to go, followed by the other men, Ojoboro also tries to rise but is pressed back gently to his seat.*]

Apele: No; stay behind and comfort your mother. You are her husband and son all in one now. And, Afokise, sit with them. We shall not be long.

[*They file out, and Tibo begins a strange act of beating herself across the shoulders with both hands as if warding off a swarm of bees, keening at the same time over and above the growing hubbub outside, as peers of Kari take up his body to carry to Obibasan, the unholy ground upon the bank of the Kiagbodo River.*]

The End

A Decade of Tongues

Selected Poems, 1958–1968

The imprisonment of Obatala

Those stick-insect figures! they rock the dance
Of snakes, dart after Him daddy-long arms,
Tangle their loping strides to mangrove stance,
And He, roped in the tightening pit of alarms,
Dangles in His front, full length,
Invincible limbs cramped by love of their strength.

And that mischievous stir, late sown or spilt
On the way between homestead and stream,
Wells up in pots long stagnant on stilt,
Brims out to where ancestral eyes gleam
Till angry waves dam His track
And caterpillars riding out of froth break their back.

One leap upon the charcoal-coloured ass
Swishing ochre urine towards palace and sun,
Kicking impatient tattoo on the grass,
And generations unborn spared the wrong.
But the cry of a child at what it knows not
Evokes trebly there the droop, mud-crack and clot.

Abiku

Coming and going these several seasons,
Do stay out on the baobab tree,
Follow where you please your kindred spirits
If indoors is not enough for you.
True, it leaks through the thatch
When floods brim the banks,
And the bats and the owls
Often tear in at night through the eaves,
And at harmattan, the bamboo walls

Are ready tinder for the fire
That dries the fresh fish up on the rack.
Still, it has been the healthy stock
To several fingers, to many more will be
Who reach to the sun.
No longer then bestride the threshold
But step in and stay
For good. We know the knife scars
Serrating down your back and front
Like the beak of the sword-fish,
And both your ears, notched
As a bondsman to this house,
Are all relics of your first comings.
Then step in, step in and stay,
For her body is tired,
Tired, her milk going sour
Where many more mouths gladden the heart.

Fulani cattle

Contrition twines me like a snake
Each time I come upon the wake
Of your clan,
Undulating along in agony,
Your face a stool for mystery:
What secret hope or knowledge,
Locked in your hump away from man,
Imbues you with courage
So mute and fierce and wan
That, not demurring nor kicking,
You go to the house of slaughter?
Can it be in the forging
Of your gnarled and crooked horn
You'd experienced passions far stronger
Than storms which brim up the Niger?

Perhaps the drover's whip no more
On your balding hind and crest
Arouses shocks of ecstasy:
Or likely the drunken journey
From desert, through grass and forest,
To the hungry towns by the sea
Does call at last for rest;
But will you not first reveal to me,
As true the long knife must prevail,
The patience flowing from your tail?

For Granny (from hospital)

Tell me, before the ferryman's return,
What was that stirred within your breast,
One night fifteen floods today,
When upon a dugout
Amid pilgrim weeds on the Niger,
You with a start strained me to your breast:
Did you that night in the raucous voice
Of yesterday's rain,
Tumbling down banks of reed
To feed a needless stream,
Then recognize the loud note of quarrels
And endless dark nights of intrigue
In Father's house of many wives?
Or was it wonder at those footless stars
Who in their long translucent fall
Make shallow silten floors
Beyond the pale of muddy waters
Appear more plumbless than the skies?

Night rain

What time of night it is
I do not know
Except that like some fish
Doped out of the deep
I have bobbed up bellywise
From stream of sleep
And no cocks crow.
It is drumming hard here
And I suppose everywhere
Droning with insistent ardor upon
Our roof thatch and shed
And through sheaves slit open
To lightning and rafters
I cannot quite make out overhead
Great water drops are dribbling
Falling like orange or mango
Fruits showered forth in the wind
Or perhaps I should say so
Much like beads I could in prayer tell
Them on string as they break
In wooden bowls and earthenware
Mother is busy now deploying
About our roomlet and floor.
Although it is so dark
I know her practiced step as
She moves her bins, bags and vats
Out of the run of water
That like ants filing out of the wood
Will scatter and gain possession
Of the floor. Do not tremble then
But turn, brothers, turn upon your side
Of the loosening mats
To where the others lie.
We have drunk tonight of a spell
Deeper than the owl's or bat's
That wet of wings may not fly.
Bedraggled up on the iroko, they stand

Emptied of hearts, and
Therefore will not stir, no, not
Even at dawn for then
They must scurry in to hide.
So let us roll over on our back
And again roll to the beat
Of drumming over all the land
And under its ample soothing hand
Joined to that of the sea
We will settle to a sleep of the innocent and free.

Agbor dancer

See her caught in the throb of a drum
Tippling from hide-brimmed stem
Down lineal veins to ancestral core
Opening out in her supple tan
Limbs like fresh foliage in the sun.

See how entangled in the magic
Maze of music
In trance she treads the intricate
Pattern rippling crest after crest
To meet the green clouds of the forest.

Tremulous beats wake trenchant
In her heart a descant
Tingling quick to her finger tips
And toes virginal habits long
Too atrophied for pen or tongue.

Could I, early sequestered from my tribe,
Free a lead-tethered scribe
I should answer her communal call
Lose myself in her warm caress
Intervolving earth, sky and flesh.

Girl bathing

Her basket of cassava, set away from reach
Of a log basking smooth on the beach,
She wades gingerly up to her high
Girdled hips, her underskirt lapping her thigh
Like calyces a corn. And as she ducks
Under, with deft fingers plucks
Loose her hair, the sweat and dirt long dried in her every pore,
Fall off her back, and in their place set once more
The unguent flow of her limbs, the fresh
Warm smell of her flesh.
O girl of the erect and rearing breast,
So ripe with joy for the blest,
Splash, splash, your teeth flashing pearls, in the whirlpool
You have made, its lively cool
Waters, all lambent through your veins,
A tonic to the core of your bones.
And striding back to land neat
On sands golden at your feet,
How iridescent breaks all
Your porcelain skin to tattoo beads of coral!

Hands over head

Hands over my head,
Down our village lane
I ran: S.P. is come again
And none must cry for dread.

The A.D.O. in fever violence[1]
Upon his boat offshore,
Heard rumors of war,
Caused in huts royal silence:

When bees swarm over main
Men beat roof-zinc and brass.
But today, oh let them pass.
There's enough below for pain.

All said: it must be the king
Or God himself or more—
Okuakpolokpolo!
When he's done, we shall sing.

Horoscope

So you believe, bastard child,
The moon, as she twines
Her arms to that perfect round,
Can pull the waters
Three-quarters spilled about the earth;
Draw them to bow-bend
At each antipodal end,
And make oceans pound back mountain force?

[1]*A.D.O.*—Assistant District Officer, a Pooh-Bah of a functionary in the old British colonial administration of Nigeria with powers as dreaded as those of S.P., the old scourge of Small Pox, or of Okuakpolokpolo, the King of Benin, "He who asks for a hundred human heads today and gets them."

And will you in the self-same breath say the stars,
The stars millions of whom shine
In their own light
More attractive than the sun,
Have not control over the destiny
Of man, this clot
Of clay, three-quarters diluted in water?
Vain cynic, believe me, the stars
Even as they in their galaxies roll and glow,
Affect our human lot,
Day to day make us ebb and flow;
And though the intricacies of the zodiacs
Are as yet beyond our faithful compass,
Our individual flux between joys and disasters
May be that interlocking of our souls with the stars.

Pub-song

So that is what they say?
That I walk the house of bawds
Who bathe my feet from gourds
Raising smoke between me and day?

Well, if that's all you meant
Now the myth is broken
And I wild in the open
What is there left to repent?

Tide-wash

Up the laughing stream
We raced down the sun.
Who there thought such fun
Could end? We held one steam.

But the pulse that never
Gave sign fell through the sand;
Depleted now we stand
Exposed more than ever.

The water maid

Give me your water whole
And slake slake my soul
The irresistible blight
Spiriting in the night
Has come down on me
Is sapmeal eating me
Should you wait till thunder
Claps and lightning are over
I shall dry
Shall instant die.

New year

Another flood is finished to a fall
Finished finished with a roar and rush
And you and I two reeds on the bank
Go dipping hungry blades in her wash

Full fine sands rear up, how high
Each day! like manatees out on a spree
And even the sexless water lettuce
From upland go hand in hand to the sea

But you and I two reeds swaying on
The banks with the wind of world-blight
How long this hedging listing and roll
Before our self-split selves unite?

Insidious cracks of drying joints
Warn of recessions so hard to reach
I wonder this flood in the laps of the old
Will long bear us aberrants on the beach.

Ibadan dawn
(after *Pied Beauty*)

Mist-hung curtains, adrizzle-damp, draw, fall
Apart, spring a forward catch in the sky
That swift over us spreads, all
Of a lift, this fresh burst of blue, freckled dye
In running decks
Of quicksilver flakes and flecks.
It is pageant fit for a bride
Who, ah, look at! walks over there wide
Velvet greens dipping out of sight:
Rush outdoor concession-strong,
Greet her with cockerel song,
For blushing calm from flush of cam,
Morning comes breathing flowers, warm and light
Of limbs, to charm earth from vice of night.
Tumble in her flaming tan!

The year's first rain

Rain comes . . .
After long surcease in desert
Rain comes,
Hot-breathing, alert
And swift to thunder-rolls and claps
With kestrel-together-leaf flaps.
And earth all the while waiting, waiting inert,
Fallow and burdened with stone,
Shudders to her rump,
Tingles to the trump
Of the long-missed one.
Now with more than tongue can tell
Thrusts he strokes her, swamps her,
Enters all of him beyond her fell,
Till in the calm and cool after
All alone, earth yawns, limbers her stay,
Swollen already with the life to break at day.

Return of the fishermen

Pins and needles effervescent up heel,
Dabble, dabble, dip paddle blades,
And silent you furrow up from sea.

O, quick now goes the sun to sea,
Tick-twit, squirrels stow their seeds,
And low is the squirming down keel.

Come, said the Kingfisher, you feel
Beat. Behind there breaks the village
Profile, and filled is the quay.

Ibadan

Ibadan,
           running splash of rust
and gold—flung and scattered
among seven hills like broken
china in the sun.

Streamside exchange

Child: River bird, river bird,
         Sitting all day long
         On hook over grass,
         River bird, river bird,
         Sing to me a song
         Of all that pass
         And say,
             Will mother come back today?

Bird: You cannot know
         And should not bother;
         Tide and market come and go
         And so has your mother.

Easter

So death
being the harvest of God
when this breath
has blown uncertain above the sod,
what seed, cast out in turmoil

to sprout, shall in despair
not beat the air
who falls on rock swamp or the yielding soil?

In hospital,
mute with the soft pad of sheet
hung up on the wall,
I draw in my hook feet,
await the reaper's call, the rap
of his crook in the corridor,
but the poor
dupe, opening, shall find bats far gone with my sap.

The outsider

A disinterested act, stumbled on
In the tired noon
And then forgot, reels back like tide:
One mixing amala behind a shed,
Another spewing urine by the wayside;
   Now that I have slept and fed
   I teeter between rage and scorn.

Ivbie: a song of wrong

First Movement

Is it not late now in the day,
Late, late, altogether late,
Turning our doubled backs upon
   fate,

The soured man hankers
for his lost infancy

To pluck out of honey fresh milk
      fangs?
Is it not late, so awfully late,
Fingering sun-dried husks and
      shells on
Whose rank sap suckling we
      stifled our initial pangs?

You who from a far-fabled country
Reached into our virgin jungle
Passing through like therapeutic
      rays
Muscles tangled-torn out of roll,
Has the fire stopped riding the
      wind,
The fire you lit cigarettes with?

He addresses his visitors
from across the seas

Walk as on your tarmac our
      occult groves
With alien care and impunity
Walk in abandon ahead tourist
      droves
Eyes so big like a sailor's ranging
      mirage distance
To where God in heaven plunges
      to earth
How can they in the fixity
And delirium of a glance
How can they catch the thousand
      intricacies
Tucked away in crannies
And corners perhaps known only
      to rats?
How can they tell the loin-cloth
Cast away in the heat of desire
The shifts hanging in the wind
Now groins want oiling?
The sanctuary of things human is
      swathed
In menstrual rags, not in the
      market place.

"You've seen the ancient iroko
Last flood torn to bits by
   lightning?"
"The one they say witches haunt
   at cockcrow?"
"Lice, lice, my dear, may infest
Stately woman's crest."
"Shall we see them all, the whole
   lot
And in the act steal a shot?"
"As likely as not
                  so you make sure
You hold out your pennies."

Rare works of art discovered in
Tin mines! Another in Benin
Of great historical
Interest in London! Moscow!
   New York!
And still more from Olumo
   Rock,
All before the Flood!

Treasures, so many and
   beautiful,
Bartholomew Diaz and Sir John
Hawkins, wondering adrift on
A log ferry boat,
Did not know, Cellini
Dwelt among cannibals.

Dig well below wild opensteads
Dig well below dry riverbeds
The ivory bust
               the terracotta:
In the shadow of all trees
Lie holy unravelled dust
Seek out the shrines of Ifa
Creep in on both your knees
For wood carvings done in
   blood:
To win their mahogany,

Vignette: Native guide
takes around tourists with
preconceived ideas

Archaeological finds hailed
in newspapers

In Ijaw and Urhobo myth
the dead have to be ferried
to the other world of
classical myth

Ifa is the Yoruba oracle

Interest abroad is only
aesthetic, not being aware
of the mysteries behind.
The image is based on the
legend of a king who gave
his rival house such a task.
They however escaped to
found a more prosperous
settlement

Twenty thousand men wheeled
    the axe
And falling, another twenty
Received it on their backs.

Second Movement

In the irresolution   The visitors catch their
Of one unguarded moment   host napping
Thereby hangs a tale
A tale so tall in implications
Universal void cannot contain
The terrible immensity
Nor its permanence dissolve
In the flux wash of eternity:

Those unguent gums and oils   So begins the story of
Drawn in barrels off to foreign   exploitation
    mills
The soil quarried out of
    recognition
As never would erosion another
    millennium
The blood crying for blood spilt
    free
From keels away on frothing sea
The dark flesh rudely torn
And grafted on to red fetid sore
Breeding a hybrid lot
To work the land of sunset.

Sweet Mrs. Gamp, not a coward,   Their womenfolk follow and
Followed her man into the wild   try to make restitution
And wiping gentle hands on her
    eyes,
Without bias,
Delivered amid cries in the
    mission ward
A wisdom-toothed child

Is it truce or ruse   How they used the Bible
That peace which passeth all
    understanding
O big brother in heaven!

Third Movement

Out there where winds and
  clouds,
Tongues lashing, bang-clash and
Back thrash, tingling out
Of collision weird splintered
  flame,
You said you came,
Streaking out flaks
Of freak profusion and crowd
Upon a wood-awninged lake.

The strangers say they
bring "light"

Now, where are the lightning-
  spokes
That quivering should dance
Ten thousand leagues into the
  limbs of things?
Where are the broadways
Of oriflamme that opening wide
  should lance
Into the heart of darkness,
As when trembling like a fresh
Maid before her man,
Moonlight distils fluorescent
  submarine seas?

Thus pure light may act on
muddy waters in the dark

And Austin Herefords go toot
Tooting in mad rush for loot,
Go hooting,
Blazing wide trails of gold
Through the forests of the night.

The light visible is of army
and goods-trucks

Fourth Movement

Say, you communal gods at the gate
Has that whiff of carrion crept
Past your bars while you slept?
Did it roll-blowing gain the village
And without as much as a fight
From you? Did he brow-beat,
Bribe-beat you into our plight?
A man is a man for a' that
So when fallen upon in the dark
Why bleat, oh why bleat?

The betrayed man queries
his village gods

The ram in his belief that
one man can not kidnap
another never cries out for
help when himself a victim

Come into the house
Go in to bed O children
Who falls in mud
Need not smear another's blood
So come in children
An unlaid ghost
Has come into the village
Tonight out of the coast
I hear his wings flapping in the
    twigs
I smell the dank sweat
Brine of his breath
Heavy on plantain leaves and
    palm
They crinkle dry up and die
Yes I Oyin in times
Before farm-maids walked home
Upon the rainbow in fog climes
Had lived the fear beating out
    in fronds
The loud despair out there in the
    dark
We've lived through all before.

Fear him, children, O fear the
    stranger
That comes upon you
When fowls have gone to roost
Fear him his footfall soft light
As a cat's, his shadow far darker
Than forest gloom or night
And flimsy like matter in the mist.

O fear the dragon smoke-cloud
That hangs bloated, floating over
Roof-thatch mangoes and lime
Fear him that wreath-curling
    fetish-tree
Seeth-writhing beyond lofts

Mother hurries in her children. This image further worked out below is based on an actual phenomenon I have myself observed several times at home: the sudden smell of corpse blowing at night into the village in good health. Of course it is evil

Oyin is the Creator, the ultimate being in Ijaw myth. She is Woman and her name actually means "mother." Thus she is the anxious mother above. Sometimes we see the sun far into the evening behind red clouds. In the Niger Delta it is believed to be seeing home maids lost in the bush. The rainbow image therefore is not that far-fetched

Oyin, our all-knowing mother, briefs her children

When roof-thatch is burning in the day, black kites usually come hovering above—whether to seek out buried treasure or to help a mother-in-law put out the fire I cannot now exactly say

It turns out no less than he
  of the spoils

A snake-bird fell down early flat
In the market-place
Clinging quick to earth on his
  belly

There is indeed such a
bird known for its long
stay in water. The image
had to be extended. A pity
the amount of evil credited
to it here for it looks in life
innocent enough

Digging with his bristle fangs
Open communal graves amid
  confused clangs
Of race and riot
Fear the poison passed out or spat
Straight on our ancestral seat
Fear it though a trickle or dot
Fear it, the corruption,
That dissolving, will deluge all
  the earth
Fear the flood, children,
On whose repulsive waves
Two life-buoys alone bob
"Dirt and death, death and
  dirt . . ."

"Dirt and death"
And all along only the owl
Safe in her magic cowl
Saw all
I the white bearded woman
Of night fame saw all
But men heeded not my hooting
Placed instead penalty in warning
And finality in brief omen.

Every housewife thinks her
neighbor the witch
incarnate in any owl she
sees. I identify the bird
here with Oyin, the wise
old woman. The man who
first sights an omen is
immune from the impending
evil; perhaps that accounts
for men's intolerance of him
and his find

Fifth Movement

When you and I were young
Oyin bade us hold our tongue

The white-collar
generation, more white
than white

Bade us note "things don't stand
Looking into . . . so why trouble

Our heads," and later in our
 moments
Of expansion, both on the cricket
 field and
At the office desk, we clapped
 ourselves on the back;
So well-fed on sweet quotations
 and wine
Were we, with pride, we said:
"Forget O forget . . . to forgive is
 divine."

Yet in my father's house I cannot
 sleep
Nor shut myself up in peace
But loud knocks,
Absorbed in the thick of shocks,
Come beating back on my door
Crying: "Sleep no more!"

After all the fine sense of
humor and all the fine
manners, do they really
become civilized and
forget?

I cannot sleep I cannot sleep
Though not acting
Fierce floodlights flash-focus me
Our fathers rightly or wrongly
Properly drugged slept at least
And you say I ought to on this
 cup of tea
But all night I walk to and
Fro dung-polished floors
Unable to shut a little slit
That fast should fringe like flash
 at flies
Balancing the right and wrong
 of it
For does not the Holy Writ
Loud peddled abroad
To approve imperial flaws and
 fraud
Does it not say true:
"Knock and it shall be opened
 unto you"?

Tea cannot help as gin did
their forefathers

Cow dung is precious
polish for mud floor

And if I open unto them in haste
That cry out of a violated past
Shall ancient bones, safe laved
   in seas,
Not crash on crags
And if I fail
Shall bars not lifting burst of
   their own?

The suicide and the
dilemma

Talk then round the point,
   Hamlet, do talk on.
The Niger, long ago,
Faced with a similar lot,
Hedged round and till tomorrow
Goes on spinning whirlpools

It is neither new nor
peculiar, the long long
delay and indecision

The cocks begin again to crow
The night is old
And I am cold
So cold I know
Right in my bones the fear
Electrical in an old woman's
   breast
As new kites appear
Swooping in from the west.

The hen shields her brood
from the black kite; so does
Oyin her children from
invaders old and new.
The white collar generation
really doubly do not belong.

I cannot sleep nor act
And here I pace her bastard
   child,
A top twirling out of complexity
"Gnawing at my finger-tips deep
   perplexity."

Sixth Movement

Pass on then, O pass on, missile-
   hurled,
In your headlong flight to fool
   the world;
Being self-turned, how could you
   have heard

Above our wild herd
And market murmur of
    assembled waves
A song strange fallen out of
    night-caves
Like a star all of a sudden from
    the sky?
I,
Reared here on a cow-dung floor,
From antediluvian shore
Heard all, and what good it did!
"Magnificent obsession" now
    magic chords are broken!

Pass on in mad headlong flight
O pass on, your ears right
Full of throttle sound,
So winding up your kaleidoscope
Leave behind unhaunted
An innocent in sleep of the ages.

From *A Reed in the Tide*

Flight across Africa

Earth, from miles up, lies
Slaughtered, the splintered green of plantain
About her. Still the coaches and trucks
Pummel the body, their tracks
Or scars, sharp lines against the skies,
Horizontal spits and stakes that pin
Down the calf. As shrine-attendant
Years back with others now initiate,
We stripped entrails, wet and warm, wide
Open in the streams. And the tide
Whichever way it came, took
Care of the mess and shook
Us all free. But those valleys and
Fields, showing ulcerated in the sun,
And highlands, so carved clean,
The butchers no longer care to beat off
Flies, certainly are strange sacrifice
Not even this soap-sud sea we ride
Can flood . . . And so the wild expectant take-off
Broke no bones, no banks, though it tore down
The bloody baft—which is enough touchdown.

Emergency commission

Self-tossed out of heart
No outside hand could touch,
Still the storm howls on,
Heads, rock and root adrift.
And before cock crows a third
Time, yet another tree that
Seemed beyond reach of wind

And bolt, topples down,
  Or shows the blast.

Good God! What great grove
Is this under whose spell
We have these several
Seasons dug up old secrets
Of the soil, though aboard
Stars, when mahoganies
Show a center too rotten
For rings, and twigs and grass,
Already denied room and sun,
  Carry the crush and shock?

The leader

They have felled him to the ground
Who unannounced home from abroad
Wrestled to a standstill his champion
Cousin the Killer of Cows. Yes,
In all that common
And swamp, pitched piecemeal by storks,
No iguana during a decade of tongues
Could throw or twist him round
While he rallied the race and clan.
Now like an alligator he lies
Trussed up in a house without eyes
And ears:
  Bit of bamboo,
Flung to laggard dogs by drowning
Nearest of kin, has quite locked his jaws.

His Excellency the masquerader

He serves
To ford between swamp and sand,
He serves!

The bridge stands,
All that stone and steel put togehter,
It stands;

But bolts drop,
And steel that should be blue
At close grip

Shows brown . . .
And for such service, songs more than
Water and sand:

In Ojoto
So they worship the masks,
Although in season—

The masks!
O take off the mask! And behind?
What wind! What straw!

A child asleep

He who plucked light
From under shade of a tree
Sat so in dust, but in silence,
Passing like a spear clean into
The pith of things. But you,
Graft to an old bombax tree,
Raised on fullness of sap science
Cannot give, breed flies
In the oil of our evening,

Have sat dropsical feeding
On desire: it squashes, like the dried
Out ribs of tobacco an old woman
Is turning into snuff you tried
To wreck with stones—
But there, look at what we spies
Have missed! In the sand
Here at our feet already fallen is
Your stool, and how clean
Past our fingers, teasing and
Tugging, you have slumped down
A natal stump, there shed
Distended in the dust
As a primeval shadow
Tumbling head over heels into the arms of light.

Who bade the waves

Who bade the waves, like horsemen of Bornu, stop
A foot short
Of swamping the stand, rode
Them breast-breaking to sea and
Back, dry-shod,
Does not touch my heart, will not
Ride me rodeo one step. No! My heart
That is no stallion
Or lion in its cage
Encased with slabs of stone,
Rears in no rage
But against itself that cannot
Devour, savor all. After
Earthquake, stumble out the survivors
By no means the fittest. No so
Some. My heart that knows a thousand
Rifts, vents to heaven! with mouth
Of them crushed under stone,

Intercelled still in flesh, not
On the third night alone
Cries out for escape, knocks
For release as long as cocks
Crow—but release and escape oh
To where, and how then tell?
Who holds out hand
Of deliverance, drank
Dreg, paled upon nails, sank
In dust. And the body
Flames out still a thousand tongues, blind
As waves, deaf as dunes. Oh why
Does their cup fill out wind,
And I
All boiling with stone?

Boeing crossing

My head is in the clouds,
Literally, and but for this occasional
Reel and lurching to get
Through or round clumps and cliffs
That hover between water and air,
I shouldn't for a moment think
I was in one place in particular—or
For that matter, going anywhere
One knows of.
The lady
At my elbow, only lately clear
Of her belt, engages with the glove
She's knitting half by rote for some
Beloved hand, no doubt already outstretched,
Or perhaps otherwise occupied
At the other end; but for all that, she is
So bent on keeping pace with her reading,
She flicks through two, three pages

Of poetry, and I still on one. Another
Straight in front, I can just see
The tired tassel top of her, unwinds
Herself in blue black purls
Of smoke out of a holder as much
Aflame as those talons or tongs
She preens herself on. And
That old-timer over there
Across the aisle, a tycoon
Of some sort I'd bet my pants, lifted well
Outside the fluid frontiers of his empire,
Figures out safe solutions for today's
Crossword puzzle in *The Times*. But what
Cross-current of tongues
Above the wake of wings
And wind, and what flutter down
And up the corridor, in fact, so sure-footed, fresh
Rumors and echoes of a possible wet
Finish or fire are already dispelled
Which two sweet voices earlier on
Could not settle.
Now Sinbad
The Sailor, they say, got caught
Between the beak of Roc, and though dangling
Asleep, under unfailing spell,
Was whisked among the several
Wonders of his world. And according
To others, the whale that shuns
Stars and sun, in a manner
Not really unlike ours, delivered
Jonah early enough to keep
Date with a certain destiny, still denied
The tribe . . .
New York, however,
Weather and wear permitting, is
Where we are scheduled for the come-down
(That mine!) with a thud and
A dash or more, should certainly send
Us all packing and about our several ways
And wares which customs and
Firemen stand all round the clock to check.

Oh you,
Who have faith in the fable of fowl
And fish, and in the V.I.P.
Each gave passage, pray
That we who today prowl
The skies and bowels of the sea,
And so successfully play
Pranks with both distance and
Dawn, twisting Time's own tail
So far back into its jaws,
That old dragon does seem to pause
In its path, pray
We have the common sense to tell
When we hit either ceiling or floor
Please pray before we all
Lose our heads in the clouds.

Cuba confrontation

With my hammer head
I'll smash up the earth,
Said
The lizard:
And up reared
The aroused crown,
And then down
The blow
Came—like a courtesan's head,
Deep in her pillow.

I wake to the touch

Last night, times out of dream,
I woke
To the sight of a snake
Slithering in the field, livid
Where the grass is
Parched, merged up where it runs
All shades of green—and suddenly!
My brother in India, up, stick
In hand, poised to strike—
But ah, himself is struck
By this serpent, so swift,
So silent, with more reaction
Than a nuclear charge . . .

And now this morning with eyes still
To the door, in thought of a neck
Straining under the sill,
I wake
To the touch of a hand as
Mortal and fair, asking
To be kissed, and a return
To bed, my brothers
In the wild of America!

Home from Hiroshima

By decree
Of the President of the United States
Of America, unchallenged
By factions on the hill,
The eagle across the seal
Has turned eyes
Away from the arrows to the olive

Shoot, so praise them who prospered most in war
And now will live
By peace, Yet in city
And field, from coast to coast,
The hails
Of plumes, plucked, scattered free
From the original breed,
Shriek, thrash, rend the skies
Till vengeance is
Theirs, and likely
At its own instance
The wild west wreck the world.

Service

A dime
　in the slot,
And anything
　from coke to coffee
Spews down your throat,
　from crackers to candy
Breaks against the enamel
　wear of your teeth,
(And as T.V. minstrels
　Will have it ahead
Of the Congo
　and Guernica) tobacco
Enough to plant
　another Garden:
Now, old Moses
　for whom, they say,
Manna fell in the desert,
　　did he push a button as this,
　　and who knows at what price?

Times Square

Day fell here:
Like a drift of dead leaves,
Day fell facewise among the blocks,
And suddenly! down the overgrown plots,
The great tall figures, all sterile
And faceless before, are in woods
Of a festal night conifer-like trees
Ablossom with fruit. All
Who earlier in the fall
Milled here to pluck or pick at a price
The apple or peach, have forced
Through the harvest, bitten by
Bugs, have followed nuts
Home to rabbit-holes,
To nests up among boles.
How stripped of sensations now the stalls
And stand—even like a strip-teaser
Without breast or hair!
Two figures,
Fugitive from light, go kicking
Their shadows down steps belching up
The corner. Just then, as if in affectionate
Recognition, a wake of wrappings
Fingers have fondled, tongues
Have sucked to stumps, blow
Them kisses with the gum-wetness
Of a wind limping also to bed.
And I am
As the bum washed up on
The street, when markets are full
To fiesta, lesser by far than the scarecrow
Left over a farm, long after
Elephant trumpet and chorus of locust.

Cave call

The caves of Manhattan call out to me
In Times' neutral Square, at noon
Emerged from running colors that clash
By night. Tantalized, I take the steps down,
Descending at a dead loss. Escalating
Crowds, cross-current underground, dispute
The passage, each after shadows
Thrown in that pit and close
To reliefs out of a dream of mescalin:
I look for my own in the wild clot
And jumble, till like thunder tunnelling
The earth, the centipede train
Lunges full into station
And pulls us all to attention.
Multiple doors of their own slide
Open all at once down the platform,
Each the magnetic yawn
Of a monster. And already eaten
Up, I squash past the mass
Of flesh issuing forth. Then
At one blink, lights go out, and
Willy-nilly, the beast is tugging
Me blind by the front into his bowels
Of night. "Hold on!" "Hey, there,
Hold on!" tongues briefly untie
And tangle again in one intestinal
Rumble—
    Except that for me reeling
Sick, no string pays out now to clear
The meandering incubus caves to Manhattan . . .
At Washington
Square, a hot disc still dancing
The twitch up my left temple,
I lugged my trunk up the littered stairways—
    And didn't
The heart take a hop, although alone
Once more in those siren streets and afternoon!

From *Casualties*

I   Song

I can look the sun in the face
But the friends that I have lost
I dare not look at any. Yet I have held
Them all in my arms, shared with them
The same bath and bed, often
Devouring the same dish, drunk as soon
On tea as on wine, at that time
When but to think of an ill, made
By God or man, was to find
The cure prophet and physician
Did not have. Yet to look
At them now I dare not,
Though I can look the sun in the face.

II   Skulls and cups

"Look, JP,
How do you tell a skull
From another?" asked Obi.
"That this, could you find where he fell,
Was Chris, that Sam, and[2]
This there in the sand

[2]*Chris*—Christopher Okigbo, the poet and publisher: killed in action in September 1967 in the Nigerian Civil War, fighting as a major on the secessionist side.

Sam—Sam Agbam, a diplomat: executed in Enugu in September 1967 along with other activists wanting a return to the Federation.

Of course Emman. Oh yes,[3]
How does one tell a cup on the floor
From another, when the spirit is emptied?
And the goblets are legion,
Broken up the fields after Nsukka."

III   Vulture's choice

The vulture wanted a child
Six years was a long time
To be married and no child
What if the fetus should drop?
Then I shall eat it for breakfast.
What if the wife should die?
Then I shall eat her for lunch.
What if mother and child should die?
Then I shall eat both for the night.
The vulture wanted a child
Six years is a long time
To be married and no child!

[3]*Emman*—Major Emmanuel Ifeajuna: leader of the Army revolt of 15 January 1966, that toppled the civilian government of Sir Abubakar Tafawa Balewa; was held in detention along with other executors of the coup by Major-General Aguiyi-Ironsi who was himself overthrown on 29 July 1966; released by the then military Governor of the former Eastern Region of Nigeria Lieutenant-Colonel Odumegwu Ojukwu; executed in September 1967 for planning a counter-coup to return Eastern Nigeria to the Federation.

IV   *The burden in boxes*

Boxes were brought by night[4]
Boxes were left at crossroads
As gifts for the people
Without distinction
With no keys to the locks
No bearer at hand to take back
Baskets, take back platters with rabbit ears

Open the boxes was the clamor
Of monkeys above tides. *Open them all!*
Cows in the plains mooed over grass. But
Into cold storage the high priest
Of crocodiles moved the boxes,
Draping them in sacks muzzled at
The neck, into cold storage
He stowed them of unknown number.

Bring us the bearers of the gifts,
The gifts left us in boxes at
The crossroads, bring them out, we say,
So we may see them in the market place.
But in cold storage he left the lot,
The high priest of crocodiles who skipped
Over hedge in the dark, then leapt back,
Into sharp sunlight, hearing the cheer
Given voice by sea and desert,
Into cold storage he carted the boxes,
All making ominous music on the way.

---

[4]*Boxes*—In the first flush of the coup, Nigerians saw it as a gift from the gods, but when the coffins began to be counted, the Pandora character of the gift became apparent. Killed were the civilian leaders Sir Abubakar Tafawa Balewa, the Prime Minister of Nigeria; his party leader Sir Ahmadu Bello, the Sardauna of Sokoto and Premier of Northern Nigeria; their allies, the Premier of Western Nigeria, Chief S. L. Akintola, and Chief F. S. Okotie-Eboh of the Mid-West Region, the Federal Minister of Finance; and killed also were the senior Army officers Brigadier Zak Maimalari, Brigadier Ademulegun, Colonel Shodeinde, Colonel Pam, Lieutenant-Colonel Lagema, and Colonel Unegbe—a pattern of killing partial to the Eastern axis of the country. It changed the complexion of the coup, although a man of character other than General Ironsi's could still have rescued the situation for the country.

V   *The usurpation*

Caucuses at night, caucuses by day,
With envoys, alien and local,
Coming and going, in and out
Of the strongroom. What briefs
In their cases? The state,
Like a snake severed of its head,
Lies threshing in blood, and
Unless a graft at once is found,
The bird will flee the tree.

VI   *The cockerel in the tale*

At the desert end of a great road
To the sea, he who woke up the lion
And burnt down his den over his crest,
He who the same night bagged
A rogue elephant, not sparing his brood,
He who in the heat of that hunt
Shot in the eye a bull with horns
They say never gored a fly, hooves
That never trod on cocoa or groundnut farm,
Stood,
Alone on the trembling loft of the land,
And like the cockerel in the tale, proclaimed[5]
The break of day uncertain then
Where the sun should rise.
He lent the winds of the world
His name, that morning he lent them forever.

[5] *The Cockerel*—Major Chukwuma Kaduna Nzeogwu, in the eyes of the world the leader of
the coup of 15 January 1966.

VII   *The reign of the crocodile*

They say,
Because the alligator is stark deaf,
He runs as the torrent.
If so, the old master of the stream[6]
Must have had a hundred ears, prickly as leaves
Of the pine before wind-breath,
That summoned by a concourse on the banks
To breast a festival flood,
He punted upon his tail,
And like the whirlpool at Ganagana,
Swallowed his own head.

And so for six months a mighty river
Silted in the mouth,
Lacking distributaries;
For six months fields upon banks
Crackled to the sky,
Lacking distributaries;
And in caves flooded by them
Tied feet and tongue at pleasure of the leopard
And lion, palms peeled at palms.

To acolytes at the same time,
All nearly of one clan, and none
Out of bed when sun at noon
Paced into night, the high priest
Of crocodiles gave places
Right inside the shrine for all tribes,
Yam scrambled in palm oil
That was for gods out of land, sea, and sky.
The people cried for strokes to stem a tide.
With his left he released
To them pigeons and promises.

As if a skyful of pigeons, a sea
Of promises could drown the burden

---

[6] *The old master of the stream*—or the crocodile. Major-General Aguiyi-Ironsi was famous for his swagger-stick, a stuffed crocodile.

Heaving now in boxes like pythons.

Of him some scribes have written:
Taking a tour of his castle
By the sea, days
After the usurpation,
From parapet he moved
Into the cellar, and
After that, never rose again.

Others wrote:
He came to center stage,
Straight from the drinkhouse.
Seated long after payment,
The people cried for a song,
The song was in the street,
But like the ham he was,
He sat down to a party,
Called in his cronies, and
Not one knew the song.

VIII   Seasons of omens

When calabashes held petrol and men
  turned faggots in the streets
Then came the five hunters
When mansions and limousines made
  bonfires in sunset cities
Then came the five hunters
When clans were discovered that were not in the book
  and cattle counted for heads of men
Then came the five hunters
When hoodlums took possession of police barracks
  in defiance of bullets
Then came the five hunters
When ministers legislated from bed and
  made high office the prize for failure

Then came the five hunters
When wads of notes were kept in infant skulls
   with full blessing of prelates
Then came the five hunters
When women grew heavy with ballot papers delivering
   the house entire to adulterers
Then came the five hunters
When a grand vizier in season of arson turned
   upon bandits in a far off place
Then came the five hunters
When men lost their teeth before they cut them
   to eat corn
Then came the five hunters
When a cabinet grew so broad the top gave way
   and trapped everyone therein
Then came the five hunters

At club closure
Antelopes slept, for lions snored;
Then struck the five hunters,
But not together, not together.
One set out on his own into the night,
Four down their different spoors by the sea;
By light of stars at dawn
Each read in the plan a variant

And so one morning
The people woke up to a great smoke.
There was fire all right,
But who lighted it, where
The lighter of the fire?

Fallen in the grass was the lion,
Fallen in the forest was the jackal,
Missing by the sea was the shepherd-sheep,
His castrate ram in tow,
And all around was the blood of hounds.

IX   *What the squirrel said*

They killed the lion in his den
But left the leopard to his goats
They killed the bull without horns
But left the boar to his cassava
They killed the elephant with his brood
But left the crocodile to litter the field
They killed a sheep who played shepherd
But left the hyrax who was a hyena

The rumor sprang seed
In the throat of a squirrel
The seed grew into a trunk
Inside fangs, inside horns
Wind from its blast blew down forests,
And the rage is not done, coils
Of it about us, about our necks.

X   *Leader of the hunt*[7]

He who began it all,
Grown mad with love or hiss
Of housewife and harlot,
One night plucked out of bed
A vizier; his treasurer, taken
As well, spilling bags of bills
All the way to a shallow grave
On some wayside. That night, while others failed
Their parts, he left behind a trail
Of brass all loaded with lead,

[7]*Leader of the hunt*—Major Emmanuel Ifeajuna. After failing in Lagos, he fled to Accra from where Christopher Okigbo and I brought him back to Nigeria on 16 February 1966, a week before the Ghana coup that overthrew President Kwame Nkrumah. He, Chris and I are the characters A, B, and C of *Conversations at Accra.*

In the end fled
The prize some swear he plotted for years,
Because of the tryst a confidant
Did not keep. Foiled though through the gates,
He drove across country, blood on
His boots, bodies in his boot,
Unknown to crowds jubilant for a champion.
Kith and kin he had spared, though
More ravenous than lion or rogue elephant,
Denied him then, as they would again and
Again. So back he reeled across country,
Helped over stile by several hands with key
To surgery or bedroom, decked at one point
As a belle, in which guise he crossed
The border, shorn of beard, shorn of sleep,
Never more to wake from nightmare,
Never more know a friend.

There in another country, kept
As a thing of curiosity in a cage
Before a god about to fall,
I held him in my arms,
The friend I dare not look at again,
Though I stare the sun in the face.

XI   *Conversations at Accra*

A: The situation may change,
        It may change completely.
        Then, they who condemning the change
        By force of arms, have inherited
        The booty, may in their turn
        Be divested of the spoil it is plain
        They will feed to birds of the air.
        Brother in fact may turn
        Against brother, and the same act
        Repeated from sea to desert.

Then may I not return home
To the people, oh my people,
Clamoring for a parade
They know not the leader!

B: The clamor is not in markets only
The clamor is in cathedrals
The clamor is from minarets
And not in the morning alone
The clamor is in kitchens, in schools;
In court, in palace alone is silence.

A: Is that so? Is that so?
Then I am happy, very happy.

C: Dog does not eat dog
Why in the hunt did the pack
Fall on its own kind?

A: Because the hounds at the head of the pack
Played with the lion
Because they hunted with the lion
Because they hunted for the lion
One gave in fact fangs to the hyrax,
Called into the kennel the jackal.
And another was sent
As plague upon his breed. Oh, rabid
The day the keeper delivered
All in the grassland to the lion,
All in the forest to the leopard,
The breed fell upon every blade
To hand, in defiance of teeth filed
On latest drill, and all along,
All the course swaddled face
In handkerchief, with cheer
The breed carried in its vein rats.

C: Still, crickets and cows are crying
Whether thongs could not have served
Where fangs have torn up graves
None again can cover.

A: You mean tie a thorough hound
To a tree and set a common cur

As guard over him? Oh boy, oh boy,
Before you rush to the next post,
There would be reversal of roles, and you
At the end of the leash.

B: And the penalty is death
By fang. Oh, broken in town now
Is the pack, each pouncing on
The other asleep.

A: It was a pack the trainers left
Without union of heart or sight
Disbandment seems the one course
It can now run. Look,
I am a soldier,
Well able to look after myself
On the way home by land,
Sea, or air. But what word
Have I the general who offers
Me now in one hand a flag of no color
Has not in the other the writ of fire?
The situation, on the other hand,
May change, change utterly, and
New paths open out, whether into day
Or relapse further into night,
Which of us here can tell?

C: A group goes hunting as one man
A hunter goes into the night
With carbide eye on his forehead
His companion his gun
If one returns home without the other
Then something is wrong
The animal lies fallen in the forest
If shoulders do not bear it home together
Then something is wrong
The leader of the hunt is up on the iroko
Scattered are the group in the forest
The buffalo stumps over shrubs
The buffalo stools under the iroko
His tail stirs stool to lash it out
Further up the iroko scales the leader of the hunt

Gathered are the flies on the meat
The people may not eat.

A: I know, I know, don't I know? That night
The group accepted me leader,
Even he who took the lion.
They will follow now if I blow the horn.

B.   Then blow, blow it! Right now,
Scattered in the forest are hounds
You led to the hunt.
Stranded in the woods are dogs listening
For the hunter's horn,
And loitering in the square
Are the people hungry for a share.

C: What if the horn is broken?
What if it broke the night
Ropes of sound, ropes of light
Were cut overhead? Can
A horn be put together like cord?

A: That is the point, that is the point.
Out of four unequal pillars
To a barn like bedlam,
One taller than the rest
Together, I sought to build
A new estate of fourteen wings,
Each interlocked with the other
Around an open court.
I sought to post by each gate
A watchdog, summon to service
Hands that never held dirt,
And upon the stool in the hall
I thought to sit a man,
Burnt clean by fires he had
Himself started. Overnight,
Bricks in the act crumble down,
A pack of cards in the hands
Of a delinquent, and straws
In the wind spell no design.

XII   *Return home*

Together with Chris I brought him home
On clipped wings, on clipped wings,
He who seeing a forest fire,
Turned on a tap the crocodile
Could not stop, unknown to pilot, to crew,
As plain Fred King. There by the green lights
On the ground the red rug was rolled
From under his feet. Engaged elsewhere was
The horse that should have cantered to the midget plane,
Crawling now to its place of rest. Instead, came
A donkey to carry into the night
King Fred, Chris close at his back,
Sam holding to a restive tail,
And I alone on the tarmac
With odd items to clear,
A number of papers I did not dare declare.

XIII   *The locust hunt*

Locusts were discovered outside city walls
Locusts were decried in stranger settlements
Locusts were hunted down to women and children
With mortar, matchete, with broomsticks and rackets
In shops, in streets, in offices
Locusts were hunted down in courts and convents.

So a royal bull was slain
With all the egrets on his hump
So dog ate dog in a hunt
With a scattering of the pack in the plain
Oh, how many grasshoppers make up
The loss of one elephant?
How many ticks must there be
To eat up one mastiff?

A river under clear skies
Keeps to its channel, but let
The clouds break, let them break
And ripped below are the banks upon the plains
And let them remember on the banks
The fire struck by one spark,
In grasslands or forest,
Lights up a stockpile.

XIV   July wake[8]

For Emman and Dorcas

In the streets the jungle-geared jeeps roar,
Glint of SMG,[9] flare of mortar, tremor
Of grenades occupying ministry
And market, and like hens, men go
To bed with the setting sun, the sun
Setting over the land, with a people afraid
It will set on their individual days.

One night, walls fell upon
A cat in a mouse hide, clatter of boots
Over and around his doors,
Barricaded with any block from books
To cooker and radiogram. Four hours
He ran a marathon
In his house, uncheered by faces,
Over hedge, voices over telephone,
And even by the 999 squad
He called in. Harassed as a hen

---

[8]The days were full of terror, confusion, and general uncertainty following the openly retaliatory coup on 29 July 1966, in which Major-General Johnson Aguiyi-Ironsi was overthrown and killed together with the gallant Military Governor of Western Nigeria, Lieutenant-Colonel Adekunle Fajuyi, as well as several officers and men. This was when Christopher Okigbo and I last met—on one of those critical days in August. Partition was the theme then in the air. Chris and I agreed that we must go home, as it was a time when anybody could be killed by mere association and for the acts of others; but home to him meant Enugu in the East, while for me it was Warri in the Mid-West.

[9]The passing car of the Secretary to the Military Government, the head of administration.

By hawks when the keeper is
Gone, he clutched at last
For the roof of his caving estate,
With bare fingers to scratch there
A hole, perhaps to the sky. Too late,
The gang in green got him then
By legs lost in loosening pajama.
Crumpled, they flung him
In his sweat and discharge
Down inside their boot, passed mercifully
By now beyond despatch.
Last night to my right, tonight
To my left side and front, oh,
Let but a car come hooting by,
And I hear in its bonnet the roar
Of leopards amok from the forest.

XV   *Exodus*

They flee the altar who in
The ceremony of forging the faggot
Danced round the anvil, swung
The heaviest hammer. Others in the act
Said: "They ought to have left
Us some bars in the fire,
Some wind in the bellows." As
If rod bends over or spark goes out
Of its own for others to flourish.
More just perhaps was the charge
The clan carried in its heart
The curse of Aristotle: so fast
Through the furnace, a bubble
Sprang down its middle, that pierced,
Has scattered the cast
So quick through the kiln, so given
To toil, it was
The miracle of a generation.

XVI   August afternoon

In the blind noon
Shadows shudder,
And a column of rats
Scales over roofs
After cats.

XVII   The rat in a hole

A couchant leopard in its cage
Is a coil of steel with the catch
In a safe. One day
The creature will break
In the face of the keeper.

Cooped in my hole,
I cringe as a rat
Upon a rising mound
Of fear, the forbidden meat
I feed fat on,
My own tail my lash.

In the east is the sun,
Calling all to thunder.

XVIII   *Dirge*

Show me a house where nobody has died
Death is what you cannot undo
Yet a son is killed and a daughter is given
Out of one seed springs the tree
A tree in a mad act is cut down
Must the forest fall with it?
Earth will turn a desert
A place of stone and bones
Tears are founts from the heart
Tears do not water a land
Fear too is a child of the heart
Fear piles up stones, piles up bones
Fear builds a place of ruin
O let us light the funeral pile
But let us not become its faggot
O let us charcoal the mad cutters of teak
But let us not cut down the clan!

XIX   *The flood*

The rain of events pours down . . .
Like a million other parakeets, cunning
In their havens out on the lee,
I don my coat of running
Colors, the finest silver and
Song can acquire. Not enough,
I unfurl my umbrella, resplendent as any
That covers a chief
At a durbar. It buckles, and will
Fly out of my hand. In the grief
Gusts of rain now over all the land,
I flounder in my nest, a kingfisher,
Whose flockmates would play

At eagles and hawks, but like
Chickens, are swept away
By flood fed from septic tanks, till
Together, we drift and drown,
Who were at home on sea, air, and land.

XX   *Aburi and after*

With old faces in my mind
Retired to their wing,
I thought for a long time
They were wringing Jack Gowon's hand,
Wringing his hand for use of a rule
Too broken then in the sand
To flog a fly. Only
When bones were wrenched out of joint
In the court of a stranger,
Did we wake to the scowl
Of implacable masks in the compound,
And a keeper now at attention,
With ankle twisted, and
A prayer in his heart.

XXI   *The beast*[10]

Long pronounced in tumult underground
But not likely because of antlered heads
To rush out of cracks breaking across
The land, the dragon by five young demons

[10]On 6 July 1967, war broke out at last, although secession had been proclaimed on 30 May.

Released out of their mad love of the land,
Belches, gorged already with the feast
That creates room as it fills the guts.

Wind from the dragon takes possession
Of masks; dung from the dragon
Makes catacombs of cities and farms;
With mere drippings the dragon sets
Rivers on fire, flames of this lick
Mangroves to salt, salt more colic than
Arsenic, and debris damming a whole delta.

In the sunset sky kites of all colors take
The wind, swifts and swallows escort them.
Above, how they scream diving for flags
Of fire rooted to the heart, while below
Breath burns more sulphurate
And blood calcifies into boulders
For brother to hurl against brother.

XXII   *Death of a weaverbird*[11]

Shot,
At Akwebe,
A place not even on the map
Made available by Shell-BP,
A weaverbird,
Whose inverted house
Had a straw from every soil.
Clear was his voice as the siren's
Chirp with no fixed hour
Of ditty or discourse . . .
When plucked,
In his throat was a note
With a bullet for another:

[11]Christopher Okigo, of his volume of poems *Limits*.

I am in contact with the black-kite,
At the head of a flock I have led
To this pass.
How can I return to sing another song?
To help start a counter surge?

XXIII   *Friends*

The friends
That we have lost,
May be carried
Deep in our hearts,
But shallow is the burden
When placed beside
The loss to kin.
Though we share with the dead
Club or cult,
Our loss, large as the fellowship
We kept,
Is by that number
Relieved of the load
Which is square upon love.

XXIV   *A photograph in* The Observer

Night falls over them
The young enlisted honey-combed
In the sun
Night falls over them
Statuettes of ebony ganged together
As ibeji at an altar
Night falls over them

Heads of them bald
Bared bodies
Crackling from the tight knot
They throw on the field before
A physician
Night falls over them
And already
They are a cache certified fit
For hurling at the ogre
They all see in the dark
Night falls over us . . .

XXV *Benin sacrifice*

And yet another screen is rent
Off our bedside . . .

In the glare before dark,
Two rams are led out,
One already broken and on
A stretcher, the other still strutting
On his own steam . . .

Before a full arena
Adorned by governor, trader, and
Parlor wife, two rams are led
Hooded to stakes, anchored
To barrels of sand . . .

They are strung upright.
One seems at a standstill
With the hour, the other
Rippling as the crowd now
And many decades before . . .

Then the priest commanding
Intones the charge, and the latest
Instruments of slaughter stutter out

A message mortal at once to two rams
Now men again in the city of blood . . .

And another screen is rent
Off our bedside.

XXVI   *Party song*

Here we mill drinking by midnight
Here we mill bobbing by fairylight
Here we mill glowing by dimlight

A floor away
Other drums are beating
Other lamps are burning in a
Titanic ball

And through open gates by night and day
Brigades and villages are going out
Like lights over Lagos.

XXVII   *The casualties*

To Chinua Achebe

The casualties are not only those who are dead;
They are well out of it.
The casualties are not only those who are wounded,
Though they await burial by instalment.
The casualties are not only those who have lost
Persons or property, hard as it is
To grope for a touch that some
May not know is not there.

The casualties are not only those led away by night;
The cell is a cruel place, sometimes a haven,
Nowhere as absolute as the grave.
The casualties are not only those who started
A fire and now cannot put it out. Thousands
Are burning that had no say in the matter.
The casualties are not only those who escaping
The shattered shell become prisoners in
A fortress of falling walls.

The casualties are many, and a good number well
Outside the scenes of ravage and wreck;
They are the emissaries of rift,
So smug in smoke-rooms they haunt abroad,
They do not see the funeral piles
At home eating up the forests.
They are the wandering minstrels who, beating on
The drums of the human heart, draw the world
Into a dance with rites it does not know

The drums overwhelm the guns . . .
Caught in the clash of counter claims and charges
When not in the niche others have left,
We fall,
All casualties of the war,
Because we cannot hear each other speak,
Because eyes have ceased to see the face from the crowd,
Because whether we know or
Do not know the extent of wrong on all sides,
We are characters now other than before
The war began, the stay-at-home unsettled
By taxes and rumors, the looters for office
And wares, fearful every day the owners may return,
We are all casualties,
All sagging as are
The cases celebrated for kwashiorkor,
The unforeseen camp-follower of not just our war.

XXVIII   *Night song*

The night for me is filled with faces,
Familiar faces no season
Of masks can cover. Often,
The strange and young I never met,
Like Nyananyo, Amangala,[12]
Boro, all summoned from office[13]
Or study, from sound of highlife
And sweet taste of tongues, straight into
The siren arms of war,
Intercept the faces I loved,
And sun is blotted out that I
Believe should ripen the land anew,
Though the sowing is of hearts I knew
And hold closest still in my head.
Now winds gallop through the gates
Of their eyes. In pots their mouths make
In fields already forgotten
In the fight, grow arum lilies,
Hedges of ivory about them. Let
Me but close my eyes, and they flower
Into more mornings of faces
I dare not look at,
Though I have sat it out in the sun.

The faces recur,
Out of the iron siege of the earth,
Bright bulbs tied to tree hands

[12]*Nyananyo, Amangala*—Boardman Nyananyo and Captain George Amangala, volunteer servicemen from the classroom, killed in action in the Bonny sector of the war, fighting on the Federal side.

[13]*Boro*—Isaac Adaka Boro was born in 1936 at Odi, Rivers State; first came into the news as the student leader at Nsukka who took Sir Abubakar Tafawa Balewa, then Prime Minister of Nigeria, to court for allegedly misconducting the country's census; declared the first secession in Nigeria—of the Rivers State from the then Eastern Nigeria in February 1966 with himself as head of state; rebellion crushed by Major-General Aguiyi-Ironsi; later tried and condemned to death; reprieved by Major-General Yakubu Gowon on 3 August 1967; enlisted in the Nigerian Army as a lieutenant in September 1967 along with compatriots like Amangala, Nyananyo, Sese, and old colleagues like Nottingham Dick; killed in action as a major near Okrika as Port Harcourt was falling a few miles away in May 1968.

Flailing in a storm none
On either side can tell the end. One,
Trapped in a cell when the crocodile
In turn was trussed seated into a hole,
On his return to day, fell
Into a pit. Others, touched on
A chord resonant to the root,
Followed, at the great crossroads,
A dance into the forest. Oh,
How can woods echo a song
That filled city-halls?
How can cantors of the song
Abandon the service on the floor?

A song was begun one night;
The song should have begun
A festival of three hundred tribes.
Instead it lit for cantor
And chorus a funeral pile.
In the crash of columns and
Collapse of rafters,
Another,
Ignored by all as dumb,
Catches the strain, in
The daze of noon the song rises,
Burns down the old ramparts
Of the heart, and before
Smoke seal our eyes, mud our mouths,
Firm upon the ground appears the house
Of our dream, with a mansion
For them who followed ghosts
Into the forests of night.

Epilogue to Casualties

To Michael Echeruo

In the East Central State of Nigeria, four years
After the war, I visited again the old sites
I had frequented with friends, dead
Or gone now to their own homesteads,
Admonished gently by the administrator
Of the estate for coming when reconstruction work
Was all but complete. Even then,
The ruins that greeted me on the road,
Right from Milliken Hill to the amputated
Giant astride the River Niger, raised
Before my eyes a vision of the unnatural
Disaster that is war: the bridges,
Broken before and beyond Oji,
The bellows belching again at Awka,
The skeleton carriers, camouflaged
By grass at Abagana, and of course,
The other Ogidi, strangely without
Pock-marks, hamlet of the fabulist
Who I thought would never forgive, never forget,
Knowing the wrong in his own heart.
Yet Onitsha, whether as the birthplace
Of Emmanuel Ifeajuna, Tony Asika,
Or Nnamdi Azikiwe, came as the jolt
That broke my journey to Owerri,
Aba, Umuahia, through Ulli
Ihiala which after all was but a stretch
Of road for pirate planes to spirit off
Warriors, swearing to fight to the last man
Even as they fled orphan, widow, and batman.
Here houses, scalped and scarred past surgery,
Stared at me, sightless in their sockets, like
The relics of shell-shock that they are.
One, so mutilated, it is a miracle
The parts hung together at all,
Called to me in the crush, in it one

Plump woman, careless of her bare breast
And brood, pounding yam up on a balcony,
Tilted in face of gravity. The wreck
Seemed greatest by the river, there
Voiceless and sweeping the earth as
A widow who has also buried her seeds.
To one side of her lay that giant bridge
With knee lopped in the air, while clamorous
For comfort upon her other side struggled
The old market of dreams, a forest,
Cropped of all foliage, rising already
Above two cathedral spires still in conflict
For eastern pastures, as they were before the war.

Incidental songs for several persons

Incident at the police station, Warri

(*After The Flagellation of Jesus* by Piero della Francesca)

For Father O'Flannagan

Stripped to his penis, the convict at
His lordship's command is shooed out
Of his cell into the square to a bench,
Gleaming with grime in the sun.
"Lie down!" cracks the order, and at that,
Superfluous uniform hands as of an octopus
Grapple the prisoner down, one smart
Sergeant mounting his back. Now with the hiss
And beat of a cobra incensed,
The big stick descends deliberate and
Constant upon the shivering buttocks till
Carbolic water, blood, and tears, wrung
Free in spite of iron will,
Flow in one polluted stream, washing
Society of another individual wrong.
And the smell
Fills the air of the first flagellation with thong:
The scared, curious throng,
Mainly of women and children, twittering
At the sight of a tail shrunken
Between thighs, three very important
Looking persons discussing in one corner,
Perhaps the latest list of promotions or
Prices on the market, and in a car
Parked close by, one gallant and another
Asking the girls to more wine and song.

The Lagos–Ibadan road before Shagamu

For Sam, Sesan, Kayode and the wives

A bus groaned uphill. Trapped
In their seats, fifty odd passengers rocked
To its pulse, each dreaming
Of a different destination.
GOD'S TIME IS THE BEST, read
One legend. NO CONDITION IS
PERMANENT, said another. And on,
On over the hill Ashiru
Drove the lot, a cloud of Indian hemp
Unfolding among his robes. With
The swish over his shoulders, it
Trailed out, touched tails with the smoke
That squatted all indigo
On the hillside: like a stream
Was the going downhill, swift
Past recollection, straight into a bend
Upturned as a saucer, and
The journey spilt over in a ditch.
In the early morning sun,
To the clamor of flies that first
Answered the alarm, water
Of sewage kind washed their common
Wound, silenced their common groan.

No need of first aid,
All died on the spot,
Said the dailies. *The police,*
Well supplied with notes,
Are looking for the driver
Who escaped unhurt.

A lamp by my window

For Ayo Ogunsheye and Nekan Ademola

I have a lamp
   By my window at night
Dislodges the moon.
    Broken there as a mosaic,
It strikes me in bed
    Moon and lamp are many discs
Dancing in a stream
    Bearing me to sleep.

To my academic friends
who sit tight on their doctoral theses
and have no chair for poet or inventor

You who will drive forward
But look to the rear mirror
Look at the crashes and
Casualties holding up traffic
To the market. He drives
Well who arrives
Again and again with fresh wares.

Letter from Kampala

To Ebun

At this other end of Africa
It is of you alone
I think at home,
And the children:
I go farther in order
To get home to you.

Nairobi National Park

For Nyambura and James Ngugi

Ostrich and giraffe peek
Over bush; warthog and
Baboon amble across roads;
From lone tree to Songora
Ridge drift the heifers,
But shy in the grass
The lion lies,
And placid are the ponds
In Embakasi Plain.

Addis Ababa

For Mary Dyson

Buffaloes,
Assorted and gelded,
Scramble up burning mountains:
In the lead,
A dinosaur out
Of the Abyssinian lake.

A god is the cow

For Primila and Charles Lewis

A god is the cow
In India, never to be eaten
As is holy flesh by
Another clan.
Which is not to say
Her children deny
Her. Upon her neck is the common
Yoke for beggar-cart and plough.

The players

Union of blood or need, boy and girl
Carry in their bag no trick
As the old couple in the act.
Natural mishap is the ware
The young hustle in the street.
Thrilled today at the dazzle
Of a rupee the girl can only touch
On the way to a shallow till,
The beggar boy moves scene
For hag to play drum
Majorette to her man, caught
In a cycle-wheel and sundry kit.
How often has staff hurtled
About that crooked bole,
Flogging out of routine a trembling
Flush? Gathered are her palms
Unfolded into a bowl
After drill, but bored are
The itinerant crowds caged in
Themselves. And the flickering
In her eyes is not of the wind.

Bombay

Here nothing seems new: the rising
Estate is cancelled out by septic slums;
The very docks that gave this city
Her name Gateway to India
Smell of the old company
That made paupers of moguls;
The streets crawl with vintage
Vehicles: bullock carts, horse carts, iron
Carts, human carts, all in unison groan
For service. From gardens hanging on
A hill to a mosque afloat
In the harbor, mansion and
Shack tumble down like monsoon
Waves in the Bay of Bengal,
And all about,
Upon monument as upon men,
Grime with slime sits brandishing rags
In the wake of an empress now slut.

Calcutta

Cow and man loll about
In lice, share in streets
Of slime the same bed
And bath, as the palaces
And slums in flood.

State of the Union

Something is rotten in the state . . .
Hamlet I.iv. 1.90

For all those who have died
and suffered for her

I   Here Nothing Works

Here nothing works. Services taken
For granted elsewhere either break down
Or do not get started at all
When introduced here. So supply of water
That is basic to life after air
Re-creates for the people
Desert conditions even by the sea,
As every day darkness increases
Over the land, just as more dams go up
And rivers reach levels approved by experts,
What is it in ourselves or in our soil
That things which connect so well elsewhere,
Like the telephone, the motorway, the airways,
Dislocate our lives so much that we all
Begin to doubt our own intelligence?
It cannot be technology itself
In our hands fails us, for we pick up
The skills fast enough as all vendors know
Who sell to us round the world. But the doctor,
Playing God in his ward of death many
Outside are dying to enter, forgets
Or denies his oath, and law that should rule
The land so each may be free to cultivate
His talent for the wellbeing of all breaks down
In all departments of life, from classroom
To courthouse, for many, remembering
The principle, do not believe in its
Practice anymore. So something there must
Be in ourselves or in our times that all
Things working for good elsewhere do not work
In our expert hands, when introduced
To our soil that is no different from other lands.

II   *Progress*

The sandboats on the lagoon,
Will they make the last mile
Home by sunset? The wind,
Stalling in their sails,
Has travelled a thousand miles
Since they set out at dawn.

III   *The Cleaners*

Look at the crew
Who after each disastrous race
Take over a public place
To wash it new.
They are themselves so full
Of muck nobody can see
The bottom of the pool
For the mud they carry
And cast so freely at a few.

IV   *Return of the Heroes*

They have all come back as if nothing
Had happened, the generals in the field
And the great civilian leaders
Who fled abroad, and left surrogates
To give up the war they fought
Like leopards to share out the land.
They all arrive, are met at the airport,

And driven into town with sirens,
Receive from the latest head of state
A warm embrace. One even was told
He had the freedom of the country
Now one man was gone, as if the war
The secessionist waged had been against
The man. Now they are all back home
To the last man who was the first
To run away, while they that followed
The code to the barracks, got tried,
Did time, and today can have some comfort
They were not among the countless dead.

V   Easter 1976

What came uppermost in their minds,
Thirty-odd men walking thirty-odd
Yards to their death on an
Afternoon, a whole city emptied
Upon the shore to watch them?

A drowning man, it is said, catches
The holograph of his life in a flash:
Air, water, soil and sky, he takes
Them in in that gulp, when all
The cumulations of sense and mind
Go out as so many bubbles . . .

But thirty-odd men walking thirty-odd
Yards to their death, what scenes,
What sensations of horror or delight
Came crowding into their minds?

True, every attempt by force
To change command carries
The actors over the brink to a bank,
Dim even to the lynx by light of day,
And if it fails, they fall into a gorge

With only the echo of their cry
To mock the sky . . .

Gentlemen all, or so they swore
To act, had a woman, mother
Of one among them, known,
When at the great cross-roads of careers
To service at the top, that her child,
After leading battalions into the field,
Would walk like this one day
To be shot at a stake by the shore,
His own comrades his executioners,
She might well have chosen to pass
Blood all her yielding years.

Officers more than men
Were hunted down in the field
In offices, in hospitals, at home
Before wives, before children
In a fever that seized a nation.
It only had to be said
Such and such a man had met
An actor at the bar, or played
Polo or ludo with him, and he was
Accused of a part in the wildcat plot
Of a gang that called curfew
For morning to evening, having shot
Dead in the middle of a street
Their quarry for crimes they could not
Even pronounce, though heaven knows
The homesteads and farms are many
Crying still, after the passage
Of the buffalo a people
Have taken for their totem.

One there among them I knew well,
Or so I thought, until
The act betrayed the man,
Not the general who they say took
A hundred bullets to die
And now in death I cannot
Get out of my dreams, but

A young man, one that should
Have been close to me, if only
For plucking from the same tree,
And bearing it later fallen
To its place of rest, where
One morning a buffalo fell.

So questions were asked at the time
Under breath, and questions more are
Being asked now the matter is
Of no account to the dead, and
The living are learning again to live,
Questions that the great pushers
Of causes convenient still
Have not asked, whether a trial,
Conducted with the first rule
In the book reversed,
Could have found out which finger
In the act touched another
With the blood it did not spill.

But thirty-odd men walking thirty-odd
Yards to their death on an afternoon,
A whole city emptied upon the shore
To watch them, who will ever know
What came uppermost in their minds?

VI   *Victoria Island*

In the interest of the public
They took over land a family
Owned before the country began.
With public seal and money
They reclaimed it from swamp and sea.
Then while the people looked on
In wonder, they parcelled out the land
Among themselves, their mistresses, liars,

And sycophants from Tyre and Sidon.
Now the people may not step on the land
Overnight flooded with millionaires.
Why should the country not be sick?

VII   *Of Sects and Fellowships*

There is a tide across the land
Unstable has turned souls away
From cathedrals to the marketplace:
Streets, beaches and sitting-rooms
Now are full of men and women
In direct contact with God
On any matter from queries
At work to sale of rice, while pews
Only fill for weddings and death.

What is there in a flaming candle,
Upheld by figures in flowing gowns,
Draws flocks to their immolation
Upon a bell and a book the best
Of them, shedding incense, cannot
Even read from cover to cover?

VIII   *A Parable*

For John Alele

By the road outside a convent
The mad fed the mad, and
The sane swore to take an eye
For an eye should harm come
To him by hand of the insane.

IX   *Phaemon's Dog*[14]

A race at one time across country
Brought out the whole school roistering
In the rain, and there was not
A laggard in the group did not hug
The course, proud of a challenge
He shared and met with the best.

These days, the whistle has not gone
But the pack is off rushing for short cuts,
And nobody bothers when they return
With so much meat in their mouths.

X   *Sacrifice*

How shall I tell my children not
To love her to the point that loss
Of life, limb and property is
A sacrifice they cannot withhold
If called upon to serve in her time of need?

I have known her send out
So many of her bright, beautiful,
And young in pursuit of a course

[14]Phaemon the philosopher had a little dog whom he had trained to go to the butcher every day and bring back a lump of meat in a basket. This virtuous creature, who would never dare to touch a scrap until Phaemon gave it permission, was one day set upon by a pack of mongrels who snatched the basket from its mouth and began to tear the meat to pieces and bolt it greedily down. Phaemon, watching from an upper window, saw the dog deliberate for a moment just what to do. It was clearly no use trying to rescue the meat from the other dogs: they would kill it for its pains. So it rushed in among them and itself ate as much of the meat as it could get hold of. In fact, it ate more than any of the other dogs, because it was both braver and cleverer. (From *Claudius the God* by Robert Graves)

Still not very clear to the old
Who in their time also set out in hope

Though nothing but mounds, weeds
And thorns have sprung up in the field.

XI   *Song of the Retired Public Servant*

My own estate let me now give
Some time. In our old way we tried
To give to her something
More than she gave us. Now
It pleases her best if servant
Becomes her master and builds
Himself many a mansion,
My own estate let me give
The time I have left, before
My children turn tenants to their peers.

XII   *Out of the Tower*

For Derry for his festschrift

That air and light may come again
Clean and free into the chambers
Of my heart, I give up, perhaps
In folly, my tenure in a tower,
Built upon a place of swamp.
I had thought, standing in the cesspool,
Head, shoulders and trunk above
The stench, the rot around could not
Infect my life. But feet in boots

Over years of no reclamation
Grew fetid, and lungs that were clear
Before so much congested,
It would have been suicide
To stay any day longer,
Believing one might as well accept
The conditions, since they were
After all endemic to the country.

XIII   Election Report

It was a numbers game from the start.
First came the enumerators, issuing
Voting cards for the great month of outing.
From house to house, on hilltop and in swamp,
They went across the land, not counting heads
But taking figures, dictated by heads
Of compounds, and since no violation
To harem was meant, and the watchword
The more mouths the greater the share
Out of the national cake, each head
Of house outdid the neighbor, swelling
His family strength sometimes tenfold.
It was indeed a register of
Inflated numbers, compounded further
By political party agents, armed
With tall lists of objections and
Omissions, carrying names of people,
Fictitious, long dead, or of favorite
Children already registered in the places
Of work far away. It was all, they said,
To consolidate strongholds ethnic in
Foundation. By election days therefore,
Except among minorities, always
Squabbling about which majority
To ally with in the numbers game for power,

It was not necessary really
To call on prophet or fortune-teller to see
The new shadow falling over the land.
Safeguards, universally accepted, were
Provided, to wit, the mint-printed ballot
Papers, the ballot boxes made like safes,
The sight-proof polling booths, and the soap-proof
Staining-ink, but greatest of all, even more
Than soldier and the police who staked
All they had left to run a free and fair
Election, after thirteen years of charge
And counter-charge, was the polling officer,
Everywhere a child of the soil. Long neglected
As teacher, clerk, or the never-do-well,
Polling Day was the day he rose to his own.
And whether queues were long, short or present
At all before booths inside toilets or
Bedrooms, it was he, choosing his time,
Called the numbers as pleased his purse and people.
And since both interests often were identical,
Which party losing could press home a protest
Doing the same in its area of influence?
So figures were trumped up in excess
Of known settlements, and taken on camel
And bicycle, in pick-up and canoe,
From one election to another
For assembly and executive seats,
At state and national tiers, were delivered
To a commission with no mind and means
To untie the bag of incongruities
It had from the start adopted. In the end,
Though the sum seemed straightforward to soldier
And schoolboy, numbers, based on
A mathematical formula, argued
By lawyers to the last decimal point
Before the full supreme court of the land,
Confirmed the winner, announced by officials
And generals, discreetly out of sight.
It was, by all accounts, a numbers game.

XIV   The Patriarchs at the Return to Civilian Rule

They are at it again, the old soldiers
Who will never let the people forget
What a great war they won for their country,
When the stranger of his own gave back part
Of the lease he did not want. The old
In other lands, without forgetting, give
Way graciously for the young to possess
And, if necessary, review the field.
But here they not only hold on to their flint-
Lock guns but come the season, called by
The stranger who was never really out
Of sight, and the old soliders, no better
Than the boys they have brought up, are shooting
It out with baronial vehemence.

XV   Handshake

Bouquets are not enough
If brought in flowers;
Here handshake strictly
Is for gold, better still
If delivered abroad.

XVI   *New Currency*

Gold has rolled into a pit
Where so much counterfeit
Adorns the market.
It was not always one grade
When we began our trade.
Will the young ever find it?

XVII   *One Country*

They draw waters upcountry from the rivers;
The aborigines upon the banks are left
Dry in their tenements.
Engines upon rigs ulcerate the soil;
The aborigines upon the banks may not have
Their settlements renewed.
They cannot even sleep, for flares above
Woods and waters have so banished their nights,
The aborigines who generations
Ago kept the stranger at bay
Can only now keep wake for their rights,
The rights the majorities upcountry
Have taken away in the name of one country
To turn waste regions into garden cities.

XVIII   *Song of the New Millionaires*

So close to the desert or forest,
Out of which we all come,
We fear forest or desert will overtake
Us in our new city stronghold.

So close to the desert or forest
Out of which we all come,
How shall we find rest
In our new beds of gold?

This is why we stake
As far as eye can see.

This is why we rake
The land of all we see.

XIX   *Epitaph for Boro*

Boom of oil
Has replaced
The boom of guns,
And politicians like
Soldiers go after spoils.
When will the wells run dry,
And the guns boom again?

XX   An Epidemic without a Name

Another one gone.
It was never like this before,
Not when there is no war,
Or a dread disease widespread.
What feast among the dead
Calls them home at such a run?

Fear beats the drum
Let them run who can
Fear beats the drum.

XXI   Victoria Island Re-visited

They say the sea is raging at the Bar
Beach of Lagos, knocking at the doors
Of homes built by contract finance
On public land for a few to collect
Millions. How has it harbored
For so long this structure with a bottom
So patently false and rotten
It cannot but founder one day?

Next they will be drawing upon
The public purse to salvage the hulk.

XXII   *The Plague*

More than ten years after, the war,
Declared over in the enclave,
Has taken a different turn all
Across the land. Nobody now
May go out any time of day
For fear of gunmen as ready
To kill as be killed for a car
Or any purse, and there is
No homestead in all the country
Not under siege. When will soldier
And state wash for us to live again?

XXIII   *Concerning "My Command" and Other Accounts of the Nigerian Civil War*

Now all is being told
That was said or done
Behind masks, may tramps,
Middlemen and speculators
Not take over the market!

XXIV   Where do they all go?

Where do they all go, the big wigs
In government, when by force or choice
They leave service? Some we know
Side-step into boardrooms and buy
Themselves a little time, while a few
Ascend to thrones termites dispute.
But the bulk of these characters,
Who in their time manipulated
Millions in the name of millions,
Where do they all go, when, willing
Or not, they leave their posts on high?

They cannot all be these gentlemen
Farmers we hear desert and forest
Have reclaimed, and now utterly
Are unable to make the land yield.

XXV   The Sovereign

For Michael Echeruo

It was never a union. It was at best
An amalgamation, so said in fact
The foreign adventurer who forged it.
Four hundred and twenty three disparate
Elements by the latest count, all spread
Between desert and sea, no trace of one
Running into the rest in two thousand
Years of traffic, how can any smith out
Of fable fashion from such a bundle
An alloy known to man? Hammer upon
Anvil may strike like thunder, and the foundry
Fill with lightning, but all is alchemy
Trying to sell as gold in broad daylight
This counterfeit coin called a sovereign.

Postscript

XXVI *The Playwright and the Colonels*

To Wole Soyinka

"Indigo women are waiting
For their men across the river," said
The playwright to the colonel
Who would rule a republic,
And now wanted a kingdom
As hostage in a desperate drive
To the sea. So into the bridge state
Rode the other colonel, assured
Of free board and bed by hosts
Who betrayed a brother to let
Him in but, as it turned out,
Had not the fire nor the spirit
To help him on. The rest
Is history. Except the playwright,
When picked up like a rabbit on the road
In daytime, enroute to principals,
All set to proclaim another kingdom,
Swore between tears in the toilet:
    "A triumphant ride
    Is coming in my wake
    Will raise again the race,
    And though my friend,
    Refuse me gun by his side,
    With my pen I shall take
    Such a grape-shot, in the end
    All who read my tale,
    And do not know how lucky
    I am to get away
    With a holding charge,
    Will forget in our war
    Much more than the man died."

Other Songs on Other States

The Wreck

Although the preparation was so long
All fled his side who had fed
Out of hands with nothing left to give
Except his waste, his going, when
It came, was difficult for us to take.
A stroke felled him down stepping out
One day to dare yet another siege
Against his kind at sea. Hands and
Thighs, that had broken many a bone
In the square yet had caressed women
To sleep, lost at that instant their charge,
Left behind no rallying voice
For the wreck without warning washed
Aground at his doorstep. I saw
The great heart marooned in that carcass
That for three years rotted between
Modern and so-called traditional
Practice as well as the hope that beat
Aloud there still, when the numerous
Who came daily to cheer themselves broke down
In tears, and I can well believe
His young attendant that upon
The morning he went out into the night,
He rose to his hands and feet, eyes
Glazing in a head raised high in bed,
Until he had to be held down before
He froze into a position, that men
Would say to the very end refused rest.

Family Meeting for the Disposal of the Wreck

It was a full house, bringing home
The saying a house is not a boat,
And will not capsize for overflowing.
It was a sight that would have split
The sides of the host had he been there,
But he was not there in his chair,
And was not expected to come,
Being some miles tucked away in
A cold bed. And now this gathering
Of the family, extended to all
Ancestral cousins, was to decide
The style and time of his going home.
The items of expense, when adopted
Under the distinguished chairmanship
Of a nephew, who had summoned
The meeting in the last instance
To rescue a deteriorating state,
Amounted to a grand total
Of sixteen thousand naira, a modest
Proposal, someone said, compared with
Prevailing practice elsewhere. How well
The practice would have served the man
Had half the people there present
Turned up, when he was alive,
Wasting, waiting in bed and that chair
For so much less money and care
Than they were all so willing to tax
Themselves, now that he needed them no more.

Last Rights in Ijebu

Here custom requires
The truly ripe are carried
Home by young men, married
To girls of grand descent
From the dead. I had
No idea, until I did the rite,
A corpse is more dead
Than the wood and the lead
That are its coffin. It is right
They who eat of the luxuriant
Fruits upon a tree, should bear
It fallen in their arms where
All the truly ripe go resplendent
To their graves with choirs.

A Hymn for a Friend in His Losses

For Dejo Okediji

We seek to plumb death
Who flounder here in sleep. Dream
Is a ray refracted in the stream
We rise from each night we draw breath.

The rest is one run of tide
No light has pierced. God, how can we dream
We swim a sea who cannot cross a stream?
We wait for him to ride

Again who in every hymn
Made it to and from the other shore. Praise him!

Prognosis

For Elaine Duncan

Why should a breast that never fed
A child take life? Fondled without
Fulfilment, it seems the last
Point a life, spent in the service
For others, should find exit.
But cells that for years produced
Milk and found no release,
Broke bounds, and multiplying
Against the rule, are taking their toll.

Summary Treatment

They lopped off the limb
He would not give up for free
In the premier place he left
To keep the body all agreed
Was so beautiful.

They lopped off his limb
At swelling expense to his brother
For bed, food, drugs, surgery
And the other services elsewhere,
Like X-rays, blood tests, urine tests . . .

They lopped off his limb
For a price in some streetside place,
Knowing well the enemy
Had long taken over his body.

Translation
From the Urhobo

The orange tree bears fruit,
Bears fruit:
If it does not
Fall, there is food for thought.

Autumn in Connecticut

Why does my heart leap with the fall
Of so many leaves in the wind,
So many, their yellow and brown
Overrun the green of the grass?

Does the downpour of so much gold
Upon the ground rattle again
My rusting can of a heart? It brims over.
Fresh leaves may yet take root.

Harvest

In time, even leaves on
The ground in a garden
Are gathered home.
Where do I find the basket
To gather in my gone years?

Birthday at Wesleyan, Middletown

Days fall about me, dead leaves
Returning to earth in a dry shower.
A tree sheds leaves to put on
A new crown. It also grows
From heart to sapwood rings
Of gold that may have seen
A hundred generations. Now,
I that shed days, not by the season
Alone but all the year round,
Go without promise of fruits
Decaying from my roots.

The Coming of Age

Those times I spent
When a child in her arms
She seemed of all things
Around the one without
Change. Now she is gone,

And I grow old, I feel
Even more close to her than
When she carried me
Rocking at her back,
And I unaware

All under spell of day
Moves on into night.

Miracle in a Farm

In memory of Abdul Azeez Atta

I saw a wet, empty sack,
Crumpled upon the ground in a farm.
"Now guess again what it is," laughed
My host, but before I could
As much as say a word,
It shook, filled, and rose
To life upon four feet,
Its tongue seeking out the mother,
Wet upon the grass some steps away.

Herons at Funama

If at the end of our days here,
There is the chance of coming
Again as all faiths attest,
There is no talent I shall ask
For more than to be able
To walk, swim and fly
Like you, oh, herons
At play on my waterfront!

Faces

Whose are these faces I keep seeing
In my dreams even more than those
I have known since childhood? They are
Not the faces of people I know
In my waking hours, nor have I
Seen them in my reading or on the reeling
Screen. Does my mind, relieved of
The body asleep, recall to itself
The many faces I meet at work
Or in the course of outings in and
Out of town and country, without
Knowing they register in such
Surreal shades? Or does the state of sleep
Of its own, as a mirror to our end,
Serve as some agent to lift my mind
So clear of the body, it already
Is engaged in improbable acts
With characters the seers say are
So much with us though free of time and space?

Mandela
and other poems

—————————————————

Mandela

How does the old man spend his day
In the cage they keep him,
Knowing the wife he left behind,
When bride and bridegroom embraced a flag,
Is no freer beyond the statutory steps
That take her to him, when twice in a year,
They allow her past her garden in Soweto?
Does he, outside the routine drill of the day,
Tell the passing of the day upon
The beat of his slowing heart?
Sitting or asleep on his bed of stone,
What does he see, what does he dream
In the dark of day so slow to break?
Does the old man hear
Above the waves battering Robben Island,
Above the thunder rolling over Drakensberg,
The clamor and clangor of children in revolt,
All ready to die outside their classrooms
Rather than receive the pen
And pit reserved for their parents?
How many times, walking round his cell,
In more than a quarter century of dark,
Has he circled the earth?
And when the concourse of doubts come crowding him,
As they must during the day,
Crowing to him: "Can a man lead in solitary?"
"Can he who merges so well with the night of his cell?'
Does the old man then curse his day
He is no dissident,
Incarcerated in another land,
For whom mighty presidents, prime ministers,
Chancellors, primates, editors and dons
Roar forth human rights,
Swear never again to deal with the devil
Until the regime lets his people go?

So many thoughts in a small room!
Before the cameras of the world,
A wall of glass between,
Sit, coupled to telephones, man and woman
Who must not sleep together,
Because of the flag bride and bridegroom embraced
So that they and their children
May look the sun in the face,
Walk erect on earth as given them by God.
Children now are parents since the vow was made.
Oh, cameras in space, hurtling to pierce
Planets in search of light,
In search of life,
Show us the thoughts of an old man kept in a cage
Away from wife,
Away from life!

A Letter to Oliver Tambo
On the 75th Anniversary of the
African National Congress

Too long, Tambo, it's too long,
Seventy-five years to fight a liberation war
Is too long, much too long.
So we have been fired from far away
By a war that went on for thirty years?
But that was because a small seed came down
A mighty river, full of cataracts and shoals,
Up from mountains and gorges three thousand miles away,
To flower deserts below for a billion people.
But seventy-five whole years to fight a people's war,
And no end in sight on a fair terrain,
Is too long, Tambo, much too long.
Ask the British who are selling you the line
It should go on for a hundred years,

While you talk like gentlemen around
The huge stakes they have on your land.
Ask the Americans who are withdrawing
Their holdings now they have bought the sanctions kit,
Although their chief of state believes it
An incendiary device put together
By your communist friends, and in his heart
Would rather have you ""'dead than red.'"
Oh, yes, ask the French who talk so fast
From both ends of their mouth any fool can tell,
As with their friends, their mouth is where
Their belly is. As for the West Germans,
Do not ask them for whom the Boers fought
On the back of the unmentionable beast.
Only ask the rest, so ready to preach peace
When in fact all they are doing is
Holding your hands tight behind you,
While the enemy their brother beats
You, jails you, kills you dead
In the name of law and order they only know.
As these great allies, now friends with the beast,
How long it took each in their time to shake off
Their shackles, and acting together not so long ago,
How long to hunt down the beast.
A few years and days, Tambo, a few years
And days! And faster still were your friends,
When they took over the bear.
So why must you fight for a century,
A whole hundred years, Tambo,
When God and medicine did not give man
As many days on earth? Or is the delay
So children will take over
Who are dying already in classrooms?
Steps stalling in the hunt never killed
The boar, Tambo. Unfurling maps in the marketplace
Makes you bush meat for the enemy, Tambo.
And letting his allies choose for you
Your friends allows of no fight for heroes.
Therefore, as from this day forward, Tambo,
Resolve to fight on your own ground on your own terms
As the Kikuyu in Kenya did.

With no help of allies abroad,
Relying only on ancestral powers
From a forest, they put out the fires
Of the greatest dragon of them all,
Who belched at dawn and the world heard it at sunset.
Oh, yes, resolve today, Tambo, to fight
As the Berbers in Algeria did.
With nobody believing turbans and veils
In this day and age could win a raid,
They tossed the settlers so far out into the sea,
The waves almost overwhelmed a nation.
Today, the great triumphal arch over Africa,
Transcending ten thousand rainbows
Slung in the sky as from one bow,
One foot in Angola, the other
In Mozambique, and the crest
Over Zimbabwe, stands tottering over us,
All because one lost tribe in its lair
Sits as a beast over the treasures
Strangers have garnered from your land
The beast is a coward.
Though thirsty, it cannot stand a bath
Of the innocent, least of all its keepers.
Look how Sharpville pierced them.
Look how Soweto made them wet.
Look how the curfew they have called for day
Sends the allies reeling in the dark.
The beast by itself is a coward
In a suicide bid. So where are you, Tambo,
Where are you, Umkhonto we sizwe?
Is the hunt only to be on the boundary
To the shout of women and children?
Is the hunt to be one burst of thunder here
And another there and then silence for a year?
When will skirmishes become full engagements,
If only such as are seen in cities of the allies?
When, oh, when, Tambo of Umkhonto we sizwe?
If guns graze the beast, then use numbers!
The fight should be in the house,
It should be in the farm;
It should be in the pit;
It should be in the office;

In the factories, in the streets,
As it is in schools in Soweto
And Guguletu, until it is
All over South Africa to the last beach.
In other words, Tambo, be winners now or never.
Seventy-five years, a hundred years,
Is so long we might well all be dead
In prison or outside, in exile or at home.
This cry is from the barrel of a horn,
Blown this day by J. P. Clark from Nigeria.

The Beast in the South

At last the beast that moved south
Is exposed for all his hood.
Mere children, afraid to live
In the concentration camp
He has made of their land,
Stampede barb-wire and bullet.
As the old bury their seeds
In a field of gas, guarded by dogs,
The wailing is across the world.
Only the Witch of Whitehall
And her escort in the White House
Embrace the beast their people
Had hunted down to his den.

The Death of Samora Machel

They vowed his government will fall
In a matter of days,
If he did not behave like a good boy.
In exactly a week

He fell from the sky,
Right in their backyard,
On his way home from Zimbabwe.

Oblivious of voices, broken
With his fuselage, they combed
A mountain for his papers,
Before announcing to the world
His people could come
And collect his remains
Where they had packed a legend.

The News from Ethiopia
and the Sudan

Armies and lemmings do not go
In numbers such as come over
In waves everyday from the Sudan
And Ethiopia. All down
The Saharan belt, land that once feasted
Pharaohs and emperors no longer
Can feed livestock and peasant,
Though out in commons, millions fled
Yesterday, milk and grain
Are building lakes and pyramids,
Protected well by thirteen tribes.
How have fields that first heard
The hurrah of harvest and hunt
Become the burning grounds for cattle
And sheep no powers, past
Or present, will take for offering?
Where has the flock wandered
That father and mother beggar
Scarecrows in the field, all their seeds
Wilting at their breasts and feet?
The prophets spoke of seasons

Of plagues and pestilence;
They spoke of visitations
Of frogs, rats, locusts and bats;
They also spoke of the ruler
Who acted upon a dream, and turned
Seven lean years into a festival
In fields where the wind also blew
Sand in the face of the sun.
In our times, so briefly touched
By the string of troubadours, the mighty
Of the earth hear and see all right,
But are for their arms and skin alone.

Waiting for the Dead

In memory of Abdul Aziz Atta

The last time he came to see us,
My wife, on answering the bell,
Cried out to me in the bathroom
A ghost had come to call by day,
For there, in the black and white frame
Of the doorway, swayed
The gangling figure of my friend,
Yellow all over to his hair.
As more than secretary to the state,
Work and care that knew no hour
Could well have broken the man,
But because the ox bears his egrets,
None knew another guest
Was around eating up its host.
The next time we should have seen him,
It was at the airport,
All the state out there to receive
The traveller taken to the wrong shore,
It was impossible even to see
Him change planes for home,
Until led in concourse from the palace,
After final rites only the family
May view, I saw for the last time
My friend, at full length, lowered
In simple cloth among his kind.

Washing the Dead

Two mortuary hands, under the red glare
Of their dean, washed the big bare body
That held all who were there wondering
Whether he truly was one now with
The cold grey slab upon which he lay,
Stitched from end to end, as was the slit
Across his throat. From here blood had drained
All through the night, till it flooded his lungs
With such effect the patient drowned
In his own fluids, after a routine
Operation. A strand, astray
From their grey worn sponge, had caught in the hair
Of his groin, but before they could stop
To undo the coupling, at the point
They were wiping him dry of water
And soap to dress him up, the young woman
Doctor in attendance, out of no
Morbid concern, gathered the thing
Between her palms, while a man, who braved
The knife for a touch of beauty,
Lay sleeping beyond the reach of dreams.

Dressing the Dead

In memory of Sonny Omabegho

All indigo now as the dye in his veins,
He looked no different from the friend
His wife had often had to help
Out of his clothes, when flush with the gift
Of an additional day, he came home
At dawn, barely made it to bed,
And promptly asked for coffee. Only now,

He had to be helped into his best,
After receiving a good cold bath.
Oddly, it was his hands that would not go
Easily into those silk sleeves he loved
To dance his way into, fixed as
They were in the position
The fingers had spread and crooked,
When he was brought out of an ice bed.
And now they were interlaced in white
Across his chest perfectly at rest,
Hands that, at a simple touch, could tell
A mother why her child cried all night.

Seeing Off the Dead

I could have sworn by the veil
She wore I had never seen
The lady in the aisle, but my friend,
Leading the way, stopped by her side,
And lifting the bridal gear from her face,
Kissed her full in the mouth again
And again, as they must have done
Their first night together.
So changed, so small had she grown
In the one month since I last saw her,
When driving herself to work in her state,
She called gaily to me in the traffic,
I came to know, too late, a parasite
Can so occupy the host,
It will leave nothing over
For the next day but so displace
The body in the possession,
A mother becomes again the child
In what would be her cradle,
If the lid did not have to close
For four men to carry her to the altar.

Leaves falling

Leaves falling in numbers speak of
Themselves for all of us.
They speak a language of numbers
That all understand who have roots
In water, land or air.
They speak to us all return
To earth that spring from dust.
Only when leaves that are green
Fall in numbers do we say an upset
Of seasons has replaced rust
With ash. And if leaves, falling
In numbers out of season, fall
All in one lot, then men will speak
As oracles there is something in the soil.

A Family Procession

It seems no day passes now
But yet another child is taken home
To be laid at the foot of one tree.
From all across the country they come
In one traffic as traders to a fair,
Except that each arrival empties
A house that swelled so like a market,
From the first tide, it was heard
On shores at the other side of the sea.
Who next in line in a line,
Stretched fourteen times round itself?
What commodities of another world,
Displayed only to its chosen ones,
And what accounts, left to settle

In the ruins of their numinous yard,
Bring them home to a market now
A burial-ground among the creeks
Of a great river no vessels plow?
As all the world on the road watches
And waits with wonder, a family,
Perhaps more than five thousand strong,
Trembles to announce its latest dead.

A Royal Welcome

They had forgotten to switch off
The power before going
To receive him at the terminal,
And now that he was home
And everybody crying to see him,
As they had not clamored
For anyone in sixty years,
He could not be seen,
Because he had on no clothes.
So for a whole night and a day,
While cannons rumbled down
A river, and drum and dance
Reeled to mandatory rites and songs,
The family labored behind doors
To free his head and limbs
In the great iron bed
Where he lay fixed,
Face to one side, hands crossed
Over his chest, and therefore
Unacceptable to the people.

Death of a Lady

Death can be so lazy at times
On purpose he took many months
Claiming a lady nobody knew
Attracted him for years more than
Her sisters much riper in
All things a man wants. Although
She cried from time to time he had
His hand early on her breast,
None saw a lamb under the paw
Of a leopard, so filled with flesh
From the forest, it played
With a pet dish as a spoilt child
Does before his mother. And not
Until she had learnt to breathe
Again with everybody believing
The leopard had gone back
Into the bush did he turn
And take her piece by piece,
As a cob of corn is picked
Between thumbs, in the end
Her eyes that refused to close
In death threw a green suffused light
Upon the bare pole of her body,
Asking: "Who now will he take?"

A Passing at New Year

Now the white sheet he objected to,
When he came out of a day-long coma,
Was spread fully over his face.
So they considered him already
A corpse, he gasped, as he champed at

The tube down his throat. Then he would get up,
He swore, and go him, regardless of cost,
Before they got him. But though he heaved
And tossed, the high tide of his blood,
Flowing with a full sweetness
On the year's last day, had so dammed
His gateways, it left him a debris
In his bed. With a catheter
In his belly, and hands strapped
To bottles running out of fluids,
It was clear to all, on both sides
Of the screen, he would need by break of day
A white sheet spread over his face.

A Tale of the Hyrax

A hyrax lives on top
Of a tree outside town.
There he barks all night
He is king of the forest.
Then all day he is asleep.
Only at night when hungry,
Does he scurry down the tree
To scratch at its foot.
So what is this story
A hyrax came into town
By day and bit the daughter
Of a prince in her room?
It is right the tailless thing
Was eaten up by fire.
Now let the hunt spread
Until the true cat is caught!

If the Dead in Their State

If the dead in their state could only see
The things relations and friends do
When they are gone, a great many
Would not want to come again as members
Of their families or to their place of birth.
Only a few, hearing the true cry of pain
And loss that they leave behind
When they go, will rise and say
They did not know they were so much loved
And missed by family and friends.

Mourner's Comfort

Night falls
For day to break.

An Old Man on Trial

I prayed so hard for old age to come
As the gift my fathers had in their time
It has come to me with such a blow
The fruit is smashed all over an estate
Where children drop like leaves,
Just as I reach for the full basket
They bring running and laughing
To the trustee they all now call father.
It would be easy to cry out
For exchange of parts so that dead wood

Will go back to feed the earth,
While young ones clamber for fruits
Among branches before wild birds
Nibble them with song, if the hand
That seems deflected now in granting
A boon, did not also hold
The axe that falls, when it will fall,
On any tree in any part of the garden.
So how shall I call again upon
God, oh, my fathers, when the gift
You were given to enjoy in your time
Is today a curse in my hands?

A Mother's Story

I came to this house many fear,
A child at the other end of town.
Because I had no need to set up house
Away from home, my husband,
No older than I was, gave away
My first rightful place, and not all
The voices in this compound whitemen found
As commanding as Edo's royal court,
Could prevail upon the heir presumptive,
Still feeding with his mother,
When not gaming or wrestling
Beyond his age at his father's call.
It would be folly, now I am told
I wear diamond in the house,
To count the number of times I was kicked
Like a ball to my mother only
To be returned with still more courtesy
And plea my master was all disarmed,
Until the next round of rage shook the house.
Nor will it clear the air to pick up
The footmat that my sons say I

Became to their father, as the years
Rolled like barrels of palm oil,
That I with others, not so lucky,
Paddled for years through bitter storms
On the Niger, as he followed
His fathers down the wake of a dying trade.
But it is enough God hears prayers.
Today the town is laughing from end
To end the old man of the house
With many wives cannot breathe or take
A blow unless one old woman is at his side.

Sweat in the Moonlight

Which way is the water going,
Which way going? asked the little girl
Of her mother, as she watched
The trees going by on the bank.
Look at me, said her mother at the stern,
And see my sweat in the moonlight.

Homecoming

I put off for years all thoughts
Of coming home, my one excuse
To family and friends being
The house they all agreed I should
First build as my own place of rest,
Before becoming a girl again
In the compound of my fathers.
Now that I am home,
After fifty years away on the coast,

I see ensconsed in our house
The vagrant guest everybody
Alive entertains one day.
It must be spite more than hunger
That within a year of my coming home,
Death should take six of the tender
And strong of my blood for breakfast.

Stranger in the House

In only one year of my coming home
I have seen a thing in the house
My father and mother did not see.
It burns more than fire
It weighs more than stone
It chills more than ice
In only one year of my coming home
I have seen in the house a thing
My father and mother did not see.

The Last Wish

Now that where I am going
Is nearer than where I began,
May I be like the emerging child,
If the arrival is into light.

The Order of the Dead

The dead in other lands are settled
It communes away from town, and although
Town in time may grow to encircle commune,
The dead of other lands sleep sound
Within their walls, and no amount
Of traffic, screaming outside their gates,
Can wake them from their set dream
Of another land. But here in a land
Where the dead without blemish
Are buried in their homesteads, if blessed
With children, and in their own bedrooms,
Taken over by their heirs, if titles
Are clean, the dead do not sleep
Any more than a mother beside
Her troubled child at dead of night.
They are of an order coming after death,
Though going before birth to that source
Which is the home for all
That inhibit the land. Knowing no fixed day
That all the dead of the world must wake,
They are quick to rise, whenever there is
The slither of a snake in the house,
And all the town has no stick
Long enough to strike it dead.
And while long lines of descendants serve them,
The dead of this land, praising God,
May come again into town as children,
If at their first coming,
They went away with a sign of great wrong.